To Nelson Mandela

Windows NT™ Network Programming

How to Survive in a 32-Bit Networking World

Ralph Davis

Addison-Wesley Publishing Company
Reading, Massachusetts • Menlo Park, California • New York
Don Mills, Ontario • Wokingham, England • Amsterdam
Bonn • Sydney • Singapore • Tokyo • Madrid • San Juan
Paris • Seoul • Milan • Mexico City • Taipei

Library of Congress Cataloging-in-Publication Data
Davis, Ralph, 1947–
    Windows NT network programming: how to survive in a 32-bit
networking world / Ralph Davis.
        p. cm.
    Includes index.
    ISBN 0-201-62278-5
    1. Operating systems (Computers) 2. Windows NT. 3. Computer
networks. 4. Systems programming (Computer science) I. Title.
QA76.76.063D43   1994
005.26--dc20
                                       94-8468
                                        CIP

Sponsoring Editor: Philip Sutherland
Project Manager: Ellie McCarthy
Production Coordinator: Lora L. Ryan
Cover design: Barbara T. Atkinson
Set in 11 point Times by S.T. Associates

1 2 3 4 5 6 7 8 9 -MA- 9897969594
First printing, September 1994

Addison-Wesley books are available for bulk purchases by corporations, institutions, and other organizations. For more information please contact the Corporate, Government and Special Sales Department at (800) 238-9682.

Acknowledgments

With this book, I enter my fifth year of working with Addison-Wesley. A project like this depends on a lot more people than the author, and I feel fortunate to have Addison-Wesley's highly skilled staff participating. In particular, I want to thank Phil Sutherland for being a forward-thinking idea man; Ellie McCarthy for managing the production of the book with a keen attention to detail; and Susan Riley, the copy editor, for coming up with many elegant turns of phrase for me.

I also want to thank the people who spurred me to undertake this book. In particular, Mike Hendrickson of Technology Exchange Company was instrumental in getting me to write the course that grew into this book, and in encouraging me to follow through and do the book also. I am also very grateful to Mike, his wife Donna, and the inimitable Chester for extending me their warm hospitality on frigid New England evenings.

On the technical side, I benefited greatly from the close, rigorous reading that Steve Buck of Aurora, Colorado, gave my manuscript. His insistence on high-quality, thorough explanations, and his poring through the Microsoft documentation to verify my statements, went a long way to ensuring the high level of technical accuracy I wanted to achieve here.

And lastly, I cannot forget the Microsoft teams who produced this superb operating system.

Ralph Davis

Contents

Part 1 Introductory Comments

## Chapter 1

Introduction

Overview

This book is the latest stage in what has become an ongoing process for me. It started in mid-1992, when I wrote *Windows Network Programming* for Addison-Wesley. Much of that book centers on the implementation of one function—WNetSendMessage(). My intent was to extend the Windows message-passing paradigm so that you could direct messages to windows on remote machines. In order to implement this function—which knew nothing about communications protocols—I had to build a network-independent support layer, using DLLs that supplied a core set of functions.

The Windows 3.X environment supported only one network protocol at a time prior to Windows for Workgroups. Because Windows for Workgroups and *Windows Network Programming* emerged from the laboratory at roughly the same time, the API I developed was oriented toward the one-protocol-at-a-time limitation. The function WNetGetCaps(), which Windows 3.1 provides in USER.EXE, reports the underlying network, so I used it to decide which of my DLLs to load.

NT Network Programming Course

In early 1993, I wrote a course on Windows NT network programming for the Technology Exchange Company, a subsidiary of Addison-Wesley. Encouraged by the success of *Windows Network Programming*, I decided to derive the course material from the work I had already done there. My first step was to port the network DLLs to NT. Very early in the process, I decided to sacrifice nothing on the altar of backward compatibility. It did not

3

require much exposure to NT to see that it provided a platform for client-server applications that was far superior to Windows 3.1.

- NT is a true preemptive multitasking operating system. The non-preemptive nature of Windows 3.1 forces you to do a lot of polling, which is very inefficient. In NT, you just call a blocking function and go to sleep.
- NT is also multithreaded. This allows applications to multitask themselves and gives server applications the means to provide much higher throughput.
- NT's network services are part of the operating system. With the software that comes out of the box, you get peer-to-peer networking, which allows stations on a network to share directories, printers, and modems. There is built-in support for NetBEUI (Microsoft's network protocol), TCP/IP, Novell's IPX/SPX, and IBM's Data Link Control (DLC).

  This means that you have none of the problems integrating third-party software that are such a constant source of frustration with Windows 3.X. Even when you do need third-party software—for example, to support protocols that Microsoft does not provide, like DECNet—all protocol drivers are expected to conform to the Transport Driver Interface (TDI). By providing this standardization, Microsoft has made it possible for third-party software to be integrated into NT with a minimum of fuss and bother.

- NT supports other hardware besides Intel CPUs. These currently include the MIPS line of chips from MIPS Technologies and the Alpha series from Digital Equipment Corporation. Both of these are very fast CPUs based on Reduced Instruction Set Computer (RISC) technology. Even more importantly, NT supports multiple-processor machines. From my experience writing this book, I have come to the conclusion that this is NT's most important innovation. I have used a 100 MHz MIPS machine, a 33 MHz Intel 486, and another Intel machine with two 66 MHz 486s. The last machine turned in the best performance. Not only does NT on this platform outperform the faster MIPS with a single processor, it also beats Windows 3.1 on the same machine.
- In addition to providing its own network protocols, NT offers programming interfaces for them. Named Pipes, Windows Sockets, and Remote Procedure Calls, as well as the aging NetBIOS API, they are all supported, and they form the subject of Part 3 of this book.

Limitations of the Code in Windows Network Programming

Porting *Windows Network Programming* to NT also made me aware of the following limitations in the software I presented there:

- It allowed multiple client applications to connect to a single server application, my WNet Server. Thus, the only distributed functionality it supported was functions like WNetSendMessage(). It did not provide a truly full-featured API for peer-to-peer communications.
- Loading one network DLL at a time may have made sense under Windows 3.1, but it makes none under NT.

By adding one argument to several functions, I have expanded the API so that it is indeed a general-purpose communications layer. I have also changed the software so it loads support DLLs for all communications APIs that you configure it for. Then, when machines try to connect to each other, they determine at the last moment which protocol they need to use.

Why present my API at all? For one reason—to show you how to use the NT APIs by demonstrating how I used them in a substantial software system.

Windows NT Network Programming

When I sat down to write this book, I decided to continue the work I had done for the course. To present a topic like NT Network Programming in a four-day course requires a great deal of condensation. A full-length book, on the other hand, permits the expansive treatment that NT needs and deserves. This book has allowed me to cover the core topics in much more depth, and to add subjects that I could only allude to in a four-day course, such as the Security API, the Registry, Performance Monitoring, and the LAN Manager API for Windows NT.

I continued to make changes and enhancements to the code. For example, most of the code in this book is at least nominally in C++.

C++. I say that the code is "nominally" in C++ because, in most cases, I use C++ only so that I can declare variables where I use them. There are a few places where I have gone further and created some true C++ objects, mostly to do arithmetic on things like 64-bit integers. I have gone to C++ because Visual C++ has made a believer of me. I have not gone further with it for a couple of reasons (other than my own immaturity with the language). First, it seems many, if not most, of us still have one foot in the C world. The move to C++ does seem to be accelerating, but I don't want to leave C behind altogether just yet. Second, I want to have a much clearer idea of what kind of overhead you incur with C++, particularly for writing system-level software. There has to be some, but I don't yet know how much.

Unicode. I have also chosen to use the Unicode character set as much as possible. As NT's native character set, Unicode is more efficient than ANSI, because NT has to convert all your ANSI strings to Unicode. However, this is not a decision you can be dogmatic about, nor is it one you can make once and be done with it. There are too many inconsistencies in the Windows world around Unicode, and they are likely to be with us for some time to come. For example, Win32s doesn't support Unicode, and Win32 Chicago won't either. Also, Windows Sockets, NetBIOS, NetDDE, and the Messaging API (MAPI) don't understand Unicode. On the other hand, some APIs including the LAN Manager API for Windows NT and Performance Monitoring require Unicode.

What I often find myself doing, as you will see through the course of this book, is using both character sets. This involves forcing strings from ANSI to Unicode in one place, and from Unicode to ANSI in others. It may also require specifying the ANSI or Unicode version of particular Win32 functions. Many of these, as you may already be aware, are actually macros; their definition depends on the UNICODE constant. The header files might say something like this:

```
#ifdef UNICODE
#define GetOpenFileName     GetOpenFileNameW
#define OPENFILENAME        OPENFILENAMEW
#else
#define GetOpenFileName     GetOpenFileNameA
#define OPENFILENAME        OPENFILENAMEA
#endif
```

When a Unicode application wants to ask the user which files to send, it is reasonable for it to force the use of the ANSI character set since MAPI does not understand Unicode. In Chapter 17, you'll see code like this:

```
OPENFILENAMEA OpenFileName;

// [Initialize fields of OpenFileName]
if (GetOpenFileNameA(&OpenFileName))
   // [User selected files, send them using MAPI
```

I will concede at once that this is kludgey and ugly, but you don't have much choice when you have so many conflicting demands to satisfy. Indeed, I suspect that you will see much more code for Windows NT written like this.

Structure of the Book

This book consists of four parts. Part 1 (Chapters 1–2) presents introductory remarks and a brief look at the architecture of Windows NT. Part 2 (Chapters 3–8) discusses advanced NT techniques that are essential for writing effective network programs, though they are not directly network-related. Part 3 (Chapters 9–13) presents the built-in peer-to-peer communications APIs and the implementation of my generic API on top of them. Finally, Part 4 (Chapters 14–17) presents additional APIs that, unlike the ones in Part 2, are not indispensable but are very useful nonetheless.

At the end of each chapter, I include a section called "Suggested Readings." NT is a very large subject; no one book can possibly cover it all. There are many places where my coverage of a topic is narrowly focused because I discuss it in the context of Windows NT network programming. Often, other people have written books that discuss the same topic in greater detail because it is more central to their purpose. I think it's better to tell you where you can get more information than to try to be all things to all people.

Jeff Richter, for instance, has done a masterful job of covering advanced NT techniques in his book *Advanced Windows NT*. I discuss many of the same topics in Part 2 of this book, though not at the same length as he does. For me, these topics are a means to an end—writing effective distributed programs under Windows NT. For him, they are the entire subject of his book. There are some points of emphasis where I disagree with him, but I have no hesitation in suggesting that you read his book from cover to cover. Having done so, though, don't skip my Part 2; it lays the foundation for what comes after, and it presents the same subject matter from my particular point of view.

Helen Custer's *Inside Windows NT* is the definitive work on the architecture of Windows NT, which I discuss briefly in Chapter 2. My intention is to introduce some terms and to give you general familiarity with how things work. Her book, on the other hand, is an in-depth analysis of Windows NT by a person who is deeply versed in operating system theory and design. If you are familiar with her work, you probably can skip Chapter 2.

Installing the Source Code Disk

The disk that comes with this book includes source code without binaries. The batch file INSTALME.CMD in the root directory puts the source code into the \NTNET directory on the drive indicated by your HOMEDRIVE environment variable. It also executes the batch file MAKEALL.CMD, which it installs in the \NTNET\CODE directory.

If you look at MAKEALL.CMD, you will see that for each source code directory, it goes to the %Cpu% directory under it. This is where MAKEALL.CMD actually builds the software. Here's the portion of the file that builds the applications and DLLs in \NTNET\CODE:

```
cd \ntnet\code\%Cpu%
nmake -f ..\wnetdfc.mak all %1
nmake -f ..\wnetlvl1.mak all %1
nmake -f ..\wnetrpc.mak all %1
nmake -f ..\wnetmain.mak all %1
nmake -f ..\wnetmsgs.mak all %1
del *.pch
```

This structure came about because I had a single source-code bed on my NT Advanced Server and wanted to build binaries for Intel and MIPS, the two platforms that I currently have under my roof. (I intend to support the Alpha in a future version of the software.) When I discuss source code in the book, I will tell you where to find it.

Most of the binaries are copied to %HOMEDRIVE%\ NTNET\CODE\%Cpu% as the final step in the build process. The only exceptions are benchmark programs where several versions have the same names.

Conclusion

Windows NT is a superb operating system and a powerful platform for distributed applications. It requires a lot of hardware, but it will reward your investment. Of particular interest is its ability to run on fast RISC processors like MIPS and Alpha CPUs. Its most powerful impact, however, is likely to come from its support of multiple processors. This is where it can give you its greatest performance, and where it presents its most serious challenge to current market leaders.

One word of advice: don't nickel-and-dime NT. It's powerful, but it needs to be fed. Don't get less than 32 MB of RAM, or less than 450 MB of hard disk space. And if you can, get a couple of CPUs.

## Chapter 2

The Architecture of Windows NT

Overview

This chapter will take a brief look at the way Windows NT is put together. It is not my intention to give any exhaustive coverage to the subject; after all, as Helen Custer has so ably demonstrated, it is a book-length topic. The architecture of the operating system is not of concern to those developing software for it. My goal here is primarily to introduce some terms that I will use from time to time through the rest of the book. And although the system architecture is not of crucial importance to us as developers, the way that networking has been built into Windows NT from the very start greatly improves the environment we have to work with. Those of you who have developed distributed applications for Windows 3.X know that it is a constant battle to keep your Windows drivers and your network drivers cooperating with each other. With Windows NT, most of these frustrations go away, and the pleasure of working with a well-designed system replaces them.

One of my premises is that there should be a single Win32 API for peer-to-peer communications. Those of you who have read *Windows Network Programming* know that, in that book, I developed such an API for Windows 3.X. Here, I extend the work that I began there, but my emphasis changes because NT has answered many—but not all—of the concerns I expressed. In *Windows Network Programming*, it was necessary to build my networking API on top of drivers supplied, for the most part, by third-party vendors like Novell, Banyan, or TCP/IP software houses. In this book, my API will be built on top of those that are already part of Windows NT. What makes this book necessary is that there is still no single API set for peer-to-peer communications. You have to choose between Named Pipes, Windows

9

Sockets, NetBIOS, and RPC, each of which has its advantages and disadvantages. The API I present relieves application software from this burden because it decides at runtime which underlying API set is the best for communicating with a given host. Windows NT comes tantalizingly close to providing the API that I'm looking for. There is indeed a single, generic API for network communications—the Transport Driver Interface (TDI)—but it is at the driver level and is not exposed to applications. I still look forward to the day that the work I have done here and in *Windows Network Programming* becomes obsolete because Microsoft will finally have built it into the operating system.

The Architecture of the Operating System

Windows NT is designed to support multiple operating system environments at the application level and to run on multiple hardware platforms. Its architecture reflects these design goals. In the simplest terms, Windows NT consists of user-mode components—principally the Environment Subsystems—layered on top of the kernel-mode components, to which the NT Executive provides the interface. Figure 2-1 shows the overall structure of Windows NT.

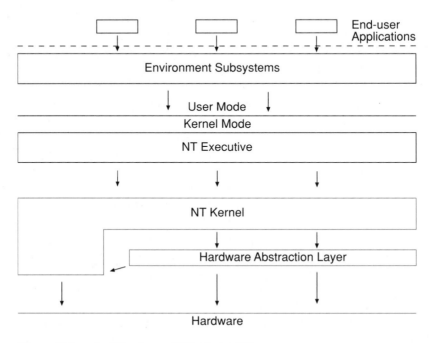

Figure 2-1.   Architecture of Windows NT

Environment Subsystems

User-level applications interface to the Environment Subsystems, which emulate the environment of a given operating system. Currently supported subsystems are Win32, MS-DOS, Win16, OS/2 1.X, and POSIX. The Environment Subsystems run in user mode, so they are protected from each other, as well as from application programs. They in turn request services of the NT Executive, which provides the interface to kernel-mode services. This interface is not exposed to application programs, though much of it is accessible through the Win32 API.

The Win32 subsystem provides keyboard and mouse input and screen output to all the other subsystems. Because it exposes the most facilities of the NT kernel, it offers the most powerful vehicle for developing NT applications. The Win32 subsystem consists of the executable file CSRSS.EXE (Client-Server Runtime Subsystem) and four Dynamic Link Libraries:

- USER32.DLL is the Window Manager for Windows NT. It is responsible for managing higher-level interface objects like windows, menus, and dialog boxes.
- GDI32.DLL handles lower-level graphic primitives.
- KERNEL32.DLL supports operations like multithreading, synchronization, object creation and management, and memory allocation.
- CONSOLE.DLL supports character-mode applications.

Many of the functions in these DLLs are actually stub routines that package their arguments and ship them to the Win32 subsystem (CSRSS.EXE) using the Local Procedure Call (LPC) Facility. This client-server exchange is transparent to the application program.

The Security Subsystem

The Security Subsystem is referred to as an integral subsystem because it provides system-wide services. In concert with the Logon Process, the Security Subsystem validates user logon requests and generates an access token for the currently logged-in user. This token is then attached to every process started by the user, and is used by the Security Reference Monitor component of the NT Executive to determine if the user has rights to a given object.

The NT Executive

The Windows NT Executive is the gateway to the kernel-mode services offered by Windows NT. It offers a common interface to the environment subsystems, which use those services to emulate their target operating systems. The NT Executive consists of six subcomponents: the Process Manager, the Object Manager, the Security Reference Monitor, the Virtual Memory Manager, the Local Procedure Call (LPC) Facility, and the I/O Manager.

The Process Manager. The Process Manager manages threads and processes. Processes are an executable image along with its virtual address space and any objects it owns. Threads are the active units that the Process Manager schedules for execution in the CPU. The Process Manager has no concept of hierarchical relationships among processes. This is left to the environment subsystems to implement according to the behavior of their emulated operating system.

The Object Manager. The Object Manager is responsible for creating, naming, sharing, and protecting NT system objects. Managed objects include mutexes, events, semaphores, files, pipes, processes, threads, file systems, and file-mapping objects. The Object Manager uses a hierarchical naming scheme for all NT objects. This scheme is modeled after a hierarchical file system.

The Security Reference Monitor. The Security Reference Monitor implements local security policy. It controls access to all NT objects and generates requested audit messages.

The Virtual Memory Manager. The NT Virtual Memory Manager controls memory protection, the translation of virtual addresses into physical addresses, and the policy that NT uses to determine how to page memory blocks to and from the swap file.

The Local Procedure Call (LPC) Facility. The Local Procedure Call (LPC) Facility implements the client-server model by which applications request services from subsystems. It closely models the way the Remote Procedure Call (RPC) mechanism works, but optimizes it for client-server exchanges on the same machine.

The I/O Manager. The I/O Manager supports all input/output operations in the NT environment. It uses a scheme whereby file system drivers and network drivers are layered on top of actual device drivers, which they access using a common interface. This gives the NT I/O Manager the flexibility to support multiple file system drivers and multiple networks. The I/O Manager also supports network redirection. The network server and redirector modules are written as NT file system drivers. They are supported by transport-layer drivers that implement the Transport Driver Interface (TDI), which is in turn underlain by network adapter drivers written to the Network Device Interface Specification (NDIS).

The NT Kernel

The Windows NT Kernel is responsible for scheduling, multiprocessor synchronization, hardware exceptions, interrupt processing, and power-failure handling. It also exports a set of objects to the NT Executive, some of which are exposed through the Win32 API. These include mutexes, events, semaphores, files, file-mapping objects, pipes, mailslots, processes, threads, and communication devices. The NT Kernel is intended to be very primitive. It does not determine operating system policy—it just effects the policies of the NT Executive.

The Hardware Abstraction Layer (HAL)

The lowest level of the Windows NT operating system is the Hardware Abstraction Layer. It is meant to isolate hardware dependencies so that device drivers and the kernel can be ported to different hardware platforms more readily.

NT Network Architecture

The network architecture of Windows NT is designed to provide a high level of connectivity. Windows NT supports multiple network redirectors using multiple protocol stacks inside machines that have multiple network cards installed. Thus, for example, you can have redirectors for NT, NetWare, and NFS, using NetBEUI, TCP/IP, and IPX/SPX, connected to an EtherNet and a Token-Ring network. Network drivers can be loaded and unloaded at runtime.

At the application level, requests for I/O operations are evaluated to see if they should be carried out locally or remotely. If they need remote servicing,

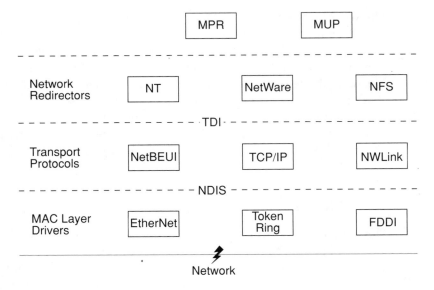

Figure 2-2.   Windows NT Network Modules

two user-mode NT components, the Multiple UNC Provider (MUP) and the Multiple Provider Router (MPR), determine how to find the responsible host machine. Figure 2-2 shows the way the NT network modules are layered.

The Multiple UNC Provider (MUP)

UNC is an acronym for Universal Naming Convention. UNC names have the format \\<server name>\<share name>\<path>\<file>. If an application tries to open a file or file-like device (like a named pipe) using a UNC name, the Multiple UNC Provider is asked to figure out how to talk to the server machine—that is, which network provider knows how to communicate with it.

The Multiple Provider Router (MPR)

If an application accesses a file using a filename that includes a redirected drive, then the Multiple Provider Router (MPR) resolves the request. It is also responsible for dispatching calls to the built-in WNet functions; they are supported in the DLL MPR.DLL. The Multiple UNC Provider and the Multiple Provider Router pass the request along to the component at the next level down, the Network Redirector.

The Network Redirector

The Network Redirector takes remote I/O requests and sends them to the machine responsible for processing them. In the Windows NT environment, more than one Network Redirector may be active. On my network, the NT stations use both the Windows NT Redirector and the Client Services for NetWare (CSNW), which is provided by Microsoft for connectivity to NetWare file servers. In resolving a remote I/O request, the Multiple UNC Provider and the Multiple Provider Router pass it to each Network Redirector they find until one of them accepts it. The Network Redirector packages the request and forwards it to the target host. At the receiving end, the Network Server accepts it, issues it locally, and returns the results to the station that issued it.

Network Redirectors are implemented as file system drivers. The most important implication of this is that they can use all of NT's security features.

The Network Server

The Network Server is the software component responsible for sharing local directories and print queues. When a remote station asks to access a file on the local machine, the Network Server translates the call into a local I/O operation, issues the appropriate function call, and returns any output information over the network to the calling station. Like the Network Redirector, the Network Server is a file system.

Transport Driver Interface (TDI) and Network Device Interface Specification (NDIS)

So that Windows NT can support multiple concurrent protocol stacks, the Network Redirector and the Network Server communicate with transport layer drivers via a standard programming interface, the Transport Driver Interface. The transport protocols, in turn, communicate with the lower-layer drivers using another standard API, the Network Device Interface Specification.

Just as the Transport Driver Interface allows multiple protocol stacks to run simultaneously, the Network Device Interface Specification allows a computer to have more than one network adapter card installed. Both interfaces are documented in the Windows NT Device Driver Kit.

Conclusion

Windows NT uses a microkernel architecture that provides for a great deal of flexibility. This has ramifications in several areas. At the highest level, the end-user level, it allows NT to emulate the operating environments of different operating systems. This is accomplished by implementing the user interface layer in environment subsystems. The principal subsystem—the native one, if you will—is Win32. Of the other supported environments, the most important are Win16 and MS-DOS. The OS/2 and POSIX environments are much more limited.

At the lowest level of the operating system, NT offers portability to a variety of platforms by isolating as many hardware dependencies as it can in the Hardware Abstraction Layer (HAL). This allows it to run at present on Intel, MIPS, and DEC Alpha platforms, on both single- and multiprocessor machines. In the future, you can expect to see it ported to other hardware platforms, like the PowerPC.

For networking, flexibility means, among other things:

- Multiple network providers give you connectivity to diverse network environments, including Windows NT, Windows for Workgroups, NetWare, the Network File System (NFS), and IBM's Systems Network Architecture (SNA).
- These providers in turn have their choice of a multiplicity of transport protocols, all of which can run concurrently. NT ships with NetBEUI, TCP/IP, IPX/SPX, and IBM's DCL. Because the transport layer services are accessed via a standard interface—the Transport Driver Interface (TDI)—new transport drivers can be provided without rewriting the base operating system.
- At the lowest level—the network adapter card—NT allows a machine to have multiple adapters, supporting divergent network technologies, such as EtherNet, Token Ring, and FDDI. Here again, it is a standardized interface—the Network Device Interface Specification— that makes this possible.

Suggested Readings

Custer, Helen. *Inside Windows NT*. Redmond, WA: Microsoft Press, 1992.
Microsoft Corporation. *Windows NT Resource Kit*, Volume I. Chapter 1 and Chapters 15–22. Redmond, WA: Microsoft Press, 1993.

Part 2 Advanced NT Techniques

Chapter 3

Structured Exception Handling

Overview

Structured Exception Handling is a means by which applications can handle unexpected events. These can include both software- and hardware-generated error conditions, called **exceptions**. Structured Termination Handling, which is an adjunct to Structured Exception Handling, protects a body of code from being abandoned while resources, such as synchronization objects, are in a locked or indeterminate state.

Uses

Structured Exception Handling and Structured Termination Handling can be used for several purposes. By trapping your own exceptions, you can prevent the summary termination of your application and do something less drastic, such as rolling back the activity where the exception occurred. You can use Structured Exception Handling as a debugging mechanism to determine the precise source of an exception by catching the exception and printing out __FILE__ and __LINE__ information. You can also use it quite deliberately to implement algorithms, such as lazy memory allocation. (See the virtual memory allocation discussion in Chapter 4.)

Structured Termination Handling can guarantee that a function will have a single exit point regardless of how many *return* statements are scattered throughout the function body. Thus, all resource cleanup can be localized in a single block of code.

Syntax

As the name implies, Structured Exception Handling and Structured Termination Handling are implemented by the Windows NT C/C++ compiler using structured programming principles. They add four keywords to the language: *try, except, leave,* and *finally.* Actually, these are macros defined in the header file \MSTOOLS\H\EXCPT.H. The keywords to which they map depend on the target machine. For example, *try* becomes _ _ *try* on an Intel host, and *_builtin_try* on MIPS or Alpha machines.

Here is the skeletal framework of an exception handler:

```
try
    {
    // Guarded code
    }
except ([exception-filter expression])
    {
    // [Exception-handling logic]
    }
```

The curly braces are mandatory, even if the *try* and *except* blocks consist of a single statement. The *try* blocks cannot stand by themselves; they must be followed by either an *except* or a *finally.*

Semantics of Structured Exception Handling under Windows NT

First, the *try* block is executed. If an exception occurs, NT tries to notify a debugger. If the process is not being debugged, or if the debugger does not handle the exception, NT begins climbing back up the stack ("unwinding") to find an exception handler. If it finds one, it evaluates the exception-filter expression. As you will see, this can be coded inline, or it can call a function to evaluate the exception. If the expression resolves to EXCEPTION_EXECUTE_HANDLER (1), NT will enter the *except* block. The exception filter can also be EXCEPTION_CONTINUE_EXECUTION (-1), telling NT to retry the machine instruction that failed, or EXCEPTION_CONTINUE_SEARCH (0), indicating that the associated exception handler cannot deal with the exception that has occurred. If NT does not find an application-defined exception handler, it tries to notify the debugger again. If there is no debugger, or the debugger still does not handle the exception, NT executes its own exception-handling logic. On machines where the Win32 SDK is not present, a message box appears, informing the user that an error has occurred; data describing the exception is written to the application log file using the application name Dr. Watson. It can be viewed using the NT Event Viewer, whose icon is located in the Administrative Tools group box.

When the Win32 SDK has been installed from a supported CD-ROM drive, post-mortem debugging is handled instead by WinDbg. This time, the message box offers to debug the application if you press the Cancel button. This is generally more useful than the information that Dr. Watson writes to the system log.

Possible Exceptions

Undoubtedly, the most typical exception is a memory access violation (0xC0000005), defined as the constant EXCEPTION_ACCESS_ VIOLATION. This indicates that somewhere in your application you have strayed into memory that you do not have permission to access. Table 3-1 lists all the exception codes that are currently defined. The codes are divided into bit fields as follows (the *typedef* is my own):

```
typedef struct _EXCEPTION_CODE
{
    unsigned dwSeverity  : 2;   // Bits 31 and 30
    unsigned dwOwner     : 1;   // Bit 29
    unsigned dwReserved  : 1;   // Bit 28
    unsigned dwFacility  : 12;  // Bits 27-16
    unsigned dwException : 16;  // Bits 15-0
} EXCEPTION_CODE;
```

The values for *dwSeverity* are:

- 0: success
- 1: informational
- 2: warning
- 3: error

\MSTOOLS\H\WINNT.H provides macros for extracting and testing the error level. APPLICATION_ERROR_MASK (0x20000000) can be used to strip off the low 30 bits. The remaining two will then be one of these values:

- ERROR_SEVERITY_SUCCESS (0): success
- ERROR_SEVERITY_INFORMATIONAL (0x40000000): informational
- ERROR_SEVERITY_WARNING (0x80000000): warning
- ERROR_SEVERITY_ERROR (0xC0000000): error

All the codes listed in Table 3-1 are either warnings or errors.

dwOwner indicates whether the code is generated by Microsoft (0) or defined by the developer (1). *dwReserved* is always 0; NT clears it automatically when processing an exception. Both *dwFacility* and *dwException* are defined according to the needs of the application. All the codes in Table 3-1 have *dwFacility* set to 0.

The #*defines* for the EXCEPTION_ codes are in WINBASE.H; #*defines* for the STATUS_ constants are in WINNT.H. Both these headers are included by WINDOWS.H.

Table 3-1.   Windows NT Exception Codes

Code	Defined As	Level
EXCEPTION_ACCESS_VIOLATION	STATUS_ACCESS_VIOLATION (0xC0000005)	Error
EXCEPTION_DATATYPE_MISALIGNMENT	STATUS_DATATYPE_MISALIGNMENT (0x80000002)	Warning
EXCEPTION_BREAKPOINT	STATUS_BREAKPOINT (0x80000003)	Warning (used by debuggers)
EXCEPTION_SINGLE_STEP	STATUS_SINGLE_STEP (0x80000004)	Warning (used by debuggers)
EXCEPTION_ARRAY_BOUNDS_EXCEEDED	STATUS_ARRAY_BOUNDS_EXCEEDED (0xC000008C)	Error
EXCEPTION_FLT_DENORMAL_OPERAND	STATUS_FLOAT_DENORMAL_OPERAND (0xC000008D)	Error
EXCEPTION_FLT_DIVIDE_BY_ZERO	STATUS_FLOAT_DIVIDE_BY_ZERO (0xC000008E)	Error
EXCEPTION_FLT_INEXACT_RESULT	STATUS_FLOAT_INEXACT_RESULT (0xC000008F)	Error
EXCEPTION_FLT_INVALID_OPERATION	STATUS_FLOAT_INVALID_OPERATION (0xC0000090)	Error
EXCEPTION_FLT_OVERFLOW	STATUS_FLOAT_OVERFLOW (0xC0000091)	Error
EXCEPTION_FLT_STACK_CHECK	STATUS_FLOAT_STACK_CHECK (0xC0000092)	Error
EXCEPTION_FLT_UNDERFLOW	STATUS_FLOAT_UNDERFLOW (0xC0000093)	Error
EXCEPTION_INT_DIVIDE_BY_ZERO	STATUS_INTEGER_DIVIDE_BY_ZERO (0xC0000094)	Error
EXCEPTION_INT_OVERFLOW	STATUS_INTEGER_OVERFLOW (0xC0000095)	Error

Table 3-1.   Windows NT Exception Codes (continued)

Code	Defined As	Level
EXCEPTION_PRIV_INSTRUCTION	STATUS_PRIVILEGED_INSTRUCTION (0xC0000096)	Error
EXCEPTION_IN_PAGE_ERROR	STATUS_IN_PAGE_ERROR (0xC0000006)	Error
EXCEPTION_ILLEGAL_INSTRUCTION	STATUS_ILLEGAL_INSTRUCTION (0xC000001D)	Error
EXCEPTION_NONCONTINUABLE_EXCEPTION	STATUS_NONCONTINUABLE_EXCEPTION (0xC0000025)	Error
EXCEPTION_STACK_OVERFLOW	STATUS_STACK_OVERFLOW (0xC00000FD)	Error
EXCEPTION_INVALID_DISPOSITION	STATUS_INVALID_DISPOSITION (0xC0000026)	Error
EXCEPTION_GUARD_PAGE	STATUS_GUARD_PAGE_VIOLATION (0X80000001)	Warning
CONTROL_C_EXIT	STATUS_CONTROL_C_EXIT (0xC000013A)	Error
STATUS_NO_MEMORY	0xC0000017	Error

In addition to EXCEPTION_ACCESS_VIOLATION, programming errors may also trigger EXCEPTION_PRIV_INSTRUCTION or EXCEPTION_ILLEGAL_INSTRUCTION violations. EXCEPTION_ PRIV_INSTRUCTION means that the CPU encountered an instruction in the code stream that is reserved for operating system software, such as an ARPL (Adjust Requestor Privilege Level) on an Intel chip. EXCEPTION_ILLEGAL_INSTRUCTION means that the CPU was given an instruction that it was unable to decode. These exceptions are most likely to result from attempting to execute data, from executing code that has been overwritten, or from calling a routine in a DLL that is no longer present in memory. EXCEPTION_BREAKPOINT and EXCEPTION_SINGLE_STEP are used by debuggers. EXCEPTION_DATATYPE_MISALIGNMENT indicates that a piece of data is not aligned on the proper byte boundary for the host processor. For instance, the following excerpt from the function _WNetEnumStations(), presented in Chapter 9, triggers a datatype misalignment exception on a RISC processor, but not on an Intel platform. When I first wrote this function for *Windows Network Programming*, WNET_SIGNATURE was defined as "WNET", and WNET_SIG_LENGTH as 5.

```
typedef enum tagWNetRequest
{
    POST_MESSAGE,
    SEND_MESSAGE,
    FIND_WINDOW,
    ENUM_STATIONS,
    ENUM_STATION_RESPONSE,
    MESSAGE_BOX,
    WIN_EXEC,
    WNET_GET_USER
} WNET_REQUEST;

LPBYTE lpPacket;
static BYTE byEnumStationPacket[255];

lpPacket = (LPBYTE) byEnumStationPacket;
lstrcpy(lpPacket, WNET_SIGNATURE);
lpPacket += WNET_SIG_LENGTH;
*((WNET_REQUEST FAR *) lpPacket) = ENUM_STATIONS;
```

The last line of code in the preceding block assigns a 32-bit value to a memory location that is not aligned on an 32-bit boundary. The solution to this problem was quite simple; I redefined WNET_SIGNATURE as "WNET$$$" and WNET_SIG_LENGTH as 8.

The EXCEPTION_FLT_ and EXCEPTION_INT_ codes are triggered by errors that occur in floating-point and integer arithmetic operations. EXCEPTION_NONCONTINUABLE_EXCEPTION means that you attempted to retry an instruction after an exception that has been tagged as noncontinuable. EXCEPTION_GUARD_PAGE means that you tried to access a page of memory that you have designated as a guard page. CONTROL_C_EXIT means that the user pressed Control-C; it will be received only by console applications. STATUS_NO_MEMORY is used to report memory-allocation errors under certain conditions (see Chapter 4).

The Exception Filter

Simple expression filters can be coded inline. Here are two examples.

```
// Do the exception handler unconditionally
except (EXCEPTION_EXECUTE_HANDLER)

// Handle access violations
// Pass all other exceptions back to NT
except (GetExceptionCode() == EXCEPTION_ACCESS_VIOLATION ?
        EXCEPTION_EXECUTE_HANDLER :
        EXCEPTION_CONTINUE_SEARCH)
```

More complex filter expressions require the invocation of a filter function. In particular, you cannot request the reexecution of an instruction unless you call a filter function. As you will see, this can be a powerful way to use Structured Exception Handling. It allows you, for instance, to delay allocating memory until you actually need it and then to allocate only as much as you actually need.

Win32 provides two pseudofunctions (they are actually macros) that allow you to determine what caused the exception. GetExceptionCode() returns a DWORD containing the exception code (see Table 3-1).

```
DWORD GetExceptionCode(VOID);
```

GetExceptionCode() can be called in either the filter expression or the *except* block; it cannot be called from a filter function.

GetExceptionInformation() returns complete information about the exception and the instruction that triggered it.

```
LPEXCEPTION_POINTERS GetExceptionInformation(VOID);
```

The return value is a pointer to an EXCEPTION_POINTERS structure, which contains pointers to two other structures.

```
typedef struct _EXCEPTION_POINTERS
    {
    PEXCEPTION_RECORD ExceptionRecord;
    PCONTEXT          ContextRecord;
    } EXCEPTION_POINTERS;
```

The EXCEPTION_RECORD structure that *ExceptionRecord* points to describes the exception in a machine-independent way. *ContextRecord* points to a CONTEXT structure, which is a snapshot of the register contents at the time the exception occurred. The EXCEPTION_RECORD is defined as follows:

```
typedef struct _EXCEPTION_RECORD
{
    DWORD ExceptionCode;
    DWORD ExceptionFlags;
    struct _EXCEPTION_RECORD *ExceptionRecord;
    PVOID ExceptionAddress;
    DWORD NumberParameters;
    DWORD ExceptionInformation[EXCEPTION_MAXIMUM_PARAMETERS];
} EXCEPTION_RECORD;
```

ExceptionCode reports the exception that occurred; it is the same value as that returned by GetExceptionCode(). *ExceptionFlags* indicates whether the instruction can be retried or not. NT uses the *ExceptionRecord* field to build a linked list of EXCEPTION_RECORDs if nested exceptions (which are exceptions in exception handlers or filter functions) occur. *ExceptionAddress* points to the instruction that the application was executing when the exception was triggered. *NumberParameters* and *ExceptionInformation* contain any additional information required to more precisely describe the exception. At present, they are used only with access violations (*ExceptionCode* == EXCEPTION_ACCESS_VIOLATION). In this case, the first element in the *ExceptionInformation* array is 0 if the application was attempting to read the address, and 1 if it was trying to write to it. The second element is the virtual address of the data that the application was accessing.

GetExceptionInformation() can be called only from the filter expression. It cannot be called in a filter function or an exception handler. The restrictions on where you can use GetExceptionCode() and GetExceptionInformation() may appear rather arbitrary. However, they make sense when you consider that GetExceptionCode() and GetException-Information() are macros, not functions. They are expanded in-line, and the stack environment is volatile during exception processing.

To summarize, there are three locations of interest during the processing of an exception. Each has different restrictions on the use of GetExceptionCode() and GetExceptionInformation(). One is the exception filter expression, contained in the parentheses following the *except* statement. Here, you can call either GetExceptionCode() or GetExceptionInformation(). Another is the filter function that is called from the filter expression. It may call neither GetExceptionCode() nor GetExceptionInformation(). The third is the exception handler, which is the code in curly braces after the *except* statement. It can call GetExceptionCode(), but not GetExceptionInformation(). The easiest way to accommodate these restrictions is to pass the return value of GetExceptionCode() or GetExceptionInformation() as an argument to a filter function. The filter function can use this information as it needs to. Fortunately, you don't have to memorize these rules—the compiler displays a "bad context for intrinsic function" message—but it doesn't hurt to know what they are.

Here's a code fragment demonstrating the use of a filter function. It uses GetExceptionInformation() to obtain both the exception code and information on register contents.

```
char *p;
try
```

```
     {
     strcpy(p, "Hi, folks");
     }
except (CheckPointer(GetExceptionInformation(),
        &p))
     {
     // p could not be allocated
     MessageBox(NULL,
                "Memory allocation error",
                "My Application", MB_OK);
     ExitProcess(1);
     }
```

p is not initialized, so the strcpy() triggers an exception. CheckPointer(), the function called by the filter expression, examines the exception to determine how to proceed. If the exception was EXCEPTION_ACCESS_VIOLATION, CheckPointer() allocates memory for *p*. If the allocation is successful, CheckPointer() returns EXCEPTION_CONTINUE_EXECUTION. If it fails, CheckPointer() returns EXCEPTION_EXECUTE_HANDLER. The exception handler puts up a message box informing the user of the error. For any other exception, CheckPointer() returns EXCEPTION_CONTINUE_SEARCH. The exception handler does not know how to deal with any other type of exception.

Here is the listing for CheckPointer():

```
DWORD CheckPointer(LPEXCEPTION_POINTERS lpExc, char **pp)
{
    char *p;
    if (lpExc->ExceptionRecord->ExceptionCode !=
         EXCEPTION_ACCESS_VIOLATION)
      return EXCEPTION_CONTINUE_SEARCH;
    p = malloc(255);
    if (p == NULL)
      return EXCEPTION_EXECUTE_HANDLER;
    *pp = p;

    // We also have to change the register
    // contents by modifying a field
    // in the CONTEXT structure

#if _X86_
    // This is 80386-specific
    lpExc->ContextRecord->Edi = (DWORD) p;
#elif _MIPS_
    lpExc->ContextRecord->IntA0 = (DWORD) p;
    lpExc->ContextRecord->IntV1 =
```

```
            lpExc->ContextRecord->IntA0 + 1;
#endif
    return EXCEPTION_CONTINUE_EXECUTION;
}
```

Notice that CheckPointer(), in addition to allocating memory and storing its address in *p*, must also put the newly allocated pointer into the appropriate fields of the CONTEXT structure, pointed to by the *ContextRecord* field of the EXCEPTION_POINTERS structure. For an Intel platform, this field is the *Edi* field, representing the contents of the EDI register. For a MIPS processor, the *IntA0* and *IntV1* fields are the relevant ones. *IntA0* represents the A0 register and *IntV1* (the V1 register), which contains *p + 1*. When NT reexecutes the instruction, it reloads the registers from the CONTEXT structure. This code is both machine- and compiler-specific. Ordinarily, programming NT this way is a terrible practice; to get the greatest advantage out of NT, you don't want to make any assumptions about the hardware you're running on. My intention here is only to show you how to do this if you ever need to—not to suggest that you do it regularly.

Raising Your Own Exceptions

You can use the exception-reporting mechanism for your own purposes by invoking the function RaiseException().

```
VOID RaiseException(DWORD    dwExceptionCode,
                    DWORD    dwExceptionFlags,
                    DWORD    dwArguments,
                    LPDWORD  lpdwArguments);
```

dwExceptionCode is the exception that you want to raise. It will be reported in the ExceptionCode field of the EXCEPTION_RECORD or returned by GetExceptionCode(). It can be one of the predefined exceptions, or a code you define for your own purposes. As I discussed earlier in this chapter, exception codes are formatted as a bitfield, shown again here:

```
typedef struct _EXCEPTION_CODE
{
    unsigned dwSeverity  : 2;   // Bits 31 and 30
    unsigned dwOwner     : 1;   // Bit 29
    unsigned dwReserved  : 1;   // Bit 28
    unsigned dwFacility  : 12   // Bits 27-16
    unsigned dwException : 16   // Bits 15-0
} EXCEPTION_CODE;
```

dwFacility and *dwException* can be whatever you want them to be. By NT convention, *dwSeverity* uses a value of 1 to indicate an informational exception, 2 to indicate a warning, and 3 to specify an error. Set *dwOwner* to 1 to stamp this code as one of your own. *dwReserved* must be 0; in fact, NT will automatically clear it. Here is an easy way to distinguish programmer-defined exceptions from those used by Microsoft: the high byte for programmer-defined codes will always be 0x60, 0xA0, or 0xE0, whereas for Microsoft's it will be 0x40, 0x80, or 0xC0.

dwExceptionFlags has one possible non-zero setting, EXCEPTION_ NONCONTINUABLE. This indicates that the offending instruction cannot be retried, and any attempt to do so will itself trigger an exception (EXCEPTION_NONCONTINUABLE_EXCEPTION). Passing this argument as 0 says that the instruction can be reexecuted—provided, of course, that there is an exception filter function that knows how to remedy the situation. For most exceptions, it is probably reasonable to reattempt the instruction, or at least give yourself the option to do so. Noncontinuable exceptions should be reserved for truly serious error conditions. *dwExceptionFlags* is returned in the *ExceptionFlags* field of the EXCEPTION_RECORD.

dwArguments and *lpdwArguments* allow you to pass yourself additional information. They will be reported in the *NumberParameters* and *ExceptionInformation* fields of the EXCEPTION_RECORD.

In the DLLs I present later in this book, I use RaiseException() to report memory allocation errors. Raising an exception is quicker and easier than testing return values at many levels of a call tree. The exception I raise is STATUS_NO_MEMORY, which is the exception raised by the Heap Allocation routines under certain conditions (see Chapter 4). There is no reason to make this a noncontinuable exception; a smart exception filter function might be able to adjust memory-usage conditions so that the request could be retried and succeed—though I don't provide one. I also pass the number of bytes I tried to allocate as the first element in the *lpdwArguments* array.

Structured Termination Handling

Windows NT also offers C/C++ syntax for termination handlers. This sets up code that will be executed no matter how a block of code terminates. The only exclusion from this behavior is a statement that kills the running thread or process, such as ExitThread() or ExitProcess(). (This includes implicit calls, caused by using C run-time functions like exit() and abort()). In this case, the *finally* will not be executed.

```
try
    {
    // [Normal flow of execution]
    }
finally
    {
    // [Cleanup code here]
    }
```

Note that termination handlers and exception handlers must be separate. This code, for example, won't compile:

```
try
    {
    // [Guarded statements]
    }
except (EXCEPTION_EXECUTE_HANDLER)
    {
    // [Exception handler]
    }
finally
    {
    // [Termination handler]
    }
```

However, this will:

```
try
    {
    try
        {
        // [Guarded statements]
        }
    except (EXCEPTION_EXECUTE_HANDLER)
        {
        // [Exception handler]
        }
    }
finally
    {
    // [Termination handler]
    }
```

The pseudofunction AbnormalTermination() can be used in the *finally* block (and only in the *finally* block) to determine whether the *try* block terminated with some kind of specific transfer of control (*return, break, goto, or an exception*):

```
BOOL AbnormalTermination(VOID);
```

If the *try* block executes to completion, it will fall through into the *finally* block, and AbnormalTermination() will return FALSE. Any statement that causes an abnormal termination can be expensive because it causes NT to search backward up the stack for termination and exception handlers. For instance, using *return* inside a *try* block in response to an error or as the last statement in a *try* block is considered an incorrect use of *try/finally*. Therefore, Microsoft C/C++ for Windows NT provides an additional keyword, *leave*, which breaks out of a *try* block without triggering either an abnormal termination or an unwind. There is a very good discussion of *leave* in Jeff Richter's *Advanced Windows NT*. It behaves the way a *break* statement behaves in a *for* loop, but its natural habitat is the *try* block of a *try/finally*.

Here is the function _WNetAddStationToList(), a component of the DLLs presented later in this book. The first listing shows *return* statements embedded in the *try* block. Though the function works just fine this way, this is the expensive way to do it. (Don't worry about the details of this function; it uses techniques and API calls that we have not discussed yet.)

```
BOOL WINAPI _WNetAddStationToList(LPSTATION_INFO lpStationInfo,
                                  WORD wNameLength)
{
    int i;

    // Use hEnumStationsMutex to protect this code
    WaitForSingleObject(hEnumStationsMutex, INFINITE);

    try
        {
        for (i = 0; i < MAX_NAMES; ++i)
            {
            if (lpStationTable[i].szStationName[0] == '\0')
                break;
            if (lstrcmpi(lpStationTable[i].szStationName,
                        lpStationInfo->szStationName) == 0)
                // Already in the list
                {
                return TRUE;        // Expensive!
```

```
            }
        }
    if (i == MAX_NAMES)
        {
        return FALSE;          // Expensive!
        }
    lpStationTable[i] = *lpStationInfo;
    return TRUE;                  // Expensive and unnecessary!
    }
finally
    {
    ReleaseMutex(hEnumStationsMutex);
    }
}
```

Here is a better implementation that uses *leave* instead of *return* in the *try* block, then does the *return* after the termination handler:

```
BOOL WINAPI _WNetAddStationToList(LPSTATION_INFO lpStationInfo,
                                  WORD wNameLength)
{
    int i;
    BOOL bRetcode = TRUE;

    // Use hEnumStationsMutex to protect this code
    WaitForSingleObject(hEnumStationsMutex, INFINITE);

    try
        {
        for (i = 0; i < MAX_NAMES; ++i)
            {
            if (lpStationTable[i].szStationName[0] == '\0')
                break;
            if (lstrcmpi(lpStationTable[i].szStationName,
                        lpStationInfo->szStationName) == 0)
                // Already in the list
                {
                leave;             // Much better
                }
            }
        if (i == MAX_NAMES)
            {
            bRetcode = FALSE;
            leave;                 // And cheaper
            }
        lpStationTable[i] = *lpStationInfo;
        }
```

```
finally
    {
    ReleaseMutex(hEnumStationsMutex);
    }
return bRetcode;
}
```

Conclusion

The Microsoft documentation states:

> Structured exception and termination handling is an integral part of the Win32 system and it enables a very robust implementation of the system software. It is envisioned that application developers also will use these mechanisms to create consistently robust and reliable applications.

(Microsoft Win32 Programmer's Reference, Volume 2, page 434)

The more I work with NT, the more I see how pervasive the impact of Structured Exception Handling and Structured Termination Handling is, for several reasons:

- In addition to the normal flow of execution through your code (the horizontal flow, if you will), there is a vertical flow that you must be prepared to handle. Termination and exception handlers allow you to detect a vertical exit from your code, and handle it cleanly.
- Termination handlers make your life much easier. They allow you to have only one exit point from a function, no matter how much cleanup must be done. They also guarantee that operating system resources will not be left in an unknown state.
- Correct use of termination and exception handlers is essential to harnessing the power of NT. It is particularly important when developing RPC applications, as many RPC errors are reported as exceptions, not function return values.
- As you will see in Chapter 4, Structured Exception Handling can be an integral part of sophisticated algorithms for memory management.

Suggested Readings

Richter, Jeff. *Advanced Windows NT*. Redmond, WA: Microsoft Press, 1993. Chapter 10.

Structured Exception Handling Overview in the Win32 on-line help. Published as Chapter 64 of the *Win32 Programmer's Reference, Volume 2*.

Goodman, Kevin. "Clearer, More Comprehensive Error Processing with Win32 Structured Exception Handling." *Microsoft Systems Journal*, Vol. 9, No. 1, January 1994.

Microsoft Corporation. *Microsoft Knowledge Base*, supplied with the *Win32 SDK* as WIN32KB.HLP, has some good articles on specific details of Structured Exception Handling. For instance:

"Correct Use of Try/Finally"

"Try/Finally with Abort() in Try Body"

"try/finally with return in finally Body Preempts Unwind"

"Initiating an Unwind in an Exception Handler"

"Using volatile to Prevent Optimization of Try"

"Trapping Floating-Point Exceptions under NT"

"Noncontinuable Exceptions"

"Postmortem Debugging under Windows NT"

"Choosing the Debugger that the System Will Spawn"

## Chapter 4

Memory Allocation in Windows NT

Overview

Memory management has changed radically from Windows 3.X to Windows NT, at least at the operating system level. Because the underlying architecture is so different, the Win32 API adds two function sets for memory allocation—the Virtual Memory API and Heap Memory API. The Virtual Memory API is the closest to how the operating system itself actually does things. The Heap Memory API provides a layer on top of the Virtual API that is somewhat easier to work with. This is not to say that the Virtual API set is difficult to use; it is not. As you will see, there are certain tradeoffs that you have to make in choosing which API set to use. The situation is clouded further by the fact that the Global and Local allocation routines (GlobalAlloc(), LocalAlloc(), and their related functions) are still supported, and by the reemergence of the C runtime functions such as malloc() and calloc() as viable options.

Windows NT uses a virtual memory scheme in which every process runs in its own separate address space. As befits a 32-bit environment, each process has 4 GB of virtual memory available to it. The upper 2 GB are used by the operating system; the lower 2 GB are available to the application. The mapping of virtual addresses to physical addresses uses a page-based scheme. Because the page is the unit used by this scheme, it is the unit of granularity for NT memory allocation. On Intel chips, a page is 4096 bytes. On the DEC Alpha, a page is 8192 bytes. On MIPS machines, the page size is configurable; NT uses a page size of 4096 bytes. You need never assume a particular page size; the GetSystemInfo() function reports this information.

Since the virtual address space of 4 GB is unlikely to be supported by that much real memory, NT swaps pages of physical memory to disk to satisfy memory allocation requests. Every process has a set of pages known as its **working set**; these are the pages of memory belonging to the process that are currently resident in RAM. NT will dynamically adjust the working set of processes to respond to changing usage conditions. When a process requests a new page of memory and none is available, NT swaps one of the other pages belonging to that process to disk on a first-allocated, first-discarded basis. In addition, NT uses a demand-paging strategy; even after pages are allocated, they are not brought into physical memory until they are actually accessed.

States of Memory

NT associates a couple of attributes with each page of virtual memory. One describes the measure in which the page has been allocated to a process. The three possibilities are

- The page is **free**; it has not been allocated.
- The page is **reserved**. The process has been granted a given virtual address (or range of virtual addresses), but no physical memory or swap file space has been associated with it.
- The page is **committed**. Here, a virtual address is fully supported by physical storage.

There are also three fundamental levels of memory access:

- No access is allowed. Free and reserved memory, by definition, cannot be accessed. In addition, you can deny all access to a committed block for some algorithmic purpose, like having a guard page to detect the need for more heap space. (However, NT also allows you to set up a page as a guard page and generates an EXCEPTION_GUARD_PAGE exception to inform you that you have entered it.)
- The page may be accessed on a read-only basis. Committed memory can be set to allow read-only access. You might do this, for instance, to prevent sensitive data from being accidentally overwritten.
- The page may be read from and written to. This allows full access to a page of committed memory and is the most common usage.

The Virtual Memory Allocation API

The Virtual Memory Allocation API set most closely reflects the underlying NT memory management scheme. It consists of a small group of functions, of which the most important, as you would expect, are the ones that allocate and free memory—VirtualAlloc() and VirtualFree().

The unique innovation that Win32 provides is that memory allocation can be either a one-step or two-step process, depending on how you call VirtualAlloc(). This is because memory has three possible states (free, reserved, or committed), rather than just two (free or allocated). Thus, VirtualAlloc() lets you reserve memory for later commitment, commit memory that you have previously reserved, or reserve and commit memory in a single step.

```
LPVOID VirtualAlloc(
        LPVOID    lpAddress,
        DWORD     dwSize,
        DWORD     dwAllocationType,
        DWORD     dwProtect);
```

lpAddress is the virtual address of the region you are allocating. The first time you allocate a block, you will most likely pass *lpAddress* as NULL, although you can specify a base virtual address if you have some reason for doing so. If the address is already in use, VirtualAlloc() will return NULL. If you reserve memory first and commit it later, you need to supply a non-NULL address when calling VirtualAlloc() to commit the memory.

dwSize is the number of bytes you want to reserve or commit. NT will scale *lpAddress* and *dwSize* so that they describe an even multiple of the system page size. Assuming a page size of 4096 bytes, if you call VirtualAlloc() with an *lpAddress* of NULL and *dwSize* of 16000, NT will allocate a region of 16384 bytes. If you try to commit 100 bytes starting at address 5000, NT will commit 4096 bytes at address 4096. You do not need to adjust your requests; NT will do this automatically. It will not fail the request.

dwAllocationType specifies whether you want to reserve memory, commit it, or do both at once. To reserve memory, pass the constant MEM_RESERVE; to commit it, pass MEM_COMMIT. For a one-step reserve/commit, you may OR the two together, though MEM_COMMIT is sufficient.

The *dwProtect* argument indicates what level of access you desire to the newly allocated memory. Even if you are reserving memory, this argument is relevant. You should request the access that you will later need when you commit the memory. This makes the subsequent commitment work a little more efficiently. The most important values for dwProtect are PAGE_NOACCESS, PAGE_READONLY, and PAGE_READWRITE. Other less-used possibilities are PAGE_WRITECOPY, which requests NT to make a new copy of the page when it is written to; PAGE_EXECUTE, PAGE_EXECUTE_READ, PAGE_EXECUTE_READWRITE, and PAGE_EXECUTE_WRITECOPY, which also grant permission to execute the block of memory. There are two page-protection modifiers, PAGE_GUARD and PAGE_NOCACHE, which can be ORed with one of the other protection constants. PAGE_GUARD causes NT to raise an EXCEPTION_GUARD_PAGE exception when the page is entered. This operates as a signal that a data structure (like a stack) needs to be expanded. PAGE_NOCACHE is more esoteric and of little use to application programs; its principal relevance is in device drivers.

Here is an example that reserves a block of memory, then commits it in response to an exception. This is a very common and important use of Virtual Memory Allocation in conjunction with Structured Exception Handling. Notice also the use of a termination handler to release the memory when you are through with it, and the nesting of a *try-except* within a *try-finally*. You will find this example on the source code disk as \NTNET\CODE\MEMORY\EXAMPLE4.CPP.

```
/********
*
* EXAMPLE4.CPP
*
* Demonstrates using an exception handler
* to commit memory only as needed.
*
* It first tries to write to a buffer that has been reserved,
* but not committed.
*
* The exception filter function commits the memory, then returns
* EXCEPTION_CONTINUE_EXECUTION (if the commit succeeded, of course).
*
********/

#include <windows.h>
#include <stdio.h>

DWORD CheckPointer(DWORD dwException, char **p)
{
```

```
   printf("\nCheckPointer() entered");
   if (dwException != EXCEPTION_ACCESS_VIOLATION)
      {
      printf("\nCheckPointer() returning EXCEPTION_CONTINUE_SEARCH");
      return EXCEPTION_CONTINUE_SEARCH;
      }

   *p = (char *) VirtualAlloc(*p, 4096, MEM_COMMIT, PAGE_READWRITE);

   if (*p == NULL)
      {
      printf("\nCheckPointer() returning EXCEPTION_EXECUTE_HANDLER");
      return EXCEPTION_EXECUTE_HANDLER;
      }
   printf("\nCheckPointer() returning EXCEPTION_CONTINUE_EXCEPTION");
   return EXCEPTION_CONTINUE_EXECUTION;
}

void main(int argc, char *argv[])
{
   char *p;

   p = (char *) VirtualAlloc(NULL, 4096, MEM_RESERVE,
                             PAGE_READWRITE);

   try
      {
      try
         {
         strcpy(p, "Hi, folks");
         }
      except (CheckPointer(GetExceptionCode(), &p))
         {
         printf("\nMemory allocation error");
         ExitProcess(1);
         }
      }
   finally
      {
      if (p != NULL)
         {
         printf("\n%s\n", p);
         VirtualFree(p, 0, MEM_RELEASE);
         }
      }
   ExitProcess(0);
}
```

Why Reserve Memory?

I have found in trying to explain this material that, inevitably, the question arises: alright, so you *can* do things this way, but why would you *want* to?

The primary reason is that reserving memory mimics NT policy of not consuming a resource until it is actually needed. The preceding example does not dramatically illustrate the value of this principle. Suppose, however, you have an array that under maximum (but highly unlikely) conditions could reach 10 MB in size. Under most circumstances, it will probably never get bigger than 1 MB. It is extremely wasteful and causes severe performance degradation to sit on 10 MB of memory that you will probably never use. However, you must have contiguous virtual addresses since the data structure you are creating must be treated as an array.

The two-step reserve/commit provides a very clean solution to this problem. When you first allocate the data structure, you reserve a 10-MB region by calling VirtualAlloc().

```
LPBYTE lp;
lp = VirtualAlloc(NULL, 10 * 1024 * 1024, MEM_RESERVE,
                  PAGE_READWRITE);
```

You then surround reads and writes to the array with *try/except* logic. Your exception filter function will look very much like the one in the preceding example. This way, you have an object that looks to you like a simple large array but that uses only the physical memory that you really need.

By the way, note that the exception filter function just presented does not assume that the call to committing the memory succeeds. Indeed, you cannot make this assumption; you must check to see if VirtualAlloc() returns NULL. Reserving the memory only assigns virtual address space; it does not in any way guarantee that the physical memory will be there when you need it.

VirtualFree() reverses the allocation process. Like VirtualAlloc(), it can be done in a one-step or two-step fashion. Thus, you can decommit a committed block of memory. In this case, the virtual addresses continue to be reserved; they are available to be recommitted at a later time. The physical memory is returned to the operating system. You can also release a block of memory, thereby relinquishing both the virtual addresses and the underlying physical memory.

VirtualFree() takes one less argument than VirtualAlloc()—the access mode is irrelevant. Here too you specify the base address, the number of bytes being affected, and the operation you want to perform (decommit or release).

```
BOOL VirtualFree(
        LPVOID  lpAddress,
        DWORD   dwBytes,
        DWORD   dwFreeType);
```

As with VirtualAlloc(), *lpAddress* will be rounded down to a page boundary, and *dwSize* will be rounded up to a multiple of the page size. *dwFreeType* can be either MEM_DECOMMIT or MEM_RELEASE. If you are releasing memory rather than decommitting it, these three conditions must be met:

- *lpAddress* must be the base of the region you originally reserved when you called VirtualAlloc().
- *dwBytes* must be zero.
- All pages in the region must be in the same state (committed or reserved). You can satisfy this requirement by first decommitting the entire block. There is no requirement that all pages be committed for a decommit request to succeed.

```
LPBYTE pBase = (LPBYTE) VirtualAlloc(
                        NULL,
                        1024 * 1024,
                        MEM_RESERVE,
                        PAGE_READWRITE);
//
// [Use memory here, committing it as needed]
//
// Now decommit the memory, then release it
VirtualFree(pBase, 1024 * 1024, MEM_DECOMMIT);
VirtualFree(pBase, 0, MEM_RELEASE);
```

The only caveat is that if you reserve a very large block, decommitting the entire block (whether or not you have committed it) is time-consuming. It is more efficient to decommit only the number of bytes that you have actually committed (assuming that you are committing from the base of the block and not fragmenting the block into reserved and committed sections). You can do this by either maintaining a running count of the number of committed bytes or by calling VirtualQuery() to find out the size of the committed region. This way, you will know exactly how many bytes you need to decommit, and the decommit request will execute much more quickly. You should also check to make sure the number of committed bytes is not zero. Decommitting an entire block where no bytes have been committed is also expensive.

Here's a revision of the previous example that uses VirtualQuery() to determine how many bytes have been committed:

```
MEMORY_BASIC_INFORMATION mbi;
LPBYTE pBase = (LPBYTE) VirtualAlloc(
                         NULL,
                         1024 * 1024,
                         MEM_RESERVE,
                         PAGE_READWRITE);
//
// [Use memory here, committing it as needed]
//
ZeroMemory(&mbi, sizeof (MEMORY_BASIC_INFORMATION));
VirtualQuery(pBase, &mbi, sizeof (MEMORY_BASIC_INFORMATION));
if (mbi.State == MEM_COMMIT && mbi.RegionSize > 0)
   VirtualFree(pBase, mbi.RegionSize, MEM_DECOMMIT);
VirtualFree(pBase, 0, MEM_RELEASE);
```

Other Virtual-Memory Functions

The other virtual-memory functions are of less significance, though they can be useful under certain circumstances. VirtualProtect() and VirtualProtectEx() change the access mode of a block of memory. This can be valuable in protecting sensitive data after you have allocated memory for it and written the data into the memory. Here are their prototypes:

```
BOOL VirtualProtect(
        LPVOID  lpAddress,
        DWORD   dwSize,
        DWORD   dwNewProtect,
        PDWORD  lpdwOldProtect);
BOOL VirtualProtectEx(
        HANDLE  hProcess,
        LPVOID  lpAddress,
        DWORD   dwSize,
        DWORD   dwNewProtect,
        PDWORD  lpdwOldProtect);
```

lpAddress points to the region you want to change. *dwSize* is the number of bytes. As with all the Virtual Memory functions, they will be scaled so that they describe complete pages of memory in the region. *dwNewProtect* is the new access mode, and *lpdwOldProtect* returns the previous protection assigned to the memory. All pages in the indicated region must be committed; otherwise, the request will fail.

VirtualProtectEx() allows you to manipulate memory belonging to another process; it takes an additional argument, *hProcess*. This is the handle of the process that owns the memory.

VirtualQuery() and VirtualQueryEx() return information about a given block of virtual memory. VirtualQueryEx(), like VirtualProtectEx(), works with the virtual memory of a remote process.

```
BOOL VirtualQuery(
        LPCVOID lpBaseAddress,
        PMEMORY_BASIC_INFORMATION lpMBI,
        DWORD   dwLength);
BOOL VirtualQueryEx(
        HANDLE  hProcess,
        LPCVOID lpBaseAddress,
        PMEMORY_BASIC_INFORMATION lpMBI,
        DWORD   dwLength);
```

They populate a MEMORY_BASIC_INFORMATION structure, whose definition is as follows:

```
typedef struct _MEMORY_BASIC_INFORMATION
{
    PVOID   BaseAddress;
    PVOID   AllocationBase;
    DWORD   AllocationProtect;
    DWORD   RegionSize;
    DWORD   State;
    DWORD   Protect;
    DWORD   Type;
} MEMORY_BASIC_INFORMATION;
```

Each call to VirtualQuery() will report on the largest contiguous range of memory starting at *lpBaseAddress* for which all the pages have identical characteristics. *RegionSize* is the number of bytes in the region being reported. *State* is MEM_FREE, MEM_COMMIT, or MEM_RESERVE. *Protect* is the current access mode of the region; *AllocationProtect* is the access mode that was requested when the region was first allocated. *Type* can be MEM_IMAGE, indicating that the pages are an executable file image; MEM_MAPPED, designating a memory-mapped view of a file; or MEM_PRIVATE, specifying that the memory is private to this process. *BaseAddress* is the beginning of the region being described; *AllocationBase* is the base of the block from which this region has been carved. In other words, *AllocationBase* is the address returned by the first call to VirtualAlloc(); *BaseAddress* was returned by a subsequent call that changed the state or access mode of this memory.

Heap Memory Allocation

In Windows NT, heap memory allocation has two meanings. One connotes the API set known as the Heap Memory Allocation API. The other is a more general usage, referring to all the memory allocation API sets that manage memory in the default heap of a process. These include the LocalAlloc() and GlobalAlloc() APIs inherited from Windows 3.X, the malloc() family of functions, and the Heap Memory Allocation API itself. They are all built on top of Virtual Memory allocation, but shield applications from the additional complexity of the Virtual Memory functions. They also provide subsegment allocation capabilities. The granularity of the Virtual Memory functions is rather coarse; the minimum amount of memory you can allocate is one page—which currently means either 4096 or 8192 bytes, depending on the hardware your program is running on. The other API sets give you much finer granularity. In exchange, they give you less control over how memory is managed and do not provide as much memory protection.

The Heap Memory Allocation API

The Heap Allocation functions, like the Virtual Memory Allocation functions, are new to Win32. They expose some of the underlying memory-management scheme, though not as much as the Virtual API. There are only a few functions, the most important of which are HeapAlloc() and HeapFree(). The other functions in the group are:

- HeapCreate() and HeapDestroy(), which you can use to allocate and release a new region for subsegment allocation
- HeapReAlloc(), which lets you resize a memory object allocated by HeapAlloc()
- HeapSize(), which reports the size of an object

In addition, GetProcessHeap() returns a handle to the default heap of the process. When HeapAlloc() and HeapFree() are used in this manner, they are exactly equivalent to GlobalAlloc(), LocalAlloc(), and malloc(). That is, the memory is all allocated from the same block of virtual address space, and you can use the functions from the different API sets interchangeably. You can obtain a piece of memory by calling malloc(), then free it by calling HeapFree(). Of course, there are no good reasons to do things this way.

GetProcessHeap() takes no arguments and returns a handle.

```
HANDLE GetProcessHeap(VOID);
```

You can use the handle as input to HeapAlloc() to allocate memory from the default heap, or you can create a new heap by calling HeapCreate().

```
HANDLE HeapCreate(DWORD dwOptions,
                  DWORD dwInitialCommitted,
                  DWORD dwTotalReserved);
```

If *dwOptions* is passed as zero, then (by default) memory allocations that fail will return NULL pointers, and NT will automatically serialize access to the heap by multiple threads within your application. This is probably the behavior you will want most of the time; if you want to change it, you can specify two flags, HEAP_GENERATE_EXCEPTIONS and HEAP_NO_ SERIALIZE. HeapAlloc() and HeapFree() also include a flags argument. If you pass the zero flag to HeapCreate(), you can override the default behavior by setting the corresponding flag for those functions.

dwInitialCommitted is the number of bytes you want allocated in committed pages; typically, you will pass this as a small number, somewhere between 4096 and 16384. *dwTotalReserved* is the number of bytes you want allocated as reserved memory. The Heap Allocation routines will automatically commit new pages from this region when it becomes necessary. The committed portion of the heap will always grow, but never shrink; once a page in the heap has been committed, NT will not decommit it. You can pass *dwTotalReserved* as zero to indicate that you want the heap to be able to grow to all of available memory.

The HANDLE returned by either HeapCreate() or GetProcessHeap(), which is just the base virtual address of the heap, is then passed to the rest of the heap functions: HeapAlloc(), HeapFree(), HeapDestroy(), HeapReAlloc(), and HeapSize().

HeapAlloc() allocates memory from a heap.

```
LPVOID HeapAlloc(HANDLE hHeap, DWORD dwFlags, DWORD dwBytes);
```

hHeap and *dwBytes* should be obvious. *dwFlags* can be the same non-zero values as specified above for HeapCreate(), HEAP_GENERATE_ EXCEPTIONS, and HEAP_NO_SERIALIZE. No matter what you passed to HeapCreate(), these flags will take precedence if you set them when calling

HeapAlloc(). If you do not set them, they will inherit whatever values you passed to HeapCreate(). To reiterate, HEAP_GENERATE_EXCEPTIONS means that if the allocation request cannot be satisfied, NT will generate a STATUS_NO_MEMORY (0xC0000017) exception, rather than return a NULL pointer. HEAP_NO_SERIALIZE means that access to the heap will not be serialized among multiple threads during this call to HeapAlloc().

You can pass one additional flag, HEAP_ZERO_MEMORY. This tells NT to clear the allocated block to zeroes. Ordinarily, NT does this automatically; in fact, the heap itself is zeroed when you call HeapCreate(). However, by the time you call HeapAlloc(), your process is already considered to own the heap, so NT does not rezero individual subsegments that you allocate from it unless you set the HEAP_ZERO_MEMORY flag.

HeapFree() releases memory obtained from HeapAlloc().

```
BOOL HeapFree(HANDLE hHeap, DWORD dwFlags, LPVOID lpMem);
```

lpMem is the pointer returned by HeapAlloc(); *hHeap*, again, is the handle generated by HeapCreate() or returned by GetProcessHeap(). HEAP_NO_SERIALIZE is the only setting currently defined for *dwFlags*, and means the same thing as it does with HeapAlloc()—don't serialize access to the heap while you are executing this function.

HeapDestroy() releases the memory originally allocated for the heap when you called HeapCreate(). Presumably, HeapDestroy() calls VirtualFree() twice, once with MEM_DECOMMIT and once with MEM_RELEASE. As I said earlier, the Heap Allocation functions will commit new pages as they need them. Once a page is committed, it will not be decommitted. You should not call HeapDestroy() with the heap handle returned by GetProcessHeap().

Less important functions are HeapSize(), which returns the size of an allocated block within a heap, and HeapReAlloc(), which resizes a previously allocated block.

```
DWORD HeapSize(HANDLE hHeap, DWORD dwFlags, LPCVOID lpMem);
```

lpMem is the pointer returned by HeapAlloc(). The only possible setting for *dwFlags* at this time is HEAP_NO_SERIALIZE. The return value of the function is the size of *lpMem*; it is zero if the function fails.

```
LPVOID HeapReAlloc(HANDLE hHeap,
                   DWORD dwFlags,
                   LPVOID lpMem,
                   DWORD dwBytes);
```

dwBytes is the new size that you desire for *lpMem*. *dwFlags* can take on all the values described above for HeapAlloc() (HEAP_GENERATE_ EXCEPTIONS, HEAP_NO_SERIALIZE, and HEAP_ZERO_MEMORY), as well as one additional setting, HEAP_REALLOC_IN_PLACE_ONLY, which prevents NT from moving the block to satisfy the request. The return value is the new virtual address where the memory resides (unless the request cannot be satisfied, in which case you either get a NULL pointer or a STATUS_NO_MEMORY exception).

Global and Local Memory Allocation

The time-honored global and local memory allocation API sets are still supported in Windows NT. After all, there is a great deal of code that has been written using these functions; breaking them would cause major side effects and was no doubt adjudged to be politically impossible. However, they have none of their previous semantics; in fact, they are now just different names for the same functions. You can use the local and global functions interchangeably with the same piece of memory. For instance, this code is perfectly acceptable:

```
LPSTR lp;
lp = LocalAlloc(LPTR, 255);
...
GlobalFree(lp);
```

Of course, it makes no sense to do this. The point I am making here is not that it is now appropriate to engage in questionable coding practices; rather, because there is no distinction between NEAR and FAR pointers in Windows NT, the LocalAlloc() and GlobalAlloc() family of functions behave exactly the same. These functions reflect the memory management environment that Microsoft created for Windows 2.1, where memory had to be maintained in two states: as a handle most of the time and as a pointer when you needed to access it. This scheme became irrelevant when Windows 3.0 went to protected mode. From that time on, there has been no need to LocalAlloc() or GlobalAlloc() a HANDLE, then LocalLock() or GlobalLock() it to convert it to a pointer. In protected mode, pointers are just virtual addresses, so Windows can let you keep track of unchanging pointers and still be free to move memory around as it sees fit. In Windows 3.X, the distinction between NEAR and FAR pointers is still pertinent; it is rooted in the segmented architecture of 16-bit Intel chips. Of course, the 80286 is now obsolete as well. There are still a few lying around, but it is silly to limit what you can do on 32-bit machines because of restrictions imposed by 16-bit machines that you may never encounter. With Windows NT, segmented memory also disappears; for all intents and purposes, local and global memory allocation is obsolete.

Surprisingly, though, much of the sample code coming out of Microsoft uses LocalAlloc(). It is certainly understandable that Microsoft did not want to stop supporting LocalAlloc() and GlobalAlloc(); what is less clear is why new applications should continue to use them, except in places where they have to (with the clipboard, for instance). On the low side, there are two new API sets that more closely reflect NT's way of doing things; on the other side, it is now all right to use malloc() and calloc() to do Windows memory allocation. With this rich panoply of options, why would you choose LocalAlloc()?

A Little PWALK through Memory

In this section, I present a sample application, MEMTEST.EXE, whose source code is in \NTNET\CODE\MEMORY\MEMTEST.CPP. In concert with the Win32 SDK utility PWALK.EXE (Process Walker), it demonstrates how the various memory allocation APIs behave. From this, the relative advantages and disadvantages of each emerge in pretty clear relief.

Figure 4-1 and Figure 4-2 show the PWALK screens that appear when MEMTEST.EXE first starts up.

In Figure 4-1, I have highlighted the lines showing the process's stack (beginning at virtual address 0x00030000) and its default heap (at address 0x00130000). Notice that the stack begins with a region of 1,040,384 bytes that has been reserved. Next comes a single page that has been committed and given PAGE_READWRITE access; it has also been flagged as a guard page. Following this is the currently active stack region, consisting of 4096 bytes of committed, read-write memory. When the stack needs more than 4096 bytes of memory, the guard page is entered, which triggers an EXCEPTION_GUARD_PAGE exception. At this point, NT's exception handler removes the guard page protection on the guard page and commits a new guard page out of the bottom of the reserved portion.

The default heap for the process is the 1-MB region that begins at 0x00130000. The first three pages have been committed. If this proves insufficient, the committed portion of the heap will grow into the reserved area at virtual address 0x00133000. As you will see, all calls to GlobalAlloc(), LocalAlloc(), malloc(), and HeapAlloc(GetProcessHeap(), ...) are satisfied from this location.

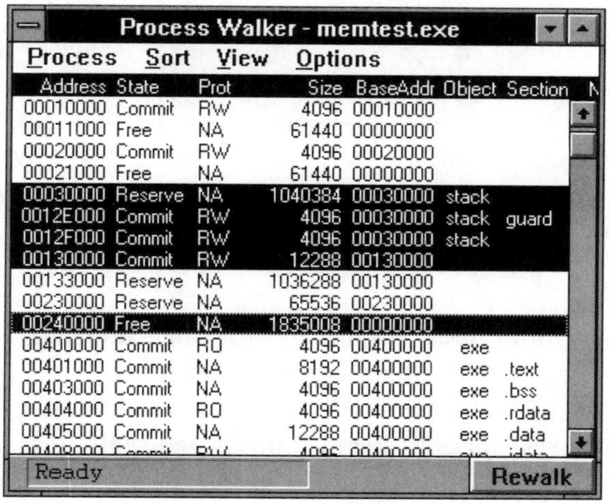

Process Walker - memtest.exe

Process Sort View Options

Address	State	Prot	Size	BaseAddr	Object	Section	N
00010000	Commit	RW	4096	00010000			
00011000	Free	NA	61440	00000000			
00020000	Commit	RW	4096	00020000			
00021000	Free	NA	61440	00000000			
00030000	Reserve	NA	1040384	00030000	stack		
0012E000	Commit	RW	4096	00030000	stack	guard	
0012F000	Commit	RW	4096	00030000	stack		
00130000	Commit	RW	12288	00130000			
00133000	Reserve	NA	1036288	00130000			
00230000	Reserve	NA	65536	00230000			
00240000	Free	NA	1835008	00000000			
00400000	Commit	RO	4096	00400000	exe		
00401000	Commit	NA	8192	00400000	exe	.text	
00403000	Commit	NA	4096	00400000	exe	.bss	
00404000	Commit	RO	4096	00400000	exe	.rdata	
00405000	Commit	NA	12288	00400000	exe	.data	
00408000	Commit	RW	4096	00400000	exe	.idata	

Ready Rewalk

Figure 4-1. PWALK Display at Startup—Screen 1

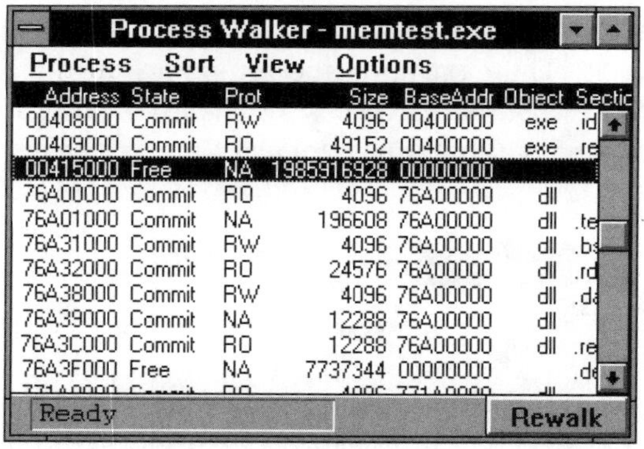

Process Walker - memtest.exe

Process Sort View Options

Address	State	Prot	Size	BaseAddr	Object	Sectic
00408000	Commit	RW	4096	00400000	exe	.id
00409000	Commit	RO	49152	00400000	exe	.re
00415000	Free	NA	1985916928	00000000		
76A00000	Commit	RO	4096	76A00000	dll	
76A01000	Commit	NA	196608	76A00000	dll	.te
76A31000	Commit	RW	4096	76A00000	dll	.b
76A32000	Commit	RO	24576	76A00000	dll	.rd
76A38000	Commit	RW	4096	76A00000	dll	.da
76A39000	Commit	NA	12288	76A00000	dll	
76A3C000	Commit	RO	12288	76A00000	dll	.re
76A3F000	Free	NA	7737344	00000000		.de
771A0000	Commit	RO	4096	771A0000	dll	

Ready Rewalk

Figure 4-2. PWALK Display at Startup—Screen 2

At the bottom of Figure 4-1, I have highlighted the 1,835,008 region of free memory beginning at address 0x00240000. I will soon make several calls to VirtualAlloc(), and they will be apportioned from this area. After this, the next virtual address the process is using is 0x00400000, the universal instance handle. This is the virtual memory address where, by default, NT maps a process's executable file, and is the value reported by the *hInstance* argument to WinMain().

In Figure 4-2, I have highlighted a free region at 0x00415000. I will create a private heap with HeapCreate(); it will be allocated at the next 64K boundary, 0x00420000. Notice the size of the region; it's almost 2 GB.

In Figure 4-3, look at the description of the area at 0x77C6E000.

This is another large chunk of free memory (127 MB). When you call VirtualAlloc() with a non-NULL base address and a MEM_COMMIT request, it will return NULL until you ask it for 0x7F470000. However, if you only ask NT to reserve the memory, you get a non-NULL result much sooner.

MEMTEST has three menu items: the first one allocates memory, the second tests memory access violations, and the third tests writes to released memory. Figure 4-4 shows the memory allocations that occur when you walk the virtual address space trying to commit a non-NULL base address.

The program first calls VirtualAlloc() with a base address of NULL and asks for 32 bytes. This is represented by the pointer *lpVirtual1*. As Figure 4-4 shows, the address assigned is 0x003D0000. Next it adds 4096 bytes to *lpVirtual1* and calls VirtualAlloc() to commit 32 bytes at this specific address. It keeps adding 4096 bytes until it gets a non-NULL address. This is the pointer *lpVirtual3*—you had to walk a long way (all the way to 0x7F470000) to find it! The next thing the program does is VirtualAlloc() another buffer using a NULL base address; this is *lpVirtual2*. As Figure 4-4 shows, this is allocated 65,536 bytes past *lpVirtual1*.

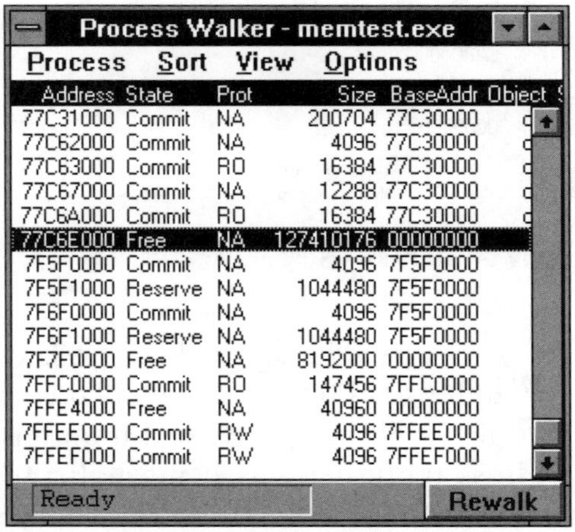

Figure 4-3.   PWALK Display Showing Large Block of Free Virtual Memory

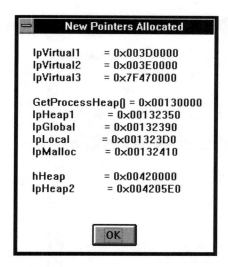

Figure 4-4. Initial Memory Allocations—Screen 1

To test the heap allocation routines [HeapAlloc(), GlobalAlloc(), LocalAlloc(), and malloc()], MEMTEST next allocates four pointers from the default process heap. The function GetProcessHeap() returns the HANDLE of the process's heap; as you can see, it is just the base address of the heap (0x00130000). *lpHeap1* is returned by a call to HeapAlloc(Get ProcessHeap(), ...). *lpGlobal* results from a call to GlobalAlloc(), *lpLocal* from one to LocalAlloc(), and *lpMalloc* is generated by malloc(). Finally, MEMTEST creates a new heap by calling HeapCreate() and asking for 8192 bytes of committed memory from a total of 65,536 bytes reserved. This is the variable *hHeap*; it is the base virtual address of a newly committed region of memory. *lpHeap2* is HeapAlloc()'d from this new heap.

Figure 4-5 and Figure 4-6 show the new memory dumps produced by PWALK.

In Figure 4-5, I have highlighted the default process heap again; the pointers from HeapAlloc(GetProcessHeap(), ...), GlobalAlloc(), LocalAlloc(), and malloc() are all from this region (0x00132350, 0x00132490, 0x001323D0, and 0x00132410). Notice that these pointers are 64 bytes apart, although the amount of memory requested was only 32 bytes. Presumably, the extra 32 bytes is control information used by the subsegment allocator.

The last four lines I have highlighted at the bottom of Figure 4-5 show the memory allocated for *lpVirtual1* and *lpVirtual2*. Although I only asked for 32 bytes for each of them, I got 4096–and this is not the only overhead.

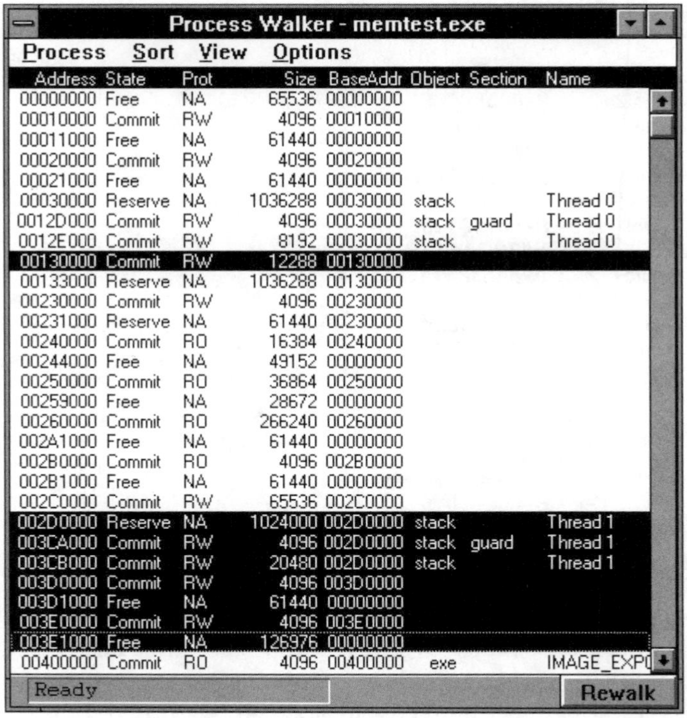

Address	State	Prot	Size	BaseAddr	Object	Section	Name
Process Walker - memtest.exe							
Process Sort View Options							
Address State	Prot		Size BaseAddr	Object Section			Name
00000000 Free	NA		65536 00000000				
00010000 Commit	RW		4096 00010000				
00011000 Free	NA		61440 00000000				
00020000 Commit	RW		4096 00020000				
00021000 Free	NA		61440 00000000				
00030000 Reserve	NA		1036288 00030000	stack			Thread 0
0012D000 Commit	RW		4096 00030000	stack	guard		Thread 0
0012E000 Commit	RW		8192 00030000	stack			Thread 0
00130000 Commit	RW		12288 00130000				
00133000 Reserve	NA		1036288 00130000				
00230000 Commit	RW		4096 00230000				
00231000 Reserve	NA		61440 00230000				
00240000 Commit	RO		16384 00240000				
00244000 Free	NA		49152 00000000				
00250000 Commit	RO		36864 00250000				
00259000 Free	NA		28672 00000000				
00260000 Commit	RO		266240 00260000				
002A1000 Free	NA		61440 00000000				
002B0000 Commit	RO		4096 002B0000				
002B1000 Free	NA		61440 00000000				
002C0000 Commit	RW		65536 002C0000				
002D0000 Reserve	NA		1024000 002D0000	stack			Thread 1
003CA000 Commit	RW		4096 002D0000	stack	guard		Thread 1
003CB000 Commit	RW		20480 002D0000	stack			Thread 1
003D0000 Commit	RW		4096 003D0000				
003D1000 Free	NA		61440 00000000				
003E0000 Commit	RW		4096 003E0000				
003E1000 Free	NA		126976 00000000				
00400000 Commit	RO		4096 00400000	exe			IMAGE_EXP0
Ready							Rewalk

Figure 4-5.   PWALK Display After Initial Allocation—Screen 1

Notice that the 4096 bytes of committed memory at 0x003D0000 is followed by 61,440 bytes of free memory. Part of the experiment I was doing in TestMemoryAllocations() was to see if there was any way I could get to this additional memory (starting at 0x003D1000). There isn't. No matter what you do, the rest of the 64K starting at *lpVirtual1* is unavailable. In other words, an allocation of 32 bytes consumes 4K (actually, one pageful) of physical memory and 60K of virtual memory!

The three highlighted lines above this, describing the region beginning at 0x002D0000, show the stack that is allocated for TestMemoryAllocations(). Because this function has the potential of taking a very long time, I spin it off as a separate thread. The committed portion is larger (20,480 bytes) than the stack for Thread 0 because I purposely declared a 16K variable to see how it would affect the stack.

Figure 4-6 shows the second page of output from PWALK.

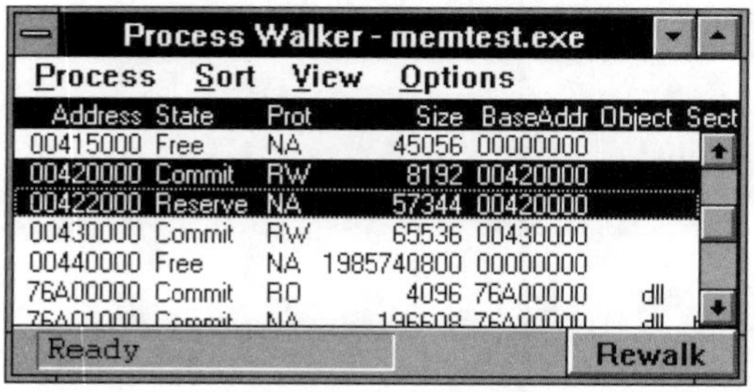

Figure 4-6. PWALK Display After Initial Allocations—Screen 2

This contains the listing for the newly created heap, represented by *hHeap* (0x00420000). It has exactly the characteristics we requested: 8192 bytes in committed pages, and 64K reserved.

Figure 4-7 points out the block allocated by VirtualAlloc(), when we walked through memory trying to commit specific virtual addresses. This is *lpVirtual3* in Figure 4-4, at 0x7F470000.

I was quite surprised to find that I had to go all the way to 0x7F470000 to get VirtualAlloc() to cooperate with me. It then occurred to me that I might get a lower address if I first tried to reserve the memory, then committed it afterwards. That's just what happened. Figure 4-8 shows the message box displayed by TestMemoryAllocations() in this case. Now, *lpVirtual1*, *lpVirtual2*, and *lpVirtual3* are 64K apart from each other; *lpVirtual3* is allocated before *1pVirtual2*.

Clearly, the prime disadvantage of using VirtualAlloc() is its exceedingly coarse granularity.

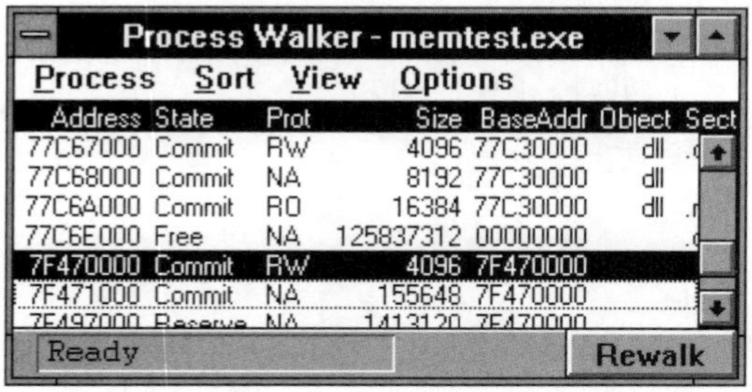

Figure 4-7. PWALK Display—Memory Allocated at 0x7F470000

Figure 4-8.   Initial Memory Allocations—Screen 2

Here is the function TestMemoryAllocations():

```
DWORD WINAPI TestMemoryAllocations(HWND hWnd)
{
    CHAR  szMessage[16384];
    DWORD dwOperation;
    SYSTEMTIME SystemTime;

    lpVirtual1 = (LPBYTE) VirtualAlloc(NULL, 32, MEM_COMMIT,
                            PAGE_READWRITE);
    lpVirtual2 = lpVirtual1 + 4096;

    GetSystemTime(&SystemTime);

    if (SystemTime.wSecond % 2 == 0)
        dwOperation = MEM_RESERVE;
    else
        dwOperation = MEM_COMMIT;

    while (TRUE)
        {
        // An interesting phenomenon occurs here
        // If we try to reserve the next page up from lpVirtual1,
        // it fails, but as soon as we get to the next
        // 64K boundary, we're in business.
```

```
      // However, if we try to commit lpVirtual3 in this
      // call to VirtualAlloc, it does not succeed until
      // we get into virtual addresses over 0x7F000000

      lpVirtual3 = (LPBYTE) VirtualAlloc(
          lpVirtual2, 32, dwOperation, PAGE_READWRITE);
      if (lpVirtual3 != NULL)
          break;
      lpVirtual2 += 4096;
      }
  // This commit call succeeds
  if (dwOperation == MEM_RESERVE)
     VirtualAlloc(lpVirtual3, 32, MEM_COMMIT, PAGE_READWRITE);

  // But this one fails
  VirtualAlloc(lpVirtual1, 8192, MEM_COMMIT, PAGE_READWRITE);

  lpVirtual2 = (LPBYTE) VirtualAlloc(NULL, 32, MEM_COMMIT,
                          PAGE_READWRITE);

  lpHeap1 = (LPBYTE) HeapAlloc(GetProcessHeap(), 0, 32);
  lpGlobal = (LPBYTE) GlobalAlloc(GPTR, 32);
  lpLocal = (LPBYTE) LocalAlloc(LPTR, 32);
  lpMalloc = (LPBYTE) malloc(32);

  hHeap = HeapCreate(0, 8192, 65536);
  lpHeap2 = (LPBYTE) HeapAlloc(hHeap, 0, 32);

  wsprintf(szMessage, "lpVirtual1        = 0x%08X\n"
                      "lpVirtual2        = 0x%08X\n"
                      "lpVirtual3        = 0x%08X\n\n"
                      "GetProcessHeap() = 0x%08X\n"
                      "lpHeap1           = 0x%08X\n"
                      "lpGlobal          = 0x%08X\n"
                      "lpLocal           = 0x%08X\n"
                      "lpMalloc          = 0x%08X\n\n"
                      "hHeap             = 0x%08X\n"
                      "lpHeap2           = 0x%08X\n",
      lpVirtual1, lpVirtual2, lpVirtual3,
      GetProcessHeap(), lpHeap1, lpGlobal, lpLocal, lpMalloc,
      hHeap, lpHeap2);

  // We use an event to govern our response
  // to WM_INITMENUPOPUP
  SetEvent(hEvent);
  MessageBox(hWnd, szMessage, "New Pointers Allocated", MB_OK);
```

```
if (((int) GetVersion()) > 0)   // Not Win32S
   ExitThread(0);
return 0;
}
```

The second thing MEMTEST tests is what you have to do to trigger an exception. My hypothesis was that only memory accesses outside of committed, read-write pages would trigger exceptions. Thus, if you are doing heap allocations, you can read or write anywhere within the heap within causing an exception. In other words, if you use the heap allocation APIs, your memory objects are protected from other processes, but they are not protected from you. Let's see what the results show us.

Figure 4-9 shows the message box displayed by the function TestAccessViolations(), which tries to find the point where an exception will happen.

With *lpVirtual1*, it calls VirtualQuery() to get the size of the allocated region, then reads the next byte. For heap objects (*lpHeap1, lpGlobal, lpLocal, lpMalloc*, and *lpHeap2*), it calls the corresponding function that reports the size of the object [HeapSize(), GlobalSize(), LocalSize(), and _msize()]. It then reads the byte that should be one byte past the end of the

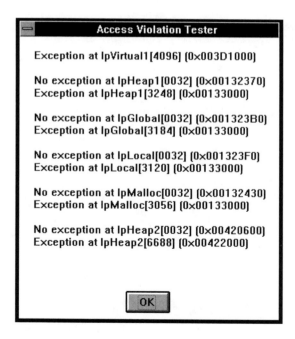

Figure 4-9. Exceptions Caused by Invalid Memory Accesses

object. For instance, with a size of 32, it first tries to read *lpHeap1[32]*. If this succeeds (which it does), it then keeps bumping the array index and reading the next byte until it gets an exception. Figure 4-9 shows that the read from *lpVirtual1[4096]* triggers an exception, but that with all the heap objects, no exception is triggered while you are reading a byte within the pages of committed memory that belong to the heap. The first time you read from the reserved page that follows it, you get an exception. You can see in Figure 4-5 and Figure 4-6 that the sensitive addresses are 0x00133000 and 0x00422000—exactly where Figure 4-9 tells us that exceptions finally occurred.

The conclusion here is inescapable: heap objects cannot be protected from each other. On the other hand, memory objects gotten from VirtualAlloc() are secure, with one exception: if you commit a region of 65536 bytes (or some multiple of it), then commit the following page, a read or write past the end of the first region will not cause an exception. Here's a code fragment that demonstrates this:

```
LPBYTE lpVirtual1, lpVirtual2;
lpVirtual1 = (LPBYTE) VirtualAlloc(NULL, 65536, MEM_COMMIT,
                                   PAGE_READWRITE);
lpVirtual2 = (LPBYTE) VirtualAlloc(NULL, 4096, MEM_COMMIT,
                                   PAGE_READWRITE);
// lpVirtual2 will equal lpVirtual1 + 65536
// This line of code will NOT cause an exception
lpVirtual1[65536] = '\0';
// No exception occurs until you write to lpVirtual1[65536 +
4096],
// which is past the region you have committed for lpVirtual2
```

Here is the listing for TestAccessViolations() and the function it calls, TryMemoryAccess():

```
VOID TestAccessViolations(HWND hWnd)
{
    char szMsg[16384];
    MEMORY_BASIC_INFORMATION mbi;
    DWORD   dwGlobalSize, dwLocalSize, dwMallocSize;

    // Remember the sizes of our heap-based memory objects
    dwGlobalSize = GlobalSize((HGLOBAL) lpGlobal);
    dwLocalSize = LocalSize((HLOCAL) lpLocal);
    dwMallocSize = _msize(lpMalloc);

    lstrcpy(szMsg, "");
```

```
    // Try to read from lpVirtual1[size of lpVirtual1]
    // This will trigger an exception
    VirtualQuery(lpVirtual1, &mbi, sizeof (mbi));

    TryMemoryAccess(szMsg, lpVirtual1, mbi.RegionSize, "lpVirtual1", TRUE);

    // Try reading from lpHeap1 + HeapSize(lpHeap1)
    // This should not trigger an exception

    TryMemoryAccess(szMsg, lpHeap1,
        HeapSize(GetProcessHeap(), 0, lpHeap1), "lpHeap1", TRUE);

    // Try reading from lpGlobal + GlobalSize(lpGlobal)
    // This should not trigger an exception

    TryMemoryAccess(szMsg, lpGlobal, dwGlobalSize,
        "lpGlobal", TRUE);

    // Try reading from lpLocal + LocalSize(lpLocal)
    // This should not trigger an exception

    TryMemoryAccess(szMsg, lpLocal, dwLocalSize, "lpLocal", TRUE);

    // Try reading from lpMalloc + _msize(lpMalloc)
    // This should not trigger an exception

    TryMemoryAccess(szMsg, lpMalloc, dwMallocSize, "lpMalloc", TRUE);

    // Try reading from lpHeap2 + HeapSize(lpHeap2)
    // This should not trigger an exception

    TryMemoryAccess(szMsg, lpHeap2,
        HeapSize(hHeap, 0, lpHeap2), "lpHeap2", TRUE);

    MessageBox(hWnd, szMsg, "Access Violation Tester", MB_OK);
}

VOID TryMemoryAccess(LPSTR lpszMsg, LPBYTE lpMem, DWORD dwOffset,
                     LPSTR lpVariable, BOOL bContinueUntilException)
{
    BOOL bExceptionRaised = FALSE;
    BYTE byMem;

    // Try reading from lpMem + dwOffset

    try
        {
        byMem = lpMem[dwOffset];
        }
```

```
except (EXCEPTION_EXECUTE_HANDLER)
    {
    bExceptionRaised = TRUE;
    }

if (bExceptionRaised)
    wsprintf(&lpszMsg[lstrlen(lpszMsg)],
        "Exception at %s[%04d] (0x%08X)\n",
        lpVariable, dwOffset, lpMem + dwOffset);
else
    {
    wsprintf(&lpszMsg[lstrlen(lpszMsg)],
        "No exception at %s[%04d] (0x%08X)\n",
        lpVariable, dwOffset, lpMem + dwOffset);

    if (bContinueUntilException)
        {
        // See how far we have to go till we get an exception
        while (!bExceptionRaised)
            {
            try
                {
                byMem = lpMem[++dwOffset];
                }
            except (EXCEPTION_EXECUTE_HANDLER)
                {
                bExceptionRaised = TRUE;
                }
            }
        wsprintf(&lpszMsg[lstrlen(lpszMsg)],
            "Exception at %s[%04d] (0x%08X)\n",
            lpVariable, dwOffset, lpMem + dwOffset);
        }
    }

lstrcat(lpszMsg, "\n");
}
```

And, as you can see in Figure 4-10, it gets worse; even after you free a heap object, you can **still** read and write it.

Figure 4-10 is generated by the routine TestMemoryReleases(), which frees the memory allocated by TestMemoryAllocations(), then tries to read it. It VirtualFree()s *lpVirtual1*, HeapFree()s *lpHeap1*, GlobalFree()s *lpGlobal*, LocalFree()s *lpLocal*, and free()s *lpMalloc*. As you have probably surmised already, only one of the subsequent reads triggers an exception: the read from *lpVirtual1*.

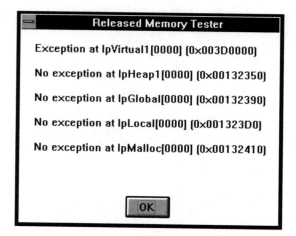

Figure 4-10.   Exceptions Triggered by Accessing Freed Memory

Here is the listing for TestMemoryReleases():

```
VOID TestMemoryReleases(HWND hWnd)
{
    char szMsg[8192];

    // Free lpVirtual1, then try to read from it
    // This will cause an exception

    VirtualFree(lpVirtual1, 0, MEM_RELEASE);

    TryMemoryAccess(szMsg, lpVirtual1, 0, "lpVirtual1", FALSE);

    // Free lpHeap1, then read from it
    // This should not cause an exception
    HeapFree(GetProcessHeap(), 0, lpHeap1);
    TryMemoryAccess(&szMsg[lstrlen(szMsg)], lpHeap1, 0, "lpHeap1",
        FALSE);

    // Free lpGlobal, then read from it
    // This should not cause an exception
    GlobalFree((HGLOBAL) lpGlobal);
    TryMemoryAccess(&szMsg[lstrlen(szMsg)], lpGlobal, 0, "lpGlobal",
        FALSE);

    // Free lpLocal, then read from it
    // This should not cause an exception
    LocalFree((HLOCAL) lpLocal);
```

```
TryMemoryAccess(&szMsg[lstrlen(szMsg)], lpLocal, 0, "lpLocal",
    FALSE);

// Free lpMalloc, then read from it
// This won't cause an exception, either
free(lpMalloc);
TryMemoryAccess(&szMsg[lstrlen(szMsg)], lpMalloc, 0, "lpMalloc",
    FALSE);

// Free other pointers just to be polite
VirtualFree(lpVirtual2, 0, MEM_RELEASE);
VirtualFree(lpVirtual3, 0, MEM_RELEASE);
HeapFree(hHeap, 0, lpHeap2);
HeapDestroy(hHeap);

// Reset event so menu can be initialized properly
ResetEvent(hEvent);
MessageBox(hWnd, szMsg, "Released Memory Tester", MB_OK);
```

By the way, when I originally wrote this test, I had it write to the memory rather than read from it. This produced identical results to those shown here. However, when I got curious to see how MEMTEST would behave under Win32S, I got a rude surprise. Writing outside the bounds of memory that you own does not trigger an exception, unless you VirtualAlloc() it. However, it was not without consequences; it rebooted my machine. So in order to get meaningful results from Win32S, I changed the operation to a read rather than a write. With that modification, MEMTEST behaves exactly the same under Win32S.

The tradeoff between Virtual Memory and heap-based memory can thus be depicted in stark detail and bold hues: you can have fine granularity or tight protection, but not both. I have not yet discovered a way to balance these two more delicately. In most of the code in this book, I lean towards VirtualAlloc(). But this is just a matter of personal preference; I have no strong, righteous feelings that this is the right way to do things, nor can I present cogent, well-reasoned arguments.

Conclusion

Windows NT offers a very powerful, flexible memory management scheme. To give developers more direct access to the underlying mechanism, the Win32 API adds two memory management APIs: the Virtual Memory API and the Heap API. Virtual Memory is the most powerful and allows you the most control over your own memory management. Its principal innovation is the ability to reserve large contiguous blocks of virtual memory without consuming any physical resources. You can then commit portions of this block, thereby obtaining physical storage, as you actually need them. You can decommit memory when you are done using it; the virtual addresses remain valid until you commit them again, or until you finally release the entire region. In conjunction with Structured Exception Handling, you can defer committing memory until the very moment when you actually access it. You can also manipulate the access allowed to a block of memory, which keeps you from accidentally overwriting read-only memory objects.

The Heap API lets you take advantage of the reserve/commit scheme without having to be aware of what goes on behind the scenes. NT reserves and commits pages on your behalf as they are needed. The Heap API allows finer granularity than the Virtual Memory API; essentially, what it gives you is a subsegment allocation API that operates within the parameters of the virtual memory management scheme.

The older Windows memory allocation APIs using LocalAlloc(), GlobalAlloc() and their related functions are still supported, as are standard C functions like malloc() and calloc(). They are essentially the same as the Heap API when it is used with the default process heap; all allocation requests are satisfied from the same block of reserved memory.

The principal disadvantage of Virtual Memory allocation is that its unit of granularity is quite coarse. Any memory allocated with VirtualAlloc(), no matter how little, results in using at least one page of physical memory, and 64K of virtual memory. On the other hand, the memory is completely protected; you cannot inadvertently overwrite the memory thus obtained without causing an exception. In contrast, allocations from heap memory made by calling HeapAlloc(), GlobalAlloc(), LocalAlloc(), or malloc() carve out much more precise units. The memory objects allocated using these functions are the size that you ask for (with, apparently, 32 additional bytes of memory management header). Unfortunately, the NT Virtual Memory Manager considers all objects residing in the same heap to be part of the same set of committed pages. Thus, wayward writes to variables in a heap can easily corrupt other objects in the heap, as well as the control information that precedes each object. These kinds of bugs can be very insidious and difficult to trace; their effects may not be felt until long after the offending code has been executed.

Suggested Readings

Richter, Jeff. *Advanced Windows NT*. Redmond, WA: Microsoft Press, 1993. Chapters 2 and 3.

Richter, Jeff. *Memory Management Overview* in the Win32 on-line help. Published as Chapter 42 in the *Win32 Programmer's Reference, Volume 2*.

Custer, Helen. *Inside Windows NT*. Redmond, WA: Microsoft Press, 1992. Chapter 6.

Yao, Paul. "An Introduction to Windows NT Memory Management Fundamentals." *Microsoft Systems Journal*, Vol. 7, No. 4, July/August 1992.

Richter, Jeff. "An Introduction to Win32 Heap and Virtual Memory Management Routines." *Microsoft Systems Journal*, Vol. 8, No. 3, March 1993.

Kath, Randy. "The Virtual-Memory Manager in Windows NT." *Microsoft Developer Network CD*. 1992.

Kath, Randy. "Managing Virtual Memory in Win32." *Microsoft Developer Network CD*. 1993.

Kath, Randy. "Managing Heap Memory in Win32." *Microsoft Developer Network CD*. 1993.

Microsoft Knowledge Base for Win32 SDK articles:
"VirtualLock Only Locks Pages into Working Set"
"Memory Management via Malloc()"
"PAGE_READONLY May Be Used as Discardable Memory"
"Maximum Memory Handles"
"Windows NT Virtual Memory Manager Uses FIFO"
"How Windows NT Provides 4 Gigabytes of Memory"
"Non-Address Range in Address Space"
"Determining Memory Usage under Windows NT"

Chapter 5

Multithreading

Overview

In exploring how to multithread an NT application, very little discussion needs to revolve around the actual mechanics. The API set is simple; it centers on the CreateThread() function, which is neither difficult nor complex. Instead, most of the discussion concerns integrating a multi-threaded design into applications, particularly server-side applications. The question, then, is not how to implement a multithreaded application—simply put, you invoke functions through CreateThread() rather than calling them directly. The question instead is deciding what kinds of applications lend themselves particularly well to multithreading, and, within that context, what the best division of labor is among the threads you create.

What Are Threads?

Threads are the basic objects that NT schedules for execution and they compete for and share the CPU (or CPUs). Threads allow a single application to multitask its own execution. On a single-processor machine, threads give the appearance of simultaneous, concurrent execution. On a multiple-processor machine, multiple threads do indeed execute simultaneously.

Purposes of Threads

Threads provide four essential services. First, they allow portions of an application to execute asynchronously and in parallel. Second, they let you run multiple copies of a code section so that you can do things like provide identical services to multiple clients. Third, they make it possible to call functions that are likely to block without keeping your program's user from doing other things with it. Fourth, only multithreaded applications can take advantage of a multiprocessor machine.

Parallel, Asynchronous Execution

The first benefit provided by threads is allowing asynchronous and parallel execution. Frequently, the component tasks that make up an application do not need to execute consecutively. As long as task B does not need the output of task A, it is not necessary to make task B wait for task A to complete before it can commence operations. A single-threaded operating system forces sequential execution; a multithreaded one allows a design that more accurately reflects the interrelationships among parts of an application.

For instance, here are two functions that perform separate, unrelated tasks:

```
int a = 2, b = 3, c;
int d = 4, e = 5, f;

VOID FuncA()
{
    c = a + b;
}

VOID FuncB()
{
    f = d + e;
}
```

A single-threaded environment forces you to call FuncA(), wait for it to complete, and then call FuncB().

```
FuncA();
FuncB();
```

However, FuncB() deals with data that is entirely different from that manipulated by FuncA(). There is no need to make FuncB() stand in line behind FuncA(); why not do something like this (assuming a programming language statement "spin off")?

```
spin off FuncA();
spin off FuncB();
```

Now, the calling module can go about its business. Only when it needs the output of FuncA() and FuncB() does it need to make sure they're finished.

Suppose, for instance, that you have a function FuncC(), that returns the sum of *c* and *f*.

```
int FuncC()
{
    return c + f;
}
```

You cannot call FuncC() until you know that FuncA() and FuncB() have calculated the correct values of *c* and *f*. Thus, the top-level module needs to do something like this:

```
spin off FuncA();
spin off FuncB();
do other stuff
make sure FuncA() and FuncB() are done
printf("\nc + f = %d", FuncC());
```

Executing Multiple Copies of Code Simultaneously

The second benefit provided by threads is the ability to run multiple copies of a given code stream. This is important, for instance, in a Named Pipes server application, where a one-thread-per-client division of labor is often an intelligent design. A single function in the server application might listen for connection requests, then accept incoming requests for data or services, responding to them as appropriate. For each instance of the pipe, a new copy of the function can be executed in a separate thread; the more client activity the server expects, the more threads it can start up. This allows the server to provide a higher level of throughput than it can achieve with a single thread of execution.

Shielding Users from the Effects of Blocking Calls

The third benefit provided by threads is the harmless execution of functions that block. When a thread running under NT issues a blocking function call, it goes to sleep until the function completes. If the function call is issued by the main thread of an application (the one that manages the user interface), it shuts the application down; the user can do nothing with it. Some blocking functions—particularly those involving network communications—may block for a long time. This situation is rendered innocuous by making the blocking call in a secondary thread, perhaps one created for that sole purpose. When the function completes, the threads can use some kind of asynchronous notification, like posting a message, to let the responsible authorities know what has happened.

Symmetric Multiprocessing

A final benefit provided by threads is that only multithreaded applications can take advantage of a multiprocessor machine. Multiprocessing is one of the major advances that NT provides, and it may be the single feature that causes it to replace NetWare as the network operating system of choice. A single-threaded application cannot possibly reap the performance benefits that multiple CPUs can yield. My own tests with a dual-486 machine indicate that these benefits are substantial.

CreateThread()

CreateThread() is the Win32 function that starts up a new thread.

```
HANDLE CreateThread(
    LPSECURITY_ATTRIBUTES  lpSecurityAttributes,
    DWORD                  dwStackSize,
    LPTHREAD_START_ROUTINE lpThreadFunction,
    LPVOID                 lpArgument,
    DWORD                  dwFlags,
    LPDWORD                lpdwThreadID);
```

lpSecurityAttributes points to a SECURITY_ATTRIBUTES structure that determines whether the thread handle can be inherited by child processes, and who can do what with the handle.

```
typedef struct _SECURITY_ATTRIBUTES
{
    DWORD   nLength;
    LPVOID  lpSecurityDescriptor;
    BOOL    bInheritHandle;
} SECURITY_ATTRIBUTES;
```

nLength is used for version control; you always set it to *sizeof* (SECURITY_ATTRIBUTES). *bInheritHandle* indicates whether the handle can be inherited by child processes. *lpSecurityDescriptor* points to a SECURITY_DESCRIPTOR structure, which is used to specify what rights other processes will have to the thread handle. The SECURITY_ DESCRIPTOR structure is an opaque type; that is, its format is not published, and applications may only access it indirectly, through the functions in the Security API (see Chapter 14).

For example, you can use the thread handle to determine when the thread terminates; this requires what is referred to as SYNCHRONIZE access. To set the thread's priority, you must have THREAD_SET_INFORMATION authorization; to get information like its priority or its exit code, you need THREAD_QUERY_INFORMATION rights. To suspend and resume a thread, you need THREAD_SUSPEND_RESUME permission. The HANDLE returned by CreateThread() has all rights to the thread object. You can limit what other processes can do with it by passing the *lpSecurityDescriptor* member as a non-NULL value. With thread handles, though, there is seldom a need to do this; ordinarily, if you use security attributes at all, it is only to make the thread handle inheritable.

The second argument to CreateThread(), *dwStackSize*, specifies the number of bytes to allocate for the thread's stack. Every thread gets its own stack space; some of the figures in Chapter 4 show the stack space that NT has set aside for the MEMTEST application. Unless you tell the linker otherwise, NT gives the startup thread of a process a 1 MB reserved area. Pages at the bottom are committed, and the page above them is committed and flagged as a guard page. The stack grows dynamically by triggering guard-page exceptions; however, if an application overflows the 1 MB reserved area, NT raises an EXCEPTION_STACK_OVERFLOW exception as a protection against infinite recursion. If you pass *dwStackSize* to CreateThread() as zero, NT will give the new thread a stack having the same size as the process's startup thread. Passing it as non-zero asks NT to commit more or fewer bytes at the bottom of the stack than it would otherwise; the reserved area is still the same size as that reserved for the startup thread. If you are reasonably certain that your stack will not grow beyond a certain size, you can economize on your use of physical memory by making *dwStackSize* small—keeping in mind that at least one page of memory will be committed.

The third argument to CreateThread(), *lpThreadFunction*, is a pointer to the function where NT will enter the thread. LPTHREAD_START_ROUTINE represents a function with the following prototype:

```
DWORD WINAPI ThreadFunction(LPVOID lpv);
```

You will see that the DWORD return type is somewhat incorrect; the function behaves more like a VOID function.

The fourth argument to CreateThread(), *lpArgument*, is any data you want to provide to the thread entry-point function. If it will not fit in 32 bits, or if there is more than one piece of information, you typically allocate memory for some type of structure or a C++ object and pass its address. It is important that any pointer be valid for the life of the thread. If the function that creates the new thread passes a pointer to a stack variable, then exits, the pointer stands a good chance of being invalid in the thread, thereby triggering an EXCEPTION_ACCESS_VIOLATION error.

The *dwFlags* parameter controls the initial scheduling of the thread. If you set it to zero, NT will immediately schedule the thread for execution. The only non-zero flag, CREATE_SUSPENDED, indicates that you do not want the thread to run until you specifically release it by passing its handle to ResumeThread().

The last argument, *lpdwThreadID*, points to a DWORD variable that returns the thread ID assigned by the NT Process Manager. Although the thread ID is generally of little interest, you cannot pass *lpdwThreadID* as NULL. The thread ID, incidentally, is not the same as the HANDLE returned by CreateThread(). The handle is generated by the NT Object Manager and behaves like a standard NT kernel object. Therefore, the handle can be used for synchronization, and it embodies the security protection requested in the security attributes. As a synchronization object, the thread handle stays nonsignalled as long as the thread is running.

Most thread management functions need the thread handle. Only a few take the thread ID, the most useful of which is PostThreadMessage(). If you do not intend to use the thread handle, it is best to close it as soon as you create it. This has no effect on the thread itself; closing the thread handle is not equivalent to killing the thread. At some point, you do need to close thread handles (like all NT object handles). Failing to do so leaves system resources allocated, but not used, until your program finally exits.

The Thread Entry-Point Function

The thread entry-point function acts like any callback function in a Windows program. However, because it typically implements some kind of background task, it often runs in an infinite loop. You will see that Win32 provides no direct way to kill a thread; you must use some kind of indirect mechanism. The ExitThread() function explicitly terminates the thread that calls it.

```
VOID ExitThread(DWORD dwExitCode);
```

ExitThread() has a VOID return value for a very good reason: it doesn't return. *dwExitCode* is recorded as the final status of the thread; it can be retrieved by calling GetExitCodeThread().

```
BOOL GetExitCodeThread(
   HANDLE hThread,
   LPDWORD lpdwExitCode);
```

As long as the thread is running, GetExitCodeThread() reports the exit code as STILL_ACTIVE.

If the thread entry-point function issues a *return* statement, NT does an implicit ExitThread() on its behalf, passing whatever value was included in the *return*. This is why the entry-point function is typed with a DWORD return value. However, I am not fond of "implicit" mechanisms, so I usually call ExitThread() explicitly. Doing so makes a *return* statement unnecessary and irrelevant; this is why I said that a thread function behaves more like a VOID function. If the function is specified to return a DWORD, the compiler will bellyache if you omit the *return*, so I normally include that, too. You don't really have to define a thread entry point to return a DWORD; you can just as well specify it as VOID, then cast its address to an LPTHREAD_START_ROUTINE when you call CreateThread(). Compilers are extremely fussy and pedantic; after all, that's what they get paid to do.

Other less important functions in the API set allow you to stop and restart a thread (SuspendThread() and ResumeThread()); to get and set the thread's priority (GetThreadPriority() and SetThreadPriority()); to obtain handles and IDs for the current thread (GetCurrentThread() and GetCurrentThreadID()); and to abort a running thread (TerminateThread()). When a thread first starts, it takes on the priority class of its owning process and runs at normal priority within that class. You should adjust the priority of a thread very carefully, and only if necessary. A thread whose priority gets reduced may get starved for CPU time; a thread whose priority gets boosted may hog the CPU. NT's policy for scheduling threads is to schedule them in the order of their priorities. All threads at the same priority are **said** to run in first-in, first-out order. However, I have met people whose empirical observations do not confirm first-in, first-out scheduling. If for some reason this is important to an application you're developing, don't assume it.

Killing Threads

ExitThread() initiates a normal thread shutdown. The memory allocated for the thread's stack is released, and any DLLs that the process is using are notified of the thread's disappearance. However, ExitThread() does not specify a particular thread; it affects the thread that calls it. There is no analogous function that includes the thread handle or ID. TerminateThread() allows you to specify a thread handle, but it is an abortive termination—the

stack is not released and DLLs are not informed. It should be used only if no
other strategy works.

```
BOOL TerminateThread(
    HANDLE hThread,
    DWORD  dwExitCode);
```

To kill a thread that is running as an infinite loop, you have to use some
kind of back-door contrivance. I have found two methods that are effective.
The first is as follows:

1. Pass the thread a pointer that you VirtualAlloc(). Within the loop, the
    thread refers to the pointer.
2. When you want to kill the thread, VirtualFree() the pointer. The
    thread includes an exception handler that detects the exception and
    handles it by breaking out of the loop.

Note that this will only work with a pointer created by VirtualAlloc(). As
discussed in Chapter 4, pointers allocated by other means (HeapAlloc(),
GlobalAlloc(), LocalAlloc(), or malloc()) do not cause exceptions when you
write to the memory after freeing the pointer.

The second method uses PostThreadMessage():

```
BOOL PostThreadMessage(
    DWORD   dwThreadID,
    UINT    uMsg,
    WPARAM  wParam,
    LPARAM  lParam);
```

PostThreadMessage() is one of the few functions that takes the thread ID,
rather than the thread handle. PostThreadMessage() has the appearance of a
standard message-passing function, like PostMessage() or SendMessage(),
but it targets a thread, not a window. You can post either a user-defined
message or a predefined message that the thread knows how to interpret, like
WM_COMMAND, WM_DESTROY, or WM_QUIT. The thread can check
its messages by calling GetMessage(), which will block until a message
comes in, or PeekMessage(), which returns immediately. A better alternative,
which lets you avoid blocking forever or polling relentlessly, is
MsgWaitForMultipleObjects(). This function indicates if you have any
messages, but also lets you specify a determinate timeout period. I present an
example that uses it later in this chapter.

If the thread that is the target of a PostThreadMessage() has created
windows, it will also have to retrieve messages for them. In Windows NT,

only the thread that creates a window gets messages for it. However, a thread message has no target window; the *hwnd* member of the MSG structure is reported as NULL. So it will not be enough for the thread to do a traditional message loop like this one:

```
MSG msg;
while (GetMessage(&msg, NULL, 0, 0))
   {
   TranslateMessage(&msg);
   DispatchMessage(&msg);
   }
```

DispatchMessage() will not be able to determine which window procedure to call; it retrieves this information by calling GetWindowLong (lpMsg->hwnd, GWL_WNDPROC). As a result, the message loop must be prepared for NULL window handles and deal with them appropriately. Here is a revised message loop that can manage messages posted by PostThreadMessage():

```
MSG msg;
while (GetMessage(&msg, NULL, 0, 0))
   {
   if (msg.hwnd == NULL)
      {
      // Deal with thread-specific message
      }
   else
      {
      TranslateMessage(&msg);
      DispatchMessage(&msg);
      }
   }
```

Thread Synchronization

Unlike separate processes, each of which runs in its own virtual address space, all threads of a process share its virtual address space. Therefore, they can all access the static data of the process. They also share all objects owned by the process—window handles, GDI objects, file handles, and synchronization objects, to name some of them. Thus, threads are very tightly coupled, and you must synchronize their access to any process-wide data items or objects. NT provides a wide array of tools for doing this (see Chapter 6).

Compiler and Linker Switches for Building
Multithreaded Applications and DLLs

To generate a thread-safe executable, you need to define _MT when you compile, then link with the multithreaded C runtime library, LIBCMT.LIB. The easiest way to do this is to take advantage of macros defined in NTWIN32.MAK, which is provided with the Win32 SDK. The macro *cvarsmt* compiles a multithreaded application; *cvarsdll* generates thread-safe code for a dynamic-link library. Then, in the linker command line, the macros *guilibsmt, conlibsmt, conlibsdll,* and *guilibsdll* tell the linker to link with the multithreaded GUI, console, or DLL support libraries.

Here are the compiler command lines I use to build standalone executables and DLLs, respectively. *cvarsdll* includes *cvarsmt;* it also defines the constant_DLL. In all these command lines, the lower-case macros are defined in NTWIN32.MAK; the upper-case ones are mine.

```
# Compile standard multithreaded executable
$(cc) $(cflags) $(cvarsmt) $(cdebug) -YX $*.cpp

# Compile for DLL (implicitly multithreaded by definition
# of cvarsdll)
$(cc) $(cflags) $(cvarsdll) $(cdebug) -YX $*.cpp
```

I have three linker command lines: one for windowed applications, one for console applications, and one for DLLs.

```
# Link windowed app
$(PROG).exe: $(OBJ) $(PROG).rbj
    $(link) $(linkdebug) $(guiflags) -out:$(PROG).exe \
            $(OBJ) $(PROG).rbj $(guilibsmt) $(WNETLIBS)

# Link console app
$(link) $(linkdebug) $(conflags) -out:$(PROG).exe \
        $(OBJ) $(conlibsmt) $(WNETLIBS)

# Link DLL
$(link) $(linkdebug)        \
        -dll                \
        -entry:_DllMainCRTStartup$(DLLENTRY)    \
        -out:$(PROG).dll    \
        $(PROG).exp $(OBJ) $(guilibsdll) $(WNETLIBS) \
        netapi32.lib wsock32.lib
```

Code Listings

The Windows Network Manager (\NTNET\CODE\%Cpu%\WNET.EXE on the disk) includes a dialog box that demonstrates Structured Exception Handling, Virtual Memory Allocation, and Multithreading. Figure 5-1 shows what it looks like on my NeTpower NT Advanced Server box.

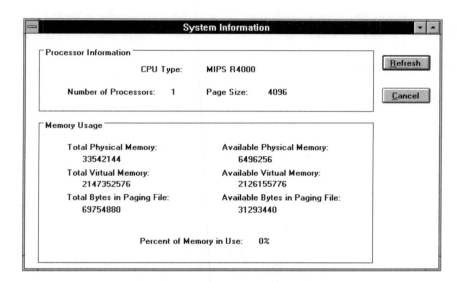

Figure 5-1.   Windows Network Manager System Info Dialog Box

The information in the Processor Information group box is constant; it is retrieved during program initialization by a call to GetSystemInfo(), and the fields are populated during the processing of the WM_INITDIALOG message. On the other hand, the Memory Usage statistics on the bottom of the screen are dynamic. For this reason, the dialog box is modeless; you can leave it running on the screen without impeding your ability to use other parts of the Windows Network Manager. Rather than capturing the statistics once in response to WM_INITDIALOG, the dialog procedure spins off a thread that runs in an infinite loop. The loop works as follows:

1.   It captures the memory statistics by calling GlobalMemoryStatus().
2.   It displays them in the fields of the dialog box.
3.   It gathers its strength for the next cycle by sleeping for five seconds.

In order to support the Cancel button that you see in the dialog box, you need some way to kill the thread. For the reasons I discussed earlier, I do not consider TerminateThread() an acceptable solution. Therefore, when the dialog procedure starts the thread, it passes it a pointer that it obtains from VirtualAlloc(). This points to a structure typed as follows:

```
typedef struct tagSystemInfo
{
    HWND hDlg;                  // The window handle for the dialog box
    TCHAR szBuffer[150];        // A buffer the thread can use
                                // for constructing messages
} SYSTEM_INFO_PARMS;
```

Here is the fragment of code that allocates the memory and spins off the thread:

```
static SYSTEM_INFO_PARMS *lpSystemInfo;
...
lpSystemInfo =
    (SYSTEM_INFO_PARMS *) VirtualAlloc(NULL,
                             sizeof (SYSTEM_INFO_PARMS),
                             MEM_COMMIT,
                             PAGE_READWRITE);
if (lpSystemInfo != NULL)
    lpSystemInfo->hDlg = hDlg;

hThread = CreateThread(
            NULL, 0,
            (LPTHREAD_START_ROUTINE) SystemInfoThread,
            (LPVOID) lpSystemInfo,
            0, &dwThreadID);
if (hThread != NULL)
    CloseHandle(hThread);
```

When the user presses the Cancel button, the dialog procedure posts itself a WM_CLOSE, in response to which it calls VirtualFree() to release the memory.

```
switch (uMessage)
    {
    case WM_COMMAND:
        switch (LOWORD(wParam))
            {
            case IDCANCEL:
                PostMessage(hDlg, WM_CLOSE, 0, 0);
                return TRUE;
            // [Other wParam cases follow here]
            }
```

```
case WM_CLOSE:
    if (lpSystemInfo != NULL)
        VirtualFree(lpSystemInfo, 0, MEM_RELEASE);
    DestroyWindow(hDlg);
    hSystemInfoDlg = NULL;  // Global variable that remembers
                            // dialog window handle

    return TRUE;
}
```

When the thread wakes up, it tries to write to the dialog box using the window handle in the structure and gets an EXCEPTION_ACCESS_ VIOLATION. It traps this and breaks out of the infinite loop.

To implement the Refresh button, you need a way to wake the thread up if it is in its five-second nap. And this is where it will spend 99.99999999 percent of its time. If the thread just calls Sleep(5000), there is nothing you can do to roust it out. Therefore, the thread calls MsgSleep(), coded as follows.

```
BOOL WINAPI MsgSleep(DWORD dwMilliseconds)
{
    return (MsgWaitForMultipleObjects(0, NULL, FALSE,
            dwMilliseconds, QS_ALLINPUT)
        == 0);
}
```

MsgWaitForMultipleObjects() normally deals with an array of object handles, but in this case there are none; the first argument indicates a zero-element array and the second is a NULL pointer to it. The fourth argument is the timeout value, with the special value INFINITE (-1), saying to wait forever. Finally, the last argument is a flag specifying what kinds of messages should wake the thread up. QS_ALLINPUT means that you want to know about everything that happens. (QS is an abbreviation for Queue Status; the full suite of flags is documented with the GetQueueStatus() function.) MsgWaitForMultipleObjects() returns either the zero-based index into the array of handles of the object that satisfied the wait or the count of handles if a message arrives. We have an empty array, so a return value of zero indicates a message. The only other possible response using MsgWaitForMultipleObjects() this way is WAIT_TIMEOUT, which means that the timeout period expired. (See Chapter 6 for a discussion of MsgWaitForMultipleObjects() and synchronization objects.)

As you can see, MsgSleep() provides the same syntax and functionality as Sleep(), with the added dimension that it will wake up if a message is received. It returns TRUE if a message arrives, FALSE if the timeout

expires. This is ideal for implementing the Refresh button; I post the thread a
message with PostThreadMessage(). It doesn't matter what message I post,
but I use WM_COMMAND because it makes sense in this context. Here is
the code that handles a click on the Refresh button:

```
switch (uMessage)
    {
    case WM_COMMAND:
        switch (LOWORD(wParam))
            {
            // [Other wParam cases are here]
            case IDB_REFRESH:
                // Check for click
                if (HIWORD(wParam) == BN_CLICKED)
                    {
                    // Wake the thread up
                    PostThreadMessage(dwThreadID, WM_COMMAND, 0, 0);
                    }
                return TRUE;
            }
    }
```

Here are the listings of the thread function, SystemInfoThread(), and the
supporting dialog procedure, SystemInfoDlgProc(). The source file on the
disk is \NTNET\CODE\WNETDLGS.CPP.

```
// Thread function for system info dialog box
// putting it here keeps us from having to put a prototype somewhere

DWORD WINAPI SystemInfoThread(LPVOID lp)
{
    SYSTEM_INFO_PARMS *lpSysInfo = (SYSTEM_INFO_PARMS *) lp;
    MEMORYSTATUS MemoryStatus;
    MSG     msg;
    BOOL    bContinue = TRUE;

    while (bContinue)
        {
        MemoryStatus.dwLength = sizeof (MEMORYSTATUS);
        GlobalMemoryStatus(&MemoryStatus);

        try
            {
            SetDlgItemInt(lpSysInfo->hDlg, IDB_TOTAL_PHYSICAL,
                        MemoryStatus.dwTotalPhys, FALSE);
            SetDlgItemInt(lpSysInfo->hDlg, IDB_AVAIL_PHYSICAL,
                        MemoryStatus.dwAvailPhys, FALSE);
```

```
            SetDlgItemInt(lpSysInfo->hDlg, IDB_TOTAL_VIRTUAL,
                    MemoryStatus.dwTotalVirtual, FALSE);
            SetDlgItemInt(lpSysInfo->hDlg, IDB_AVAIL_VIRTUAL,
                    MemoryStatus.dwAvailVirtual, FALSE);
            SetDlgItemInt(lpSysInfo->hDlg, IDB_TOTAL_PAGING,
                    MemoryStatus.dwTotalPageFile,
                    FALSE);
            SetDlgItemInt(lpSysInfo->hDlg, IDB_AVAIL_PAGING,
                    MemoryStatus.dwAvailPageFile,
                    FALSE);
            wsprintf(lpSysInfo->szBuffer, TEXT("%d%%"),
                    MemoryStatus.dwMemoryLoad);
            SetDlgItemText(lpSysInfo->hDlg, IDB_MEMORY_PERCENT,
                    lpSysInfo->szBuffer);
            }
        except (EXCEPTION_EXECUTE_HANDLER)
            {
            break;
            }

        // Sleep for five seconds, but check for
        // messages

        if (MsgSleep(5000))
            {
            // Got a message—we'll look for WM_DESTROY
            // as a terminate message, although nobody's
            // sending it to us right now
            // WM_COMMAND means refresh the memory display

            if (PeekMessage(&msg, NULL, 0, 0, PM_REMOVE) &&
                msg.message == WM_DESTROY)
                bContinue = FALSE;
            }
        }
    printfConsole(TEXT("\nSystemInfoThread terminating"));
    ExitThread(0);
    return 0;
}

BOOL CALLBACK SystemInfoDlgProc(HWND hDlg, UINT uMessage,
                                WPARAM wParam, LPARAM lParam)
{
    static HANDLE hThread;
    static DWORD  dwThreadID = 0xFFFFFFFF;
    LPTSTR lpProcessorType;
```

```
// It's OK to do lpSystemInfo as a static
// This dialog box only gets created once
static SYSTEM_INFO_PARMS *lpSystemInfo;
switch (uMessage)
    {
    case WM_INITDIALOG:
        // Populate the static fields, and spin off
        // a background thread to continually update the
        // memory usage fields
        switch (SystemInfo.dwProcessorType)
            {
            case PROCESSOR_INTEL_386:
                lpProcessorType = TEXT("Intel 386");
                break;
            case PROCESSOR_INTEL_486:
                lpProcessorType = TEXT("Intel 486");
                break;
            case PROCESSOR_INTEL_PENTIUM:
                lpProcessorType = TEXT("Intel Pentium");
                break;
            case PROCESSOR_INTEL_860:
                lpProcessorType = TEXT("Intel 860");
                break;
            case PROCESSOR_MIPS_R2000:
                lpProcessorType = TEXT("MIPS R2000");
                break;
            case PROCESSOR_MIPS_R3000:
                lpProcessorType = TEXT("MIPS R3000");
                break;
            case PROCESSOR_MIPS_R4000:
                lpProcessorType = TEXT("MIPS R4000");
                break;
            case PROCESSOR_ALPHA_21064:
                lpProcessorType = TEXT("DEC Alpha");
                break;
            default:
                lpProcessorType = TEXT("Unknown processor");
                break;
            }
        SetDlgItemText(hDlg, IDB_PROCESSOR_TYPE, lpProcessorType);
        SetDlgItemInt(hDlg, IDB_PROCESSOR_COUNT,
                    SystemInfo.dwNumberOfProcessors, FALSE);
        SetDlgItemInt(hDlg, IDB_PAGE_SIZE,
                    SystemInfo.dwPageSize, FALSE);

        lpSystemInfo =
            (SYSTEM_INFO_PARMS *) VirtualAlloc(NULL,
                                    sizeof (SYSTEM_INFO_PARMS),
```

```
                                        MEM_COMMIT,
                                        PAGE_READWRITE);
            if (lpSystemInfo != NULL)
                lpSystemInfo->hDlg = hDlg;
            hThread = CreateThread(
                        NULL, 0,
                        (LPTHREAD_START_ROUTINE) SystemInfoThread,
                        (LPVOID) lpSystemInfo,
                        0, &dwThreadID);
            if (hThread != NULL)
                CloseHandle(hThread);
            return TRUE;
        case WM_SETFOCUS:
            // Refresh the window by posting the thread a message
            // It appears that we never get this message—
            // the window proc for the built-in dialog class
            // must handle and suppress it.
            PostThreadMessage(dwThreadID, WM_COMMAND, 0, 0);
            break;
        case WM_COMMAND:
            switch (LOWORD(wParam))
                {
                case IDCANCEL:
                    PostMessage(hDlg, WM_CLOSE, 0, 0);
                    return TRUE;
                case IDB_REFRESH:
                    // Check for click
                    if (HIWORD(wParam) == BN_CLICKED)
                        {
                        // Wake the thread up
                        PostThreadMessage(dwThreadID, WM_COMMAND, 0, 0);
                        }
                    return TRUE;
                }
            break;
        case WM_CLOSE:
            if (lpSystemInfo != NULL)
                VirtualFree(lpSystemInfo, 0, MEM_RELEASE);
            DestroyWindow(hDlg);
            hSystemInfoDlg = NULL;
            return TRUE;
        }
    return FALSE;
}
```

Conclusion

Multithreading allows you to create software that more closely reflects the way logical components of an application interact with each other. Instead of imposing a sequential, serial mode of execution, applications can be written to run concurrently and asynchronously. This is the only way a Win32 application can take advantage of a multiprocessor hardware platform; multiple threads of an application can run on any available CPU. Part 3 of this book demonstrates that multithreading is critical to writing effective server applications. It is not so essential on the client side, but it does allow an application to remain responsive to the end user even while waiting for a lengthy network operation to complete.

The thread management API is not complex; CreateThread() is the most important function, and it may be the only one you'll use in many applications. SuspendThread() and ResumeThread() allow you to suspend and resume threads, and SetThreadPriority() lets you control their relative priority. A thread calls ExitThread() to stop its own execution.

Challenges arise in three areas when using threads:

- Because there is no direct way for one thread to stop another thread, you have to use indirect means, such as purposely causing exceptions or posting thread-specific messages.
- Threads are tightly coupled; they share the same virtual address space, the same static data, and the same object handles. Therefore, without proper synchronization they can get in each other's way. The use of synchronization objects is essential in managing the interaction among threads.
- Much design work and thinking needs to happen before writing a multithreaded application. When I implement a Named Pipes server application in Chapter 10, you will see some of the considerations that are involved. You must still decide if multithreading is a good idea for your application, what the best division of labor is among the threads, and what the tradeoffs are between having one thread bear too much responsibility and having too many threads competing for CPU time.

Suggested Readings

Custer, Helen. *Inside Windows NT*. Redmond, WA: Microsoft Press, 1992. Chapters 4 and 7.

Richter, Jeff. *Advanced Windows NT*. Redmond, WA: Microsoft Press, 1993. Chapter 2.

Processes and Threads Overview in the on-line help. Published as Chapter 43 of the *Win32 Programmer's Reference, Volume 2*.

Richter, Jeffrey. "Creating, Managing, and Destroying Processes and Threads under Windows NT." *Microsoft Systems Journal*, Vol. 8, No. 7, July 1993.

Microsoft Knowledge Base for Win32 SDK articles:

"Creating Windows in Threads"

"Getting Real Handle to Thread/Process Requires Two Calls"

"Physical Memory Limits Number of Processes/Threads"

"CPU Quota Limits Not Enforced"

"Interrupting Threads in Critical Sections"

Chapter 6

Synchronization Objects

Overview

Synchronization objects are the traffic control mechanisms of a multitasking, multithreaded operating system (sometimes also called a real operating system). They allow threads and processes to coordinate their activities by determining things like when a certain task or operation has completed and when a shared global resource is available.

Windows NT provides three object types for interprocess as well as interthread synchronization, and one object type solely for interthread synchronization. The interprocess mechanisms are **semaphores**, **events**, and **mutexes**. They belong to the set of objects known as NT kernel objects. They are all protected by NT's security subsystem, and they are represented by HANDLEs generated by the Object Manager. **Critical sections** serve only for coordinating the threads of a single process; they are not NT kernel objects.

NT kernel objects have two significant states for synchronization purposes: signalled and nonsignalled. These are the green light and red light. When an object is signalled, any thread waiting on its handle is allowed to proceed. If the object is nonsignalled, threads waiting on it go to sleep. This behavior is common to all NT kernel objects—even those not normally considered synchronization mechanisms, such as file, thread, and process handles. Chapter 5 discussed how it applies to threads and processes, where a handle stays nonsignalled until the thread or process it represents terminates. Subsequent chapters cover how it applies to file and pipe handles.

The meaning of the signalled and nonsignalled states depends on the type of object. A semaphore is nonsignalled if its current count is 0—that is, all the resources that it is protecting are in use. Its state reverts to signalled when a thread using one of the resources surrenders ownership of the semaphore. A mutex is nonsignalled if a thread has claimed it; it is signalled otherwise. An event is nonsignalled while an operation with which it is linked is pending; it is signalled when the operation completes.

For the network programming techniques presented in this book, mutexes and events are the synchronization objects that need to be considered. Semaphores and mutexes are closely related; a mutex can be thought of as a semaphore whose count is always 1. Mutexes are necessary in this book to enable a dynamic link library to control access to shared global data structures. Mutexes and critical sections do exactly the same thing; they provide mutually exclusive (one-at-a-time) access to shared resources. However, since critical sections do not provide interprocess synchronization, they are of little use here.

Events are important because they are used by many of the API sets we will be considering—File I/O, Named Pipes, Windows Sockets, and NetBIOS. Therefore, a thorough understanding of events is crucial. However, before examining mutexes and events any further, I want to consider the wait functions. They are essential tools for using NT synchronization objects effectively.

The Wait Functions

The three wait functions provide the same service. They allow a thread to put itself to sleep either until needed resources become available or until an operation completes. For instance, a thread might suspend itself until it can safely write a message to a window. The main thread of an application might spin off several worker threads, then wait until all of them finish their work. Before displaying a file to the user, make sure you've finished reading it.

The wait functions provide these variations on the same theme:

- Wait for one object.
- Wait for any one of a set of objects.
- Wait for all of a set of objects.
- Wait for a set of objects (which may be empty), and also let me know if a message comes in.

Because all of these functions take a timeout value, you have control over the duration of a wait.

WaitForSingleObject() waits for one object at a time.

```
DWORD WaitForSingleObject(HANDLE hObject, DWORD dwTimeout);
```

The timeout value is in milliseconds. If specified as the constant INFINITE (-1), WaitForSingleObject() will block indefinitely. You can also pass it as 0, which allows you to test the state of the object without waiting for it to signal. There are four possible return values from WaitForSingleObject():

- WAIT_OBJECT_0: The object has entered the signalled state. With mutexes and semaphores, this also confers ownership.
- WAIT_TIMEOUT: The timeout expired before the object became available.
- WAIT_ABANDONED: The object is a mutex in the signalled state, and the thread that owned it terminated without releasing it. It is safe to use it.
- WAIT_FAILED: Uh oh! Call GetLastError(). (*hObject* is probably a bogus object handle.)

WaitForMultipleObjects() allows you to wait for a set of objects.

```
DWORD WaitForMultipleObjects(
        DWORD        dwCount,
        CONST HANDLE *lpHandles,
        BOOL         bWaitAll,
        DWORD        dwTimeout);
```

dwCount is the number of handles in the array that *lpHandles* points to. The objects do not have to be of the same type; you can pass a set consisting of thread, mutex, event, and pipe handles if it makes sense in the context of your application. *bWaitAll* indicates whether you want to wait until **all** of the objects go signalled (TRUE), or whether it will be sufficient for just **one** of them to signal (FALSE). *dwTimeout* is the timeout in milliseconds. The return value from WaitForMultipleObjects() can also be WAIT_OBJECT_0, WAIT_ABANDONED_0, WAIT_TIMEOUT, or WAIT_FAILED. In addition, because you are interested in an array of objects, the return value can be the index of the signalling object into *lpHandles* added to either WAIT_OBJECT_0 (defined as 0) or WAIT_ABANDONED_0 (which is only appropriate for mutexes).

Suppose you pass a five-element array and indicate with *bWaitAll* that you need only one of the objects to signal. The third object in the array *(lpHandles[2])* goes signalled first, so the return value is WAIT_OBJECT_ 0 + 2 (which at present happens to be just 2, since WAIT_OBJECT_0 is defined as 0). Or perhaps you have five mutexes you are interested in, again being content if only one of them signals. The fourth object *(lpHandles[3])* belongs to a thread that crashes without having a termination handler to make sure the mutex gets released. The return value will be WAIT_ ABANDONED_0 + 3.

If you need for all of the objects to go signalled, then you pass *bWaitAll* as TRUE. In this case, when the wait is satisified, the return value will be between WAIT_OBJECT_0 and WAIT_OBJECT_0 plus *dwCount* (the number of elements in the array) minus one because the index is zero-based. If the return value falls between WAIT_ABANDONED_0 and WAIT_ABANDONED_0 + dwCount - 1, then all of the objects in the array are signalled, and at least one of them is an abandoned mutex.

MsgWaitForMultipleObjects() behaves like WaitForMultipleObjects(); the first four arguments are the same.

```
DWORD MsgWaitForMultipleObjects(
        DWORD    dwCount,
        LPHANDLE lpHandles,      // sic!
                                 // prototype for
                                 // WaitForMultipleObjects()
                                 // says CONST HANDLE *
        BOOL     bWaitAll,
        DWORD    dwTimeout,
        DWORD    dwEventFlags)
```

In addition, MsgWaitForMultipleObjects() has a PeekMessage() flavoring; it will return if a message is posted to the thread's message queue. The fifth argument is a filter specifying what messages you are interested in. I normally pass this as QS_ALLINPUT, which will report any message that comes in. Other possibilities allow you to narrow the scope of messages you are interested in. They are described on the reference page for the GetQueueStatus() function.

You saw in the last chapter that MsgWaitForMultipleObjects() allows you to pass an empty array, where the first argument is 0 and the second is NULL. In this case, the function gives you the equivalent of an interruptible Sleep(), which expects only one argument—the amount of time to sleep. If in the meantime a message comes in, nothing can be done about it—you're asleep and that's all there is to it. MsgWaitForMultipleObjects() lets you say, "Put me to sleep for this much time, but wake me up if anybody calls." MsgWaitForMultipleObjects() is often preferable to PeekMessage() as well because it puts the calling thread to sleep, whereas PeekMessage() necessitates polling. Polling is always undesirable in NT because it wastes a great deal of CPU time.

The Mechanics of the API

For semaphores, mutexes, and events—and for other types of NT objects—the procedure is pretty much the same:

1. The object is created by calling the appropriate Create<object>() function, such as CreateMutex(), CreateSemaphore(), or CreateEvent().

2. If another process is synchronizing on the object using its name, it can get a handle by calling the Open<object>() function, or by just calling the Create<object>() function again. For most object types, an attempt to create an object that already exists does not fail—it just works like an open. The only difference is that the Create<object>() call implicitly requests all access to the object, whereas Open<object>() allows you to specify the exact access you want. It is more efficient to ask only for the level of access you actually need. However, I must be candid and admit that I often just ask for all access anyway; this way I know that if I get a handle to the object, I can use it however I want to. Being more precise invites unanticipated ERROR_ACCESS_ DENIED failures.

3. The threads or processes using an object gain and release control of it by calling the appropriate functions.

4. When a process is finished using an object, it closes the handle by calling CloseHandle().

The next discussion focuses on mutexes and events, the object types I will be using for the network DLLs presented in Part 3.

Mutexes

CreateMutex() is the function that creates a new mutex object.

```
HANDLE CreateMutex(
        LPSECURITY_ATTRIBUTES lpSecurityAttributes,
        BOOL                  bClaimedAtCreation,
        LPCTSTR               lpName);
```

Most of the Create<object>() functions mimic this syntax: the first argument is the SECURITY_ATTRIBUTES you want to tie to the object and the last is the name you want to assign to it. The intermediate arguments are dependent on the type of object; they are different for semaphores, mutexes, and events. The security attributes determine whether the handle can be inherited by child processes and what kinds of access other processes are allowed to have. The Win32 Security API is complicated. Until it is discussed in Chapter 14, I will pass the security attributes as NULL, except when it's necessary to do otherwise (like when a server application creates a Named Pipe). The question "Should I use security attributes?" is like "Should I program in assembler?" The answer is don't use them unless you have to; if you need to ask, you probably don't have to. With synchronization objects, NULL security attributes allow open access.

Objects are assigned names so that other processes can use them for synchronization. If you don't need to do interprocess synchronization with an object, or you're synchronizing with a child process that knows the object's handle, you don't need to name it. There are no conventions for naming NT objects, unlike Named Pipes, which have a required prefix (\PIPE\). However, to minimize the likelihood of name-space collisions, it is a good idea to adopt some discipline in how you name objects. I imitate the convention for Named Pipes. In addition to the required prefix, it is also usually suggested that you follow \PIPE\ with a component that stamps the pipe as belonging to your application, say \PIPE\WNET\. This decreases the chances that you and someone else will give a pipe the same name. Table 6-1 shows the prefixes I use for different object types. I also follow them with a signature component. I use forward slashes because the backslash is an illegal character in an NT object name.

Table 6-1.   Prefixes for Naming NT Objects

Object Type	Prefix
Semaphore	/SEMAPHORE/
Mutex	/MUTEX/
Event	/EVENT/
Shared Memory	/SHARED_MEM/
Memory-mapped File	/FILE_MAP/

The type of the name is LPCTSTR, a pointer to a string that is either 16-bit Unicode or 8-bit ANSI. LPCTSTR is actually typed as a pointer to a TCHAR array. If the constant UNICODE is defined, the *typedef* for TCHAR is a *wchar_t*, or *unsigned short*. If UNICODE is not defined, TCHAR is a *char*.

Getting back to CreateMutex(), its second argument, *bClaimedAtCreation*, allows you to create a mutex and claim ownership of it in a single atomic operation. If you pass *bClaimedAtCreation* as FALSE, the mutex is created in the unowned (signalled) state. Under most circumstances, you don't need to claim a mutex when you create it, so you will usually pass *bClaimedAtCreation* as FALSE.

Once a mutex has been created, OpenMutex() returns a handle to it.

```
HANDLE OpenMutex(DWORD    dwDesiredAccess,
                 BOOL     bInheritable,
                 LPCTSTR  lpName);
```

All the Open<object>() functions take the same set of arguments, except for those derived from previous versions of Windows. The first is the access mode you want. This will vary with the type of object. SYNCHRONIZE access allows you to claim and release a mutex and close its handle, which is all you need to do with it. The constant MUTEX_ALL_ACCESS requests "all possible access." Specifically, this grants every access right that makes sense for a mutex. An excellent article by Rob Reichel in the April 1993 issue of *Windows/DOS Developer's Journal* details how this works. Microsoft literature recommends that you request the lowest level of access that you actually need; higher levels of access require additional security checks and therefore degrade performance.

The second argument to the Open<object>() functions, *bInheritable*, indicates whether the handle can be inherited by child processes. A child process can inherit a handle and use it for synchronization without knowing its name. However, named objects are much more common for synchronization among processes—and are easier to code.

The third argument, the name of the object, must correspond to the name of an object that already exists. You can also call the Create<object>() function with the name of an existing object; for most object types, this is just interpreted as a call to Open<object>() requesting all possible access. The Create<object>() function will behave normally, returning a valid handle. You can detect this condition by calling GetLastError(); it will report ERROR_ALREADY_EXISTS.

Once you have a handle to a mutex, you claim ownership of it by calling one of the wait functions and surrender it with ReleaseMutex():

```
BOOL ReleaseMutex(HANDLE hMutex);
```

To prevent synchronization objects from getting stuck or abandoned, it's a good idea to put the release function in the *finally* block of a structured termination handler. Let's take another look at the function printfConsole(), which I first presented in Chapter 3. It uses a mutex to synchronize writes to a console window, created by a call to AllocConsole() when the Windows

Network Manager starts up. printfConsole() is in a DLL; this code fragment from the DLL's initialization code creates the mutex:

```
extern HANDLE hPrintfMutex;
hPrintfMutex = CreateMutex(NULL, FALSE,
                "/MUTEX/WNET/WNET_PRINTF_MUTEX");
```

Here is the listing of printfConsole():

```
int _CRTAPI2 printfConsole(LPCTSTR format, ...)
{
    va_list argp;
    TCHAR   szBuffer[1024];
    CHAR    szOutBuffer[1024];
    LPCVOID lpcOutBuffer;
    HANDLE  hStdout;
    DWORD   dwBytes = ((DWORD) -1);
    CPINFO  CodePageInfo;
    DWORD   dwLength;

    va_start(argp, format);

    hStdout = GetStdHandle(STD_OUTPUT_HANDLE);

    // Protect write to the console with a mutex
    WaitForSingleObject(hPrintfMutex, INFINITE);

    try
        {
        // Find out if we're using wide character code page

        wvsprintf(szBuffer, format, argp);
#ifndef WIN32S
        GetCPInfo(GetACP(), &CodePageInfo);

        if (CodePageInfo.MaxCharSize == 1)
            {
            WideCharToMultiByte(CP_ACP, 0, szBuffer, lstrlen(szBuffer) + 1,
                szOutBuffer, sizeof (szOutBuffer), NULL, NULL);
            lpcOutBuffer = (LPCVOID) szOutBuffer;
            dwLength = lstrlenA(szOutBuffer);
            }
        else
            {
            lpcOutBuffer = (LPCVOID) szBuffer;
            dwLength = lstrlen(szBuffer);
            }
```

```
        if (!WriteFile(hStdout, lpcOutBuffer, dwLength,
                    &dwBytes, NULL))
            dwBytes = (DWORD) -1;
#else
            OutputDebugString(szBuffer);
            dwBytes = lstrlen(szBuffer);
#endif
        }
    finally
        {
        // Make sure we release the mutex, no matter how we got here
        ReleaseMutex(hPrintfMutex);
        va_end(argp);
        }

    return (int) dwBytes;
}
```

Events

Events are open-ended objects that report the completion of I/O operations. They are built into the File I/O, Named Pipes, Windows Sockets, and NetBIOS APIs. When used in this context, they are set to the nonsignalled state when you make the call that starts the operation and set to the signalled state when the operation completes.

Events come in two types—auto-reset and manual-reset. An auto-reset event allows one thread to proceed when it signals, then immediately reverts to nonsignalled. A manual-reset event allows any thread to run once it has entered the signalled state. It does not go nonsignalled again until it is tied to a new I/O operation or explicitly reset by a call to ResetEvent(). For the APIs we will be dealing with, manual-reset events are required, so that is all I consider here.

As with mutexes, CreateEvent() creates a new event or returns a handle to an existing one; OpenEvent() returns a handle to an event created somewhere else.

```
HANDLE CreateEvent(
        LPSECURITY_ATTRIBUTES lpSecurityAttributes,
        BOOL    bManualReset,
        BOOL    bInitialState,
        LPCTSTR lpName);
```

lpSecurityAttributes and *lpName* are the same as they are for CreateMutex(). *bManualReset* determines the type of event—manual-reset

(TRUE) or auto-reset (FALSE). *bInitialState* indicates whether the event should be created in the signalled (TRUE) or nonsignalled (FALSE) state.

OpenEvent() has the same arguments as OpenMutex; here is its prototype:

```
HANDLE OpenEvent(
        DWORD   dwDesiredAccess,
        BOOL    bInheritable,
        LPCTSTR lpName);
```

The only difference between OpenEvent() and OpenMutex() is the types of access that are appropriate. SYNCHRONIZE access allows you to wait on the event handle, either implicitly by tying it to an I/O operation or explicitly by passing it to one of the wait functions. EVENT_MODIFY_STATE lets you change the state of the event by calling SetEvent(), ResetEvent(), or PulseEvent(). EVENT_ALL_ACCESS requests that you be given all possible access (that is, all accesses that are supported). If you pass CreateEvent() the name of an existing event, it behaves like a call to OpenEvent() with a desired access of EVENT_ALL_ACCESS. To reiterate, Microsoft recommends that you not request any higher level of access than you actually need because each additional permission requires a security check.

When an event is used with an I/O operation, there is no need to directly change its state. You associate an event with an operation by putting its handle in a field of a structure. Next, you invoke the function that begins the operation, for example, ReadFile(), and tell it to execute asynchronously. The function returns before the operation completes. You then test the status of the operation by passing the event handle to one of the wait functions, or to GetOverlappedResult() (see Chapter 7).

Three functions directly change the state of an event:

- ResetEvent(), which puts the event into the nonsignalled state.
- SetEvent(), which puts it into the signalled state.
- PulseEvent(), which signals the event, then immediately forces it back to the nonsignalled state. For manual-reset events, all waiting threads are released before the event goes nonsignalled. For auto-reset events, only one thread is released.

All of these functions take one argument, the event handle, and return TRUE or FALSE to indicate success or failure.

In Chapter 5, I showed how to use MsgWaitForMultipleObjects() to enter an interruptible sleep state. I called the function MsgSleep() because it works much like the Win32 Sleep() function. WaitForMultipleObjects() and

MsgWaitForMultipleObjects() let you pass an array of object handles. You can pass MsgWaitForMultipleObjects() an empty array, in which case you will either timeout or wake up when you get a message. When I originally wrote MsgSleep(), I used a dummy manual-reset event and passed its handle to MsgWaitForMultipleObjects() after creating the event in the nonsignalled state. Because no one else knew about it and I never tied it to any kind of operation, it never went signalled. Therefore, passing its handle to MsgWaitForMultipleObjects() gave me the functionality I needed to implement MsgSleep(). I thought this was terribly clever, until one day someone in one of my NT classes asked, "Can't you just pass MsgWaitForMultipleObjects() an empty array?" Well, I hadn't thought of that, so I tried it, and, indeed, it worked just fine. Clearly, an empty array is a superior solution because it uses fewer system resources, so I changed MsgSleep() accordingly. However, pride of paternity being what it is, I cannot resist showing you my original coding, presented here as MsgSleepEvent():

```
BOOL WINAPI MsgSleepEvent(DWORD dwMilliseconds)
{
   // Create a dummy manual-reset
   // event that is always nonsignalled
   HANDLE hDummyEvent = CreateEvent(NULL,
                                    TRUE, FALSE, NULL);
   BOOL   bRetcode =
          (MsgWaitForMultipleObjects(1,
                               &hDummyEvent, FALSE,
                               dwMilliseconds, QS_ALLINPUT)
          == (WAIT_OBJECT_0 + 1));
   // MsgWaitForMultipleObjects() returns the
   // number of elements in the array + WAIT_OBJECT_0
   // if a message comes in
   CloseHandle(hDummyEvent);
   return bRetcode;
}
```

Conclusion

Synchronization objects are an important tool for safe programming in a multithreaded environment. Windows NT provides several kinds of them. The choice of which one to use depends on what you need to accomplish. Keep these points in mind as you select your synchronization objects:

- Semaphores regulate access to a shared resource where more than one instance of the resource may be used concurrently. Examples of this are modem pools or software licenses.
- Mutexes can be thought of as semaphores where there is never more than one instance of a resource. The term mutex is shorthand for mutual exclusion. Mutexes allow one thread at a time to use a shared object.
- Critical sections are essentially mutexes that work only between threads of the same process.
- Events are open-ended objects that are used to signal the completion of an I/O operation. They are required by some of the other Win32 API sets.

Structured Termination Handling helps assure the proper use of synchronization objects because it guarantees that a thread that owns an object will relinquish it.

In the code presented in Part 3, I use mutexes to guard global resources in DLLs, most importantly shared memory tables. I use events with I/O operations, in particular Named Pipes and NetBIOS communications.

Now that you understand events and mutexes, you're ready to move on to File I/O and Dynamic Link Libraries, which are covered in Chapters 7 and 8, respectively.

Suggested Reading

Custer, Helen. *Inside Windows NT*. Redmond, WA: Microsoft Press, 1992. Chapter 3.

Richter, Jeff. *Advanced Windows NT*. Redmond, WA: Microsoft Press, 1993. Chapter 5.

Handles and Objects Overview in the on-line help. Published as Chapter 48 in the *Win32 Programmer's Reference, Volume 2*.

Synchronization Overview in the on-line help. Published as Chapter 44 in the *Win32 Programmer's Reference, Volume 2*.

Richter, Jeff. "Synchronizing Win32 Threads Using Critical Sections, Semaphores, and Mutexes." *Microsoft Systems Journal*, Vol. 8, No. 8, August 1993.

Microsoft Knowledge Base for Win32 SDK articles:
"Interrupting Threads in Critical Sections"
"Objects Inherited through a CreateProcess() Call"
"Win32 Subsystem Object Cleanup"

## Chapter 7

Win32 File I/O

Overview

Because Windows NT is a complete operating system rather than a patchwork operating environment like Windows 3.X, the Win32 API offers a complete set of file I/O functions. You can still use standard C runtime library functions, but these are provided primarily for console applications and for backward compatibility. The Win32 File I/O calls offer the most hooks into the NT kernel and are the only way to use NT's advanced capabilities, which include:

- Attaching security restrictions to files and directories on NTFS partitions
- Support for 64-bit (i.e., unlimited) file sizes
- Asynchronous I/O
- Using callback functions with read and write calls

Basic File I/O Operations

The Win32 functions that perform the basic set of operations (open, read, write, and close) are CreateFile(), ReadFile(), WriteFile(), and CloseHandle().

CreateFile()

The name CreateFile() would seem to suggest that this function is responsible for creating new files, and that OpenFile() should be used with existing files. However, the name CreateFile() is used because it is consistent with the other object functions in Windows NT; that is, it asks the NT Object Manager to create an NT file object representing some kind of a disk object. The associated disk operation is the province of the NT I/O Manager and is included as one of the arguments to CreateFile(). The old Windows function, OpenFile(), continues to be supported, but is superseded by CreateFile(). Here is the prototype for CreateFile():

```
HANDLE CreateFile(
        LPCTSTR lpFileName,
        DWORD   dwDesiredAccess,
        DWORD   dwShareMode,
        LPSECURITY_ATTRIBUTES lpSecurityAttributes,
        DWORD   dwCreationDisposition,
        DWORD   dwFlagsAndAttributes,
        HANDLE  hTemplateFile);
```

The first three arguments should be more or less self-explanatory as they are common to most file I/O APIs. The operating system needs to know the name of the file *(lpFileName)*, it needs to know how you intend to access the file *(dwDesiredAccess)*, and it needs to know what access to allow other processes while you have the file open *(dwShareMode)*. *lpFileName* is an LPCTSTR, a pointer to a Unicode or ANSI string. You can access files on remote machines (including NetWare servers or Windows for Workgroups stations) either using a redirected drive or with the full Universal Naming Convention (UNC) filename. UNC filenames have this format:

```
\\<Machine name>\<Share name>\<Rest of path to file>\<File name>
```

For instance, if the machine NUMBER1 is sharing the directory C:\ under the share name ROOT$, you use the UNC name \\NUMBER1\ROOT$\AUTOEXEC.BAT to open the AUTOEXEC.BAT file in that directory. As you will see in Chapter 10, this is how a client application opens a named pipe on a remote machine.

The next argument to CreateFile(), *dwDesiredAccess*, indicates whether you want to open the file for read access, write access, or both. The constants defined by Win32 for this purpose are GENERIC_READ and GENERIC_WRITE. *dwShareMode* specifies the ways in which other threads and processes may access the file while you are working with it. A value of zero requests exclusive access. The constants FILE_SHARE_READ and FILE_SHARE_WRITE grant read and write access and may be ORed together.

lpSecurityAttributes is significant if you are creating a new file on an NTFS partition or if you need the file handle to be inheritable. You can pass it as NULL if you do not need for child processes to use the handle and if you are not setting explicit security limitations. Be aware that creating a file with NULL security attributes or passing a SECURITY_ATTRIBUTES structure with a NULL security descriptor does not make it available to everyone. Rather, it causes the file to inherit the security restrictions of the directory where it resides. Usually, these allow administrative users (those belonging to the group Administrators) full access and give other users (members of the group Everyone) read access. You will see how to grant universal access to a file in Chapter 10 when I apply security attributes to named pipes. I defer the bulk of the discussion on NT security until Chapter 14.

Most of the syntactic complexity of CreateFile() is contained in *dwCreationDisposition* and *dwFlagsAndAttributes*. CreateFile() can do a number of things; *dwCreationDisposition* tells CreateFile() what you want it to do. Specifically, it is your instruction to the NT I/O Manager that informs it what I/O operation you want. Possible values for *dwCreationDisposition* are:

- CREATE_NEW: Create a new file, but fail the function if the file already exists.
- CREATE_ALWAYS: Create a new file unconditionally; if the file already exists, replace it.
- OPEN_EXISTING: Open an existing file, but fail the function if the file does not already exist.
- OPEN_ALWAYS: Open an existing file, and create a new one if the file does not already exist.
- TRUNCATE_EXISTING: Open an existing file, and truncate it to zero bytes. If the file does not exist, fail the function.

dwFlagsAndAttributes specifies the attributes of a newly created file. It is ignored when you open an existing file. They are the standard normal, read-only, hidden, system, and archive attributes. The corresponding Win32 constants are FILE_ATTRIBUTE_NORMAL, FILE_ATTRIBUTE_READONLY, FILE_ATTRIBUTE_HIDDEN, FILE_ATTRIBUTE_SYSTEM, and FILE_ATTRIBUTE_ARCHIVE. Another interesting attribute is FILE_ATTRIBUTE_TEMPORARY, which tells NT that you are creating the file as a temporary file. In combination with the flag bit FILE_FLAG_DELETE_ON_CLOSE, it lets you set up a temporary file that you do not have to worry about deleting when you are through with it. NT will delete it when the last handle to the file is closed. NT can also optimize your access to the file if it knows that you do not intend it to be permanent. Two other attributes are reserved for future use: FILE_ATTRIBUTE_ATOMIC_WRITE and FILE_ATTRIBUTE_XACTION_WRITE. The existence of these flags seems to indicate Microsoft's intention to add some kind of transactional protection to the NT file system.

The flag bits of *dwFlagsAndAttributes* govern the way in which the file will be accessed. The most interesting for our purposes is FILE_FLAG_OVERLAPPED. This enables overlapped (asynchronous) file I/O for both normal disk files and named pipes. FILE_FLAG_WRITE_ THROUGH may be desirable for certain kinds of named pipes; it prevents local buffering of data, forcing all writes to the named pipe to be immediately transmitted to the partner station. FILE_FLAG_RANDOM_ACCESS and FILE_FLAG_SEQUENTIAL_SCAN inform NT how you intend to access the file and influence its caching policy. Presumably, it uses this flag to decide whether to use least-recently-used or most-recently-used logic. (For sequential scans, the part of the file you are least likely to want next is the one you just looked at; therefore, it should be first in line for paging to disk).

The final argument to CreateFile(), *hTemplateFile*, is a handle to an open file whose attributes will be inherited by a newly created file. It is ignored when you are opening an existing file.

CreateFile() returns a HANDLE that you use for subsequent operations on the file. If the function fails, it returns INVALID_HANDLE_VALUE (-1), not NULL. When I first starting writing code for NT, this was one of my most common mistakes. This is an annoying inconsistency in the Win32 API: Some functions that return handles return NULL to signal failure; others return INVALID_HANDLE_VALUE. There does appear to be some rhyme and reason: the functions that return INVALID_HANDLE_VALUE —that is, CreateConsoleScreenBuffer(), CreateFile(), CreateMailslot(), CreateNamedPipe(), FindFirstChangeNotification(), FindFirstFile(), and GetStdHandle()—are primarily file-related. However, so is CreateFileMapping(), but it returns NULL if it fails.

ReadFile() / WriteFile()

Reads and writes are done using ReadFile() and WriteFile(), which have identical syntax:

```
BOOL ReadFile(
        HANDLE       hFile,
        LPVOID       lpBuffer,
        DWORD        dwBytes,
        LPDWORD      lpBytes,
        LPOVERLAPPED lpOverlapped);
```

```
BOOL WriteFile(
        HANDLE      hFile,
        LPVOID      lpBuffer,
        DWORD       dwBytes,
        LPDWORD     lpBytes,
        LPOVERLAPPED lpOverlapped);
```

The first four arguments (*hFile, lpBuffer, dwBytes,* and *lpBytes*) are standard. The operating system needs to know which file you are targeting (*hFile*), where to read the data into or write it from (*lpBuffer*), and how many bytes to read or write. It also needs to inform you how many bytes were read or written. Some file I/O APIs, like the C runtime functions _read() and _write(), use the function return value to report this. Win32 uses the *lpBytes* argument.

The last argument is the most interesting. It is a pointer to an OVERLAPPED structure. For files created with the FILE_FLAG_OVERLAPPED flag, the structure allows you to do file I/O in the background while your program goes about its other tasks. With files created for non-overlapped I/O, you can use the OVERLAPPED structure to specify the file position where you want the read or write operation to begin. Ordinarily, you do this by calling SetFilePointer() before you invoke ReadFile() or WriteFile(). The OVERLAPPED structure is defined as follows:

```
typedef struct _OVERLAPPED
{
    DWORD   Internal;
    DWORD   InternalHigh;
    DWORD   Offset;
    DWORD   OffsetHigh;
    HANDLE  hEvent;
} OVERLAPPED;
```

Not surprisingly, *Internal* and *InternalHigh* are used for internal purposes. *Offset* and *OffsetHigh* specify the file position at which the read or write should begin. NT will seek to the indicated location in the file before performing the operation. For overlapped I/O, you must specify the offset; NT does not automatically adjust the file pointer. The offset is expressed as two DWORD variables to accommodate 64-bit file sizes.

The *hEvent* field is a handle to a manual-reset event that you want to associate with an I/O operation. With a file or named pipe that has been opened for overlapped I/O, the event is automatically set to nonsignalled when the operation commences, and calls to ReadFile() and WriteFile() may return FALSE. It is possible, though, that NT will decide that it does not need to overlap the operation. In this case, ReadFile() or WriteFile() return TRUE, so you need to be prepared for that eventuality. If the operation is executing asynchronously, GetLastError() reports an error code of ERROR_IO_ PENDING. The event remains nonsignalled until the operation completes.

An overlapped operation does not update *lpBytes*, the variable reporting the number of bytes read or written. After all, the operation is still pending at this point; its final result is not known until you call GetOverlappedResult().

GetOverlappedResult()

After you have spun off overlapped operations, you can test for their completion by calling GetOverlappedResult().

```
BOOL GetOverlappedResult(
        HANDLE       hFile,
        LPOVERLAPPED lpOverlapped,
        LPDWORD      lpBytesTransferred,
        BOOL         bWait);
```

hFile and *lpOverlapped* are the file handle and OVERLAPPED structure that you previously passed to ReadFile() or WriteFile(). *lpBytesTransferred* returns the number of bytes moved. *bWait* specifies whether you want GetOverlappedResult() to block until the operation completes (TRUE), or return immediately with a code indicating the status of the operation (FALSE). If you pass *bWait* as FALSE and the operation is still not complete, GetOverlappedResult() returns FALSE, and GetLastError() reports the error as ERROR_IO_INCOMPLETE (**not** ERROR_IO_ PENDING, for some reason). Because *bWait* is a BOOL, you cannot request a timeout; you either wait forever or you return immediately.

Callback Functions with Overlapped File I/O

ReadFileEx() and WriteFileEx() allow you to specify a callback function that will be invoked when an operation completes. Here is the prototype for ReadFileEx(); WriteFileEx() is exactly the same:

```
BOOL ReadFileEx(
        HANDLE       hFile,
        LPVOID       lpBuffer,
        DWORD        dwBytesToRead,
        LPOVERLAPPED lpOverlapped,
        LPOVERLAPPED_COMPLETION_ROUTINE lpRoutine);
```

The first five arguments are the same as for ReadFile() and WriteFile(). The function pointed to by *lpRoutine* has the following prototype:

```
VOID WINAPI FileIOCompletionRoutine(
            DWORD       dwError,
            DWORD       dwBytesTransferred,
            LPOVERLAPPED lpOverlapped);
```

dwError will either be 0 to indicate successful completion of the operation, or ERROR_HANDLE_EOF if ReadFileEx() tried to read past the end of the file.

dwBytesTransferred reports the number of bytes read or written. *lpOverlapped* points to the OVERLAPPED structure that was originally passed to ReadFileEx() or WriteFileEx(). The event handle, reported in the *hEvent* field of *lpOverlapped*, is not used, so you can pass other information to the completion routine using this field if you need to.

The completion routine is executed when the thread that called ReadFileEx() or WriteFileEx() enters what is known as an alertable wait state. It does this by calling extended versions of Sleep(), WaitForSingleObject(), or WaitForMultipleObjects()—SleepEx(), WaitForSingleObjectEx(), and WaitForMultipleObjectsEx(). They have the same syntax as the non-extended versions, but add one argument that specifies whether you want to enter an alertable wait state or not. Here is the prototype for WaitForSingleObjectEx():

```
DWORD WaitForSingleObjectEx(
        HANDLE hObject,
        DWORD  dwTimeout,
        BOOL   bAlertable);
```

If *bAlertable* is passed as TRUE, the thread calling WaitForSingle ObjectEx() enters an alertable wait state, in which the I/O completion routine can be called. The I/O routine runs in the context of the thread that calls WaitForSingleObjectEx(). If, on the other hand, you pass *bAlertable* as FALSE, WaitForSingleObjectEx() becomes exactly equivalent to WaitForSingleObject().

If the callback function is invoked in response to SleepEx(), WaitForSingleObjectEx(), or WaitForMultipleObjectsEx(), the function returns the value WAIT_IO_COMPLETION. It can also return the standard values for the other wait functions that I discussed in Chapter 6. This could happen if *bAlertable* is passed as FALSE or if NT elects to perform the operation immediately, rather than asynchronously. This will probably happen if the portion of the file you are reading from or writing to is already cached in memory.

Because the callback function cannot be called until you enter an alertable wait state, using callbacks does not relieve you of having to block at some point. It does replace GetOverlappedResult() because it provides another way to get the final disposition of an operation.

Additional Win32 File I/O Functions

Win32 provides a full set of functions for all the standard file I/O operations. Like CreateFile(), they support remote file operations using UNC file names or redirected drives. Much of this API set is based on the OS/2 file I/O services. Some of the most useful functions are shown in Table 7-1.

Table 7-1.   Additional Win32 File I/O Functions

Function	Action Performed
CopyFile	Copies one file to another
CreateDirectory	Makes a new directory
DeleteFile	Erases a file
FindFirstFile	Enumerate files and directories
FindNextFile	Continues file enumeration
FindClose	Closes file enumeration
FlushFileBuffers	Forces writing of dirty buffers to disk
GetCurrentDirectory	Returns the current working directory
GetDiskFreeSpace	Gets statistics on disk usage
GetDriveType	Characterizes a drive as removable, fixed, network, CD-ROM, or RAM
GetFileAttributes	Retrieves a file's attributes
GetFileSize	Gets file size with full support for 64-bit file sizes
GetFullPathName	Returns the full path specification for a file
GetVolumeInformation	Reports file-system information for a given drive
LockFile	Locks a byte range in a file
LockFileEx	Locks a byte range in a file
MoveFile	Moves or renames a file
MoveFileEx	Moves or renames a file
RemoveDirectory	Deletes a directory
SearchPath	Searches a set of directories for a given file
SetCurrentDirectory	Changes the current working directory
SetEndOfFile	Sets the size of a file

Table 7-1. **Additional Win32 File I/O Functions (continued)**

Function	Action Performed
SetFileAttributes	Changes a file's attributes
SetFilePointer	Moves the file pointer
SetFileTime	Touches a file
UnlockFile	Unlocks a byte range in a file
UnlockFileEx	Unlocks a byte range in a file

Source Code Listings

In this section, I present Win32 versions of some standard file utilities. *cat*, *touch*, and *ls* come from UNIX. *which* finds a requested file by searching either the PATH or a given set of directories. First, though, I'd like to take a final look at printfConsole(), which I have presented already in a couple of different contexts.

printfConsole()

printfConsole() writes a formatted message to standard output. To target the standard devices with ReadFile() and WriteFile(), you have to obtain Win32 handles representing them. These are rendered by the GetStdHandle() function.

```
HANDLE GetStdHandle(DWORD dwDevice);
```

The devices are indicated by the constants STD_INPUT_HANDLE, STD_OUTPUT_HANDLE, and STD_ERROR_HANDLE. In a console application, they represent the normal I/O streams. A windowed application can also use these handles to read from or write to a console window, which is how printfConsole() uses them.

```
int _CRTAPI2 printfConsole(LPCTSTR format, ...)
{
    va_list argp;
    TCHAR    szBuffer[1024];
    CHAR     szOutBuffer[1024];
    LPCVOID  lpcOutBuffer;
    HANDLE   hStdout;
    DWORD    dwBytes = ((DWORD) -1);
    CPINFO   CodePageInfo;
    DWORD    dwLength;
```

```
        va_start(argp, format);

        hStdout = GetStdHandle(STD_OUTPUT_HANDLE);

        // Protect write to the console with a mutex
        WaitForSingleObject(hPrintfMutex, INFINITE);

        try
            {
            // Find out if we're using wide character code page

            wvsprintf(szBuffer, format, argp);
#ifndef WIN32S
            GetCPInfo(GetACP(), &CodePageInfo);

            if (CodePageInfo.MaxCharSize == 1)
                {
                WideCharToMultiByte(CP_ACP, 0, szBuffer, lstrlen(szBuffer) + 1,
                    szOutBuffer, sizeof (szOutBuffer), NULL, NULL);
                lpcOutBuffer = (LPCVOID) szOutBuffer;
                dwLength = lstrlenA(szOutBuffer);
                }
            else
                {
                lpcOutBuffer = (LPCVOID) szBuffer;
                dwLength = lstrlen(szBuffer);
                }
            if (!WriteFile(hStdout, lpcOutBuffer, dwLength,
                        &dwBytes, NULL))
                dwBytes = (DWORD) -1;
#else
            OutputDebugString(szBuffer);
            dwBytes = lstrlen(szBuffer);
#endif
            }
        finally
            {
            // Make sure we release the mutex, no matter how we got here
            ReleaseMutex(hPrintfMutex);
            va_end(argp);
            }

    return (int) dwBytes;
}
```

cat

cat is a UNIX utility that reads from standard input and writes to standard output. The name *cat* comes from the fact that multiple input files can be concatenated into a single output stream. *cat* can be implemented quite simply in standard C.

```
char szBuffer[4096];
size_t nBytes;

while ((nBytes = fread(szBuffer, sizeof (char), sizeof (szBuffer),
                    stdin)) == sizeof (szBuffer))
    fwrite(szBuffer, sizeof (char), nBytes, stdout);
// Write last part of the file
if (!ferror(stdin) && nBytes > 0)
    fwrite(szBuffer, sizeof (char), nBytes, stdout);
```

An implementation like this is generic and portable; but let's see what *cat* would look like using Win32 I/O calls instead. Let's also stipulate that we'll read from standard input using overlapped I/O. This is irrelevant, but harmless, if you are actually reading standard input instead of a disk file. You can also pass *cat* file specifications as arguments; each element of *argv* is expanded, and all the matching files are read and written to standard output. If no arguments are passed, you get a handle to standard input by calling GetStdHandle(). Otherwise, you open each requested file for overlapped I/O by calling CreateFile() as follows:

```
HANDLE hInput;
hInput = CreateFile(lpFileName,
            GENERIC_READ,
            FILE_SHARE_READ,
            NULL,
            OPEN_EXISTING,
            FILE_ATTRIBUTE_NORMAL |
            FILE_FLAG_OVERLAPPED,
            NULL);
```

You then create a manual-reset event to use for the overlapped operation and call ReadFile(). If it returns FALSE, you call GetLastError() to make sure it returns ERROR_IO_PENDING. This means you have an overlapped operation under way, so you call GetOverlappedResult() to wait for it to complete. If GetLastError() reports some other condition, or ReadFile() returns TRUE but says that zero bytes have been read, you terminate the read. Each time through the loop, you bump the offset field of the OVERLAPPED structure; NT does not move the file pointer automatically.

```cpp
// Create a manual-reset, unnamed event
// for the input operation
Overlapped.hEvent = CreateEvent(NULL, TRUE, FALSE, NULL);

// Read from input, write to output
while (TRUE)
    {
    if (!ReadFile(hInput, szBuffer, sizeof (szBuffer),
            &dwBytesRead, &Overlapped))
        {
        if (ERROR_IO_PENDING != GetLastError())
            // Read error, bail out
            break;
        if (!GetOverlappedResult(hInput,
                &Overlapped, &dwBytesRead, TRUE))
            // Error
            break;
        }

    // No bytes read means EOF
    if (dwBytesRead == 0)
        break;

    // Bump input file pointer—not done automatically
    // for overlapped I/O
    Overlapped.Offset += dwBytesRead;
    WriteFile(hOutput, szBuffer, dwBytesRead,
                &dwBytesWritten, NULL);
    }
```

Here is the complete code listing, included on the source code disk as \NTNET\CODE\WNETFUTL\CAT.CPP:

```cpp
/********
 *
 * CAT.CPP
 *
 * Copyright (c) 1993-1994 Ralph P. Davis, All Rights Reserved
 *
 * Demonstrates use of overlapped I/O with
 * handles for standard input and standard output
 *
 ********/
```

```c
/*===== Includes =====*/

#include <windows.h>
#include <stdio.h>


/*===== Function Definitions =====*/

void main(int argc, char *argv[])
{
    int i;
    HANDLE       hInput, hOutput;
    OVERLAPPED Overlapped;
    DWORD        dwBytesRead, dwBytesWritten;
    char         szBuffer[4096];
    LPSTR        lpFileName;

    // argv contains an array of file names to concatenate
    // if argc == 1, use standard input

    hOutput = GetStdHandle(STD_OUTPUT_HANDLE);

    for (i = 1; i <= argc; ++i)
        {
        if (argc == 1)
            hInput = GetStdHandle(STD_INPUT_HANDLE);
        else
            {
            if (i == argc)
                break;
            lpFileName = argv[i];
            hInput = CreateFile(lpFileName,
                    GENERIC_READ,
                    FILE_SHARE_READ,
                    NULL,
                    OPEN_EXISTING,
                    FILE_FLAG_OVERLAPPED,
                    NULL);
            }
        if (hInput != INVALID_HANDLE_VALUE)
            {
            ZeroMemory(&Overlapped, sizeof (OVERLAPPED));

            // Create a manual-reset, unnamed event
            // for the input operation
            Overlapped.hEvent = CreateEvent(NULL, TRUE, FALSE, NULL);

            // Read from input, write to output
```

```
        while (TRUE)
          {
          if (!ReadFile(hInput, szBuffer, sizeof (szBuffer),
                  &dwBytesRead, &Overlapped))
            {
            if (ERROR_IO_PENDING != GetLastError())
              // Read error, assume end-of-file
              break;
            if (!GetOverlappedResult(hInput,
                  &Overlapped, &dwBytesRead, TRUE))
              // Error
              break;
            }
          // No bytes read means EOF
          if (dwBytesRead == 0)
             break;

          // Bump input file pointer—not done automatically
          // for overlapped I/O

          Overlapped.Offset += dwBytesRead;
          WriteFile(hOutput, szBuffer, dwBytesRead,
                  &dwBytesWritten, NULL);
          }
        CloseHandle(Overlapped.hEvent);
        }
    else
        fprintf(stderr,
           "\nUnable to open %s, GetLastError() = %d",
           lpFileName, GetLastError());
    if (argc > 1)
        CloseHandle(hInput);
      }
   ExitProcess(0);
}
```

touch

touch changes the last modification time of a file. I use this, for instance, when I have a header file that my make files list as a dependency for just about every source file in an application, like \NTNET\CODE\WNET.H. If I change some insignificant constant, I don't want to have to rebuild the whole world; so I set the system date back a year, *touch* the header file, then try to remember to set the date back to today.

The Win32 implementation of *touch* uses the SetFileTime() function, but first it has to get the current time. It must also convert the system time to file-time format. The system time is retrieved by the GetSystemTime() function, and returned in a SYSTEMTIME structure:

```
typedef struct _SYSTEMTIME
{
    WORD wYear;
    WORD wMonth;
    WORD wDayOfWeek;
    WORD wDay;
    WORD wHour;
    WORD wMinute;
    WORD wSecond;
    WORD wMilliseconds;
} SYSTEMTIME;
```

SystemTimeToFileTime(), in turn, takes the SYSTEMTIME and renders it as a FILETIME:

```
typedef struct _FILETIME
{
    DWORD dwLowDateTime;
    DWORD dwHighDateTime;
} FILETIME;
```

The FILETIME is a 64-bit quantity, expressed as the number of 100-nanosecond intervals since January 1, 1601.

These are the lines of code from \NTNET\CODE\TOUCH.CPP that get the system time and convert it to file time:

```
SYSTEMTIME RightNow;
FILETIME   FileTime;

GetSystemTime(&RightNow);
SystemTimeToFileTime(&RightNow, &FileTime);
```

This is all the information needed for *touch*. However, the Win32 function that changes a file's time, SetFileTime(), requires the file handle as an argument, so you have to open the file before changing its update time. Opening it for exclusive access ensures that changing the time does not conflict with anyone else's use of the file. Here's the prototype for SetFileTime():

```
BOOL SetFileTime(
        HANDLE          hFile,
        CONST FILETIME *lpCreated,
```

```
CONST FILETIME *lpLastAccessed,
CONST FILETIME *lpLastModified);
```

Only the OS/2 High Performance File System (HPFS) and the NT File System (NTFS) support creation time and last access time. The last modification time is the item we're interested in; we pass the other two times as NULL pointers.

```
hFile = CreateFile(argv[i],
                   GENERIC_WRITE,
                   0, // exclusive access
                   NULL,
                   OPEN_EXISTING,
                   0,
                   NULL);
if (hFile != INVALID_HANDLE_VALUE)
    {
    SetFileTime(hFile, NULL, NULL, &FileTime);
    CloseHandle(hFile);
    }
```

Here is the listing for TOUCH.CPP:

```
/********
 *
 * TOUCH.CPP
 *
 * Copyright (c) 1993-1994 Ralph P. Davis, All Rights Reserved
 *
 ********/


/*===== Includes =====*/

#include <windows.h>
#include <stdio.h>


/*===== Function Definitions =====*/

void main(int argc, char *argv[])
{
    SYSTEMTIME  RightNow;
    FILETIME    FileTime;
    int         i;
    HANDLE      hFile;
    int         nTouched;
```

```
GetSystemTime(&RightNow);
SystemTimeToFileTime(&RightNow, &FileTime);

if (argc == 1)
   {
   fprintf(stderr,
       "\nUsage: touch <file name> [<additional file names>]\n");
   ExitProcess(0);
   }

for (i = 1, nTouched = 0; i < argc; ++i)
   {
   hFile = CreateFile(argv[i],
                      GENERIC_WRITE,
                      0,
                      NULL,
                      OPEN_EXISTING,
                      0,
                      NULL);
   if (hFile != INVALID_HANDLE_VALUE)
       {
       ++nTouched;
       SetFileTime(hFile, NULL, NULL, &FileTime);
       CloseHandle(hFile);
       }
   }
   printf("\n%d file(s) touched\n", nTouched);
   ExitProcess(0);
}
```

which

which uses the SearchPath() function to tell you which copy of a file it will select from a given set of directories. Suppose you have more than one copy of a utility like *ls.exe* on your path, and you want to make sure the one that gets executed is the most up-to-date version. *which* gives you that information.

Here is the prototype for SearchPath():

```
DWORD SearchPath(
        LPCTSTR    lpszPath,
        LPCTSTR    lpszFile,
        LPCTSTR    lpszExtension,
        DWORD      dwOutputBufferSize,
        LPTSTR     lpszReturnBuffer,
        LPTSTR     *lplpFileNameComponent);
```

lpszPath is the list of directories you want SearchPath() to scan. Directories in this string are delimited by semicolons. If you want SearchPath() to look in the directories that NT normally searches to run a program, you can pass *lpszPath* as NULL. In this case, the search order is:

1. The directory where the application started from.
2. The current directory.
3. The Windows system directory, identified by GetSystemDirectory(). This is \WINNT\SYSTEM32 on most of my machines.
4. The Windows directory, reported by GetWindowsDirectory() (\WINNT for me).
5. The directories listed in the PATH environment variable.

lpszFile is the name of the file you want SearchPath() to locate. *lpszExtension* is the default extension that NT will append to the filename if *lpszFile* does not include one. *dwOutputBufferSize* and *lpszReturnBuffer* describe the location where you want the answer deposited. *lplpFileNameComponent* can be handy. It will return a pointer to the last component of the file name (that is, the file name without the path preceding it). For example, if SearchPath() finds a file named D:\NTNET\CODE\WNETFUTL\LS.EXE, *lplpFileNameComponent* will point to LS.EXE. This can save you some trouble parsing the file name.

which takes one required and one optional argument. The first argument is the file you want it to locate. You also have the option of specifying the set of directories you want *which* to search. If you do not pass this, *which* passes the *lpszPath* argument to SearchPath() as NULL.

which also shows my first use of the FormatMessage() function. This is the Win32 version of perror(). Its syntax is quite a bit more complicated than perror(), but its error messages are much more informative. You can also use FormatMessage() to display application-specific messages that you have compiled with the Message Compiler and linked into your application (or a DLL). This gives you easy internationalization. My use of FormatMessage() in *which* is taken almost verbatim from the Win32 SDK Knowledge Base, article number Q94999, entitled "FormatMessage() Converts GetLastError() Codes." In *ls*, following *which*, I also use it to display my own messages, which are included on the source code disk in French and Spanish as well as English.

Here's what FormatMessage() looks like:

```
DWORD FormatMessage(
        DWORD    dwFlags,
        LPCVOID  lpSource,
```

```
DWORD    dwMessageID,
DWORD    dwLanguageID,
LPTSTR   lpBuffer,
DWORD    dwSize,
va_list  *pArgs);
```

dwFlags specifies how the output message is to be constructed. Some of the most important flags are:

- FORMAT_MESSAGE_ALLOCATE_BUFFER says that you want NT to allocate the memory for the message. When this flag is set, *lpBuffer* is a pointer to a pointer for which memory will be LocalAlloc()'d. When you are through with the message, you need to LocalFree() it.
- FORMAT_MESSAGE_FROM_SYSTEM identifies the message as a system message; *dwMessageID* is a GetLastError() code.
- FORMAT_MESSAGE_FROM_STRING indicates that *lpSource* points to a format string. It may contain "insert sequences," which are similar to *printf()* format specifiers. However, FormatMessage() uses *%n* sequences, where *n* designates a one-based index into the array pointed to by *pArgs*. The *%n* may be followed by printf()-type format codes, enclosed in exclamation points. Thus, the insert sequence *%1!08x!* says to substitute the value of the first element in *lpArgs* (that is, *lpArgs[0]*) and format it as an eight-digit hexadecimal number, padded on the left with zeroes.
- FORMAT_MESSAGE_FROM_HMODULE tells NT that the message is contained in an executable image or a DLL. *lpSource* will be either the module handle (obtained by a call to LoadLibrary() or GetModuleHandle()) or NULL to identify the current process.
- FORMAT_MESSAGE_ARGUMENT_ARRAY says that *lpArgs* is not a *va_list *, but rather an array of 32-bit data items.

lpSource is ignored unless either the FORMAT_MESSAGE_FROM_HMODULE or the FORMAT_MESSAGE_FROM_STRING flags are set.

dwMessageID identifies the message that you want to render. If FORMAT_MESSAGE_FROM_SYSTEM is set, *dwMessageID* is a GetLastError() code. The Win32 header file WINERROR.H is generated by the Message Compiler; it has the definitions of all the GetLastError() codes and includes the strings that will be returned by FormatMessage() as comments.

dwLanguageID specifies the language in which you want the message to be delivered. A version of the message in the requested language must have been defined when the Message Compiler processed the messages. For system-defined messages, you will normally pass this as either LANG_USER_DEFAULT or as GetUserDefaultLangID(), so that the message is generated in the language for which the user's machine is configured. For application-defined messages, it will be whatever numeric code you have associated with the languages you are supporting. For *ls*, I use the low 16 bits returned by GetUserDefaultLangID(). These identify the language; the high 16 bits describe dialectical flavorings, like British, American, or Australian English.

lpBuffer points to the buffer where you want the message to be placed. If you set the FORMAT_MESSAGE_ALLOCATE_BUFFER flag, NT will LocalAlloc() the memory for you. In this case, *lpBuffer* points to the pointer that you want NT to allocate. *dwSize* specifies the maximum length of a message, unless you set FORMAT_MESSAGE_ALLOCATE_BUFFER, in which case it designates the smallest size you want NT to allocate.

Finally, *lpArgs* points to the values that will be substituted into the message string for insert sequences. If the FORMAT_MESSAGE_ARGUMENT_ARRAY flag is set, this is an array of DWORDs.

Here is the complete listing of \NTNET\CODE\WNETFUTL\ WHICH.CPP:

```
/********
 *
 * WHICH.CPP
 *
 * Copyright (c) 1993-1994 Ralph P. Davis, All Rights Reserved
 *
 * Finds a given file on a given path
 *
 * USAGE:
 *
 *     which <file name> [<path>]
 *
 *     If <path> is not specified, uses NT's default searching algorithm
 *
 ********/

/*===== Includes=====*/

#include <windows.h>
#include <stdio.h>
```

```
/*===== Function Definitions =====*/

VOID main(int argc, char *argv[])
{
    LPCTSTR lpFileName;
    LPCTSTR lpPath = NULL;
    char    szPathName[MAX_PATH + 1];
    LPTSTR  lpFilePart;
    LPSTR   lpMsg;

    if (argc == 1)
        {
        fprintf(stderr, "\nUsage:  which <file name> [<path>]\n");
        ExitProcess(1);
        }

    lpFileName = (LPCTSTR) argv[1];

    if (argc < 3)
        lpPath = NULL;
    else
        lpPath = (LPCTSTR) argv[2];

    // SearchPath() returns the length of the full file name
    if (SearchPath(lpPath, lpFileName, NULL, MAX_PATH, szPathName,
                   &lpFilePart) > 0)
        printf("\n%s\n", szPathName);
    else
        {
        FormatMessage(
          FORMAT_MESSAGE_ALLOCATE_BUFFER | FORMAT_MESSAGE_FROM_SYSTEM,
          NULL, GetLastError(), LANG_USER_DEFAULT,
          (LPSTR) &lpMsg, 0, NULL );

        fprintf(stderr, "\nSearchPath() failed\n%s\n",
                lpMsg);
        LocalFree(lpMsg);
        }
}
```

ls

The last application I present here is *ls*, a Win32 implementation of the UNIX utility that lists files. The Win32 file-enumeration functions are FindFirstFile(), FindNextFile(), and FindClose().

```
HANDLE FindFirstFile(
        LPCTSTR lpszFileSpec,
        LPWIN32_FIND_DATA lpWin32FindData);
BOOL FindNextFile(
        HANDLE hSearch,
        LPWIN32_FIND_DATA lpWin32FindData);
BOOL FindClose(HANDLE hSearch);
```

The WIN32_FIND_DATA structure captures information about each enumerated file. For *ls*, the field of interest is the *cFileName* field, which reports the native name of the file in its own file system. The *cAlternateFileName* field provides an 8.3 FAT-compatible file name for HPFS and NTFS names that do not conform to FAT conventions. For instance, for the file name "george washington.c," which is legal in HPFS and NTFS, NT generates the 8.3 name GEORGE~1.C. If I have another file in the same directory called "george jones.c," *cAlternateFileName* gives it as GEORGE~2.C.

A very simple *ls* can be written with only a few lines of code. Here's what it might look like:

```
/********
 *
 * LS1.CPP
 *
 * Very simple implementation of LS using Win32 functions
 *
 ********/


/*===== Includes =====*/

#include <windows.h>
#include <stdio.h>


/*===== Function Definitions =====*/

VOID ls(LPCTSTR lpszFileSpec)
{
    HANDLE hSearch;
    WIN32_FIND_DATA Win32FindData;

    hSearch = FindFirstFile(lpszFileSpec, &Win32FindData);

    if (hSearch == INVALID_HANDLE_VALUE)
        {
```

```
        fprintf(stderr,
            "\nFindFirstFile() for %s failed, GetLastError() = %d\n",
            lpszFileSpec, GetLastError());
        return;
        }

    do
        {
        printf("\n%s", Win32FindData.cFileName);
        }
    while (FindNextFile(hSearch, &Win32FindData));

    FindClose(hSearch);
}

VOID main(int argc, char *argv[])
{
    int i;

    if (argc == 1)
        ls("./*.*");
    else
        {
        for (i = 1; i < argc; ++i)
            ls(argv[i]);
        }
    ExitProcess(0);
}
```

However, I have chosen to provide a more ambitious version that demonstrates all of the techniques we've studied so far in this book. My *ls* is multithreaded; for each *argv*, I execute the ls() function in a new thread. Each thread captures its output in a local buffer, which it concatenates to a single global buffer when it finishes. The main thread, after starting the secondary threads, waits until they all complete, then prints the contents of the global buffer.

Because multiple threads append their output to a single common buffer, their activities must be synchronized. I use a mutex for traffic control. Since you have no idea how much memory to allocate for the buffers, it makes sense to reserve an amount that is probably more than you'll need. You can then commit it as necessary when an exception occurs. I reserve 16 MB for each thread, and 16 MB times the number of threads for the global buffer. I also need an array of thread handles; I allocate this by calling HeapAlloc(GetProcessHeap(), ...).

ls uses FormatMessage() to report all errors. Even if it is unable to load the DLL that contains the messages (\NTNET\CODE\%Cpu%\ WNETMSGS.DLL), it does not use a hard-coded message. In this case, it asks the system why it couldn't load it by passing GetLastError() to FormatMessage(). It displays its messages by calling WriteFile(GetStdHandle(STD_OUTPUT_HANDLE), ...) or WriteFile (GetStdHandle(STD_ERROR_HANDLE), ...), rather than printf().

Here is the listing:

```
/********
*
* LS.CPP
*
* Copyright (c) 1993-1994 Ralph P. Davis, All Rights Reserved
*
* Win32 Multithreaded Implementation of LS
*
********/


/*===== Includes =====*/

#include <windows.h>
#include <stdio.h>
#include "wnetmsgs.h"     // Generated by the Message Compiler


/*===== Constants =====*/

#define LOCAL_BUFFSIZE (16384 * 1024)


/*===== Global Variables =====*/

LPSTR      lpBuffer     = NULL;
HANDLE     hMutex       = NULL;
HINSTANCE hMessageDLL = NULL;


/*===== Function Definitions =====*/

DWORD CommitBuffer(LPSTR lpBuffer)
{
    // Find out how much is committed, and commit one more
    // page
    SYSTEM_INFO SystemInfo;
    MEMORY_BASIC_INFORMATION mbi;
```

```
    if (VirtualQuery(lpBuffer, &mbi, sizeof (MEMORY_BASIC_INFORMATION))
        != sizeof (MEMORY_BASIC_INFORMATION))
        // Uh oh! lpBuffer is probably a bogus pointer
        return EXCEPTION_EXECUTE_HANDLER;

    if (mbi.State != MEM_COMMIT)
        // No memory has been committed yet,
        // start at offset zero.
        mbi.RegionSize = 0;

    // Get the system page size
    GetSystemInfo(&SystemInfo);

    if (VirtualAlloc(&lpBuffer[mbi.RegionSize], SystemInfo.dwPageSize,
            MEM_COMMIT, PAGE_READWRITE) == NULL)
        return EXCEPTION_EXECUTE_HANDLER;
    else
        return (DWORD) EXCEPTION_CONTINUE_EXECUTION;
}

DWORD WINAPI ls(LPSTR lpszFileSpec)
{
    HANDLE hSearch;
    WIN32_FIND_DATA Win32FindData;
    char  szMessage[1024];
    LPSTR lpLocalBuffer;
    DWORD dwBytes;
    DWORD dwError = NO_ERROR;
    LPSTR lpMsg;
    MEMORY_BASIC_INFORMATION mbi;
    LPSTR lpArgs[2];

    // Reserve a local buffer for this thread's output
    lpLocalBuffer = (LPSTR) VirtualAlloc(NULL, LOCAL_BUFFSIZE,
                            MEM_RESERVE, PAGE_READWRITE);

    if (lpLocalBuffer != NULL)
        {
        hSearch = FindFirstFile(lpszFileSpec, &Win32FindData);

        if (hSearch != INVALID_HANDLE_VALUE)
            {
            do
                {
                try
                    {
                    lstrcat(lpLocalBuffer, Win32FindData.cFileName);
```

```
            // If file name has an 8.3 rendition,
            // display that too
            if (lstrlen(Win32FindData.cAlternateFileName) > 0)
                {
                lstrcat(lpLocalBuffer, " (");
                lstrcat(lpLocalBuffer,
                    Win32FindData.cAlternateFileName);
                lstrcat(lpLocalBuffer, ")");
                }
            lstrcat(lpLocalBuffer, "\n");
            }
        except (CommitBuffer(lpLocalBuffer))
            {
            // Couldn't commit the memory
            // Whine to the user

            // The English message text is
            // "Unable to commit memory"

            // We use the low sixteen bits of
            // GetUserDefaultLangID().  These identify
            // the main language (English, French, German, etc.)
            // The high sixteen bits distinguish dialects

            FormatMessage(FORMAT_MESSAGE_FROM_HMODULE,
                        (LPCVOID) hMessageDLL,
                        MSG_CANTCOMMITMEMORY,
                        GetUserDefaultLangID() & 0x00FF,
                        szMessage,
                        sizeof (szMessage),
                        NULL);
            WriteFile(GetStdHandle(STD_ERROR_HANDLE), szMessage,
                lstrlen(szMessage), &dwBytes, NULL);
            ExitProcess(dwError = GetLastError());
            return dwError;
            }
        }
    while (FindNextFile(hSearch, &Win32FindData));
    FindClose(hSearch);
    }
else
    {
    // We're going to include the system-generated
    // message in one of our private message
    FormatMessage(
      FORMAT_MESSAGE_ALLOCATE_BUFFER | FORMAT_MESSAGE_FROM_SYSTEM,
      NULL, dwError = GetLastError(),
```

```
          LANG_USER_DEFAULT,
          (LPSTR) &lpMsg, 0, NULL );

     // Our message string has two insert sequences
     // Its text is:
     //    Error on file spec %1!s!: %2!s!
     //
     // %1 points to the first element in lpArgs (lpArgs[0]),
     // which is the file specification that caused the failure.
     // !s! indicates that it points to a NULL-terminated string

     // %2 (lpArgs[1]) is the text of the system error message
     // for the GetLastError() code triggered by FindFirstFile()
     lpArgs[0] = lpszFileSpec;
     lpArgs[1] = lpMsg;
     FormatMessage(
        FORMAT_MESSAGE_FROM_HMODULE |
        FORMAT_MESSAGE_ARGUMENT_ARRAY,
        (LPCVOID) hMessageDLL,
        MSG_FILESPECERROR,
        GetUserDefaultLangID() & 0x00FF,
        szMessage,
        sizeof (szMessage),
        lpArgs);
     LocalFree(lpMsg);
     WriteFile(GetStdHandle(STD_ERROR_HANDLE), szMessage,
        lstrlen(szMessage), &dwBytes, NULL);
     }
  }
else
   {
   // Our message string is "Unable to allocate memory"
   FormatMessage(FORMAT_MESSAGE_FROM_HMODULE,
      (LPCVOID) hMessageDLL,
      MSG_CANTALLOCATE_MEMORY,
      GetUserDefaultLangID() & 0x00FF,
      szMessage,
      sizeof (szMessage),
      NULL);
   WriteFile(GetStdHandle(STD_ERROR_HANDLE), szMessage,
      lstrlen(szMessage), &dwBytes, NULL);
   }

if (lpLocalBuffer != NULL)
   {
   // See if we've committed memory
   // If no memory is committed, we've got
   // nothing to report
```

```
      VirtualQuery(lpLocalBuffer, &mbi,
         sizeof (MEMORY_BASIC_INFORMATION));

   if (mbi.State == MEM_COMMIT && mbi.RegionSize > 0)
      {
      // Grab the mutex
      WaitForSingleObject(hMutex, INFINITE);

      try
         {
         try
            {
            lstrcat(lpBuffer, lpLocalBuffer);
            }
         except (CommitBuffer(lpBuffer))
            {
            FormatMessage(FORMAT_MESSAGE_FROM_HMODULE,
                        (LPCVOID) hMessageDLL,
                        MSG_CANTCOMMITMEMORY,
                        GetUserDefaultLangID() & 0x00FF,
                        szMessage,
                        sizeof (szMessage),
                        NULL);
            WriteFile(GetStdHandle(STD_ERROR_HANDLE), szMessage,
               lstrlen(szMessage), &dwBytes, NULL);
            leave;
            }
         }
      finally
         {
         ReleaseMutex(hMutex);

         // Decommit what we've committed
         VirtualFree(lpLocalBuffer, mbi.RegionSize, MEM_DECOMMIT);
         }
      }
   VirtualFree(lpLocalBuffer, 0, MEM_RELEASE);
      }

   ExitThread(dwError);

   // Humor the compiler
   return dwError;
}


VOID main(int argc, char *argv[])
{
```

```
int       nThreads;
LPHANDLE  lpThreadHandles;
DWORD     dwThreadID;
int       i;
MEMORY_BASIC_INFORMATION mbi;
DWORD     dwBytes;
char      szMessage[1024];

if (argc > 1)
   nThreads = argc - 1;
else
   nThreads = 1;

// Load our messages (they're in WNETMSGS.DLL)
hMessageDLL = LoadLibrary("WNETMSGS.DLL");
if (hMessageDLL == NULL)
   {
   lstrcpy(szMessage, "\nWNETMSGS.DLL: ");
   FormatMessage(
     FORMAT_MESSAGE_FROM_SYSTEM,
     NULL, GetLastError(),
     LANG_USER_DEFAULT,
     &szMessage[lstrlen(szMessage)],
     sizeof (szMessage) - lstrlen(szMessage),
     NULL );
   WriteFile(GetStdHandle(STD_ERROR_HANDLE), szMessage,
      lstrlen(szMessage), &dwBytes, NULL);
   ExitProcess(GetLastError());
   }

// Get a little bit of heap memory for the
// array of thread handles
lpThreadHandles = (LPHANDLE)
   HeapAlloc(GetProcessHeap(),
      HEAP_ZERO_MEMORY,
      nThreads * sizeof (HANDLE));

if (lpThreadHandles == NULL)
   {
   // Our message is "Unable to allocate memory"
   FormatMessage(FORMAT_MESSAGE_FROM_HMODULE,
      (LPCVOID) hMessageDLL,
      MSG_CANTALLOCATE_MEMORY,
      GetUserDefaultLangID() & 0x00FF,
      szMessage,
      sizeof (szMessage),
      NULL);
```

```
        WriteFile(GetStdHandle(STD_ERROR_HANDLE), szMessage,
           lstrlen(szMessage), &dwBytes, NULL);
        ExitProcess(GetLastError());
        }

    // Reserve enough memory for all our threads to use
    // the global buffer
    lpBuffer = (LPSTR) VirtualAlloc(NULL,
                       nThreads * LOCAL_BUFFSIZE,
                       MEM_RESERVE, PAGE_READWRITE);

    try
        {
        // Create an unnamed mutex
        hMutex = CreateMutex(NULL, FALSE, NULL);
        for (i = 0; i < nThreads; ++i)
            {
            // Note that we can use the forward slash for a file
            // name component.  Do you know anyone who likes
            // backslashes better?
            if (argc == 1)
                lpThreadHandles[0] = CreateThread(NULL, 0,
                    (LPTHREAD_START_ROUTINE) ls, "./*.*", 0, &dwThreadID);
            else
                lpThreadHandles[i] = CreateThread(NULL, 0,
                    (LPTHREAD_START_ROUTINE) ls, argv[i + 1], 0,
                    &dwThreadID);
            }

        // Wait for all the threads to terminate
        // Third argument (bWaitAll) is TRUE
        WaitForMultipleObjects(nThreads, lpThreadHandles, TRUE, INFINITE);

        // See if any memory has been committed
        // If not, we don't have anything to report
        VirtualQuery(lpBuffer, &mbi, sizeof (MEMORY_BASIC_INFORMATION));

        if (mbi.State == MEM_COMMIT && mbi.RegionSize > 0)
            {
            WriteFile(GetStdHandle(STD_OUTPUT_HANDLE), lpBuffer,
               lstrlen(lpBuffer), &dwBytes, NULL);
            VirtualFree(lpBuffer, mbi.RegionSize, MEM_DECOMMIT);
            }
        }
    finally
        {
        HeapFree(GetProcessHeap(), 0, lpThreadHandles);
```

```
      if (lpBuffer != NULL)
         VirtualFree(lpBuffer, 0, MEM_RELEASE);

      if (hMutex != NULL)
         CloseHandle(hMutex);
      FreeLibrary(hMessageDLL);
      }
   ExitProcess(GetLastError());
}
```

The next two listings are the header file \NTNET\CODE\WNETMSGS.H that was generated by the Message Compiler, and the message file that it was produced from (\NTNET\CODE\WNETMSGS.MC).

```
/********
*
* WNETMSGS.H
*
* Messages for WNet Modules that use the Message Compiler
*
*********/
//
//  Values are 32 bit values layed out as follows:
//
//   3 3 2 2 2 2 2 2 2 2 2 2 1 1 1 1 1 1 1 1 1 1
//   1 0 9 8 7 6 5 4 3 2 1 0 9 8 7 6 5 4 3 2 1 0 9 8 7 6 5 4 3 2 1 0
//  +---+-+-+-----------------------+-----------------------+
//  |Sev|C|R|      Facility         |          Code         |
//  +---+-+-+-----------------------+-----------------------+
//
//  where
//
//      Sev - is the severity code
//
//          00 - Success
//          01 - Informational
//          10 - Warning
//          11 - Error
//
//      C - is the Customer code flag
//
//      R - is a reserved bit
//
//      Facility - is the facility code
//
//      Code - is the facility's status code
//
```

```
//
// Define the facility codes
//


//
// Define the severity codes
//
#define STATUS_SEVERITY_WARNING          0x2
#define STATUS_SEVERITY_SUCCESS          0x0
#define STATUS_SEVERITY_INFORMATIONAL    0x1
#define STATUS_SEVERITY_ERROR            0x3


//
// MessageId: MSG_FILESPECERROR
//
// MessageText:
//
//   Error on file specification %1!s!: %2!s!
//
#define MSG_FILESPECERROR                0xA0000001L


//
// MessageId: MSG_CANTCOMMITMEMORY
//
// MessageText:
//
//   Unable to commit memory
//
#define MSG_CANTCOMMITMEMORY             0xE0000002L


//
// MessageId: MSG_CANTALLOCATE_MEMORY
//
// MessageText:
//
//   Unable to allocate memory
//
#define MSG_CANTALLOCATE_MEMORY          0xE0000003L


//
// MessageId: MSG_RPC_SERVER_FAILED
//
// MessageText:
//
//   %1!s! failed. %2!s!
//
#define MSG_RPC_SERVER_FAILED            0xE0000004L
```

```
;/********
;*
;* WNETMSGS.MC
;*
;* Messages for WNet Modules that use the Message Compiler
;*
;*********/

SeverityNames=(Success=0x0:STATUS_SEVERITY_SUCCESS
               Informational=0x1:STATUS_SEVERITY_INFORMATIONAL
               Warning=0x2:STATUS_SEVERITY_WARNING
               Error=0x3:STATUS_SEVERITY_ERROR
               )

LanguageNames=(English=0x0009:MSG00001
               French=0x000c:MSG00002
               Spanish=0x000a:MSG00003
               )

MessageId=
Severity=Warning
SymbolicName=MSG_FILESPECERROR
Language=English
Error on file specification %1!s!: %2!s!
.

Language=French
Erreur sur spécification de fichier %1!s!: %2!s!
.

Language=Spanish
Error sobre la especificación de archivo %1!s!: %2!s!
.


MessageID=
Severity=Error
SymbolicName=MSG_CANTCOMMITMEMORY
Language=English
Unable to commit memory
.

Language=French
Incapable engager à la mémoire
.

Language=Spanish
Incapaz de comprometer memoria
.
```

```
MessageID=
Severity=Error
SymbolicName=MSG_CANTALLOCATE_MEMORY
Language=English
Unable to allocate memory
.

Language=French
Incapable allouer la mémoire
.

Language=Spanish
Incapaz de destinar memoria
.


MessageID=
Severity=Error
SymbolicName=MSG_RPC_SERVER_FAILED
Language=English
%1!s! failed. %2!s!
.

Language=French
%1!s! a manqué. %2!s!
.

Language=Spanish
%1!s! fracasó. %2!s!
.
```

Conclusion

Win32 provides a complete set of File I/O APIs to support the capabilities of the NT File System. This API set is implicitly a network API because the functions can be used to access files on other machines. In Chapter 10, you will see that the Named Pipes and Mailslots API is built on top of the File I/O API, since Named Pipes and Mailslots are NT file systems. In Chapter 11, you will also see how Windows Sockets uses features of Win32 files. Win32 provides a number of advanced capabilities, including

- Support for 64-bit file sizes
- Asynchronous, or overlapped, I/O
- The use of callback functions with read and write operations
- Security restrictions on NTFS files

You will see in the next chapter how memory-mapped file I/O expands this set of tools. I defer it until my discussion on Dynamic Link Libraries because for the code in this book—network DLLs that must support a wide range of client applications—memory-mapped file I/O is most important as a vehicle for shared memory.

Suggested Readings

Richter, Jeff. *Advanced Windows NT*. Redmond, WA: Microsoft Press, 1993. Chapter 9.

Custer, Helen. *Inside Windows NT*. Redmond, WA: Microsoft Press, 1992. Chapter 8.

File Systems Overview in the Win32 SDK on-line help. Published as Chapter 46 of *Win32 Programmer's Reference, Volume 2*.

Files Overview in the Win32 SDK on-line help. Published as Chapter 45 of *Win32 Programmer's Reference, Volume 2*.

Windows NT Resource Kit. Chapter 5, "New Technology File System." *Microsoft Developer Network CD*, 1993.

Microsoft Knowledge Base for Win32 SDK articles:
"FILE_FLAG_WRITE_THROUGH and
  FILE_FLAG_NO_BUFFERING"
"Apps Should Wait to Free/Reuse WriteFileEx()'s Buffer"
"CreateFile() Using CONIN$ or CONOUT$"
"No Way to Cancel Overlapped I/O"
"Time Stamps under the FAT File System"
"Types of File I/O under Win32"
"Unexpected Result of SetFilePointer() with Devices"
"Limit on the Number of Bytes Written Asynchronously"
"Direct Drive Access under Win32"
"Win32 Equivalents for C Run-time Functions"
"Using Temporary File Can Improve Application Performance"

## Chapter 8

Dynamic-Link Libraries (DLLs) in Windows NT

Overview

In Part 3 of this book, I develop an abstract programming interface for peer-to-peer programming that enables you to write code to a single API, without regard for the underlying Win32 APIs. My functions determine what protocol and Win32 API to use to communicate with a given host machine. The plug-in capability of DLLs gives exactly the architecture needed to achieve this flexibility. DLLs are organized in two layers. The level-one layer (\NTNET\CODE\%Cpu%\WNETLVL1.DLL) provides services in a standardized, portable way. It also selects the correct level-zero DLL to use to talk to a particular host. The level-zero layer translates level-one calls into the underlying Win32 API (Named Pipes, Windows Sockets over TCP/IP, Windows Sockets over NWLink, or NetBIOS).

Before getting into the implementation of these DLLs, you need to understand the mechanics of DLLs under Windows NT. They are very different from previous versions of Windows. The code presented in Part 3 was developed as a port of the code that I originally presented in Windows Network Programming. This was the trickiest aspect of the port, simply because DLLs under Windows NT behave much differently than their Win16 relatives.

Building DLLs for Windows NT

To begin with, the procedure for building a Windows NT DLL is quite different from Windows 3.X. Like a Win16 DLL, but unlike a normal NT

133

executable, a Win32 DLL requires a module definition (.DEF) file. Only two keywords are necessary; LIBRARY names the module and EXPORTS lists all the functions that the DLL will be exporting. For Win16 DLLs, the .DEF file is fed to the linker. For Windows NT, it is first processed by the library manager, which generates an intermediate file with an .EXP extension. This file is then submitted to the linker, along with the application's object files, resource file, and link libraries.

Specifying the DLL Entry Point

Windows 3.X DLLs are entered through the LibMain() function, which is called only once, when the DLL is first loaded. Windows NT does not require an entry point and lets you call yours anything you want to. However, there seems to be some confusion about providing an entry point in Windows NT and what you should name it; one source says one thing, another says something different. The procedure I outline here—which works—is presented in a Win32 Knowledge Base article, "Changes to DLL Makefiles Made for Final Release." This article recommends that you call your function DllMain(). One of the command-line switches that you pass to the linker, *-entry:*, tells it if you have an entry point, and, if so, what its name is. With NT executables, windowed applications have the standard entry point WinMainCRTStartup(), and console applications use mainCRTStartup(). For a DLL that names its entry point DllMain(), the *-entry:* switch should be _DllMainCRTStartup(). This function takes care of initializing the C run-time library and calls your DllMain().

Here is the makefile \NTNET\CODE\WNETDLL.MAK, used to build the DLLs in this book. All lower-case make macros are defined in \MSTOOLS\H\NTWIN32.MAK, provided with the Win32 SDK. The upper-case macros are ones I have defined.

```
########
#
# WNETDLL.MAK
#
# (Subtitled "Steal This Make File")
#
########


!INCLUDE <ntwin32.mak>

.SUFFIXES: .cpp

.c.obj:
```

```
    $(cc) $(cflags) $(cvarsdll) $(cdebug) -YX $*.c

.cpp.obj:
    $(cc) $(cflags) $(cvarsdll) $(cdebug) -YX $*.cpp

$(PROG).lib: $(OBJ) $(SRCDIR)\$(PROG).def
    $(implib) -machine:$(CPU)         \
    -def:$(SRCDIR)\$(PROG).def         \
    $(OBJ)                 \
    -out:$(PROG).lib

$(PROG).dll: $(OBJ) $(SRCDIR)\$(PROG).def $(PROG).lib
    $(link) $(linkdebug) $(lflags)     \
    -dll            \
    -entry:_DllMainCRTStartup$(DLLENTRY)     \
    -out:$(PROG).dll   \
    $(PROG).exp $(OBJ) $(guilibsdll) $(WNETLIBS) \
    netapi32.lib wsock32.lib
```

The SELECT sample application in \MSTOOLS\SAMPLES\SELECT
provides a makefile that builds a DLL. Personally, I am not interested in
being an expert on makefiles, so I am quite content to cannibalize existing
ones. As the subtitle of WNETDLL.MAK indicates, you are perfectly
welcome to cannibalize mine, also.

Data in a DLL

By default, every process that uses a DLL gets its own private copy of the
DLL's data. This means, for instance, that global variables declared in the
DLL will contain different values for each client application. You can
override this behavior by adding a SECTIONS statement to your module
definition file. For example, to declare that all initialized and uninitialized
data is to be shared, add the following lines to the .DEF file:

```
SECTIONS
    .DATA   READ WRITE SHARED      ; Share initialized data
    .BSS    READ WRITE SHARED      ; Share uninitialized data
```

You can also share specific data items by putting them into named data
segments. You name a segment using the *data_seg #pragma*. By convention,
section names begin with a period. Here, the variable *nWindows* is assigned
to the .MYDATA segment:

```
#pragma data_seg(".MYDATA")
```

```
int nWindows = 0;
#pragma data_seg()
```

The declaration of *nWindows* must initialize it. Otherwise, the compiler puts it in the .BSS segment. You also need to add this SECTIONS statement to the .DEF file:

```
SECTIONS
    .MYDATA READ WRITE SHARED     ; Share .MYDATA segment
```

Normally, it is highly desirable for every process to have its own private copy of global data. Otherwise, each process using a DLL is subject to having the DLL's support data corrupted by a wayward sister. When you need to share DLL data among client processes, the most powerful and flexible way to do so is with shared memory, which I address in this chapter.

The DLL Entry Point

You saw earlier in this chapter that Windows NT does not require a DLL entry point and lets you give it any name you want to. As the Win32 Knowledge Base article I referred to recommends, I use the name DllMain(), and set the *-entry:* linker command-line switch to _DllMainCRTStartup().

In Windows 3.X, the DLL entry point, LibMain(), is called once, when the DLL is first loaded. When the DLL is freed by the last application using it, the WEP() function is invoked. Under Windows NT, the entry-point function is called on several occasions. For this reason, one of the arguments that NT passes to the entry point is a code indicating why it is being called. Here is the complete prototype:

```
BOOL DllEntryPoint(
        HINSTANCE hDll,
        DWORD     dwReason,
        LPVOID    lpReserved);
```

hDll is the module or instance handle for the DLL. Like the instance handle of a standard executable, it is the base virtual address where Windows NT maps the DLL. *dwReason* is the most important argument and may well be the only one you ever look at. It can take on one of the following values, to let the DLL know why it is being called:

- DLL_PROCESS_ATTACH says that a new client application is loading the DLL, either automatically at load time or by an explicit call to LoadLibrary().
- DLL_THREAD_ATTACH means that a new thread has been created in an attached process. DllEntryPoint() is not called on behalf of the startup thread of an application; the DLL_PROCESS_ATTACH notification is considered sufficient.
- DLL_THREAD_DETACH means that a thread in an attached process has called ExitThread(), either explicitly or implicitly.
- DLL_PROCESS_DETACH indicates that a process is detaching from the DLL, by calling either ExitProcess() or FreeLibrary(). By the way, I have found that explicit calls to FreeLibrary() in Windows NT can have unpredictable side effects when you are doing things like network programming, where a lot of behind-the-scenes activity goes on. When you call FreeLibrary(), assuming that you are the last process using the DLL, the memory where the code was loaded is freed. You know that, and Windows NT knows that; but there is no guarantee that your network drivers will know it. Although it violates the principle of cleaning up resources that you use, I prefer to let NT do the FreeLibrary() when my process terminates, rather than trying to pinpoint the precise moment where it's safe. LoadLibrary() is a very important function; it gives you the flexibility to load multiple implementations of the same functions, which is exactly what we do in Part 3. But leave FreeLibrary() alone, at least when you're doing client/server programming.

Thread-Specific Data

Because NT gives every process that uses a DLL its own copy of the DLL's static data, no effort is required to get process-specific data. There are two places where some programming effort is required, both having to do with changing this default behavior:

- When you want global data to be shared among processes
- When you want data to be private to each thread in a client process, not just to each process

Shared memory gives you the first; I will discuss it shortly. For the second, Windows NT provides the Thread Local Storage API, a small group of functions that lets you pigeonhole data on a thread-specific basis. Thread Local Storage is similar to extra bytes in a window structure becuase it gives you a very convenient place to tuck data for later retrieval.

Syntax of the Thread Local Storage API

Syntactically, the TLS API is very simple. TlsAlloc() generates a new TLS index, which can be thought of as a set of lockers, one for every thread that the process creates.

```
DWORD TlsAlloc(VOID);
```

Each process can allocate at least 64 TLS indexes, so many levels of thread-specific storage are available. Once you have a TLS index, you use TlsSetValue() to save thread-specific data for the current thread.

```
BOOL TlsSetValue(DWORD dwTlsIndex, LPVOID lpTlsValue);
```

No argument indicating which thread owns the data is needed; NT keeps track of each thread's pigeonholes for you.

TlsGetValue() retrieves the data you have stored for the current thread.

```
LPVOID TlsGetValue(DWORD dwTlsIndex);
```

Finally, when you are finished with a TLS index, you free it by passing it to TlsFree().

```
BOOL TlsFree(DWORD dwTlsIndex);
```

Using Thread Local Storage in DLLs

You can use the TLS functions anywhere you need to store information on a per-thread basis. They are not restricted to DLLs, though that is probably their most important usage. In DLLs, the TLS functions are typically used as follows:

1. When the DLL entry point gets a DLL_PROCESS_ATTACH notification, it calls TlsAlloc() to obtain as many thread local storage indexes as it needs for the new process. It can store them in global variables; by default, every attaching process gets its own copy of the global variables in a DLL. It also calls TlsSetValue() to store any thread-specific data for the initial thread of the process.
2. When the DLL entry point gets a DLL_THREAD_ATTACH message, it calls TlsSetValue() to store data on behalf of the new thread. This data will not destroy the data the DLL has stored for any other threads.

3. When a function in the DLL is called, it can call TlsGetValue() to retrieve any information pertaining to the current thread.

4. When the DLL entry point gets a DLL_THREAD_DETACH notification, it can call TlsGetValue() to retrieve the thread-specific data it has previously stored. If it allocated memory and stored a pointer, this is the time to free the memory.

5. When the DLL receives a DLL_PROCESS_DETACH notification, it calls TlsFree() to free the TLS indexes it originally allocated.

Using Storage-Class Modifiers to Obtain Thread-Specific Data

You can also declare variables to be per-thread variables using storage-class modifiers. These use the __*declspec* keyword, followed by the specific modifier you want enclosed in parentheses. Here's how you would declare a thread-specific variable *nWindows:*

```
__declspec (thread) int nWindows;
```

The declaration must be exactly as it appears above and can be applied only to global and static variables. Automatic (stack-based) variables are always thread-specific.

Memory-Mapped File I/O

The Win32 API provides a set of functions for mapping files to memory addresses. This API provides three services:

- It allows a program to view file I/O as simple memory accesses and relieves it from doing seeks, reads, and writes on the file.
- It allows two processes to share disk files.
- It allows two processes to share memory.

Because data in a DLL is private to each attached process, DLLs are one place where shared memory becomes very important.

Using the Memory-Mapping API

Mapping a view of a file is a three-step process:

1. Open the file by calling CreateFile(). It is strongly recommended that you open it for exclusive access. Otherwise, other processes can manipulate the file using standard I/O calls. The result will be that your view of the file will not reflect any changes those processes make, nor will their image of the file reflect your changes. If you are creating a shared memory region, do not call CreateFile(); use file handle 0xFFFFFFFF instead. (There is no constant defined for this, but you can use INVALID_HANDLE_VALUE as a joke.)
2. Obtain a handle for a file mapping by calling CreateFileMapping().
3. Obtain a memory address to access the file with by calling MapViewOfFile().

When you are creating a shared-memory region to use in a DLL, you will most likely do this during DLL_PROCESS_ATTACH handling.

Syntax of Memory-Mapping Functions

Here's what CreateFileMapping() looks like:

```
HANDLE CreateFileMapping(
        HANDLE   hFile,
        LPSECURITY_ATTRIBUTES lpSecurityAttributes,
        DWORD    dwProtection,
        DWORD    dwMaximumSizeHigh,
        DWORD    dwMaximumSizeLow,
        LPCTSTR  lpName);
```

hFile is the handle returned by CreateFile() (or 0xFFFFFFFF, if you are allocating shared memory). *dwProtection* specifies the access to the memory and uses the same constants as VirtualAlloc(), discussed in Chapter 4. Normally you will pass either PAGE_READWRITE or PAGE_READONLY. PAGE_READONLY makes little sense with shared memory, but can be used to set up a read-only view of a file. Another interesting usage with disk files is to pass *dwProtection* as PAGE_WRITECOPY, then request FILE_MAP_COPY access in the call to MapViewOfFile(). This initializes the memory from the contents of the file; however, if you write to the memory, it creates a new copy of the memory region that is not linked to the file. In this manner, you can prevent the underlying file from being altered. This is useful, for instance, with debugger applications, which may need to write breakpoints into the code. When NT loads an executable file, it maps a view of it into your virtual address space. If it were not loaded for PAGE_WRITECOPY access, then all instances of the processes, and the file itself, would be affected by the activity of the debugger. As it is, when the debugger alters the original contents of the executable, NT makes a new copy of it that is divorced from the underlying .EXE file.

dwProtection must be consistent with the file access specified in the call to CreateFile(). You cannot open a file for GENERIC_READ access and then map a PAGE_READWRITE view.

lpSecurityAttributes specifies whether the handle can be inherited by child processes; it can also be used to restrict how other processes can access the shared memory. If either *lpSecurityAttributes* or its member field *lpSecurityDescriptor* is NULL, access to the memory is unrestricted.

dwMaximumSizeHigh and *dwMaximumSizeLow* together specify the size of the region you want to allocate. If passed as zero, they say to map a region that is the same size as the file. There are two arguments to support 64-bit file sizes. For shared memory *(hFile == 0xFFFFFFFF)*, *dwMaximumSizeHigh* must be zero, and *dwMaximumSizeLow* must not be; a shared-memory region can be described only by a 32-bit quantity.

By the way, if you are working with a disk file and specify a non-zero value that is larger than the file's size, the file will grow to that size if you don't do anything else to change it. Suppose you have a 16384-byte file and you want to append some data to it. You can't do this with a memory-mapped view of the file if you pass *dwMaximumSizeHigh* and *dwMaximumSizeLow* as zero; NT will save the file with its original size. Well, you say, no problem; I'll map a 2 MB view of the file. You then append 4096 bytes, close the mapped view, and close the file. At this point, how big is the file? 20480 bytes? No, it's 2 MB. What you have to do is close the mapped view of the file, call SetFilePointer() to move to what you intend to be the new end of the file, then call SetEndOfFile(). It may be easier in this case to do your file I/O using ReadFile() and WriteFile(); NT will increase the file size as it needs to.

lpName is the name you want to assign to the mapping object.The name is needed only to share the view among processes; other processes can pass it to OpenFileMapping() to obtain their own handles. As you saw with synchronization objects in Chapter 6, NT does not enforce any naming constraints, but it is best to adopt some discipline. I use the names /SHARED_MEM/<app signature>/<rest of name> for shared memory and /FILE_MAP/<app signature>/<rest of name> for memory-mapped files.

Unlike CreateFile() (but like the other object creation functions discussed in Chapter 6), CreateFileMapping() returns NULL if it fails. If the object has already been created, CreateFileMapping() still succeeds. You can detect this by calling GetLastError() and checking to see if it returns ERROR_ALREADY_EXISTS. This is how you will normally use CreateFileMapping() when you set up shared memory in a DLL.

OpenFileMapping() has the same syntax as the other Open<object>() functions you have seen—OpenMutex() and OpenEvent().

```
HANDLE OpenFileMapping(
        DWORD   dwDesiredAccess,
        BOOL    bInheritHandle,
        LPCTSTR lpName);
```

OpenFileMapping() is useful if you need a handle to a memory-mapped view of a file created by someone else. It succeeds even if *lpName* designates a view of a disk file that was opened for exclusive access, provided you have been granted the access you request. This is also the only way you can share the file because you do not need to call CreateFile(). If someone has opened the file for exclusive access, CreateFile() will fail.

dwDesiredAccess can be FILE_MAP_READ, FILE_MAP_WRITE, FILE_MAP_COPY, or FILE_MAP_ALL_ACCESS (which is equivalent to FILE_MAP_WRITE). The access requested must be consistent with that given the file-mapping object by the creating thread. If CreateFileMapping() specified PAGE_READWRITE, then FILE_MAP_READ and FILE_MAP_WRITE are fine, but FILE_MAP_COPY is not. (Incidentally, FILE_MAP_WRITE is understood to imply FILE_MAP_READ; you do not have to specify FILE_MAP_READ | FILE_MAP_WRITE.) If you called CreateFileMapping() and asked for PAGE_WRITECOPY protection, then FILE_MAP_COPY is the only argument you can pass to OpenFileMapping().

Once you have obtained a handle from CreateFileMapping() or OpenFileMapping(), you call MapViewOfFile() to convert it to a pointer.

```
LPVOID MapViewOfFile(
        HANDLE hFileMapping,
        DWORD  dwDesiredAccess,
        DWORD  dwFileOffsetHigh,
        DWORD  dwFileOffsetLow,
        DWORD  dwBytesToMap);
```

hFileMapping is the handle returned by CreateFileMapping() or OpenFileMapping(). As with OpenFileMapping(), *dwDesiredAccess* can be FILE_MAP_READ, FILE_MAP_WRITE, FILE_MAP_COPY, or FILE_MAP_ALL_ACCESS. Again, it must be consistent with the access previously requested. A wag in one of my classes asked me, "How many times do you have to tell NT what kind of access you want before it gets the point?" The answer, as we have seen, is three times for a disk file and twice for shared memory. The question is a good one, though: why is it necessary to say over and over what you plan to do?

dwOffsetLow and *dwOffsetHigh* specify the offset into the file where mapping is to begin, and *dwBytesToMap* states how many bytes to include in the mapping. A value of zero says to include the entire file. Although file sizes can be 64 bits, memory pointers cannot; for this reason, you cannot map more than a DWORD's worth of bytes at once. For shared memory, *dwOffsetLow, dwOffsetHigh,* and *dwBytesToMap* are irrelevant and should be passed as zero.

There is another version of MapViewOfFile(), MapViewOfFileEx(), which adds an argument requesting a specific base address for the region. However, unless you have a good reason for wanting a certain address, you should content yourself with MapViewOfFile(). If the address is not available, MapViewOfFileEx() does not search for one that is; it just returns NULL.

You can access the mapped region through the pointers you obtain from MapViewOfFile() or MapViewOfFileEx(). No automatic synchronization is provided, however. To coordinate reads and writes to the area, you must use one of the synchronization objects discussed in Chapter 6.

Cleaning up is also a three-step process. Typically, a DLL does this during DLL_PROCESS_DETACH handling. To clean up a memory-mapped file:

1. Call UnmapViewOfFile() to disconnect from the shared memory. This also writes dirty buffers to a memory-mapped disk file.
2. Call CloseHandle() with the handle of the file mapping object.
3. If you are viewing a disk file, call CloseHandle() with the file handle. You do not want to close the file handle until after you close the file-mapping handle; doing so defeats opening the file for exclusive access. Once you have closed your file handle, anyone else can open it.

UnmapViewOfFile() requires only one argument—the pointer returned by MapViewOfFile().

```
BOOL UnmapViewOfFile(LPVOID lpBaseAddress);
```

You can also call FlushViewOfFile() from time to time to force dirty buffers to be written.

```
BOOL FlushViewOfFile(
        LPVOID lpBaseAddress,
        DWORD  dwBytesToFlush);
```

FlushViewOfFile() writes *dwBytesToFlush* bytes to the associated file, starting at the address *lpBaseAddress*.

Code Listings

The File-Management Utilities

In Chapter 7, I presented versions of *cat* and *touch* as standalone applications. On the disk, I also provide them in versions that use a DLL, called WNETFUTL.DLL; they are called *cat2* and *touch2*. In these versions, the main() function resides in the standalone executable; the work is done by a function in WNETFUTL.DLL. If you are interested only in writing *cat* or *touch*, this is probably not the best way to do it; keeping all the code in a single executable is probably more efficient. However, breaking the worker routine out and putting it into a DLL allows it to be called by other processes as well. And by writing the worker routine so that it makes no assumptions about the environment that it's running in—specifically, whether the calling application is a console or windowed application—it can be used in either situation. This example also shows some of the mechanics of building a DLL in a straightforward, simple, but nevertheless useful context. Here is CAT2.CPP, which contains the main() function. All it does is call cat() in WNETFUTL.DLL.

```
/********
 *
 * CAT2.CPP
 *
 * Copyright (c) 1993-1994 Ralph P. Davis, All Rights Reserved
 *
 ********/

/*===== Includes =====*/

#include "wnetfutl.h"
#ifdef UNICODE
#undef UNICODE
#undef _UNICODE
#endif
```

```
/*===== Function Definitions =====*/

void main(int argc, char *argv[])
{
   cat(argc, argv);
   ExitProcess(0);
}
```

WNETFUTL.DLL consists of \NTNET\CODE\WNETFUTL\
WNETFUTL.CPP, which defines a skeletal DllMain(), and the source files
that implement the individual functions. DllMain() responds only to
DLL_PROCESS_ATTACH and DLL_PROCESS_DETACH notifications.
When a process attaches, DllMain() allocates a private heap; when it
detaches, DllMain() destroys the heap. Here is WNETFUTL.CPP:

```
/********
 *
 * WNETFUTL.CPP
 *
 * Copyright (c) 1993-1994 Ralph P. Davis, All Rights Reserved
 *
 ********/


/*====== Includes =====*/

#include "wnetfutl.h"


/*===== Global Variables =====*/

HANDLE hHeap;


/*===== Function Definitions =====*/

BOOL WINAPI DllMain(HINSTANCE hInst,
                    DWORD     dwReason,
                    LPVOID    lpReserved)
{
   switch (dwReason)
      {
      case DLL_PROCESS_ATTACH:
         hHeap = HeapCreate(0, 4096, 0);
         if (hHeap == NULL)
            return FALSE;
         break;
```

```
                case DLL_PROCESS_DETACH:
                    HeapDestroy(hHeap);
                    break;
                }
            return TRUE;
        }
```

Here is CATDLL.CPP, containing the DLL-based version of cat(). This is practically identical to the listing shown in Chapter 7.

```
/********
 *
 * CATDLL.CPP
 *
 * Copyright (c) 1993-1994 Ralph P. Davis, All Rights Reserved
 *
 * Demonstrates use of overlapped I/O with
 * handles for standard input and standard output
 *
 ********/

/*===== Includes =====*/

#include "wnetfutl.h"


/*===== Function Definitions =====*/

void WINAPI cat(int argc, char *argv[])
{
    int i;
    HANDLE     hInput, hOutput;
    OVERLAPPED Overlapped;
    DWORD      dwBytesRead, dwBytesWritten;
    char       szBuffer[4096];
    LPSTR      lpFileName;

    // argv contains an array of file names to concatenate
    // if argc == 1, use standard input

    hOutput = GetStdHandle(STD_OUTPUT_HANDLE);

    for (i = 1; i <= argc; ++i)
        {
        if (argc == 1)
            hInput = GetStdHandle(STD_INPUT_HANDLE);
        else
            {
```

```
      if (i == argc)
         break;
      lpFileName = argv[i];
      hInput = CreateFile(lpFileName,
               GENERIC_READ,
               FILE_SHARE_READ,
               NULL,
               OPEN_EXISTING,
               FILE_ATTRIBUTE_NORMAL |
               FILE_FLAG_OVERLAPPED,
               NULL);
   }
if (hInput != INVALID_HANDLE_VALUE)
   {
   ZeroMemory(&Overlapped, sizeof (OVERLAPPED));

   // Create a manual-reset, unnamed event
   // for the input operation
   Overlapped.hEvent = CreateEvent(NULL, TRUE, FALSE, NULL);

   // Read from input, write to output
   while (TRUE)
      {
      if (!ReadFile(hInput, szBuffer, sizeof (szBuffer),
                  &dwBytesRead, &Overlapped))
         {
         if (ERROR_IO_PENDING != GetLastError())
            // Read error, assume end-of-file
            break;
         if (!GetOverlappedResult(hInput,
               &Overlapped, &dwBytesRead, TRUE))
            // Error
            break;
         }

      // No bytes read means EOF
      if (dwBytesRead == 0)
         break;

      // Bump input file pointer—not done automatically
      // for overlapped I/O

      Overlapped.Offset += dwBytesRead;
      WriteFile(hOutput, szBuffer, dwBytesRead,
                  &dwBytesWritten, NULL);
      }
   CloseHandle(Overlapped.hEvent);
   }
```

```
     if (argc > 1)
        CloseHandle(hInput);
     }
  return;
}
```

The module definition file, WNETFUTL.DEF, simply names the DLL and its exported functions.

```
;********
;
; WNETFUTL.DEF
;
; Copyright (c) 1993-1994 Ralph P. Davis, All Rights Reserved
;
;********

LIBRARY    WNETFUTL

EXPORTS
           DllMain
           touch
           cat
```

The Level-One DLL (WNETLVL1.DLL)

Most of the code comprising the level-one DLL is shown in Part 3 of this book. However, the DllMain() function, contained in \NTNET\CODE\ WNETINIT.CPP, uses many of the concepts and techniques discussed in this chapter. One of the tables maintained by WNETLVL1.DLL is a list of all stations on the network that are running my WNET software and the protocols that they support. This table is global; that is, the information applies to all processes using the DLL. For this reason, it must be shared in some fashion. I have chosen to share the table using memory-mapped files. In addition, access to this table must be regulated; for this purpose, I create a mutex. Both the shared memory region and the mutex are created during DLL_PROCESS_ATTACH notification and destroyed in response to DLL_PROCESS_DETACH. Here is an excerpt from DllMain() that performs those tasks, and also creates and destroys the mutex used by printfConsole().

```
INT APIENTRY DllMain(HINSTANCE  hInstance,
                     DWORD      dwReason,
                     LPVOID     lpReserved)
{
   BOOL     bInit;
   HWND     hWnd;

   switch (dwReason)
      {
      case DLL_PROCESS_ATTACH:
         dwTLSIndex = TlsAlloc();

         if (dwTLSIndex == 0xFFFFFFFF)
            return 0;

         hDLLInstance = hInstance;

         // Get shared memory for the station list
         // This code is copped from the on-line help
         hStationTable = CreateFileMapping(
             (HANDLE) 0xFFFFFFFF,
             NULL,
             PAGE_READWRITE,
             0,
             MAX_NAMES * (sizeof (STATION_INFO)),
             TEXT("/SHARED_MEM/WNET/StationTable"));
         if (hStationTable == NULL)
            {
            printfConsole(TEXT("Failure on CreateFileMapping()\n"));

            return FALSE;
            }

         // See if this is the first time we've called
         // CreateFileMapping()
         // We need to know this; the first person
         // through here will zero-initialize the table

         bInit = (GetLastError() != ERROR_ALREADY_EXISTS);

         lpStationTable = (LPSTATION_INFO) MapViewOfFile(
             hStationTable,
             FILE_MAP_WRITE,
             0,
             0,
             0);
         if (lpStationTable == NULL)
```

```
        {
        printfConsole(TEXT("Failure on MapViewOfFile()\n"));

        return FALSE;
        }
    if (bInit)
        ZeroMemory(lpStationTable,
            MAX_NAMES * (MAX_STATION_NAME_LENGTH + 1));
    // [Register window message]
    // [Get handles for some other mutexes]
    hPrintfMutex = CreateMutex(NULL, FALSE,
        TEXT("/MUTEX/WNET/WNET_PRINTF_MUTEX"));
    break;
  case DLL_THREAD_DETACH:
    hWnd = (HWND) TlsGetValue(dwTLSIndex);
    if (hWnd != NULL)
        DestroyWindow(hWnd);
    break;
  case DLL_PROCESS_DETACH:
    hWnd = (HWND) TlsGetValue(dwTLSIndex);
    if (hWnd != NULL)
        DestroyWindow(hWnd);
    UnmapViewOfFile(lpStationTable);
    CloseHandle(hStationTable);

    // [Close mutex handles]
    CloseHandle(hPrintfMutex);
    TlsFree(dwTLSIndex);
    break;
    }
  return 1;
}
```

Conclusion

DLLs in Windows NT are much more powerful than their Windows 3.X counterparts. Under Windows NT, all data in a DLL is private to each attaching process, unless you force it to be shared. This can cause confusing complications, and is a major source of difficulty in porting a DLL from Windows 3.X to Windows NT.

You can alter this default behavior in two ways. The Thread Local Storage API makes data even more private, by giving each thread its own slot for storing data. Memory-mapped files let you create data structures that are global to all processes that the DLL is supporting. Because NT does not synchronize access to shared memory, mutexes become very important. Typically, DLLs create and destroy thread-local storage, shared memory objects, and mutexes in their DllMain() function, which is called many times during the life of a DLL:

- When a new process loads the DLL (DLL_PROCESS_ATTACH)
- When an attached process creates a new thread (DLL_THREAD_ ATTACH)
- When a thread in an attached process terminates (DLL_THREAD_ DETACH)
- When an attached process terminates (DLL_PROCESS_DETACH)

DLLs support the entire NT environment. This means that they can service non-windowed console applications, as well as standard GUI ones. You should limit the assumptions your DLLs make about the environments they are supporting.

Suggested Readings

Richter, Jeff. *Advanced Windows NT*. Redmond, WA: Microsoft Press, 1992. Chapters 7 and 8.

Dynamic-Link Libraries Overview in the Win32 API on-line help. Published as Chapter 50 in *Win32 Programmer's Reference, Volume II*.

File-Mapping Overview in the Win32 API on-line help. Published as Chapter 47 in *Win32 Programmer's Reference, Volume II*.

Interprocess Communications Options in the Win32 API on-line help. Published as Chapter 85 in *Win32 Programmer's Reference, Volume II*.

Building Apps and DLLs on-line help (\MSTOOLS\BIN\BUILD.HLP).

Storage Class Modifiers on-line help (\MSTOOLS\BIN\MODIF.HLP).

Kath, Randy. "DLLs in Win32." *Microsoft Developer Network CD*. 1992.

Kath, Randy. "Managing Memory-Mapped Files in Win32." *Microsoft Developer Network CD*. 1993.

Oney, Walter. "NT Dynamic Link Libraries, Part I: The Basics." *NT Developer*, Volume 1, No. 8, November 1993.

Oney, Walter. "NT Dynamic Link Libraries, Part II: DLL Power Programming." *NT Developer*, Vol. 1, No. 9, December 1993.

Richter, Jeff. "Memory-Mapped Files in Windows NT Simplify File Manipulation and Data Sharing." *Microsoft Systems Journal*, Vol. 8, No. 4, April 1993.

Microsoft Knowledge Base for Win32 SDK articles:
"Thread Local Storage Overview"
"How to Specify Shared and Nonshared Data in a DLL"
"Exporting Data from a DLL"
"Dynamic Loading of DLLs under Windows NT"

"Changes to DLL Makefiles Made for Final Release"
"Alternatives to Using GetProcAddress() with LoadLibrary()"
"Code in DLL Causes Access Violation C0000005"
"Data Section Names Limited to Eight Characters"
"Win32 .DEF File Usage in Applications and DLLs"
"Debugging DLLs Using WinDbg"

Part 3 Peer-to-Peer Programming

Chapter 9

Peer-to-Peer Concepts and API Design

Overview

Horizontal applications are those that take advantage of peer-to-peer networking services. Windows NT offers a rich set of these services. In this chapter, I discuss the terminology and concepts of peer-to-peer communications and develop specifications for a network-independent peer-to-peer API set. Chapters 10–12 implement this API using Named Pipes, Windows Sockets, and NetBIOS.

Peer-to-Peer Communications

Peer-to-peer communications are communications on an equal basis among network stations. The defining characteristic of peer-to-peer networking is that any station can play the role of either client or server. This is the situation on a Windows NT network, whether or not you are running Windows NT Advanced Server. Any NT station can share resources with any other NT station.

Peer-to-peer communications use established communications protocols so that machines know what to expect in the data stream. The protocols represent the common language that the computers understand. Each protocol has rules dictating both the format of the data units, or packets, that the stations will exchange, as well as the sequence in which packets of varying types should be expected. It is not my purpose here to present an in-depth analysis of peer-to-peer protocols. That is a highly detailed, technical subject, on which many books have already been written. Besides, well-designed peer-to-peer programming interfaces shield developers from having to know anything about the protocols that underlie them.

NT provides built-in support for several protocols:

- NetBEUI (short for NetBIOS Extended User Interface)
- TCP/IP (the Transmission Control Protocol / Internet Protocol)
- NWLink, a Microsoft implementation of Novell's IPX / SPX (Internet Packet Exchange / Sequenced Packet Exchange)
- DLC (Data Link Control), an IBM protocol primarily intended for communication with mainframes and certain types of printers

It also supports these programming interfaces:

- Named Pipes, using NetBEUI
- Windows Sockets, over either TCP/IP or NWLink
- NetBIOS over NetBEUI or TCP/IP
- Remote Procedure Calls (RPC), over all available protocols

Types of Peer-to-Peer Service

Two types of peer-to-peer service are generally recognized as being required:

- Connectionless service, also referred to as datagram service
- Connection-oriented service, also known as virtual circuit service.

Connectionless (Datagram) Service

Connectionless service is intended for single-packet exchanges of information. It is the lowest level of service, offering speed of communication while sacrificing some reliability. On local-area networks, datagram service is normally highly reliable. It is primarily when you enter a wide-area network that it becomes more chancy. Most of the connectionless protocols specify that datagram packets can be discarded at any time by any router that detects an abnormal condition. These conditions can include

- A corrupted packet (one whose checksum does not tally correctly)
- A packet that appears to be lost (as identified by an excessively high "hop count," which simply keeps track of how many bridges and routers a packet has gone through)

Datagrams can be sent to more than one station at a time. A transmission to all network stations is called a **broadcast**; a transmission to a group of related stations is referred to as a **multicast**.

Two levels of connectionless service, **acknowledged** and **unacknowledged**, have been specified in the standards. Acknowledged connectionless service implements a simple request-response protocol. Packets are sent one at a time, and the receiving station is expected to acknowledge receipt of each packet; thus, delivery is guaranteed. Unfortunately, not many commercially available protocol suites (and none that ship with NT) implement this level of service. In contrast, unacknowledged connectionless service does not guarantee delivery. A packet is placed onto the network for transmission, but the sending station has no way of knowing if it ever arrives at its destination. As I stated earlier, if a host or router along the way detects a corrupted packet or decides that the packet is lost, it just quietly discards it.

It is also possible that a packet A sent at time X will arrive at its destination after a packet B that goes out at some later time Y. This can happen, for instance, on a network with intelligent routers and multiple paths between stations. When packet A is first transmitted, the geographically shortest route to the destination may be overloaded, and the routers will send it over a longer circuit. Then when packet B is placed onto the network, if the congestion in the shortest circuit has cleared up, B is likely to travel that route and get to its destination before packet A. This is why connection-oriented protocols also provide sequenced delivery of packets; if packet B is sent after packet A but before packet C, it will arrive after packet A and before packet C.

Because of its simplicity, connectionless service supports only two operations: sending a datagram and receiving a datagram.

Connection-Oriented Service

Connection-oriented service is intended for the reliable exchange of streams of data between two stations. Streams consist of multiple sequenced packets. It is guaranteed that they will be delivered, and in the same sequence in which they were transmitted. Specifically, the guarantee is that if a packet cannot be delivered, the sender will be informed. Packets are not just dropped without notification.

Connection-oriented service is always point-to-point (or, more precisely, end-to-end, on a wide-area network; what appears to be a point-to-point connection between one host machine and another may actually consist of several intermediate point-to-point connections). There are no connection-oriented broadcasts or multicasts.

Like connectionless service, connection-oriented service must support send and receive operations, as the exchange of data, after all, is the whole purpose of peer-to-peer communications. In addition, there are three operations required for setting up and destroying the communications channel. **Listen** makes a server application available for clients to connect to. **Call** attempts to establish a connection from a client to a server. **Hangup** destroys a connection when it is no longer needed.

Developing a Standardized API

Since all protocols implement these same basic operations, it should be possible to code to a single peer-to-peer API, without regard for the protocols that the network supports. There has indeed been a move in this direction in the UNIX environment for many years. Berkeley Sockets first, and later AT&T's Transport Layer Interface (TLI), are protocol-independent programming interfaces. Though they are primarily associated with TCP/IP, this is purely a historical association. In fact, Windows NT supports communication with NetWare and Macintosh stations using Windows Sockets (a dialect of Berkeley).

No Standardization under Windows

Although device independence is one of the cardinal tenets of Microsoft Windows, the area of networking continues to be a forgotten backwater in this regard. The situation has improved a great deal with Windows NT, but there is still no single network-independent programming interface. Instead, there are several possible APIs from which to choose:

- Named Pipes, which is inherited from NT's close cousin OS/2, adding overlapped I/O and security. Named Pipes is fast and secure. Because it is implemented as an NT file system, it is tightly integrated into the operating system. However, because Named Pipes is based on Universal Naming Convention (UNC) filenames, it cannot readily support internetworking.

- Windows Sockets, which is a graft of Berkeley Sockets onto the Windows environment. Like Named Pipes, Windows Sockets is a high-level programming interface. Because Sockets has traditionally been associated with TCP/IP, it provides the best wide-area networking capabilities. However, a brief comparison of Named Pipes and Windows Sockets makes the foreign aspect of Sockets glaringly clear; it is indeed an outside element introduced into Windows because of the great demand for TCP/IP and UNIX connectivity. Under NT, Windows Sockets provides connectivity to the TCP/IP, NetWare, and Macintosh worlds.

- NetBIOS is the granddaddy of Microsoft peer-to-peer interfaces. Like Sockets, NetBIOS is often thought of as the protocol itself, but it too is just an API. NT supports NetBIOS over both NetBEUI (for speedy local-area network communications) and TCP/IP (for internetworking). NetBIOS has some serious disadvantages as a programming interface, however. Since it began its life as an assembly-language interface, it is not as high-level and easy to use as Named Pipes or Windows Sockets. Microsoft has added some extensions that adapt it a little better to Windows NT, but it is still difficult to work with.
- Remote Procedure Calls (RPC) is an industry-standard API for client-server applications. RPC almost succeeds in being a true network-independent peer-to-peer API, but not quite. First of all, not all client-server applications lend themselves to the remote procedure call paradigm. Second, and more importantly—let's put it this way—have you heard the word "interoperable" before? The problems with RPC interoperability are the same as you may have seen in the past if you have tried to get different flavors of UNIX to cooperate. Microsoft RPC is supposed to be interoperable with OSF/DCE RPC. Even if we assume this is true without qualification, what about Sun RPC? It's also an important presence in UNIX networking, and Microsoft RPC is not interoperable with it at all.

In the future, OLE 2 will offer distributed objects, and may become a significant tool for peer-to-peer applications.

Porting Network Applications from Windows 3.X

In *Windows Network Programming*, I developed a single API for horizontal applications under Windows 3.X. When I first started presenting the material in this book as a course, I ported the code in *Windows Network Programming* to Windows NT. I was not content to scrub the code a little bit to get it to compile and run under NT. If you have network applications that work under Windows 3.X, I suggest you treat them with as little reverence as I have. I hope that the material in Part II of this book has convinced you that NT is far superior to Windows 3.X as a platform for network applications, especially server applications. You cannot write them effectively if you are concerned with maintaining backward compatibility. The code in this chapter and the several that follow makes extensive use of structured exception handling, virtual memory allocation, multithreading, synchronization objects, Win32 file I/O, DLLs, and shared memory. In later chapters, I also exploit RPC, the Registry, performance monitoring, event logging, security, and write an NT service. None of these features, or only pale shadows of them, are available in Windows 3.X.

In other words, rewrite your Windows 3.X network applications for NT. I have been working on the NT version of my system now for almost a year-and-a-half. The code was pretty stable about a year ago, but I have been able to show it to a lot of people and have gotten many good suggestions for improving it. (I also had some very sharp people spot bugs by eyeballing the source code.) I have changed the interface, the architecture, and even the emphasis of the WNet API from *Windows Network Programming*. Two factors have contributed to this: first, continued observation of my original API, and the chance to become more aware of its strengths and shortcomings, and second, the rich set of features that NT offers and my desire to take advantage of them.

The WNet() API

My premise continues to be that there is only a handful of operations that need to be supported for peer-to-peer communications, and that it should therefore be easy to implement a truly network-independent API. I have described seven operations so far in this chapter: **Call, Listen, Hangup, Send, Receive, Send Datagram,** and **Receive Datagram.**

Because it is normally a good idea to have initialization and cleanup functions, **Init** and **Shutdown** operations should also be provided.

To translate the abstract notion of these operations into callable functions, I have borrowed Microsoft's naming convention. Both Windows 3.X and Windows NT provide a small group of functions with a WNet() prefix. They are not general-purpose by any means; even in NT, they continue to be a miscellaneous API set, useful only for mapping local drives and print devices to remote resources. However, the naming convention is catchy: I'll use the WNet() prefix followed by the name of the operation. Thus, I have a nine-function API set.

Initialization and Cleanup Functions:

- WNetInit()
- WNetShutdown()

Functions for Connection-Oriented Service:

- WNetCall()
- WNetListen()
- WNetHangup()
- WNetSend()
- WNetReceive()

Functions for Connectionless Service:

- WNetSendDatagram()
- WNetReceiveDatagram()

These functions constitute the core API and are contained in \NTNET\CODE\%Cpu%\WNETLVL1.DLL (so named because it implements level one of the network-independent API). I also add a function called WNetShipData(). It is modeled after the Named Pipes call TransactNamedPipe(), which sends a packet and waits for an answer. I include WNetShipData() so that I can take advantage of it in the cases where the underlying API supports such an operation. For those APIs that have no equivalent, WNetShipData() does a WNetSend() followed by a WNetReceive().

The Level-Zero API

The level-zero API consists of the DLLs that translate these abstract operations into Win32 API calls: \NTNET\CODE\NMPIPE\%Cpu%\ WNETPIPE.DLL (Named Pipes), \NTNET\CODE\WINSOCK\TCPIP\ %Cpu%\WNETTCP.DLL (Windows Sockets over TCP/IP), \NTNET\CODE\WINSOCK\NETWARE\%Cpu%\WNETNW.DLL (Windows Sockets over NWLink), and \NTNET\CODE\NETBIOS\ %Cpu%WNETNB.DLL (NetBIOS). These DLLs contain functions with the same names as their level-one counterparts, but with an underscore prepended:

_WNetInit()
_WNetShutdown()
_WNetCall()
_WNetListen()
_WNetHangup()
_WNetSend()
_WNetReceive()
_WNetShipData() (where the API supports it)
_WNetSendDatagram()
_WNetReceiveDatagram()

How the WNet() API Works

An application wishing to use these DLLs calls WNetInit() to register, then uses the level-one functions as appropriate. In the Windows 3.X version presented in *Windows Network Programming*, only one level-zero DLL was loaded at a time; it was selected by querying the network driver. This is clearly an inadequate approach for Windows NT, which allows multiple protocols to run simultaneously. Therefore, the NT version tries to load all the level-zero DLLs it knows about. It finds the location of these DLLs from the Registry, using the standard .INI-file function GetPrivateProfileString(). The installation of the WNet() DLLs puts this into the IniFileMapping section of the Registry (see Chapter 15 for details.) The level-one WNetInit() loads the level-zero DLLs and obtains pointers to all the functions they contain. For each DLL it finds, it calls the level-zero _WNetInit() to allow the bottom layer to initialize itself.

Here's the prototype for WNetInit():

```
BOOL WINAPI WNetInit(HWND          hWnd,
                     LPVOID        lpStationName,
                     LPVOID        lpEndpoint,
                     LPINT         lpnNameIndex)
```

The *hWnd* argument is remembered in the static variable *hTopWindow*. This window handle's sole purpose is to act as the owner window for message boxes that are posted from remote stations using WNetMessageBox(). If *lpEndpoint* is NULL or "WNETSRVR", *hWnd* is not passed along to _WNetInit(). So that the registering application can be the target of my distributed function calls—WNetSendMessage(), WNetPostMessage(), WNetFindWindow(), WNetEnumStations(), and WNetMessageBox()—WNetInit() registers the appropriate window class ("WNETMASTER") and creates a window of that class. Its handle is remembered in Thread Local Storage, then passed along to _WNetInit(). This window then serves as the notification window—the window to which messages are posted saying, "Hey, you got something, take a look at it."

One side effect of this approach is that the thread that calls WNetInit() must field messages for the notification window, since it will be its owner. Therefore, if an application calls WNetInit() from a thread other than its main thread, it must be sure to include some kind of message loop in the function that implements that thread. This does not prevent console applications from using these DLLs; they can create windows, too, just by spinning off a separate thread to do so. Here is an example of how you might do that:

```
#include "wnet.h"

VOID main(int argc, char *argv[])
{
   HANDLE hThread;
   DWORD  dwThreadID;

   hThread = CreateThread(NULL, 0, WNetInitThread, ...);
   .
   .
   .

   ExitProcess(0);
}

DWORD WINAPI WNetInitThread(VOID)
{
   HWND hMyWindow;
   MSG  msg;

   hMyWindow = CreateWindow(...);
   WNetInit(hMyWindow, ...);
   while (TRUE)
      {
      GetMessage(&msg, NULL, 0, 0);
      if (msg.message == WM_DESTROY)  // Notification window
                                      // was destroyed
         break;
      DispatchMessage(&msg);
      }
   DestroyWindow(hMyWindow);
   WNetShutdown(...);
   ExitThread(GetLastError());
}
```

The *lpStationName* and *lpEndpoint* arguments are used to establish the registering application as a listening server. Normally, *lpStationName* will designate the host machine name. The *lpEndpoint* argument is new to the NT implementation and was not part of my Windows 3.X version. It identifies the software process that is registering with us. The endpoint used for the distributed function calls—referred to in *Windows Network Programming* as the WNet server—is "WNETSRVR." The previous version of the WNet DLLs only allowed client applications to connect to the WNet server for the purpose of issuing distributed function calls. The NT version presented here is a general-purpose communications library. The addition of the *lpEndpoint* to WNetInit(), and to a couple of other functions, provides this generality.

lpnNameIndex returns a client ID that is then used as input to some of the other functions to identify the application.

Here's the WNetInit() function, contained in the file \NTNET\CODE\ WNETINIT.CPP. I also show the CreateMasterWindows() function that it calls to create the notification window. Notice the use of the TEXT() macro and the TCHAR type. These yield Unicode- or ANSI-compatible strings, depending on whether the constant UNICODE is defined.

```
BOOL WINAPI WNetInit(HWND hWnd, LPVOID lpStationName,
                     LPVOID    lpEndpoint,
                     LPINT     lpnNameIndex)
{
    TCHAR           szAPI[MAX_PATH + 1];
    HINSTANCE       hNetLib;
    int   (WINAPI *lpWNetInit)(HWND hWnd,
                               LPVOID lpStationName,
                               LPVOID lpEndpoint,
                               DWORD  dwPreference);
    int             i;
    static          TCHAR *szDLLNames[MAX_PROTOCOLS] =
                            {TEXT("WNETPIPE.DLL"),
                             TEXT("WNETTCP.DLL"),
                             TEXT("WNETNB.DLL"),
                             TEXT("WNETNW.DLL"),
                             NULL};
    static          TCHAR *szININames[MAX_PROTOCOLS] =
                            {TEXT("WNETPIPE.INI"),
                             TEXT("WNETTCP.INI"),
                             TEXT("WNETNB.INI"),
                             TEXT("WNETNW.INI"),
                             NULL};
    static          HANDLE hInitMutex = NULL;
    int             nNextNameIndex;
    BOOL            bClientIDOK = FALSE;

    hTopWindow = hWnd;

    // Make sure the following code executes to completion
    // by protecting it with a mutex.
    // We want to make sure we get assigned consecutive
    // client IDs for each of the DLLs we load

    if (hInitMutex == NULL)
        hInitMutex = CreateMutex(NULL, FALSE,
            TEXT("/MUTEX/WNET/WNET_INIT"));
```

```
WaitForSingleObject(hInitMutex, INFINITE);

try
    {
    nNextNameIndex = WNetGetNextNameIndex();

    // If an endpoint other than "WNETSRVR" is being
    // registered, pass the window handle on down
    // Otherwise, create a notification window
    // Its handle will be saved in Thread Local Storage

    if (lpEndpoint == NULL ||
            lstrcmpi((LPTSTR) lpEndpoint, TEXT("WNETSRVR")) == 0)
        {
        if (!CreateMasterWindows(hDLLInstance, dwTLSIndex))
            return FALSE;
        hWnd = (HWND) TlsGetValue(dwTLSIndex);
        }

    for (i = 0; i < MAX_PROTOCOLS && szDLLNames[i] != NULL; ++i)
        {
        // Get full path name of DLL to load from the Registry
        GetPrivateProfileString(TEXT("NETWORK"),
            TEXT("NETDLL"), szDLLNames[i],
            szAPI, sizeof (szAPI), szININames[i]);

        hNetLib = LoadLibrary(szAPI);

        if (hNetLib == NULL)
            {
            // Flag entry in name table
            WNetSetName(i, TEXT("UNUSED"), 7);
            continue;
            }

        // Get address of _WNetInit()
        (FARPROC &) lpWNetInit = GetProcAddress(hNetLib, "_WNetInit");

        if (lpWNetInit == NULL)
            {
            WNetSetName(i, TEXT("UNUSED"), 7);
            continue;
            }

        // We also need _WNetShutdown()—it will be called
        // if WNetInit() fails
        (FARPROC &) lpWNetShutdown[i] =
            GetProcAddress(hNetLib, "_WNetShutdown");
```

```
        printfConsole(TEXT("\nLoading %s"), szAPI);

        if (lpWNetInit(hWnd, lpStationName, lpEndpoint,
          (i + 1)) == (-1))
          {
          WNetSetName(i, TEXT("UNUSED"), 7);
          printfConsole(TEXT("\n\tUnable to load"));
          continue;
          }
        SetWindowLong(hWnd, 0, nNextNameIndex);

        printfConsole(TEXT("\n\tLoad successful"));
        if (!bClientIDOK)
          bClientIDOK = TRUE;

        // Load all function pointers

        (FARPROC &) lpWNetCall[i] =
          GetProcAddress(hNetLib, "_WNetCall");
        (FARPROC &) lpWNetListen[i] =
          GetProcAddress(hNetLib, "_WNetListen");
        (FARPROC &) lpWNetSend[i] =
          GetProcAddress(hNetLib, "_WNetSend");
        (FARPROC &) lpWNetReceive[i] =
          GetProcAddress(hNetLib, "_WNetReceive");
        (FARPROC &) lpWNetHangup[i] =
          GetProcAddress(hNetLib, "_WNetHangup");
        (FARPROC &) lpWNetSendDatagram[i] =
          GetProcAddress(hNetLib, "_WNetSendDatagram");
        (FARPROC &) lpWNetShipData[i] =
          GetProcAddress(hNetLib, "_WNetShipData");
        (FARPROC &) lpWNetReceiveDatagram[i] =
          GetProcAddress(hNetLib, "_WNetReceiveDatagram");
        }
      }
    finally
        {
        ReleaseMutex(hInitMutex);
        }
    if (bClientIDOK)
        *lpnNameIndex = nNextNameIndex;
    return bClientIDOK;
}

static BOOL CreateMasterWindows(HINSTANCE hInstance, DWORD dwTLSIndex)
{
    WNDCLASS wndClass;
    HWND     hWnd;
```

```
    ZeroMemory(&wndClass, sizeof (WNDCLASS));
    wndClass.lpszClassName = TEXT("WNETMASTER");
    wndClass.lpfnWndProc   = WNetWndProc;
    wndClass.hInstance      = hInstance;
    wndClass.style          = 0;

    if (!RegisterClass(&wndClass))
        return FALSE;

    hWnd = CreateWindow(
            TEXT("WNETMASTER"),
            NULL,
            WS_OVERLAPPEDWINDOW,
            CW_USEDEFAULT,
            CW_USEDEFAULT,
            CW_USEDEFAULT,
            CW_USEDEFAULT,
            NULL,
            NULL,
            hInstance,
            NULL);

    if (hWnd == NULL)
        return FALSE;

    TlsSetValue(dwTLSIndex, hWnd);

    ZeroMemory(&wndClass, sizeof (WNDCLASS));

    // Register class for DDE agent window
    wndClass.lpszClassName = TEXT("DDEAgent");
    wndClass.lpfnWndProc = DDEAgentWndProc;
    wndClass.hInstance      = hInstance;
    wndClass.hCursor        = NULL;
    wndClass.hIcon          = NULL;
    wndClass.hbrBackground = NULL;
    wndClass.lpszMenuName = NULL;
    wndClass.style  = 0;
    wndClass.cbClsExtra = 0;
    wndClass.cbWndExtra = 16; // Four long integers
                              // GWL_CONNECTION
                              // GWL_REMOTE_HWND
                              // GWL_LOCAL_HWND
                              // GWL_LPARAM

    if (!RegisterClass(&wndClass))
        return FALSE;
    else
        return TRUE;
}
```

The level-zero versions of _WNetInit() invoke the API functions that allow the calling application to offer services to clients over the network. This normally involves creating some kind of resource, like a named pipe or a socket, then calling _WNetListen() to make the application available for clients to connect to. For this reason, it is not necessary to call WNetListen() directly. _WNetInit() also calls _WNetReceiveDatagram() so that the stations on the network can exchange datagrams. The WNet server uses datagrams for stations to broadcast their presence, find out who else is out there, and negotiate protocol compatibility. This is done with the level-one support function WNetEnumStations(), which sends a broadcast over the network saying, "Hi, I'm running the WNet server, and I support these APIs. Who else is out there, and what APIs do you like?" The exchanged information is saved in a global table in shared memory. (See Chapter 8 for details about how memory for this table is allocated.)

WNetCall() and WNetSendDatagram(). Most of the level-one functions are just conduits between applications and the level-zero functions; that is, they do nothing but pass their arguments along to their level-zero counterparts. However, some additional intelligence is required for WNetCall() and WNetSendDatagram(). Specifically, they must determine which level-zero DLL to use to communicate with the requested host. Here's the algorithm they use:

1. If the station has advertised its presence and announced what APIs it likes, find one that we both understand and use it.
2. Otherwise, try the operation using each level-zero DLL until you succeed.

The APIs are prioritized as follows:

- Named Pipes
- Windows Sockets over TCP/IP
- NetBIOS
- Windows Sockets over NWLink

In the listing of WNetCall(), you will notice that several conditions cause you to try all protocols.

- It has no information about the other station [WNetGetPreferred Protocol() returns -1].
- It cannot support the partner station's preferred protocol ($lpWNetCall[i]$ == NULL).

- It cannot establish a connection using the partner's preferred protocol (*lpWNetCall[i]* returns zero).

If the connection is established, the level-zero DLL returns a connection handle, a type that I declare in WNET.H with the DECLARE_HANDLE() macro, defined in WINNT.H.

```
DECLARE_HANDLE(HCONNECTION);
```

DECLARE_HANDLE() was first introduced in Windows 3.1. It lets you create a new HANDLE type that is sensitive to whether strict type-checking is enabled or not. If you define the constant STRICT, the compiler can tell the difference, say, between an HPEN, an HBRUSH, and an HCONNECTION. Otherwise, they are all reduced to the same base type, and look the same to the compiler.

HCONNECTION is a logical representation of the connection. It abstracts whatever object corresponds to a connection in the API being used. For instance, for Named Pipes it is a pipe handle; for Windows Sockets, it is a socket; for NetBIOS, it is a local session number (LSN). So that you can determine which level-zero DLL to use for subsequent data exchanges on this connection [WNetSend(), WNetReceive(), and WNetHangup()], I add a biasing factor to the connection handle. This factor is 50000 times the one-based position of the API in the order of preference. For Named Pipes, therefore, the bias is 50000; for Windows Sockets over TCP/IP, it is 100000; for NetBIOS, it is 150000; for Windows Sockets over NWLink, it is 200000. The bias is then stripped off when I call WNetSend(), WNetReceive(), or WNetHangup().

Here is the listing for WNetCall(). WNetSendDatagram() is very similar. Both functions reside in \NTNET\CODE\WNETFUNC.CPP.

```
HCONNECTION WINAPI WNetCall(int     nNameIndex,
                            LPVOID lpTargetStation,
                            LPVOID lpEndpoint)
{
    int i;
    HCONNECTION hConnection = 0;

    // Do we know about this station?
    i = WNetGetPreferredProtocol((LPTSTR) lpTargetStation);

    if (i != (-1))
        {
        // We know about him
        // Do we support his preferred protocol?
```

```
        if (lpWNetCall[i] == NULL)
            i = -1;  // Try to find a protocol we like
        else
            {
            // We both like the same protocol—call him
            hConnection = lpWNetCall[i](nNameIndex + i,
                           lpTargetStation, lpEndpoint);
            if (hConnection != 0)
                (DWORD &) hConnection += ((i + 1) * PROTOCOL_BIAS);
            else
                // Couldn't get ahold of him for some reason
                // Look for another protocol
                i = -1;
            }
        }
    if (i == (-1))    // Look for a mutually agreeable protocol
        {
        printfConsole(TEXT("\nNo preferred protocol found for %s %s"),
            lpTargetStation,
            lpEndpoint != NULL ? lpEndpoint: TEXT("WNETSRVR"));
        hConnection = 0;
        for (i = 0; i < MAX_PROTOCOLS && hConnection == 0; ++i)
            {
            if (lpWNetCall[i] == NULL)
                // We don't support the protocol
                continue;
            hConnection = lpWNetCall[i](nNameIndex + i,
                           lpTargetStation, lpEndpoint);
            if (hConnection != 0)
                // OK, we've got a hit!
                (DWORD &) hConnection += ((i + 1) * PROTOCOL_BIAS);
            }
        }
    return hConnection;
}
```

WNetSend(). WNetSend() shows how the biasing factor is used to determine which level-zero function to call.

```
BOOL WINAPI WNetSend(HCONNECTION hConnection,
                              LPVOID lpData,
                              WORD wDataLength)
    {
        int nSlot;

        nSlot = ((DWORD) hConnection) / PROTOCOL_BIAS;
```

```
    (DWORD &) hConnection -= (nSlot * PROTOCOL_BIAS);

    --nSlot;
    if (lpWNetSend[nSlot] == NULL)
        return FALSE;

    return lpWNetSend[nSlot](hConnection, lpData, wDataLength);
}
```

Additional Software Layers

The code on the disk includes two additional DLLs, NTNET\CODE\
%Cpu%\WNETRPC.DLL and \NTNET\CODE\%Cpu%\WNETDFC.DLL.

Remote Procedure Calls. WNETRPC.DLL includes some RPC client
routines that are used by the Windows Network Manager sample application,
described towards the end of this chapter. These include

- WNetGetRemoteUser(), which returns the name of the user logged in
  on a remote station
- WNetSetLocalUser(), which uses local RPC to tell the WNet RPC
  server (discussed in Chapter 13) who you are logged in as
- WNetWinExec(), which allows you to run programs on other machines
- IsWNetServerRunning(), which asks the WNet RPC server on a target
  station if there is a WNet server window [FindWindow(TEXT
  ("WNETMASTER"), NULL) != NULL]

Both these functions and the WNet RPC server that handles them are
covered in Chapter 13 when I discuss RPC.

Distributed Function Calls. WNETDFC.DLL contains functions that are
pretty much ported directly from *Windows Network Programming*. These are
the distributed function calls (DFC) that allow you to invoke Win32
functions on remote stations, and, most importantly, to send and post
Windows messages across the network. These functions are

- WNetSendMessage() and WNetPostMessage(), which are distributed
  versions of SendMessage() and PostMessage().
- WNetFindWindow(), a distributed FindWindow().
- WNetEnumStations(), which announces a machine supporting the
  WNet server, asks other stations to enumerate themselves, and
  disseminates protocol information.

- WNetMessageBox(), which allows you to put up a message box on a remote station.
- WNetEnumServers(), which uses the LAN Manager function NetServerEnum() to find out what other stations are on the network. (See Chapter 16 for a discussion of the LAN Manager API for Windows NT.)

The WNet Server Notification Mechanism. I mentioned earlier that when an application registers the "WNETSRVR" endpoint, WNetInit() in the level-one DLL automatically creates a notification window. The next several chapters illustrate how the level-zero DLLs alert this window to the arrival of data by calling my function SendMsgFromSharedMem(). This function places the data into shared memory, then sends a private message to the notification window. The message number is obtained by calling RegisterWindowMessage() and passing it the message name "WMU_PACKET_RECEIVED". (The WMU prefix stamps this as a user-defined message.) All software components participating in my WNet scheme must register this string so that they will recognize messages percolating up from the bottom network layers. The message is accompanied by the following information:

- *wParam* is set to the handle of the connection on which the data has arrived (using the abstract HCONNECTION type), or zero if the packet is a datagram. This handle includes the biasing factor, so it can be submitted as is to any of the other WNet() functions in the DLL.
- *lParam* is the number of bytes of data available. The data has been deposited in a shared memory region named "/SHARED_MEM/WNET/RECEIVED_DATA"; a handle to the region can be obtained by calling either CreateFileMapping() or OpenFileMapping().

Strictly speaking, this notification mechanism is not level-one functionality; it is associated with the distributed function calls. I put it in the level-one DLL (WNETLVL1.DLL) so that when an application registers the WNETSRVR endpoint, it does not need to do anything else to receive incoming calls. If it were located in WNETDFC.DLL, (where, it might be reasonably argued, it would be more germane), you would have to make a distributed function call before you could receive one. This did not seem like a justifiable restriction.

Here is the code for SendMsgFromSharedMem(), from \NTNET\CODE\ WNETMISC.CPP. Notice that I use SendMessage() to deliver the data. It is necessary to deliver the message synchronously, rather than asynchronously, because the receiving application is going to retrieve the data from shared memory. It is important that the shared memory region still be there. If I create it here, post the message, then destroy it, there is no guarantee that the receiving application will ever see the shared memory—indeed, it is quite likely that it won't.

Also notice that I am fussy about allowing only one process through here at a time. You have to guard shared memory when more than one process may access it. NT does not provide any automatic synchronization.

```
BOOL WINAPI SendMsgFromSharedMem(HWND hNotifyWnd, LPBYTE lpMsg,
                                 HCONNECTION hConnection,
                                 DWORD dwBytesToSend)
{
    HANDLE hMapObject = NULL;
    LPVOID lpSharedMem = NULL;
    BOOL   bReturnCode = FALSE;

    WaitForSingleObject(hSendMsgMutex, INFINITE);

    try
        {
        hMapObject = CreateFileMapping(
                    (HANDLE) 0xFFFFFFFF,
                    NULL,
                    PAGE_READWRITE,
                    0,
                    dwBytesToSend,
                    TEXT("/SHARED_MEM/WNET/RECEIVED_DATA"));
        if (hMapObject != NULL)
            {
            lpSharedMem = MapViewOfFile(
                        hMapObject,
                        FILE_MAP_WRITE,
                        0, 0, 0);
            if (lpSharedMem != NULL)
                {
                try
                    {
                    CopyMemory(lpSharedMem, lpMsg, dwBytesToSend);
                    SendMessage(hNotifyWnd, WMU_PACKET_RECEIVED,
                        (WPARAM) hConnection,
                        (LPARAM) dwBytesToSend);
                    bReturnCode = TRUE;
                    }
                except (EXCEPTION_EXECUTE_HANDLER)
                    {
```

```
                    bReturnCode = FALSE;
                    printfConsole(
                        TEXT("\nException in SendMsgFromSharedMem()"));
                    }
                }
            }
        }
    finally
        {
        if (lpSharedMem != NULL)
            UnmapViewOfFile(lpSharedMem);
        if (hMapObject != NULL)
            CloseHandle(hMapObject);
        ReleaseMutex(hSendMsgMutex);
        }
    return bReturnCode;
}
```

WNetMessageBox() and WNet_OnMessageBox(). For an example of how
my distributed function call protocol works, you can look at
WNetMessageBox() and WNet_OnMessageBox(). These functions are the
client and server ends of a distributed MessageBox(). Here is the prototype
for WNetMessageBox() from \NTNET\CODE\WNETDFC.H. The middle
four arguments are the standard ones for MessageBox(). The first argument
is the HCONNECTION of a connection already established with the WNet
server on another machine. The last is a BOOL that indicates whether you
need to know the return value of the remote MessageBox(), which tells you
what button the user on the remote station pushed to close the message box.

```
int WINAPI WNetMessageBox(
            HCONNECTION  hConnection,
            HWND         hOwnerWnd,
            LPCTSTR      lpszMessage,
            LPCTSTR      lpszCaption,
            UINT         uType,
            BOOL         bWaitForResponse);
```

WNetMessageBox() wraps the arguments into a packet, then calls
WNetShipData(). The packet has a header identifying the request you are
making, described by the WNET_MSG structure, also from WNETDFC.H.

```
struct WNET_MSG
{
    TCHAR        szSignature[WNET_SIG_LENGTH]; // "WNET$$$"
    WNET_REQUEST WNetRequest;
```

```
    MSG            Message;
    BOOL           bIsLParamPtr;
    WORD           wDataLength;
    WORD           wOutDataLength;
};
```

WNET_REQUEST is an enumerated type that defines constants for the distributed function calls I have implemented. It is defined as follows in WNET.H:

```
enum WNET_REQUEST
{
    POST_MESSAGE,
    SEND_MESSAGE,
    FIND_WINDOW,
    ENUM_STATIONS,
    ENUM_STATION_RESPONSE,
    MESSAGE_BOX
};
```

WNetMessageBox() resides in \NTNET\CODE\WNETMBOX.CPP, which follows:

```
/*******
*
* WNETMBOX.CPP
*
* Copyright (c) 1993-1994 Ralph P. Davis, All Rights Reserved
*
*******/


/*===== Includes =====*/

#include "wnetdfc.h"


/*===== Function Definitions =====*/

int WINAPI WNetMessageBox(HCONNECTION hConnection,
                          HWND    hOwnerWnd,
                          LPCTSTR lpszMessage,
                          LPCTSTR lpszCaption,
                          UINT    uType,
                          BOOL    bWaitForResponse)
{
```

```
int      nResult = -1;
LPTSTR   lpBuffer, lpTemp;
WORD     wLength;

if (lpszMessage == NULL)
   return -1;

wLength = WNET_SIG_LENGTH +
          sizeof (WNET_REQUEST) +
          sizeof (HWND) +
          lstrlen(lpszMessage) + 1 +
          (lpszCaption == NULL ? 1 :
           lstrlen(lpszCaption) + 1) +
          sizeof (UINT) + sizeof (BOOL);

lpBuffer = (LPTSTR) VirtualAlloc(NULL, wLength * sizeof (TCHAR),
                     MEM_COMMIT, PAGE_READWRITE);
if (lpBuffer != NULL)
   {
   lpTemp = lpBuffer;
   lstrcpy(lpTemp, WNET_SIGNATURE);
   lpTemp += WNET_SIG_LENGTH;
   *((WNET_REQUEST *) lpTemp) = MESSAGE_BOX;
   lpTemp += sizeof (WNET_REQUEST);
   *((HWND *) lpTemp) = hOwnerWnd;

   lpTemp += (sizeof (HWND));
   lstrcpy(lpTemp, lpszMessage);
   lpTemp += (lstrlen(lpszMessage) + 1);

   if (lpszCaption == NULL)
      lpszCaption = __TEXT("");
   lstrcpy(lpTemp, lpszCaption);

   lpTemp += (lstrlen(lpszCaption) + 1);
   *((UINT *) lpTemp) = uType;
   lpTemp += sizeof (UINT);
   *((BOOL *) lpTemp) = bWaitForResponse;

   nResult = (int) WNetShipData(NULL, hConnection,
      lpBuffer, wLength * sizeof (TCHAR), NULL, 0L);
   VirtualFree(lpBuffer, 0, MEM_RELEASE);
   }
return nResult;
}
```

On the receiving end, the packet gets unwrapped in the function WNet_OnMessageBox(), defined in \NTNET\CODE\WNETINIT.CPP.

```cpp
void WNet_OnMessageBox(HCONNECTION hConnection, LPTSTR lpPacket)
{
    HWND            hOwnerWnd;
    LPCTSTR         lpszMessage;
    LPCTSTR         lpszCaption;
    UINT            uType;
    int             nRetVal;
    BOOL            bWaitForResponse;

    lpPacket += (WNET_SIG_LENGTH + sizeof (WNET_REQUEST));
    hOwnerWnd = *((HWND *) lpPacket);

    if (hOwnerWnd == NULL)
        hOwnerWnd = GetLastActivePopup(hTopWindow);

    // Activate the window's top-level parent
    // (if he isn't already active)
    if (GetActiveWindow() != GetTopLevelParent(hOwnerWnd))
        SetActiveWindow(GetTopLevelParent(hOwnerWnd));

    lpPacket += sizeof (HWND);
    lpszMessage = (LPCTSTR) lpPacket;
    lpPacket += (lstrlen(lpszMessage) + 1);

    lpszCaption = (LPCTSTR) lpPacket;
    lpPacket += (lstrlen(lpszCaption) + 1);

    if (*lpszCaption == TEXT('\0'))
        lpszCaption = NULL;

    uType = *((UINT *) lpPacket);
    lpPacket += sizeof (UINT);
    bWaitForResponse = *((BOOL *) lpPacket);

    if (!bWaitForResponse)
        {
        nRetVal = IDOK;
        WNetSend(hConnection, (LPVOID) &nRetVal, sizeof (int));
        }
    nRetVal = MessageBox(hOwnerWnd, lpszMessage, lpszCaption, uType);

    SetFocus(hOwnerWnd);
```

```
if (bWaitForResponse)
    {
    WNetSend(hConnection, (LPVOID) &nRetVal, sizeof (int));
    }
}
```

The Windows Network Manager. The Windows Network Manager (\NTNET\CODE\%Cpu%\WNET.EXE) is a sample application that uses the WNet DLLs. In Chapter 5, I presented one of its dialog boxes as an example of multithreading, virtual memory allocation, and structured exception handling. Figure 9-1 shows the View Stations dialog box.

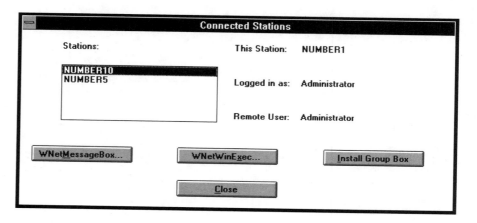

Figure 9-1.   The Windows Network Manager View Stations Dialog Box

The Stations listbox is populated as follows:

1. Call WNetEnumStations() (contained in \NTNET\CODE\ WNETENUM.CPP). This function iterates through the list of stations where the WNet server is running, then clears the list and rebroadcasts our presence. The station list is reconstructed as response packets come in.
2. Enumerate stations that are not running the WNet server by calling WNetEnumServers(), which in turn uses the LAN Manager function NetServerEnum(), discussed in Chapter 16.

The local station name is discovered by a call to GetComputerName(), and the user name from GetUserName(). For the currently selected station in the Stations listbox, I find out who is logged in there by calling

WNetGetRemoteUser(), which makes an RPC call to the WNet RPC server on that machine. The WNetMessageBox... pushbutton is enabled if there is a WNet server window active on the remote station. This too is discovered by calling the WNet RPC server. WNetWinExec... uses the WNet RPC server to start programs on the selected station. Install Group Box does DDE with the local Program Manager; it creates a group box called "NT Network Programming" that contains icons relevant to the subject.

Here are pertinent excerpts from the code that processes the WNetMessageBox... pushbutton. The complete code is in the function GetCommandDlgProc(), found in \NTNET\CODE\WNETDLGS.CPP. After putting up another dialog box to collect the message the user wants to send, the Windows Network Manager establishes a connection to the WNet server on the target station, then calls the WNetMessageBox() function.

```
TCHAR szUserName[255];
TCHAR szComputerName[MAX_COMPUTERNAME_LENGTH + 1];
TCHAR szRemoteComputer[MAX_COMPUTERNAME_LENGTH + 1];
DWORD dwLength;
TCHAR szCommandText[255];
TCHAR szCaption[255];
int   nNameIndex;
HCONNECTION hConnection;

dwLength = sizeof (szComputerName);
GetComputerName(szComputerName, &dwLength);
dwLength = sizeof (szUserName);
GetUserName(szUserName, &dwLength);
wsprintf(szCaption,
    TEXT("Message from User %s on Station %s"),
    szUserName, szComputerName);
hConnection = WNetCall(
                nNameIndex,          // Returned by WNetInit()
                szRemoteComputer,    // Currently selected
                                     // item in Stations listbox
                NULL);               // "WNETSRVR" endpoint
if (hConnection != NULL)
    {
    WNetMessageBox(hConnection,
                NULL,                // No owner window
                szCommandText,       // Entered by user
                szCaption,
                MB_OK,               // Just put up an OK button
                FALSE);              // Don't wait for response
    WNetHangup(hConnection);
    }
```

Conclusion

The theory and practice of peer-to-peer communications has evolved over the last 25 years into a stable and mature body of thought. A standard set of operations is widely agreed to be required; these operations lend themselves to standardization in a generic API. Such an API has never existed under Windows and still does not exist. In Windows 3.X, developers were required to support a dizzying array of third-party APIs. In Windows NT, the situation has improved quite a bit. Networking is built into the operating system, even if you do not have Windows NT Advanced Server. NT supports several important protocols, among them NetBEUI, TCP/IP, Novell's IPX/SPX, and IBM's DLC. On top of these protocols, NT provides several programming interfaces: Named Pipes and Mailslots, Windows Sockets, NetBIOS, and RPC. Developers must still choose to support one or the other and hope they make the right choice.

The following chapters implement the generic API presented in this chapter over the built-in peer-to-peer APIs that NT offers. As we have seen, there is no need to decide at design time what protocol or API to use. The answer is to use all of them, and let your code decide how to reach a particular target at runtime.

Suggested Readings

Davis, Ralph. *Windows Network Programming*, Reading, MA: Addison-Wesley Publishing Company, 1993. Chapter 2.

Stallings, William. *Handbook of Computer-Communications Standards. Volume 1: The Open Systems (OSI) Model and OSI-Related Standards.* Carmel, IN: SAMS, 1990.

Stallings, William. *Handbook of Computer-Communications Standards. Volume 2: Local Area Network Standards.* Carmel, IN: SAMS, 1990.

Stallings, William. *Handbook of Computer-Communications Standards. Volume 3: The TCP/IP Protocol Suite.* Carmel, IN: SAMS, 1989.

Named Pipes and Mailslots

Overview

The Named Pipes and Mailslots API is a high-level, convenient programming interface for peer-to-peer communications. It is the API whose syntax is most native to the Win32 environment since Named Pipes and Mailslots are implemented as Windows file system drivers. The main part of the data exchange (sending and receiving) uses standard Win32 file I/O. The rest of the interface involves making server applications available for clients to connect to. There are also a couple of functions that optimize request-response types of exchanges.

The Named Pipes API on the Server Side

Named Pipes provide connection-oriented service. Therefore, there must be a way for server applications to listen for connection requests. They do this by

1. Creating a named pipe with a call to CreateNamedPipe().
2. Waiting for clients to request connections by calling ConnectNamedPipe().

Pipes have several characteristics, which are set in the call to CreateNamedPipe():

- **Direction**: A named pipe can be two-way, client-to-server only, or server-to-client only.

- **Write mode**: Pipes are also written to in byte or message mode. A pipe can be written in message mode and read in byte mode. The reverse is not true.
- **Read mode**: A named pipe can be read in byte or message mode. In byte mode, the data is read and written as a stream of bytes. Reads and writes do not have to be balanced. In message-read mode, each write to the pipe defines a discrete message, and data must be read as a complete message. Attempts to read more than a message will return only the data comprising the message. Attempts to read a partial message will appear to fail. That is, ReadFile() will return FALSE, though it will retrieve the amount of data that was requested. To indicate that the read fetched an incomplete message, GetLastError() will return ERROR_MORE_DATA.
- **Blocking mode**: Either blocking or non-blocking. This determines whether or not the ConnectNamedPipe() call will block. Non-blocking pipes are obsolete and are included only for compatibility with OS/2 named pipes.

Like standard files, pipes can be opened for overlapped (asynchronous) I/O. In this case, a pointer to an OVERLAPPED structure is passed to ConnectNamedPipe(), ReadFile(), WriteFile(), and TransactNamedPipe().

CreateNamedPipe()

CreateNamedPipe() creates a server endpoint. Here is its prototype:

```
HANDLE CreateNamedPipe(
        LPCTSTR lpName,
        DWORD   dwOpenMode,
        DWORD   dwPipeMode,
        DWORD   dwMaxInstances,
        DWORD   dwOutBufferSize,
        DWORD   dwInBufferSize,
        DWORD   dwDefaultTimeout,
        LPSECURITY_ATTRIBUTES lpSecurity);
```

lpName is the name you want to assign to the pipe. Named pipes use pseudodirectory names in UNC format. The first component following the machine name must be \PIPE\. CreateNamedPipe() can create a pipe only on the local machine, so the name must use the special syntax \\.\PIPE\<pipe name>. (A dot in the machine name portion is always understood to mean the local machine.) The pipe name portion can contain further path separators; no actual directory or file is created. By convention, the component following \PIPE\ is some kind of application signature. For example, the Named Pipes level-zero DLL (\NTNET\CODE\NMPIPE\ %Cpu%\WNETPIPE.DLL) uses the pipe name \PIPE\WNET\WNETSRVR.

dwOpenMode is similar to the *dwFlagsAndAttributes* argument to CreateFile(). It can be used to request overlapped I/O on the pipe by setting the FILE_FLAG_OVERLAPPED bit. It can also request that writes to byte-mode pipes be immediately transmitted to the partner station by setting the FILE_FLAG_WRITE_THROUGH bit. By default, NT does not send data on a byte-mode pipe until one of two thresholds is exceeded:

- The amount of data exceeds a certain byte count
- No data has been sent for a certain amount of time, and there is data to send

For instance, assume that the byte-count threshold is 512 and the timeout is 500 milliseconds. After 100 milliseconds, 512 bytes have been written to the pipe; NT will transmit them. Then another 500 milliseconds go by during which only 128 bytes are written; NT will transmit only those 128 bytes.

dwOpenMode also specifies the direction of the pipe; this can be thought of as the read-write access of a file. PIPE_ACCESS_DUPLEX creates a two-way pipe this is similar to GENERIC_READ | GENERIC_WRITE file access. These are by far the most common pipes. PIPE_ACCESS_ INBOUND creates a client-to-server pipe; it is equivalent to GENERIC_READ access. Finally, PIPE_ACCESS_OUTBOUND creates a server-to-client pipe and corresponds to GENERIC_WRITE access. PIPE_ACCESS_DUPLEX, as you might suspect, is nothing more than PIPE_ACCESS_INBOUND | PIPE_ACCESS_OUTBOUND; you can use either syntax to create a two-way pipe.

dwPipeMode specifies the blocking mode, the read mode, and the write mode of the pipe. Each of these properties has its own set of mutually exclusive flags. The blocking mode is either PIPE_WAIT (0) or PIPE_NOWAIT (1). As I mentioned earlier, PIPE_NOWAIT is an obsolete usage. The read mode is PIPE_READMODE_BYTE (0) or PIPE_ READMODE_MESSAGE (2). The write mode is PIPE_TYPE_BYTE (0) or PIPE_TYPE_MESSAGE (4). As you can see, if you pass *dwPipeMode* as zero, you get a blocking pipe that will be read and written in byte mode. It is permissible to create a pipe that is written in message mode and read in byte mode (PIPE_TYPE_MESSAGE | PIPE_READMODE_BYTE). This makes sense on the server side especially, for the following reasons:

- Because the pipe will be written in message mode, clients can read it in message mode using TransactNamedPipe(), which yields superior performance to WriteFile() followed by ReadFile(). Servers, on the other hand, will be responding to client requests and are less likely to need TransactNamedPipe(). The semantics of TransactNamedPipe() are as follows: ask a question, wait for an answer. Server applications normally provide answers and don't ask questions.

- By reading the pipe in byte mode, the server avoids having to deal with partially read messages. It can read data that's available, then go back and get any data that's left. Reading a pipe in message mode requires a little more fancy footwork to make sure you get a complete message.

Passing *dwPipeMode* as PIPE_TYPE_BYTE | PIPE_READMODE_ MESSAGE will cause CreateNamedPipe() to fail.

dwMaxInstances specifies the maximum number of instances of the pipe that can be created. It can be a number from 1 to 254, or the constant PIPE_UNLIMITED_INSTANCES. Each call to CreateNamedPipe() with the same pipe name creates a new instance of the pipe, and each instance can service only one client application. Thus, to service more clients, create more instances.

dwDefaultTimeout is of marginal importance. It sets the timeout value for client applications that call WaitNamedPipe() and specify a timeout of NMPWAIT_USE_DEFAULT_WAIT. You can pass *dwDefaultTimeout* as zero, which tells NT "I couldn't care less; you figure it out." (I will discuss WaitNamedPipe() later in this chapter.)

CreateNamedPipe( ) is the first function I have presented where you cannot punt on the SECURITY_ATTRIBUTES by passing *lpSecurity* as NULL. Here is the layout of the structure again:

```
typedef struct _SECURITY_ATTRIBUTES
{
   DWORD    nLength;
   LPVOID   lpSecurityDescriptor;
   BOOL     bInheritHandle;
} SECURITY_ATTRIBUTES;
```

lpSecurity cannot be ignored for the simple reason that passing it as NULL is a significant action; it creates the pipe with "a default security descriptor," according to the Win32 documentation. The effect is to limit access to the pipe to users who are at least as trusted as the user creating it. Thus, if the pipe is created by a user with administrator status, only administrators can connect to it. Passing a non-NULL SECURITY_ ATTRIBUTES but setting the *lpSecurityDescriptor* member to NULL is also insufficient. This has the exact same effect as passing *lpSecurity* as NULL;

the only difference is that you can make the handle inheritable. In order to make the pipe accessible to any user wanting to use the server application, you must pass a non-NULL security descriptor containing a NULL discretionary access control list (DACL). The DACL says who is allowed to access the pipe and in what fashion. A non-NULL security descriptor with a NULL DACL allows anyone to access the pipe. In Chapter 14, I discuss the Win32 Security API in more detail. For now, I just present the code required to set up the SECURITY_ATTRIBUTES correctly.

```
SECURITY_ATTRIBUTES SecurityAttributes;
SECURITY_DESCRIPTOR SecurityDescriptor;

InitializeSecurityDescriptor(&SecurityDescriptor,
   SECURITY_DESCRIPTOR_REVISION);
SetSecurityDescriptorDacl(&SecurityDescriptor,
                          TRUE,   // DACL is present
                          NULL,   // Allow unlimited access
                          FALSE); // Explicitly specified DACL
SecurityAttributes.nLength =
   sizeof (SECURITY_ATTRIBUTES);
SecurityAttributes.bInheritHandle = FALSE;
SecurityAttributes.lpSecurityDescriptor =
   &SecurityDescriptor;
```

ConnectNamedPipe()

Once you have created instances of a named pipe, you call Connect NamedPipe() to wait for clients to connect.

```
BOOL ConnectNamedPipe(
        HANDLE        hNamedPipeInstance,
        LPOVERLAPPED  lpOverlapped);
```

ConnectNamedPipe() behaves differently, depending on how you originally created the pipe. For a blocking pipe that was not created for overlapped I/O, ConnectNamedPipe() does not return until a client request arrives (or the pipe closes abnormally). In the interim, the calling thread goes to sleep. In many, and perhaps most, situations, this is exactly what you want. There is one special-case situation that may arise—when a client connection request arrives between the server's calls to CreateNamedPipe() and ConnectNamedPipe(). In this case, ConnectNamedPipe() returns FALSE, but GetLastError() indicates ERROR_PIPE_CONNECTED. The connection has been established, and you can proceed to exchange data.

With a non-blocking pipe, ConnectNamedPipe() immediately returns FALSE, and GetLastError() reports ERROR_PIPE_LISTENING. ConnectNamedPipe() will return TRUE when a client request comes in. It will never block. This sounds a lot like polled I/O, which is almost always undesirable in Windows NT. Every time you ask NT, "OK, is anybody trying to connect to me?" it uses CPU time. Most of the time, the answer will be "No." It is much more effective to use a strategy that puts the calling thread to sleep at some point. Whether it goes to sleep at once when it calls ConnectNamedPipe(), or sometime later (as it will with overlapped I/O) does not matter. The important thing is that it not pester the CPU asking it if anything is happening.

On a pipe created for overlapped I/O, you must pass the *lpOverlapped* argument as a pointer to an OVERLAPPED structure.

```
typedef struct _OVERLAPPED
{
    DWORD    Internal;
    DWORD    InternalHigh;
    DWORD    Offset;
    DWORD    OffsetHigh;
    HANDLE   hEvent;
} OVERLAPPED;
```

The only significant field for named pipes is the event handle (except that the offset fields must be set to zero). Recall from Chapter 7 that *hEvent* represents a manual-reset event, which will be automatically set to the nonsignalled state when you call any appropriate function. With an overlapped pipe, ConnectNamedPipe() returns immediately; the event signals when a client connects to you. You detect this by calling one of the wait functions (WaitForSingleObject(), WaitForMultipleObjects(), or MsgWaitForMultipleObjects()).

Several strategies for multithreading a Named Pipes server are presented later in this chapter.

Named Pipes API—The Client Side

A client application requests a connection with a Named Pipes server by calling CreateFile() to open the named pipe. The pipe can be on the same machine as the client, in which case it specifies the pipe name as \\\PIPE\<pipe name>. If it is on a remote machine, the client uses the full UNC name of the pipe, \\<machine name>\PIPE\<pipe name>. You can also connect to a named pipe on the local machine using its full name. However, using \\.\PIPE\ yields a huge improvement in performance, as you will see. When a client station calls CreateFile(), the target server application wakes up from its call to ConnectNamedPipe() (or whatever wait function it is using).

SetNamedPipeHandleState()

When the client opens the pipe, it starts out as a blocking, byte-read pipe. To change either of these properties, the client calls SetNamedPipe HandleState(). It is often desirable to change the read mode to message mode (PIPE_READMODE_MESSAGE) because this allows you to use TransactNamedPipe(). TransactNamedPipe() is about 10 percent faster than issuing a WriteFile() followed by a ReadFile().

```
BOOL SetNamedPipeHandleState(
        HANDLE  hNamedPipe,
        LPDWORD lpMode,
        LPDWORD lpMaxCollectionCount,
        LPDWORD lpCollectDataTimeout);
```

lpMode points to a DWORD that specifies the blocking mode (PIPE_WAIT or PIPE_NOWAIT) and the read mode (PIPE_ READMODE_BYTE or PIPE_READMODE_MESSAGE). The client cannot change the write mode; only the server has control over this. If *lpMode* includes the PIPE_TYPE_MESSAGE bit, SetNamedPipe HandleState() fails.

lpMaxCollectionCount and *lpCollectDataTimeout* are the byte-count and timeout thresholds used for buffering data on the client end of byte-write pipes. NT collects data on the local station until either of these thresholds is exceeded. You can disable this by setting the FILE_FLAG_WRITE_ THROUGH bit in the call to CreateFile().

Named Pipes Version of _WNetCall()

The Named Pipes implementation of my level-zero function _WNetCall() uses CreateFile() to connect to the server and SetNamedPipeHandleState() to turn on message-read mode. The source file is \NTNET\CODE\ NMPIPE_WNETCAL.CPP.

The invocation of CreateFile() opens the pipe for GENERIC_READ | GENERIC_WRITE access. This corresponds to the server's declaration of the pipe as PIPE_ACCESS_DUPLEX in its call to CreateNamedPipe().

```cpp
/********
 *
 * _WNETCAL.CPP
 *
 * Copyright (c) 1993-1994 Ralph P. Davis, All Rights Reserved
 *
 ********/


/*===== Includes =====*/

#include "wnetpipe.h"
#include <string.h>


/*===== Function Definitions =====*/

HCONNECTION WINAPI _WNetCall(int nNameIndex,
                             LPVOID lpTargetStation,
                             LPVOID lpEndpoint)
{
   TCHAR  szPipeName[MAX_PATH + 1];
   HANDLE hPipe;
   DWORD dwMode = PIPE_WAIT | PIPE_READMODE_MESSAGE;
   TCHAR szComputerName[MAX_COMPUTERNAME_LENGTH + 1];
   DWORD dwNameLength = MAX_COMPUTERNAME_LENGTH;

   GetComputerName(szComputerName, &dwNameLength);

   if (lpEndpoint == NULL)
      lpEndpoint = TEXT("WNETSRVR");

   // See if we're trying to talk to the local station
   // If so, use machine name '.'—it's much faster
   if (lstrcmpi(szComputerName,
       (LPTSTR) lpTargetStation) == 0)
      lpTargetStation = TEXT(".");

   wsprintf(szPipeName, TEXT("\\\\%s\\PIPE\\WNET\\%s"),
            lpTargetStation, lpEndpoint);

   // Open the file for overlapped I/O
   hPipe = CreateFile(szPipeName, GENERIC_READ | GENERIC_WRITE,
                      FILE_SHARE_READ | FILE_SHARE_WRITE,
```

```
                   NULL, OPEN_EXISTING,
                   FILE_FLAG_OVERLAPPED |
                   SECURITY_IMPERSONATION,
                   NULL);
    if (hPipe == INVALID_HANDLE_VALUE)
        return 0;

    SetNamedPipeHandleState(hPipe, &dwMode, NULL, NULL);

    return ((HCONNECTION) hPipe);
}
```

Named Pipes API—Data Exchange

Once the pipe is connected, the client and server applications use WriteFile()
and ReadFile() to exchange data. At this point, the difference between the
pipe and a standard disk file is transparent to both parties.

When the communication involves a request-response interaction, you can
also use TransactNamedPipe(). This function writes a message to the pipe,
then waits for a response. Like ConnectNamedPipe(), ReadFile(), and
WriteFile(), it can be called in overlapped mode. My tests indicate that
TransactNamedPipe() does indeed provide better performance than just
calling WriteFile() followed by ReadFile(), just as advertised. The
benchmark data is presented at the end of the chapter.

```
BOOL TransactNamedPipe(
        HANDLE       hNamedPipe,
        LPVOID       lpInBuffer,
        DWORD        dwInBufferSize,
        LPVOID       lpOutBuffer,
        DWORD        dwOutBufferSize,
        LPDWORD      lpBytesRead,
        LPOVERLAPPED lpOverlapped);
```

lpInBuffer, *dwInBufferSize*, *lpOutBuffer*, and *dwOutBufferSize* describe
the send and receive buffers. If the pipe is not being accessed in overlapped
mode, TransactNamedPipe() will block until a response comes in, and
lpBytesRead will indicate the number of bytes received from the partner
station. For overlapped I/O, you use the techniques discussed in Chapter 7;
because Named Pipes is an NT file system, the pipe is just another file as far
as NT is concerned.

Other Client-Side Functions

A Named Pipes server can service only one client for each instance of a pipe. If more clients desire to connect than there are pipe instances to support them, WaitNamedPipe() blocks a client application until an instance becomes available. It takes the UNC name of the pipe the client wants to access and a timeout value in milliseconds. WaitNamedPipe() does not actually open a client-side handle to the pipe: it merely signals that an instance is available.

```
BOOL WaitNamedPipe(
        LPCTSTR lpPipeName,
        DWORD   dwTimeout);
```

dwTimeout is either the number of milliseconds or NMPWAIT_WAIT_FOREVER, which puts the client to sleep indefinitely. Another more esoteric constant is NMPWAIT_USE_DEFAULT_WAIT, which says to use the default timeout requested by the server in its call to CreateNamedPipe(). The server can also tell NT to use its own default by passing this value as zero, in which case NMPWAIT_USE_DEFAULT_WAIT means "use the default default."

A return value of TRUE means that an instance is available. You'd better call CreateFile() in a hurry, though; WaitNamedPipe() does not reserve an instance of the pipe for you. It is entirely possible that someone else will get the pipe between your calls to WaitNamedPipe() and CreateFile(). In order to use WaitNamedPipe(), you have to call it in a loop.

```
HANDLE hPipe;
DWORD  dwError;
while (TRUE)
   {
   if (WaitNamedPipe(...), 50000))
      {
      hPipe = CreateFile(...);
      // Have to check for race condition—
      // no guarantee that CreateFile() will
      // succeed!
      if (hPipe != INVALID_HANDLE_VALUE)
         break;
      if ((dwError = GetlastError()) != ERROR_PIPE_BUSY)
         ExitProcess(dwError);
      }
   }
```

CallNamedPipe() can be used by a client station on a message-write pipe (one that the server has created with the PIPE_TYPE_MESSAGE bit set in its call to CreateNamedPipe()). It combines calls to WaitNamedPipe(), CreateFile(), TransactNamedPipe(), and CloseHandle(). It is useful when the client only needs to send a single message and receive a single answer.

```
BOOL CallNamedPipe(
        LPCTSTR    lpPipeName,
        LPVOID     lpInBuffer,
        DWORD      dwInBufferSize,
        LPVOID     lpOutBuffer,
        DWORD      dwOutBufferSize,
        LPDWORD    lpBytesRead,
        DWORD      dwTimeout);
```

The arguments to CallNamedPipe() combine those for TransactNamedPipe() and WaitNamedPipe(). Because the pipe is not yet open, the pipe name, rather than the pipe handle, is required. The five interior arguments are the same as for TransactNamedPipe(); they describe the input and output buffers and provide a variable that returns the number of bytes read. Finally, *dwTimeout* is the same as the timeout argument to WaitNamedPipe(). There is one additional constant, NMPWAIT_NOWAIT, which directs CallNamedPipe() to fail if an instance of the pipe is not immediately available.

Terminating a Named Pipes Connection

A Named Pipes connection normally terminates when the client application calls CloseHandle() with its pipe handle. At this point, the server application detects a failure—most likely ReadFile() returns FALSE and GetLastError() says ERROR_PIPE_BROKEN. In response, the server calls DisconnectNamedPipe().

```
BOOL DisconnectNamedPipe(HANDLE hPipe);
```

DisconnectNamedPipe() puts the pipe instance back into the listening state. It does not destroy the pipe. When the server is done using a pipe instance, it calls CloseHandle() with the handle to that instance. NT destroys the pipe when the last instance is closed.

Strategies for Multithreading a Named Pipes Server

There are many ways to design a multithreaded Named Pipes server. This section covers several possible strategies.

One Thread per Instance with a Blocking, Non-Overlapped Pipe

In this scenario, a pipe is created for blocking, non-overlapped I/O. This permits a very simple, but nonetheless effective, multithreading strategy. For each instance of the pipe you create, you spin off a thread that listens for connection requests, then waits for data after a connection has been established. Here's an example:

```
const short PIPE_INSTANCES = 5;
HANDLE hPipeInstance[PIPE_INSTANCES],
       hPipeThread[PIPE_INSTANCES];

for (int i = 0; i < PIPE_INSTANCES; ++i)
    {
    hPipeInstance[i] = CreateNamedPipe(...);
    if (hPipeInstance[i] != INVALID_HANDLE_VALUE)
        {
        hPipeThread[i] =
            CreateThread(NULL, 0, NamedPipeThread,
                hPipeInstance[i],...);
        }
    }

DWORD WINAPI NamedPipeThread(HANDLE hPipeInstance)
{
    DWORD dwError;
    BYTE  byBuffer[4096];
    DWORD dwBytes;

    while (ConnectNamedPipe(hPipeInstance, NULL) ||
           GetLastError() == ERROR_PIPE_CONNECTED)
        {
        while (ReadFile(hPipeInstance, byBuffer,
                sizeof (byBuffer), &dwBytes, NULL))
            {
            // Do something with the incoming data
            }
        DisconnectNamedPipe(hPipeInstance);
        }
    ExitThread(dwError = GetLastError());
    return dwError;
}
```

One Thread for All Instances with an Overlapped Pipe

When you create a named pipe for overlapped I/O, you have other strategies available. Now, ConnectNamedPipe() will not block, so you need to check for client connections by calling one of the wait functions (WaitForSingleObject(), WaitForMultipleObjects(), or MsgWaitFor MultipleObjects()).

The strategy I used when I first wrote the Named Pipes level-zero DLL used one thread to handle all incoming activity for all my pipe instances. This meant one additional piece of bookkeeping: I had to remember the current state of each pipe instance. This was not complex, as the only possible states are listening or connected.

First I created an array of event handles and called WaitForMultiple Objects() to detect when one of them went signalled. At this point, my next action depended on the current state of the pipe. If it was in the listening state, then a client had connected, and it was entering the connected state. All I needed to do was spin off an overlapped ReadFile() and go back to the WaitForMultipleObjects(). If it was already connected, then a data packet had arrived. I sent it along to the client application and issued another ReadFile(). ReadFile() failed, and GetLastError() reported ERROR_PIPE_BROKEN, when the client closed his end of the pipe. At this point, I called the local routine ReenterListeningState(), which called DisconnectNamedPipe() and ConnectNamedPipe() after making a note of the state change.

The problem with this approach is that only one thread handles all the server background activity. This means I cannot possibly take advantage of a multiprocessor machine. It also means I cannot use the function ImpersonateNamedPipeClient() to take on the security context of a connecting client because it alters the security characteristics of the calling thread. With only one thread running, each call to ImpersonateNamed PipeClient() would change the security environment.

One Thread per Instance with an Overlapped Pipe

The approach I now use combines the two described above. I use an overlapped pipe but spin off a separate thread for each instance of the pipe. The threads are created in _WNetInit(). Two pieces of information are passed down: the handle of the pipe instance that the thread is responsible for and the window handle of the top-level notification window.

The thread still needs to keep track of the state of its pipe instance and must allocate read buffers when the instance enters the connected state.

Fields for these purposes are included in the structure passed to the thread. These are the relevant types and constants from \NTNET\CODE\ NMPIPE\WNETPIPE.H:

```
enum PIPE_STATE
{
   PIPE_STATE_LISTENING,
   PIPE_STATE_CONNECTED
};
struct NP_THREAD_PARMS
{
   HANDLE      hPipeHandle;
   HWND        hNotifyWnd;
   PIPE_STATE  PipeState;
   LPBYTE      lpReadBuffer;
};
```

Here is the code for my Named Pipes server thread, from \NTNET\CODE\NMPIPE_WNETINI.CPP:

```
DWORD WINAPI NamedPipesThread(LPVOID lp)
{
   NP_THREAD_PARMS *pThreadParms = (NP_THREAD_PARMS *) lp;
   OVERLAPPED      Overlapped;
   DWORD           dwBytes;
   DWORD           dwError = NO_ERROR;

   ZeroMemory(&Overlapped, sizeof (Overlapped));

   Overlapped.hEvent = CreateEvent(NULL, TRUE, FALSE, NULL);
   ConnectNamedPipe(pThreadParms->hPipeHandle, &Overlapped);
   pThreadParms->PipeState = PIPE_STATE_LISTENING;

   try
       {
      while (TRUE)
         {
         // Wait for the event to signal
         if (WaitForSingleObject(
             Overlapped.hEvent,
             INFINITE) != WAIT_OBJECT_0)
            {
            dwError = GetLastError();
            leave;
            }
         else
            {
```

```
    if (GetOverlappedResult(pThreadParms->hPipeHandle,
                            &Overlapped,
                            &dwBytes,
                            TRUE))
    {
    switch (pThreadParms->PipeState)
       {
       case PIPE_STATE_LISTENING:
          pThreadParms->PipeState = PIPE_STATE_CONNECTED;
          pThreadParms->lpReadBuffer =
             (LPBYTE) VirtualAlloc(NULL, 4096,
                MEM_COMMIT, PAGE_READWRITE);
          if (pThreadParms->lpReadBuffer == NULL)
             // Memory allocation error—we're in trouble
             {
             dwBytesTriedToAlloc = 4096;
             RaiseException(STATUS_NO_MEMORY, 0, 1,
                &dwBytesTriedToAlloc);
             dwError = STATUS_NO_MEMORY;
             leave;
             }
          if (!ImpersonateNamedPipeClient(
             pThreadParms->hPipeHandle))
             {
             printfConsole(
                TEXT(
                   "\nImpersonateNamedPipeClient() failed"));
             printfConsole(TEXT("\nGetLastError() = %d"),
                         GetLastError());
             }
          if (!ReadFile(pThreadParms->hPipeHandle,
             pThreadParms->lpReadBuffer,
             4096,
             &dwBytes, &Overlapped))
             {
             if (GetLastError() == ERROR_BROKEN_PIPE)
                // Client said goodbye
                ReenterListeningState(pThreadParms,
                   &Overlapped);
             }
          break;

       case PIPE_STATE_CONNECTED:
          // Data was read—forward it and read some more
          // Add Named Pipes bias to connection handle
          SendMsgFromSharedMem(pThreadParms->hNotifyWnd,
             pThreadParms->lpReadBuffer,
             (HCONNECTION)
```

```
                        (((DWORD) pThreadParms->hPipeHandle) +
                         (PROTOCOL_BIAS * dwPrecedence)),
                         dwBytes);
                if (!ReadFile(pThreadParms->hPipeHandle,
                        pThreadParms->lpReadBuffer, 4096,
                        &dwBytes, &Overlapped))
                    {
                    if (GetLastError() == ERROR_BROKEN_PIPE)
                        // Client said goodbye
                        ReenterListeningState(pThreadParms,
                            &Overlapped);
                    }
                break;
                }
            }
        else
            {
            // GetOverlappedResult() failed
            switch (pThreadParms->PipeState)
                {
                case PIPE_STATE_CONNECTED:
                    // Connection was broken, start over
                    ReenterListeningState(pThreadParms,
                        &Overlapped);
                    break;
                case PIPE_STATE_LISTENING:
                    // Pipe probably closed
                    dwError = NO_ERROR;
                    leave;
                default:
                    break;
                }
            }
        }
    }
finally
    {
    CloseHandle(Overlapped.hEvent);
    }
ExitThread(dwError);
return dwError;
}

static VOID ReenterListeningState(NP_THREAD_PARMS *pThreadParms,
                               LPOVERLAPPED lpOverlapped)
{
    pThreadParms->PipeState = PIPE_STATE_LISTENING;
```

```
FlushFileBuffers(pThreadParms->hPipeHandle);
VirtualFree(pThreadParms->lpReadBuffer, 0,
   MEM_RELEASE);
RevertToSelf();
DisconnectNamedPipe(pThreadParms->hPipeHandle);
ConnectNamedPipe(pThreadParms->hPipeHandle,
   lpOverlapped);
}
```

There are a couple of details I want to call to your attention. In ReenterListeningState(), notice the call to FlushFileBuffers() just before DisconnectNamedPipe(). FlushFileBuffers() makes sure that any data that is between the server and client stations gets fully delivered before the connection is destroyed.

Also, notice that after the server reads incoming data, it calls SendMsgFromSharedMem() to transmit it to higher-level software. This is a function included in the level-one DLL (\NTNET\CODE\%Cpu%\ WNETLVL1.DLL), and described in Chapter 9. It puts the data into shared memory, then sends the application a WMU_PACKET_RECEIVED message. It would be sufficient to simply post the message upstairs, pointing *lParam* at the data, as I did in *Windows Network Programming,* but for one thing: you can create only one instance of a given mailslot. Therefore, the first application that loads WNETPIPE.DLL creates the mailslot and spins off the background thread to receive incoming datagrams; all subsequent user applications borrow the mailslot and its thread. For this reason, the read buffer of the mailslot belongs only to the first process; you cannot pass a pointer to it to a window belonging to any other process. Mailslots are the only vehicle in this book that requires this kind of treatment; for all the others (Named Pipes, Windows Sockets, and NetBIOS) it should be sufficient to just call PostMessage(). However, since I had to create SendMsgFromSharedMem() for Mailslots, the receiving end (also in \NTNET\CODE\%Cpu%\WNETLVL1.DLL) has to retrieve the data from shared memory. The level-one DLL must not be required to know where the data is coming from, so I use the same transmission medium for all APIs.

Mailslots

Mailslots provide a datagram extension to the connection-oriented services offered by Named Pipes. The protocol is simple:

- The server side creates a mailslot and can only read from it.
- The client side opens a mailslot and can only write to it.

A mailslot can be created only on the local machine. The same process can obtain both server-side (read-only) and client-side (write-only) handles to the mailslot.

The Mailslot API

CreateMailslot() creates a mailslot and returns a server-side handle.

```
HANDLE CreateMailslot(
        LPCTSTR lpName,
        DWORD   dwMaxMessageSize,
        DWORD   dwReadTimeout,
        LPSECURITY_ATTRIBUTES lpSecurity);
```

Mailslots use a naming convention that is similar to the one used for Named Pipes. The name must be in the format \\<machine name>\MAILSLOT\<mailslot name>. For CreateMailslot(), the mailslot name must use the machine name '.', since the mailslot can only be created locally.

dwMaxMessageSize specifies the maximum byte count of a message. Passing it as zero tells NT that messages can be of any size. *dwReadTimeout* gives the number of milliseconds to wait when ReadFile() is called with the mailslot handle. Zero means don't wait; MAILSLOT_WAIT_FOREVER means block indefinitely. This is the only way you can control the behavior of ReadFile(). There is no such thing as an overlapped mailslot, and ReadFile() does not include a timeout argument. The security attributes are used the same as with CreateNamedPipe()—to permit or restrict access to the mailslot.

To repeat: only one instance of a mailslot can be created. Once a mailslot exists, any subsequent calls to CreateMailslot() using the same mailslot name return INVALID_HANDLE_VALUE. This is not a problem; as my mailslot handler shows, a single mailslot can service multiple clients. It becomes a problem only when the application that owns the mailslot goes away, because at that point the mailslot is destroyed.

When a client station wants to write to a mailslot, it opens it by calling CreateFile(). The mailslot uses the full UNC format, \\<machine name>\MAILSLOT\<mailslot name>. To obtain a handle that can be used for broadcasting, pass the machine name as "*". For example, to broadcast to all stations that have created the mailslot \MAILSLOT\WNET\WNETSLOT, call CreateFile() as follows:

```
HANDLE hMailslot;
hMailslot =
   CreateFile(TEXT("\\\\*\\MAILSLOT\\WNET\\WNETSLOT"), ...);
```

You can also do multicasts by using a Windows NT domain name instead of the name of a specific machine.

The function GetMailslotInfo() tells you if there are messages waiting to be read, but it returns immediately. In the NT multithreaded environment, it is better to call ReadFile() and create the mailslot with *dwReadTimeout* set to MAILSLOT_WAIT_FOREVER. This causes ReadFile() to block until a message arrives. Note that even though your call to ReadFile() on a mailslot will block, you can configure it to time out in the *dwReadTimeout* argument to CreateMailslot(). Mailslots are the only objects for which ReadFile() behaves this way.

A Mailslot Server

The WNet DLLs listen for datagrams to arrive in the background. The WNet server (endpoint "WNETSRVR") uses datagrams so stations that have registered this endpoint can announce their presence on the network and let other stations know what protocols they support. In the _WNetInit() function, the Named Pipes and Mailslot server tries to create a mailslot for each client application that registers. Only the first CreateMailslot() call succeeds. All others return INVALID_HANDLE_VALUE, but as long as GetLastError() says ERROR_ALREADY_EXISTS, there's no problem. Here are the relevant lines of code:

```
wsprintf(szPipeName, TEXT("\\\\.\\MAILSLOT\\WNET\\%s"),
        lpEndpoint);

   // Make pipe and mailslot available for everyone
   InitializeSecurityDescriptor(&sd,
      SECURITY_DESCRIPTOR_REVISION);
   SetSecurityDescriptorDacl(&sd, TRUE, NULL, FALSE);

   hMailslot = CreateMailslot(szPipeName,
                              0,
                              MAILSLOT_WAIT_FOREVER,
                              &PipeSecurity);

   if (hMailslot == INVALID_HANDLE_VALUE &&
      GetLastError() != ERROR_ALREADY_EXISTS)
      return -1;
```

lpEndpoint is one of the arguments passed to _WNetInit() and is the signature that identifies the server application.

As with the pipe instances I created, I spin off a background thread to receive incoming datagrams. Because mailslots are a more primitive animal, this thread is much simpler than the Named Pipes thread you have already seen. _WNetInit() passes the Mailslot thread two pieces of information in an MS_THREAD_PARMS structure, typed as follows:

```
struct MS_THREAD_PARMS
{
    HANDLE hMailslot;
    HWND   hNotifyWnd;
};
```

hMailslot is the handle returned by CreateMailslot(), and *hNotifyWnd* is the window handle of the top-level client window. The thread itself does very little. All it needs to do is sit on a call to ReadFile() and forward the data when it arrives.

```
DWORD WINAPI MailslotThread(LPVOID lp)
{
    MS_THREAD_PARMS *pMSThreadParms = (MS_THREAD_PARMS *) lp;
    BYTE    byReadBuffer[4096];
    DWORD   dwBytes;

    // Just read the mailslot until we get tired
    while (ReadFile(pMSThreadParms->hMailslot, byReadBuffer,
                sizeof (byReadBuffer), &dwBytes, NULL))
    {
        SendMsgFromSharedMem(pMSThreadParms->hNotifyWnd, byReadBuffer,
                    (HCONNECTION) 0, dwBytes);
    }
    ExitThread(0);
    return 0;
}
```

Additional Code Listings

Much of the work of the Named Pipes server is done in the initialization function, _WNetInit(). It performs the following tasks:

- It creates several instances of a named pipe.
- It creates a server-side mailslot.
- For each instance of the pipe, NamedPipesThread() is spun off to listen for client connections. The application that succeeds in creating the mailslot starts up MailslotThread() to receive incoming datagrams.

- _WNetInit() stores thread-specific information in a Thread Local Storage slot so that it can be easily retrieved by other functions in the DLL. Because I store information describing the application using the DLL in thread local storage, there is a one user per thread limitation. That is, any process wishing to use these DLLs can do so as many times as it wants to, as long as each new use—that is, each new call to WNetInit()—comes from a new thread.

Because the background threads carry out many of the passive operations associated with server applications—listening for connection requests, listening for asynchronous data packets, and listening for datagrams—the implementation of these functions is trivial. Before you look at them, though, here is the full listing of _WNetInit(). The *dwDesiredPrecedence* argument supports a Registry-based implementation of the level-one DLL presented in Chapter 15. As you will see, it makes the loading order of the level-zero DLLs configurable.

```c
int WINAPI _WNetInit(HWND hWnd, LPVOID lpStationName,
                     LPVOID lpEndpoint,
                     DWORD  dwDesiredPrecedence)
{
    TCHAR  szPipeName[MAX_PATH + 1];
    int    i, j;
    NP_THREAD_PARMS *pNPThreadParms[PIPE_INSTANCES] =
        {NULL};
    MS_THREAD_PARMS *pMSThreadParms = NULL;
    NP_TLS_DATA     *pTLSData = NULL;
    HANDLE hNPThread[PIPE_INSTANCES] = {NULL}, hMSThread = NULL;
    DWORD  dwThreadID;
    TCHAR  szComputerName[MAX_COMPUTERNAME_LENGTH + 1];
    DWORD  dwNameLength = MAX_COMPUTERNAME_LENGTH;
    TCHAR  szEndpoint[256];
    int    nNameIndex;
    SECURITY_DESCRIPTOR sd;
    SECURITY_ATTRIBUTES PipeSecurity = {sizeof (SECURITY_ATTRIBUTES),
                                        &sd,
                                        FALSE};

    // Win32S only supports client-side operations—
    // can't create named pipes or mailslots and can't spin off threads

    UNREFERENCED_PARAMETER(lpStationName);

    if (TlsGetValue(dwTLSIndex) != NULL)
        // Only one registration per thread
        return -1;
```

```
// Get our computer name
GetComputerName(szComputerName, &dwNameLength);

nNameIndex = WNetGetNextNameIndex();

if (nNameIndex == (-1))
   // No more slots
   return -1;

WNetSetName(nNameIndex, szComputerName, (WORD) dwNameLength + 1);

if (lpEndpoint == NULL)
   lpEndpoint = TEXT("WNETSRVR");

// That's all we can do under Win32S
if (ISWIN32S())
   return nNameIndex;

pTLSData = (NP_TLS_DATA *)
            VirtualAlloc(NULL, sizeof (NP_TLS_DATA),
                        MEM_COMMIT,
                        PAGE_READWRITE);
if (pTLSData == NULL)
   {
   dwBytesTriedToAlloc = sizeof (NP_TLS_DATA);
   RaiseException(STATUS_NO_MEMORY, 0, 1, &dwBytesTriedToAlloc);
   return -1;
   }

// Make sure endpoint name is in Unicode
ANSIToUnicode((LPSTR) lpEndpoint, szEndpoint, sizeof (szEndpoint));
lpEndpoint = szEndpoint;

// Create our mailslot, \\.\MAILSLOT\WNET\<lpEndpoint>

wsprintf(szPipeName, TEXT("\\\\.\\MAILSLOT\\WNET\\%s"), lpEndpoint);

// Make pipe and mailslot available for everyone
// by attaching a NULL DACL to the SECURITY_DESCRIPTOR
InitializeSecurityDescriptor(&sd, SECURITY_DESCRIPTOR_REVISION);
SetSecurityDescriptorDacl(&sd, TRUE, NULL, FALSE);

hMailslot = CreateMailslot(szPipeName,
                           0,
                           MAILSLOT_WAIT_FOREVER,
                           &PipeSecurity);

if (hMailslot == INVALID_HANDLE_VALUE &&
```

```
      GetLastError() != ERROR_ALREADY_EXISTS)
    return -1;

// We'll create the pipe
// "\\.\PIPE\WNET\<lpEndpoint>"
wsprintf(szPipeName, TEXT("\\\\.\\PIPE\\WNET\\%s"), lpEndpoint);

for (i = 0; i < PIPE_INSTANCES; ++i)
    {
    // Open two-way pipes for overlapped I/O
    // Create them in message mode for writing,
    // and byte mode for reading
    // We use byte-read mode so we don't have to worry
    // about partial-message-read (ERROR_MORE_DATA) errors

    // Make them blocking (as necessary for overlapped I/O)
    hPipeHandles[i] = CreateNamedPipe(szPipeName,
                                      PIPE_ACCESS_DUPLEX |
                                      FILE_FLAG_OVERLAPPED |
                                      WRITE_DAC,
                                      PIPE_TYPE_MESSAGE |
                                      PIPE_READMODE_BYTE |
                                      PIPE_WAIT,
                                      PIPE_UNLIMITED_INSTANCES,
                                      0, 0, 0,
                                      &PipeSecurity);

    if (hPipeHandles[i] == INVALID_HANDLE_VALUE)
        {
        if (i == 0)
            return -1;
        else
            break;
        }
    }

// OK, now let's spin off threads who will wait for
// any of the pipe instances to get a connection request.

for (j = 0; j < i; ++j)
    {
    pNPThreadParms[j] = (NP_THREAD_PARMS *)
                    VirtualAlloc(NULL, sizeof (NP_THREAD_PARMS),
                                 MEM_COMMIT,
                                 PAGE_READWRITE);
    if (pNPThreadParms[j] == NULL)
        {
        if (j == 0)
```

```
            {
            dwBytesTriedToAlloc = sizeof (NP_THREAD_PARMS);
            RaiseException(STATUS_NO_MEMORY, 0, 1,
                &dwBytesTriedToAlloc);
            return -1;
            }
        else
            break;
        }

    pNPThreadParms[j]->hPipeHandle = hPipeHandles[j];

    pNPThreadParms[j]->hNotifyWnd = hWnd;

    hNPThread[j] = CreateThread(NULL, 0, NamedPipesThread,
                                (LPVOID) pNPThreadParms[j],
                                0, &dwThreadID);
    if (hNPThread[j] == NULL)
        {
        if (j == 0)
            {
            VirtualFree(pNPThreadParms[j], 0, MEM_RELEASE);
            return -1;
            }
        else
            break;
        }
    pTLSData->pNPThreadParms[j] = pNPThreadParms[j];
    pTLSData->hNPThread[j]      = hNPThread[j];
    }
if (hMailslot != INVALID_HANDLE_VALUE)
    {
    pMSThreadParms = (MS_THREAD_PARMS *)
                    VirtualAlloc(NULL, sizeof (MS_THREAD_PARMS),
                                 MEM_COMMIT,
                                 PAGE_READWRITE);
    if (pMSThreadParms == NULL)
        {
        dwBytesTriedToAlloc = sizeof (MS_THREAD_PARMS);
        RaiseException(STATUS_NO_MEMORY, 0, 1, &dwBytesTriedToAlloc);
        return -1;
        }

    pMSThreadParms->hMailslot  = hMailslot;
    pMSThreadParms->hNotifyWnd = hWnd;

    hMSThread = CreateThread(NULL, 0, MailslotThread,
                             (LPVOID) pMSThreadParms, 0, &dwThreadID);
```

```
    if (hMSThread == NULL)
        {
        VirtualFree(pMSThreadParms, 0, MEM_RELEASE);
        return -1;
        }
    }
pTLSData->pMSThreadParms = pMSThreadParms;
pTLSData->hMSThread      = hMSThread;

TlsSetValue(dwTLSIndex, pTLSData);
if (dwDesiredPrecedence == 0xFFFFFFFF)
    dwPrecedence = PROTOCOL_NP + 1;
else
    dwPrecedence = dwDesiredPrecedence;

return nNameIndex;
}
```

Other Passive Server-Side Operations

_WNetListen(), _WNetReceiveDatagram(), and a non-blocking
_WNetReceive() essentially have nothing to do, because the background
threads are already doing the necessary work. For example, here's the file
\NTNET\CODE\NMPIPE_WNETLIS.CPP, containing _WNetListen():

```
/********
*
* _WNETLIS.CPP
*
* Copyright (c) 1993-1994 Ralph P. Davis, All Rights Reserved
*
********


/*===== Includes =====*/

#include "wnetpipe.h"


/*===== Function Definitions =====*/

BOOL WINAPI _WNetListen(int nNameIndex, HWND hWnd)
{
    // We're already listening in the background,
    // not supported under Win32s
    return (!ISWIN32S());
}
```

The code for a non-blocking receive is as sparse as _WNetListen(). A blocking receive is a little more complicated because of the overlapped I/O on the pipe. You have to create a manual-reset event, issue a ReadFile(), then wait for the event to signal.

```cpp
/*******
 *
 * _WNETRCV.CPP
 *
 * Copyright (c) 1993-1994 Ralph P. Davis, All Rights Reserved
 *
 ********/


/*===== Includes =====*/

#include "wnetpipe.h"


/*===== Function Definitions =====*/

BOOL WINAPI _WNetReceive(HCONNECTION hConnection,
                         LPVOID lpData,
                         WORD   wDataLength,
                         DWORD  dwTimeout,
                         int    nNameIndex,
                         HWND   hWnd)
{
    OVERLAPPED Overlapped;
    DWORD      dwBytes;
    BOOL       bReturnCode;

    if (dwTimeout == 0)
        {
        // We're already doing this in the background,
        // not supported under Win32S
        return (!ISWIN32S());
        }
    ZeroMemory(&Overlapped, sizeof (OVERLAPPED));
    Overlapped.hEvent = CreateEvent(NULL, TRUE, FALSE, NULL);

    if (ReadFile((HANDLE) hConnection, lpData, wDataLength,
                &dwBytes, &Overlapped))
        {
        if (Overlapped.hEvent != NULL)
            CloseHandle(Overlapped.hEvent);
        return TRUE;
```

```
   }

if (GetLastError() != ERROR_IO_PENDING)
   {
   if (Overlapped.hEvent != NULL)
      CloseHandle(Overlapped.hEvent);
   return FALSE;
   }

switch (WaitForSingleObject(Overlapped.hEvent, dwTimeout))
   {
   case WAIT_TIMEOUT:
   case WAIT_FAILED:
      bReturnCode = FALSE;
      break;
   default:
      bReturnCode = GetOverlappedResult((HANDLE) hConnection,
                       &Overlapped, &dwBytes, TRUE);
      break;
   }

if (Overlapped.hEvent != NULL)
   CloseHandle(Overlapped.hEvent);
return bReturnCode;
}
```

Transmitting Data over a Named Pipes Connection— _WNetSend() and _WNetShipData()

_WNetSend() uses WriteFile() to transmit a buffer of data. Chapter 9 discussed the WNetShipData() function, which is provided to emulate TransactNamedPipe() over APIs that do not have a similar call. The Named Pipes DLL provides a level-zero _WNetShipData() that uses TransactNamedPipe(). First, let's look at _WNetSend(). Because both client and server ends of the pipe are opened for overlapped I/O, _WNetSend() has a few more lines of code than it would if you were doing simple, synchronous I/O. Here is the file \NTNET\CODE\NMPIPE\ _WNETSND.CPP:

```
/********
*
* _WNETSND.CPP
*
* Copyright (c) 1993-1994 Ralph P. Davis, All Rights Reserved
*
********/
```

```
/*===== Includes =====*/

#include "wnetpipe.h"


/*===== Function Definitions =====*/

BOOL WINAPI _WNetSend(HCONNECTION hConnection, LPVOID lpData,
                      WORD wDataLength)
{
    OVERLAPPED Overlapped;
    BOOL       bReturnCode;
    DWORD      dwBytes;

    ZeroMemory(&Overlapped, sizeof (OVERLAPPED));
    Overlapped.hEvent = CreateEvent(NULL, TRUE, FALSE, NULL);

    if (WriteFile((HANDLE) hConnection, lpData, wDataLength,
                             &dwBytes, &Overlapped))
       {
       if (Overlapped.hEvent != NULL)
          CloseHandle(Overlapped.hEvent);
       return (dwBytes == (DWORD) wDataLength);
       }

    if (GetLastError() != ERROR_IO_PENDING)
       {
       if (Overlapped.hEvent != NULL)
          CloseHandle(Overlapped.hEvent);
       return FALSE;
       }

    bReturnCode = GetOverlappedResult((HANDLE) hConnection,
                                       &Overlapped,
                                       &dwBytes, TRUE);

    if (Overlapped.hEvent != NULL)
       CloseHandle(Overlapped.hEvent);

    return (bReturnCode && (dwBytes == (DWORD) wDataLength));
}
```

_WNetShipData() uses TransactNamedPipe(), but only waits five seconds for a reply from the partner. This is an advantage to doing overlapped I/O on the pipe. Otherwise, TransactNamedPipe() blocks indefinitely until the partner responds. TransactNamedPipe() won't get bored, but your users may.

On a permanently blocked network call, there's nothing you can do but Ctrl-Esc to bring up the task list and click the End Task button.

Here is the file \NTNET\CODE\NMPIPE_WNETSHP.CPP, containing _WNetShipData():

```
/********
*
* _WNETSHP.CPP
*
* Copyright (c) 1993-1994 Ralph P. Davis, All Rights Reserved
*
********/

/*===== Includes =====*/

#include "wnetpipe.h"


/*===== Function Definitions =====*/

LRESULT WINAPI _WNetShipData(HWND         hWnd,
                             HCONNECTION hConnection,
                             LPVOID       lpData,
                             WORD         wDataLength,
                             LPVOID       lpDataOut,
                             WORD         wOutDataLength)
{
   LRESULT    lResult = -1L;
   LPBYTE     lpReceiveBuffer, lpTemp;
   BOOL       bReturnCode;
   DWORD      dwOutDataLength;
   OVERLAPPED Overlapped;

   ZeroMemory(&Overlapped, sizeof (Overlapped));

   // Create a manual-reset event
   Overlapped.hEvent = CreateEvent(NULL, TRUE, FALSE, NULL);

   if (Overlapped.hEvent == NULL)
      return -1L;

   lpReceiveBuffer = (LPBYTE) VirtualAlloc(NULL, wOutDataLength +
                                           sizeof (LRESULT),
                                     MEM_COMMIT,
                                     PAGE_READWRITE);
   if (lpReceiveBuffer == NULL)
      {
```

```
        dwBytesTriedToAlloc = ((DWORD) wOutDataLength) + sizeof (LRESULT);
        RaiseException(STATUS_NO_MEMORY, 0, 1, &dwBytesTriedToAlloc);
        CloseHandle(Overlapped.hEvent);
        return -1L;
        }

    bReturnCode =
        TransactNamedPipe((HANDLE) hConnection,
            lpData, wDataLength,
            lpReceiveBuffer, sizeof (LRESULT) + wOutDataLength,
            &dwOutDataLength, &Overlapped);

    if (!bReturnCode && GetLastError() == ERROR_IO_PENDING)
        {
        if (WaitForSingleObject(Overlapped.hEvent, 5000) ==
                WAIT_OBJECT_0)
            bReturnCode = GetOverlappedResult((HANDLE) hConnection,
                                              &Overlapped,
                                              &dwOutDataLength,
                                              TRUE);
        else
            bReturnCode = FALSE;
        }

    if (bReturnCode)
        {
        wOutDataLength = (WORD) dwOutDataLength;
        lResult = *((LRESULT *) lpReceiveBuffer);
        lpTemp = (LPBYTE) lpDataOut;
        dwOutDataLength -= (sizeof (LRESULT));
        lpReceiveBuffer += (sizeof (LRESULT));

        if (lpTemp != NULL)
            CopyMemory(lpTemp, lpReceiveBuffer, dwOutDataLength);
        }
    else
        lResult = -1;

    CloseHandle(Overlapped.hEvent);
    VirtualFree(lpReceiveBuffer, 0, MEM_RELEASE);
    return lResult;
    }
```

Closing a Conversation—_WNetHangup()

_WNetHangup() has very little to do. Its sole argument is the
HCONNECTION corresponding to a client-side pipe handle, so all it needs
to do is call CloseHandle(). The server side will not call _WNetHangup();

doing so destroys an instance of the pipe, thereby rendering it unusable to client applications.

The listing appears in \NTNET\CODE\NMPIPE_WNETHGP.CPP.

```
/********
 *
 * _WNETHGP.CPP
 *
 * Copyright (c) 1993-1994 Ralph P. Davis, All Rights Reserved
 *
 ********/


/*===== Includes =====*/

#include "wnetpipe.h"


/*===== Function Definitions =====*/

void WINAPI _WNetHangup(HCONNECTION hConnection)
{
    CloseHandle((HANDLE) hConnection);
}
```

Transmitting Data over a Mailslot

_WNetSendDatagram() sends a datagram by opening a client-side mailslot handle, then calling WriteFile() to transmit the data. If the target station is the string "WNET_DOMAIN" (represented by the constant WNET_DOMAIN), it opens the mailslot using the machine name "*", which is the way to broadcast a datagram using Windows NT Mailslots. Because mailslots are one-way, the call to CreateFile() requests only GENERIC_WRITE access.

```
/********
 *
 * _WNETSDG.CPP
 *
 * Copyright (c) 1993-1994 Ralph P. Davis, All Rights Reserved
 *
 ********/
```

```
/*===== Includes =====*/

#include "wnetpipe.h"


/*===== Functions Definitions =====*/

BOOL WINAPI _WNetSendDatagram(LPVOID lpTargetStation,
                              LPVOID lpEndpoint,
                              LPVOID lpData,
                              WORD wDataLength,
                              int nNameIndex)
{
   TCHAR  szMailslotName[MAX_PATH + 1];
   HANDLE hMailslot;
   BOOL   bReturnCode;
   DWORD  dwBytes;

   if (lstrcmp((LPTSTR) lpTargetStation, WNET_DOMAIN) == 0)
      lpTargetStation = TEXT("*");

   if (lpEndpoint == NULL)
      lpEndpoint = TEXT("WNETSRVR");

   // Passing lpTargetStation as '*' broadcasts to all stations
   wsprintf(szMailslotName, TEXT("\\\\%s\\MAILSLOT\\WNET\\%s"),
         lpTargetStation, lpEndpoint);

   hMailslot = CreateFile(szMailslotName, GENERIC_WRITE,
                          FILE_SHARE_READ, NULL,
                          OPEN_EXISTING, FILE_FLAG_WRITE_THROUGH,
                          NULL);
   if (hMailslot == INVALID_HANDLE_VALUE)
      return FALSE;

   bReturnCode = WriteFile(hMailslot, lpData, wDataLength, &dwBytes,
                           NULL);

   CloseHandle(hMailslot);
   return (bReturnCode && (dwBytes == (DWORD) wDataLength));
}
```

Shutting Down

An application calls WNetShutdown() when it is done using the WNet DLLs. The Named Pipes _WNetShutdown() closes the pipe handles and the mailslot, then waits for the threads to terminate.

```
/********
*
* _WNETSHD.CPP
*
* Copyright (c) 1993-1994 Ralph P. Davis, All Rights Reserved
*
********/


/*===== Includes =====*/

#include "wnetpipe.h"


/*===== Function Definitions =====*/

void WINAPI _WNetShutdown(int nNameIndex)
{
    int i;
    NP_TLS_DATA *lp;

    lp = (NP_TLS_DATA *) TlsGetValue(dwTLSIndex);

    if (lp != NULL)
        {
        // Close all pipe instances
        for (i = 0; i < PIPE_INSTANCES; ++i)
            CloseHandle(lp->pNPThreadParms[i]->hPipeHandle);
        // Wait for server background threads to complete
        WaitForMultipleObjects(PIPE_INSTANCES,
            lp->hNPThread, TRUE, INFINITE);
        // Release thread parameter memory
        for (i = 0; i < PIPE_INSTANCES; ++i)
            VirtualFree(lp->pNPThreadParms[i], 0, MEM_RELEASE);

        if (lp->pMSThreadParms != NULL)
            {
            CloseHandle(lp->pMSThreadParms->hMailslot);
            WaitForSingleObject(lp->hMSThread, INFINITE);
            VirtualFree(lp->pMSThreadParms, 0, MEM_RELEASE);
            }
        VirtualFree(lp, 0, MEM_RELEASE);
        }
}
```

Named Pipes Benchmarks

In order to compare the different APIs that Windows NT has to offer and the different ways of using them, I developed a simple benchmark test. It uses a single-threaded server application that creates a single-instance named pipe, then listens for client connections. The client application waits for the pipe to become available by calling WaitNamedPipe(), then sends packets of data to the server. The server sends them right back to the client. The purpose of this test is to determine how many bytes of data can be sent per second. There are two versions of the test; one uses WriteFile() and ReadFile(), and the other uses TransactNamedPipe().

First, here is the source code for the benchmark server, \NTNET\CODE\NMPIPE\WNETBNCH.CPP:

```
/********
 *
 * WNETBNCH.CPP
 *
 * Copyright (c) 1993-1994 Ralph P. Davis, All Rights Reserved
 *
 * Named pipes benchmark server
 *
 ********/

/*===== Includes =====*/

#include <windows.h>
#include <stdio.h>


/*===== Global Variables =====*/

BYTE *byBuffer;


/*===== Function Definitions =====*/

void main(int argc, char *argv[])
{
    HANDLE hFile;
    DWORD  dwBytes;
    SECURITY_DESCRIPTOR sd;
    SECURITY_ATTRIBUTES sa;
```

```
// Attach a NULL discretionary access control list
// to the pipe to optimize access to it
InitializeSecurityDescriptor(&sd, SECURITY_DESCRIPTOR_REVISION);
SetSecurityDescriptorDacl(&sd, TRUE, NULL, FALSE);

sa.nLength = sizeof (SECURITY_ATTRIBUTES);
sa.lpSecurityDescriptor = &sd;
sa.bInheritHandle = FALSE;

byBuffer = (BYTE *) VirtualAlloc(NULL, (1024 * 1024), MEM_COMMIT,
            PAGE_READWRITE);

if (byBuffer == NULL)
   {
   printf("\nMemory allocation error");
   ExitProcess(1);
   }
hFile = CreateNamedPipe("\\\\.\\PIPE\\WNET\\WNETBNCH",
                        PIPE_ACCESS_DUPLEX,
                        PIPE_TYPE_MESSAGE | PIPE_READMODE_BYTE |
                           PIPE_WAIT,
                        1,
                        32768,
                        32768,
                        0,
                        &sa);
if (hFile == INVALID_HANDLE_VALUE)
   {
   printf("\nUnable to create pipe\n");
   ExitProcess(1);
   }

printf("\nWaiting for client connections...\n");

try
   {
   while (ConnectNamedPipe(hFile, NULL))
      {
      while (ReadFile(hFile, byBuffer, 100000, &dwBytes, NULL))
         {
         if (!WriteFile(hFile, byBuffer, dwBytes, &dwBytes, NULL))
            break;
         }
      FlushFileBuffers(hFile);
      DisconnectNamedPipe(hFile);
      }
   }
```

```
       finally
          {
          CloseHandle(hFile);
          printf("\nNamed Pipes Benchmark Server terminating\n");
          VirtualFree(byBuffer, 0, MEM_RELEASE);
          }
       ExitProcess(0);
   }
```

There are two versions of the benchmark client, WNETCLI.CPP and WNETCLI2.CPP. WNETCLI.CPP uses WriteFile() and ReadFile(); WNETCLI2.CPP uses TransactNamedPipe(). Here are the two files:

```
/********
 *
 * WNETCLI.CPP
 *
 * Copyright (c) 1993-1994 Ralph P. Davis, All Rights Reserved
 *
 * Named pipes benchmark client
 *
 ********/

/*===== Includes =====*/

#include <windows.h>
#include <math.h>
#include <stdio.h>
#include <stdlib.h>


/*===== Global Variables =====*/

BYTE byBuffer[65536];


/*===== Function Definitions =====*/

void main(int argc, char *argv[])
{
   HANDLE hFile;
   DWORD  dwBytes;
   DWORD  dwStartTime, dwEndTime;
   DWORD  dwPackets;
   DWORD  dwPacketSize = sizeof (byBuffer);
   DWORD  i;
```

```
TCHAR  szPipeName[MAX_PATH + 1];

if (argc > 1)
   dwPackets = atoi(argv[1]);
else
   dwPackets = 250;

if (argc > 2)
   dwPacketSize = atoi(argv[2]);

if (argc > 3)
   // Last argument is server name
   sprintf(szPipeName, "\\\\%s\\PIPE\\WNET\\WNETBNCH",
      argv[3]);
else
   lstrcpy(szPipeName, "\\\\NUMBER1\\PIPE\\WNET\\WNETBNCH");

while (TRUE)
   {
   if (WaitNamedPipe(szPipeName, 5000))
      {
      printf("\nWaitNamedPipe() returned TRUE");
      hFile = CreateFile(szPipeName,
                         GENERIC_READ | GENERIC_WRITE,
                         0, NULL, OPEN_EXISTING,
                         FILE_ATTRIBUTE_NORMAL,
                         NULL);
      if (hFile == INVALID_HANDLE_VALUE)
         {
         printf("\nCan't access named pipe\n");
         if (GetLastError() != ERROR_PIPE_BUSY)
            ExitProcess(0);
         }
      else
         break;
      }
   else
      printf("\nWaitNamedPipe() returned FALSE");
   }

printf("\nConnected to server\n");

for (i = 0, dwStartTime = GetCurrentTime(); i < dwPackets; ++i)
   {
   if (WriteFile(hFile, byBuffer, dwPacketSize, &dwBytes, NULL))
      {
      if (!ReadFile(hFile, byBuffer, dwBytes, &dwBytes, NULL))
         break;
```

```
            }
        else
           break;
        }
    dwEndTime = GetCurrentTime();
    FlushFileBuffers(hFile);
    CloseHandle(hFile);

    printf("\nGetLastError() = %d", GetLastError());
    printf("\n%d packets transmitted in %d milliseconds", i * 2,
        dwEndTime - dwStartTime);
    printf("\nAverage is %d packets per second\n",
        (i * 2000) / (dwEndTime - dwStartTime));

    double dTotalBytes = ((double) dwPacketSize) *
                         ((double) i) * 2000.0;
    double dEndTime = (double) dwEndTime;
    double dStartTime = (double) dwStartTime;

    printf("\nBytes per second = %.2f\n",
        dTotalBytes / (dEndTime - dStartTime));
    ExitProcess(0);
}


/********
*
* WNETCLI2.CPP
*
* Copyright (c) 1994 Ralph P. Davis, All Rights Reserved
*
* Named pipes benchmark client using TransactNamedPipe()
*
********/

/*===== Includes =====*/

#include <windows.h>
#include <math.h>
#include <stdio.h>
#include <stdlib.h>


/*===== Global Variables =====*/

BYTE byBuffer[65536];


/*===== Function Definitions =====*/
```

```
void main(int argc, char *argv[])
{
   HANDLE hFile;
   DWORD  dwBytes;
   DWORD  dwStartTime, dwEndTime;
   DWORD  dwPackets;
   DWORD  dwPacketSize = sizeof (byBuffer);
   DWORD  i;
   DWORD  dwMode = PIPE_WAIT | PIPE_READMODE_MESSAGE;
   TCHAR  szPipeName[MAX_PATH + 1];


   if (argc > 1)
      dwPackets = atoi(argv[1]);
   else
      dwPackets = 250;

   if (argc > 2)
      dwPacketSize = atoi(argv[2]);

   if (argc > 3)
      // Last argument is server name
      sprintf(szPipeName, "\\\\%s\\PIPE\\WNET\\WNETBNCH",
         argv[3]);
   else
      lstrcpy(szPipeName, "\\\\NUMBER1\\PIPE\\WNET\\WNETBNCH");

   while (TRUE)
      {
      if (WaitNamedPipe(szPipeName, 5000))
         {
         printf("\nWaitNamedPipe() returned TRUE");
         hFile = CreateFile(szPipeName,
                            GENERIC_READ | GENERIC_WRITE,
                            0, NULL, OPEN_EXISTING,
                            FILE_ATTRIBUTE_NORMAL,
                            NULL);
         if (hFile == INVALID_HANDLE_VALUE)
            {
            printf("\nCan't access named pipe\n");
            if (GetLastError() != ERROR_PIPE_BUSY)
               ExitProcess(0);
            }
         else
            break;
         }
      else
         printf("\nWaitNamedPipe() returned FALSE");
```

```
    }


    SetNamedPipeHandleState(hFile, &dwMode, NULL, NULL);

    printf("\nConnected to server\n");

    for (i = 0, dwStartTime = GetCurrentTime(); i < dwPackets; ++i)
        {
        if (!TransactNamedPipe(hFile, byBuffer, dwPacketSize,
                 byBuffer, dwPacketSize, &dwBytes, NULL))
           break;
        }
    dwEndTime = GetCurrentTime();
    FlushFileBuffers(hFile);
    CloseHandle(hFile);

    printf("\nGetLastError() = %d", GetLastError());
    printf("\n%d packets transmitted in %d milliseconds", i * 2,
       dwEndTime - dwStartTime);
    printf("\nAverage is %d packets per second\n",
       (i * 2000) / (dwEndTime - dwStartTime));

    double dTotalBytes = ((double) dwPacketSize) *
                         ((double) i) * 2000.0;
    double dEndTime = (double) dwEndTime;
    double dStartTime = (double) dwStartTime;

    printf("\nBytes per second = %.2f\n",
        dTotalBytes / (dEndTime - dStartTime));

    ExitProcess(0);
}
```

WriteFile()/ReadFile() versus TransactNamedPipe()

The first test compares the use of WriteFile() and ReadFile() with
TransactNamedPipe(). These tests were run with both the client and server
on the same machine, a 100 MHz NeTPower MIPS machine. Packet sizes
varied from 1024 to 32768 bytes. In each test, 100 packets were transmitted.
The byte transfer rate listed here is the round-trip transfer rate. Table 10-1
and Figure 10-1 present the data.

Table 10-1. WriteFile()/ReadFile() versus TransactNamedPipe()

Packet Size	1024	2048	4096	8192	16384	32768
WriteFile()/ReadFile()	195047	280547	424455	411658	421182	440134
TransactNamedPipe()	305671	390095	538947	494984	518481	547045
% Improvement	57%	39%	27%	20%	23%	24%

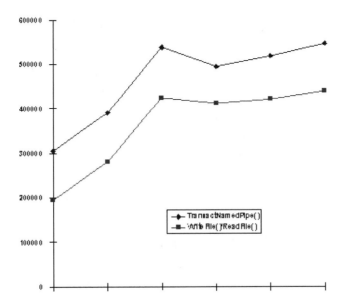

Figure 10-1. WriteFile()/ReadFile() versus TransactNamedPipe()

Clearly, TransactNamedPipe() provides a significant improvement in performance.

Local Named Pipes with Explicit Machine Name versus Machine Name of "."

The second test compares the use of an explicit machine name for a local connection with using the machine name ".". In the first case, CreateFile() is called with the pipe name \\NUMBER1\PIPE\WNET\WNETBNCH. In the second, the pipe name is \\.\PIPE\WNET\WNETBNCH. Both tests use TransactNamedPipe(). The results are shown in Table 10-2 and Figure 10-2.

Table 10-2.   Use of Explicit Machine Name versus "."

Packet Size	1024	2048	4096	8192	16384	32768
\\NUMBER1	305671	390095	538947	494984	518481	547045
\\.	2560000	4096000	6301538	6826666	6971914	6362718
% Improvement	738%	950%	1069%	1279%	1245%	1063%

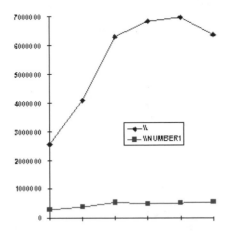

Figure 10-2.   Use of Machine Name versus "."

Using the machine name "." is approximately ten times faster! Apparently, the use of "." allows NT to bypass the normal mechanism for delivering data via a named pipe. The numbers certainly make it clear that it is worth checking to see if a client is trying to connect to a server application on the same machine.

Remote Named Pipes

The third set of data (shown in Table 10-3 and Figure 10-3) repeats the first test, but now the client station is a 66 MHz 486, and the server is a 100 MHz MIPS-based NeTPower. They are connected by a 10 MB-per-second 10BASE2 EtherNet LAN. The MIPS station is running Windows NT Advanced Server; the Intel station is a Windows NT workstation.

Table 10-3. WriteFile()/ReadFile() versus TransactNamedPipe() (Remote Stations)

Packet Size	1024	2048	4096	8192	16384	32768
WF/RF	213111	309833	467579	446917	455744	457653
TNP	252527	349488	514249	478364	492085	504200
% Improvement	18%	13%	10%	7%	8%	10%

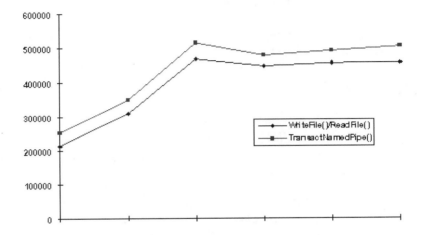

Figure 10-3. WriteFile()/ReadFile() versus TransactNamedPipes() (Remote Stations)

Here, too, TransactNamedPipe() clearly outperforms WriteFile() / ReadFile().

I will repeat these benchmark tests with the other API sets to see how each one performs.

Conclusion

Named Pipes and Mailslots are high-level APIs for peer-to-peer communication. Because they are file system drivers, they are tightly integrated into the NT environment, and the APIs are highly compatible with other Win32 APIs. Data exchange uses the standard file I/O calls WriteFile() and ReadFile(), though Win32 also provides two functions TransactNamedPipe() and CallNamedPipe(), that optimize request-response transactions. Ironically, it is precisely their implementation as file system drivers that imposes their most severe limitation—their poor suitability for internetworking. Because client applications use UNC filenames to connect to remote named pipes, and UNC names specify only a host name, there is little you can do to connect to a computer outside your immediate environment.

The data I present confirms that TransactNamedPipe() indeed offers better performance than WriteFile()/ReadFile(), when it is appropriate to the kind of exchange that is taking place. It also dramatically demonstrates that, for local Named Pipes, it is very important for clients to connect using machine name ".", rather than the explicit host name returned by GetComputerName().

Suggested Readings

Pipes Overview in the Win32 SDK on-line help. Printed as Chapter 54 in *Win32 Programmer's Reference, Volume 2*.

Mailslots Overview in the on-line help. Printed as Chapter 55 in *Win32 Programmer's Reference, Volume 2*.

Microsoft Knowledge Base for Win32 SDK articles:
    "Restrictions on Named-Pipe Names"
    "Impersonation Provided by ImpersonateNamedPipeClient()"

## Chapter 11

Windows Sockets

Overview

The Windows Sockets API is a specification developed by a consortium of companies to standardize the TCP/IP programming interface under Windows. TCP (the Transmission Control Protocol) and IP (the Internet Protocol) have an established history dating back a quarter of a century. They were originally developed to support the U.S. Defense Department's DARPA Internet. DOD has continued to play an important role in the extension of TCP and IP as the Internet has expanded to include civilian networks.

Several programming interfaces have evolved to allow applications to communicate over a TCP/IP network. The most widely used is the Berkeley Sockets interface, developed at the University of California (Berkeley) as one of Berkeley's extensions to the UNIX operating system. Berkeley's version of UNIX is referred to as the Berkeley Software Distribution (BSD). The Windows Sockets API is based on Berkeley Sockets, BSD version 4.3.

Another, more recent API is AT&T's Transport Layer Interface (TLI), developed at Bell Labs as a protocol-independent interface for requesting network transport services. Though superior to Berkeley Sockets in many ways, TLI does not yet have the acceptance enjoyed by Berkeley Sockets. However, Novell's stake in UNIX and their present emphasis on TLI could give it a significant boost.

TCP/IP has become widely associated with UNIX. This association is purely historical; there is no technical necessity for it. It is this association of UNIX and TCP/IP that has caused TCP/IP and Berkeley Sockets to be considered nearly synonymous. However, Berkeley Sockets, like TLI, is protocol-independent. Under Windows NT, Windows Sockets serves as the programming interface to the NWLink implementation of Novell's IPX/SPX. This chapter will explore Windows Sockets over both TCP/IP and NWLink.

One of the original goals of Windows Sockets was to facilitate the porting of code already written for Berkeley Sockets so that Windows stations could be easily integrated into TCP/IP networks. With some exceptions, Windows Sockets supports the complete Berkeley Sockets API. Windows Sockets also provides extended functions that are tailored to the message-passing environment of Windows. They all have WSA prefixes in their names (WSA stands for Windows Sockets Asynchronous), and they use a notification mechanism very similar to the one I have sketched in Chapters 9 and 10. One of the WSA functions, WSAAsyncSelect(), is a very powerful tool for building Windows Sockets server applications. It gives you implicit, built-in buffering and multithreading with very little work on your part. Much of my server-side code, as you will see, relies on WSAAsyncSelect().

Implementation of Windows Sockets under Windows NT

Under Windows NT, the Windows Sockets API resides in the DLL WSOCK32.DLL. It is in turn supported by helper DLLs like WSHTCPIP.DLL (for TCP/IP) and WSHNWLK.DLL (for NWLink). Its constants, types, and function prototypes are in the header file WINSOCK.H, and you link with the import library WSOCK32.LIB. Additional types and constants needed for Windows Sockets over NWLink are found in WSIPX.H.

The original Windows Sockets specification, the document published by the Windows Sockets committee, was written with Windows 3.X in mind. For this reason, it is quite emphatic in discouraging you from using blocking calls. Indeed, this was one of the biggest challenges I faced in *Windows Network Programming* —how to appear to block without actually blocking. In Windows 3.X, blocking calls can shut down the entire system. Under Windows NT, this problem no longer exists. Windows NT, like the UNIX platform that the Berkeley Sockets interface was first developed for, is a preemptive multitasking system. For this reason, generic Berkeley Sockets code will port much more easily to Windows NT than to Windows 3.X.

Berkeley Sockets to Windows Sockets

Elsewhere in this book, I am not greatly concerned with writing portable code because you cannot take advantage of the power of NT without using the Win32 API, which is only minimally portable. However, portability deserves a little more respect here because porting code between Windows Sockets and Berkeley Sockets is feasible. From what I have seen in my wanderings, it is also something that people want to do. Therefore, I will first discuss the most generic (that is, Berkeley-compatible) way to use Windows Sockets, then look more closely at the Windows extensions.

Basic Windows Sockets

WSAStartup()

Before making any other Windows Sockets calls, you must initialize the Windows Sockets DLL by calling WSAStartup(), which, of course, is not portable.

```
int WSAStartup(
      WORD        wVersionRequired,
      LPWSADATA lpWSAData);
```

wVersionRequired indicates the highest version of the Windows Sockets DLL you need. You use it to negotiate version compatibility with the DLL. The low byte specifies the major version you want, and the high byte indicates the minor version. MAKEWORD(1, 1), or 0x0101, requests version 1.1, currently the only version supported by Windows NT. If the DLL cannot support the version you request, WSAStartup() returns -1, and WSAGetLastError(), which is the Sockets equivalent to GetLastError(), reports WSAVERNOTSUPPORTED. A return value of zero indicates a successful initialization.

Windows Sockets includes version negotiation because under Windows 3.X many vendors offer Sockets implementations. The situation is very different with NT because WSOCK32.DLL ships with the operating system.

lpWSAData points to a WSADATA structure that returns information on the configuration of the DLL. Here is its *typedef* from \MSTOOLS\ H\WINSOCK.H:

```
typedef struct WSAData
{
    WORD                wVersion;
    WORD                wHighVersion;
    char                szDescription[WSADESCRIPTION_LEN+1];
    char                szSystemStatus[WSASYS_STATUS_LEN+1];
    unsigned short      iMaxSockets;
    unsigned short      iMaxUdpDg;
    char FAR *          lpVendorInfo;
} WSADATA;
```

wVersion is the version of Windows Sockets that the DLL thinks the application will use; *wHighVersion* is the highest version it can support. Normally, these two fields are the same. *szDescription* is a signature string, and *szSystemStatus* can be used to report status or configuration information. NT puts "Microsoft Windows Sockets Version 1.1." in *szDescription*, and "Running." in *szSystemStatus* when you call WSAStartup().

iMaxSockets is the maximum number of sockets available to the application; *iMaxUdpDg* is the largest datagram the application can send. NT Windows Sockets returns 32,767 and 65,467 in these fields. *lpVendorInfo* is not defined in the documentation; its use is vendor-specific.

Once you have initialized the DLL by calling WSAStartup(), you are ready to begin using Windows Sockets. The next thing a server application must do is obtain a socket to use in listening for client connection requests. It does this by calling the socket() function, then calling bind() to associate the socket with its machine address and service endpoint.

Opening a Socket

socket() opens a socket. Sockets are analogous to HANDLEs; they are just communications channels. As with HANDLEs, it is not necessary to know what they are to use them effectively in applications. (In fact, as you will see, in NT a socket *is* a HANDLE.)

```
typedef unsigned int SOCKET;
SOCKET PASCAL FAR socket(int af, int type, int protocol);
```

af denotes the address family. For Internet addresses, the address family is AF_INET or PF_INET (both defined as 2). For NetWare addressing, the address family is AF_NS, where NS comes from XNS (Xerox Network Systems) or AF_IPX.

type specifies whether you want to do connection-oriented or datagram communications. SOCK_DGRAM requests datagram service. Over TCP/IP,

SOCK_STREAM specifies connection-oriented service. Over NWLink, you can also request a socket type of SOCK_SEQPACKET (sequenced-packet socket) for connection-oriented service using SPX. You get better performance with a sequenced-packet socket than with a stream socket over IPX/SPX.

For Internet addresses, the address family and socket type determine the protocol, so you just pass *protocol* as zero. Stream sockets use TCP; datagram sockets use UDP (the User Datagram Protocol). This is not the case for NetWare addresses; you must pass *protocol* as NSPROTO_IPX for a SOCK_DGRAM socket, or as NSPROTO_SPX or NSPROTO_SPXII for a SOCK_STREAM or SOCK_SEQPACKET socket.

Binding to a Machine Address and Service Endpoint

The next thing the server must do is bind the socket to its machine address and service endpoint. The bind() function accomplishes this.

```
int PASCAL bind(SOCKET s, const struct sockaddr *addr, int namelen);
```

s is the socket returned by socket(). Because machine addresses and endpoints vary from one address family to another, *addr* points to a structure that represents the information in a neutral way.

```
struct sockaddr
{
   u_short sa_family;
   char    sa_data[14];
};
typedef struct sockaddr SOCKADDR, *PSOCKADDR, FAR *LPSOCKADDR;
```

sa_family is the address family and describes the format of the address. The *sa_data* field maps to a protocol-specific address representation.

For TCP/IP, the *sockaddr_in* type holds this specific data:

```
struct sockaddr_in
{
   short   sin_family;
   u_short sin_port;
   struct  in_addr sin_addr;
   char    sin_zero[8];
};
typedef struct sockaddr_in SOCKADDR_IN, *PSOCKADDR_IN,
                           FAR *LPSOCKADDR_IN;
```

The *sa_data* field of the *sockaddr* corresponds to *sin_port, sin_addr,* and *sin_zero* in the *sockaddr_in. sin_addr* is a 4-byte Internet address; the *struct in_addr* is actually a union that lets you view the address as four bytes, two shorts, or one long. *sin_zero* is padding, but must be set to zero for the bind() call.

For an IPX address, the address is represented by a *struct sockaddr_ipx,* defined in WSIPX.H:

```
typedef struct sockaddr_ipx
{
    short   sa_family;
    char    sa_netnum[4];
    char    sa_nodenum[6];
    unsigned short sa_socket;
} SOCKADDR_IPX, *PSOCKADDR_IPX, FAR *LPSOCKADDR_IPX;
```

An IPX machine address consists of a 4-byte network number (*sa_netnum*) followed by a 6-byte node number (*sa_nodenum*). The service endpoint is an IPX socket (*sa_socket*).

Before you can bind to your address, you need to find out what it is. The way you do this differs between TCP/IP and NWLink. I'll first explain how to determine a TCP/IP address.

TCP/IP Addresses. The TCP/IP binding process takes a human-readable host name, service name, and protocol, then maps it to a binary address. How the mapping is done depends on the underlying TCP/IP implementation. Some versions use database files; by convention, these are called **hosts** and **services** and stored in the /etc directory on UNIX systems. Other implementations use a Distributed Name Server (DNS), where the address translation requires a network exchange. NT supports either scheme; I have my network configured to use local hosts and services files, which are stored in \%SystemRoot%\SYSTEM32\DRIVERS\ETC. My hosts file provides for machines named NUMBER1 through NUMBER12; each of these maps to a fictitious Internet address from 126.0.0.1 to 126.0.0.12. Here's what it looks like:

```
# Copyright (c) 1993 Microsoft Corp.
#
# This is a sample HOSTS file used by Microsoft TCP/IP for Windows NT
# 3.1
#
# This file contains the mappings of IP addresses to host names. Each
# entry should be kept on an individual line. The IP address should
```

```
# be placed in the first column followed by the corresponding host name.
# The IP address and the host name should be separated by at least one
# space.
#
# Additionally, comments (such as these) may be inserted on individual
# lines or following the machine name denoted by a '#' symbol.
#
# For example:
#
#      102.54.94.97       rhino.acme.com          # source server
#       38.25.63.10       x.acme.com              # x client host

127.0.0.1          localhost

126.0.0.1          NUMBER1
126.0.0.2          NUMBER2
126.0.0.3          NUMBER3
126.0.0.4          NUMBER4
126.0.0.5          NUMBER5
126.0.0.6          NUMBER6
126.0.0.7          NUMBER7
126.0.0.8          NUMBER8
126.0.0.9          NUMBER9
126.0.0.10         NUMBER10
126.0.0.11         NUMBER11
126.0.0.12         NUMBER12
```

The binary Internet address (in dot notation) is the first field on the line. The translation scheme finds the requested machine name and returns the corresponding Internet address as a long integer in high-low format. For instance, a request to look up the address of my MIPS server (NUMBER1) returns the bytes **0x7E 0 0 1**, in that order.

In Berkeley Sockets, gethostbyname() maps a name to an Internet address. Here is the prototype from WINSOCK.H:

```
struct hostent FAR * PASCAL FAR gethostbyname(const char FAR *name);
```

WINSOCK.H also defines a Microsoft-style type LPHOSTENT for the return value. The FAR specifiers vanish under Windows NT; here's a simplified prototype, using Microsoft types:

```
LPHOSTENT PASCAL gethostbyname(LPCSTR name);
```

name is the human-readable machine name. The *hostent* structure is defined as follows (omitting the unnecessary and irritating FARs):

```
struct hostent
{
    char    *h_name;
    char    **h_aliases;
    short    h_addrtype;
    short    h_length;
    char    **h_addr_list;
#define h_addr h_addr_list[0]
};
```

h_name gives back the *name* argument that you passed to gethostbyname(). A machine can also be known by aliases; these follow the primary name on the line of the hosts file. *h_aliases* is an array of pointers to them. *h_addrtype* is the address family. *h_length* tells you how long the address is, and *h_addr_list* is an array of addresses. The definition of *h_addr* as *h_addr_list[0]* is for backward compatibility. Normally, *h_addr* is the machine address you need to bind to.

The Berkeley Sockets function getservbyname() takes a service name and protocol and returns the corresponding port number. Here is its Microsoft-style prototype:

```
LPSERVENT PASCAL getservbyname(LPCSTR name,
                               LPCSTR proto);
```

In a file-based TCP/IP implementation like mine, this information is fetched from the services file (%SystemRoot%\SYSTEM32\DRIVERS\ ETC\SERVICES). This file is quite long; it has entries for all the standard TCP/IP services. I show here only the portion that describes ports and protocols that I use.

```
# Copyright (c) 1993 Microsoft Corp.
#
# This file contains port numbers for well-known services as defined by
# RFC 1060 (Assigned Numbers).
#
# Format:
#
# <service name>  <port number>/<protocol>  [aliases...]  [#<comment>]
#
wnetsrvr          20000/tcp
wnetsrvr          20001/udp
wnetbnch          30000/tcp
wnetsrvr          26437/ipx      # 0x4567 in network byte order
wnetsrvr          22342/spx      # 0x4657 in network byte order
wnetbnch          17733/spx      # 0x4545 in network byte order
```

The service name is the first field on the line. The next field has the port number and protocol name.

getservbyname() returns a pointer to a *struct servent*.

```
struct servent
{
    char        *s_name;
    char        **s_aliases;
    short       s_port;
    char        *s_proto;
};
```

s_name and *s_proto* parrot the arguments passed to getservbyname(). Like hosts, services can also have aliases, and these are reported in *s_aliases*. Most importantly, *s_port* is the endpoint needed for binding.

The addresses returned by gethostbyname() and getservbyname() point to thread-specific static buffers. Any subsequent calls from the same thread will overwrite whatever was stored there previously.

Here is the function _WNetGetHostAddress() from the level-zero TCP/IP library, \NTNET\CODE\%Cpu%\WNETTCP.DLL. It takes a machine name, service name, and protocol name, and returns a SOCKADDR structure formatted so that it can be immediately passed to bind().

```
// _WNetGetHostAddress() populates a SOCKADDR structure with the
// Internet address of the local machine, and the port number of
// the requested process

BOOL WINAPI _WNetGetHostAddress(LPCSTR lpszHost, LPCSTR lpszService,
                                LPCSTR lpszProto,
                                LPSOCKADDR lpAddr)
{
    LPHOSTENT lpHost;
    LPSERVENT lpServ;
    SOCKADDR_IN sin;

    lpHost = gethostbyname(lpszHost);
    if (lpHost != NULL)
        {
        sin.sin_family = PF_INET;
        CopyMemory(&sin.sin_addr, lpHost->h_addr_list[0],
                lpHost->h_length);
        lpServ = getservbyname(lpszService, lpszProto);
        if (lpServ != NULL)
            {
            sin.sin_port = lpServ->s_port;
```

```
        ZeroMemory(sin.sin_zero, sizeof (sin.sin_zero));
        CopyMemory(lpAddr, &sin, sizeof (SOCKADDR));
        return TRUE;
        }
    }
   return FALSE;
}
```

For example, to get the binding address of the WNETSRVR service using TCP on the local machine, call _WNetGetHostAddress() as follows:

```
SOCKADDR sa;
char szMyName[256];

// gethostname() is the Berkeley function that tells you
// who you are
// It will normally return the same answer as GetComputerName(),
// but a machine can be configured so the two names are different.
gethostname(szMyName, sizeof (szMyName));
_WNetGetHostAddress(szMyName, "wnetsrvr", "tcp", &sa);
```

IPX Addresses. Binding to an IPX address is more complicated, for the simple reason that IPX has never had a human-readable scheme for naming stations. It has always used binary addresses. This forces you either to implement your own name-to-address mapping scheme or present your users with gobbledy-gook like **00000001:00C0D1800E65** (the IPX address of my MIPS server). To integrate NetWare into my network management scheme, I had to come up with a name mapping strategy. The first one I developed is modeled on the TCP/IP scheme: a NWHOSTS.INI file that lists the stations on my network and their IPX addresses. By the way, I cannot park this file in the Registry, as you ordinarily should. I use these machine names in a variety of situations, where the underlying IPX addresses are different.

```
;********
;
; NWHOSTS.INI
;
; NetWare name-to-station address mapping file
;
;********


[HOSTS]
NUMBER1=00000001:00C0D1800E65
NUMBER10=00000001:00001B3D4FF5
```

I could not shake the feeling that this was a terrible implementation, so I devised a second method. It uses the NetBIOS Find Name command, which queries the network for a station with the requested name and returns its node address if it finds one. Though not a perfect solution, this is certainly superior to the use of an .INI file. (Chapter 12 discusses the NETBIOS API.)

The Sockets function gethostbyname() knows nothing about either of these mapping schemes, so the IPX/SPX version of _WNetGetHost Address() has its own support function, NWGetHostByName(). getservbyname(), by contrast, works fine, as long as we fool it by adding the appropriate lines to the SERVICES file, such as

```
wnetsrvr        26437/ipx
wnetsrvr        22342/spx
```

(The numbers 26437 and 22342 are 0x4567 and 0x4657 in network byte order. These are IPX socket numbers that I pulled out of my hat, within the range specified for application-private sockets.)

Here is the listing of \NTNET\CODE\WINSOCK\NETWARE\ _WNETGHA.CPP. _WNetGetHostAddress() has not changed much, but the support routines are quite different. Notice that if the NetBIOS Find Name succeeds, I return the network number as zero. NWLink fills it in automatically.

```
/********
 *
 * _WNETGHA.CPP
 *
 * Copyright (c) 1992-1994 Ralph P. Davis, All Rights Reserved
 *
 * Contains IPX/SPX version of _WNetGetHostAddress()
 *
 ********/


/*===== Includes =====*/

#include "wnetws.h"
#include <nb30.h>
#include <string.h>


/*===== Local Functions =====*/

static BOOL NWGetHostByName(LPCSTR lpszHost, SOCKADDR_IPX *psipx);
static char *HexStringToBinary(char *pIn, char *pOut, char cChar);
```

```
/*===== Function Definitions =====*/

// _WNetGetHostAddress() populates a SOCKADDR_IPX structure with the
// IPX address of the requested machine, and the IPX socket of
// the requested process

BOOL WINAPI _WNetGetHostAddress(LPCSTR lpszHost, LPCSTR lpszService,
                                LPCSTR lpszProto,
                                LPSOCKADDR lpAddr)
{
   LPSERVENT lpServ;
   SOCKADDR_IPX sipx;

   if (NWGetHostByName(lpszHost, &sipx))
      {
      sipx.sa_family = AF_NS;
      lpServ = getservbyname(lpszService, lpszProto);
      if (lpServ != NULL)
         {
         sipx.sa_socket = lpServ->s_port;
         CopyMemory(lpAddr, &sipx, sizeof (SOCKADDR));
         return TRUE;
         }
      }
   return FALSE;
}

static BOOL NWGetHostByName(LPCSTR lpszHost, SOCKADDR_IPX *psipx)
{
   char  szName[256];
   char *pTemp;
   BOOL  bContinue = TRUE;
   NCB   NCBFindName;
   struct
      {
      FIND_NAME_HEADER FindNameHeader;
      FIND_NAME_BUFFER FindNameBuffer;
      } NBFindName;
   NCB   NCBReset;
   UCHAR uReturnCode;

   FillMemory(psipx, sizeof (SOCKADDR_IPX), '\0');
   psipx->sa_family = AF_NS;

   // Try NetBIOS Find Name first
   // If it fails, we'll look for NWHOSTS.INI,
   // which is the worst way to do things here.
   while (bContinue)
```

```
    {
    bContinue = FALSE; // Will be set to TRUE if we have to do a RESET
    ZeroMemory(&NBFindName, sizeof (NBFindName));
    ZeroMemory(&NCBFindName, sizeof (NCB));

    FillMemory(NCBFindName.ncb_callname, NCBNAMSZ, ' ');

    // Have to force name to upper case for NetBIOS
    // We also have to force the use of the ANSI
    // version of CharUpperBuff()
    CopyMemory(NCBFindName.ncb_callname,
        lpszHost, lstrlenA(lpszHost));
    CharUpperBuffA((LPSTR) NCBFindName.ncb_callname,
        lstrlenA(lpszHost));
    NCBFindName.ncb_command = NCBFINDNAME;
    NCBFindName.ncb_buffer = (PUCHAR) &NBFindName;
    NCBFindName.ncb_length = sizeof (NBFindName);

    if ((uReturnCode = Netbios(&NCBFindName)) != NRC_GOODRET)
        {
        if (uReturnCode == NRC_ENVNOTDEF)
            {
            // NRC_ENVNOTDEF is returned when no one has done
            // a NetBIOS RESET, so do one
            ZeroMemory(&NCBReset, sizeof (NCB));
            NCBReset.ncb_command = NCBRESET;
            NCBReset.ncb_num = 64;
            if (Netbios(&NCBReset) == NRC_GOODRET)
                bContinue = TRUE;
            }
        }
    else
        {
        // It worked, copy the net node up
        // Reported in source_addr field of FIND NAME buffer
        CopyMemory(psipx->sa_nodenum,
            NBFindName.FindNameBuffer.source_addr,
            sizeof (psipx->sa_nodenum));
        return TRUE;
        }
    }

GetPrivateProfileStringA("HOSTS", lpszHost, "",
    szName, sizeof (szName), "NWHOSTS.INI");

if (szName[0] == '\0')
    return FALSE;
```

```
    // Extract network number
    pTemp = HexStringToBinary(szName, psipx->sa_netnum, ':');

    // Now get the node number
    HexStringToBinary(++pTemp, psipx->sa_nodenum, '\0');
    return TRUE;
}

static char *HexStringToBinary(char *pIn, char *pOut, char cChar)
{
    BOOL bToggle = TRUE;

    while (*pIn != cChar)
        {
        if (*pIn >= '0' && *pIn <= '9')
            {
            *pOut += (*pIn++ - '0');
            if (bToggle)
                *pOut <<= 4;
            else
                ++pOut;
            }
        else if (*pIn >= 'a' && *pIn <= 'f')
            {
            *pOut += (*pIn++ - 'a' + 0x0a);
            if (bToggle)
                *pOut <<= 4;
            else
                ++pOut;
            }
        else if (*pIn >= 'A' && *pIn <= 'F')
            {
            *pOut += (*pIn++ - 'A' + 0x0a);
            if (bToggle)
                *pOut <<= 4;
            else
                ++pOut;
            }
        bToggle = !bToggle;
        }
    return pIn;
}
```

Once the server has bound a socket to its address and endpoint, it is ready to call listen(). This makes it fully available for client applications to connect to. From this point on, there are only a few minor differences between TCP/IP and IPX/SPX.

Putting a Server into the Listening State

listen() takes the server application from the bound to the listening state.

```
int PASCAL listen(SOCKET s, int backlog);
```

backlog indicates the number of connection requests you are willing to have queued at the socket; it must be from one to five. If you pass an argument outside this range, Windows Sockets will quietly scale it so that it is within the limits; it won't fail the function. The *backlog* is in addition to any client already being serviced. With a *backlog* of one, for example, one client application can connect to the server and exchange data. While this is going on, another client application that tries to connect on a blocking socket will go into orbit. To be precise, it will think that it has actually connected to the server, but its first attempt to transmit data will block until the server calls accept().

Accepting Client Connections

As soon as the server has called listen(), it must turn around and invoke accept(). The call to listen() puts the socket into the listening state. It does not block. accept(), on the other hand, does not return until a client request comes in.

```
SOCKET PASCAL accept(SOCKET s, LPSOCKADDR lpAddr, LPINT lpLength);
```

s is the socket that the server is listening on. *lpAddr* will return the address of a connecting client, and *lpLength* will report the length of the address. The return value from accept() is a new socket descriptor; this socket is the one that the server uses to exchange data with the client. The socket that you pass to listen() is never used for any other purpose.

Client-Side Calls

To establish a connection to a server, a client must also open a socket in the same manner as the server. It is not necessary for the client to bind the socket; Windows Sockets will assign an unbound socket a unique binding identifier when it connects to a server. The function that requests a connection is connect().

```
int PASCAL connect(SOCKET s, const struct sockaddr *name, int namelen);
```

s is the socket that the client has obtained by calling socket(). *name* is a SOCKADDR containing the machine address and service endpoint of the server. This must be populated in the same way that the server found out its own address, using the calls shown above in _WNetGetHostAddress().

Exchange of Data

Once a connection is established, the partner stations have several ways to exchange data.

recv()/send(). One option uses the recv() and send() functions, which are standard Berkeley Sockets calls. They have nearly identical arguments.

```
int PASCAL send(SOCKET s, LPCSTR buf, int len, int flags);

int PASCAL recv(SOCKET s, LPSTR buf, int len, int flags);
```

flags is the only argument needing explanation. For send(), the flag MSG_OOB indicates that the data should be sent on an urgent basis (OOB stands for out-of-band). There is also an NT extension to Windows Sockets, the MSG_PARTIAL flag. This indicates to the underlying transport driver that the packet you are sending constitutes a fragment of a larger message, and that more transmissions will follow. For recv(), the MSG_OOB flag says that you want to receive out-of-band data. MSG_PEEK can be used to peek at the data without removing it from the incoming queue. The use of MSG_OOB is discouraged, because the TCP/IP community has still not settled on what its precise semantic significance should be.

The send() and recv() functions return the number of bytes written or read, or SOCKET_ERROR (-1) if they fail. As with all Windows Sockets functions, you can get the specific error code by calling WSAGetLastError().

Windows Sockets implements send() and recv() exactly the same as Berkeley Sockets. Therefore, this is the most Berkeley-compatible way to exchange data.

_read()/_write(). Under UNIX, it is more common to use _read() and _write(), because UNIX treats sockets as files. Their syntax is very much like send() and recv(), omitting only the *flags* argument.

```
int _read(int handle, void *buffer, unsigned int count);
int _write(int handle, const void *buffer, unsigned int count);
```

You can use these functions with Windows Sockets on NT, but you cannot pass a socket as the first argument. You have to convert it to a file handle by calling _open_osfhandle(), which is a Win32 extension to the C runtime library.

```
int _open_osfhandle (long osfhandle, int flags);
```

Pass the socket as the *osfhandle* argument; *flags* takes on the same values as when you open a file: _O_RDWR (read-write access), _O_RDONLY (read-only access), _O_BINARY or _O_TEXT (to request raw or translated I/O). The return value is a handle you can then pass to _read() or _write(). For example:

```
#include <winsock.h>
#include <io.h>
#include <fcntl.h>
SOCKET s;
int    nFileHandle;
s = socket(AF_INET, SOCK_STREAM, 0);
nFileHandle = _open_osfhandle(s, _O_RDWR | _O_BINARY);
```

Now, you can use *nFileHandle* as input to _read() and _write().

ReadFile()/WriteFile(). By default, Windows NT opens sockets as overlapped NT file handles (which are not equivalent to C runtime file handles). Therefore, you can pass a socket to ReadFile() or WriteFile() without modification. The socket behaves exactly as the file handles discussed in Chapter 7 and the pipes covered in Chapter 10. Because it is opened for overlapped I/O, you have to follow the procedure I outlined in those chapters:

1. Create a manual-reset event, and put its handle into an OVERLAPPED structure.
2. Call ReadFile() or WriteFile(), passing the socket as the first argument and a pointer to the OVERLAPPED structure as the last.
3. If the return value is FALSE and GetLastError() returns ERROR_IO_PENDING, call WaitForSingleObject(), passing it the handle of the event you created in step 1 and the timeout you want.
4. If WaitForSingleObject() returns WAIT_OBJECT_0, call GetOverlappedResult() to find out how many bytes were successfully transferred.

You can force your sockets to be created in non-overlapped mode by calling the setsockopt() function with the SO_OPENTYPE socket option.

```
int nOption = SO_SYNCHRONOUS_NONALERT;
setsockopt(INVALID_SOCKET, SOL_SOCKET, SO_OPENTYPE,
    (char *) &nOption, sizeof (int));
```

This call to setsockopt() affects only sockets created after you call it, and only those sockets belonging to the current thread. setsockopt(), by the way, is standard Berkeley, but SO_OPENTYPE is not even part of Windows Sockets—it is a Windows NT extension.

Of these options, send() and recv() are the simplest and most Berkeley-compatible, as they do not require any special handling. _read() and _write() oblige you to convert a socket into a C runtime file handle. With ReadFile() and WriteFile(), you have to make the additional calls to WaitForSingleObject() and GetOverlappedResult(), since you are dealing with an overlapped Win32 file handle. I have not observed any significant difference in performance among these three approaches.

Datagram Service

For datagram service, there is no need for the server to call listen(), nor for the client to call connect().To receive datagrams, however, a station must bind to a local endpoint using a datagram protocol (either UDP or IPX). Also, to send a datagram using IPX, the sender must bind its local socket. This is not necessary over TCP/IP.

Once the datagram sockets are opened, the stations send and receive data using sendto() and recvfrom(). sendto() and recvfrom() take the same arguments as send() and recv(), but add two for the partner station.

```
int PASCAL sendto(SOCKET s, LPCSTR buf, int len, int flags,
                  const struct sockaddr *to, int tolen);

int PASCAL recvfrom(SOCKET s, LPSTR buf, int len, int flags,
                    LPSOCKADDR from, LPINT fromlen);
```

With sendto(), *to* and *tolen* indicate where to send the data. With recvfrom(), *from* and *fromlen* capture the address of the sending station. sendto() and recvfrom() are actually more general versions of send() and recv(). They can also be used with connection-oriented sockets, in which case the last two arguments are ignored. With datagrams, the *flags* argument cannot be MSG_OOB. After all, it doesn't make sense to send an urgent message using a protocol that doesn't guarantee delivery.

You can also use _read()/_write() or ReadFile()/WriteFile(), as I discussed earlier, but sendto() and recvfrom() provide the simplest and most Berkeley-compatible means of data exchange on a datagram socket.

Closing a Socket

Finally, when you are done exchanging data, you close the socket. In standard Berkeley Sockets, you can just call close() because the socket is a file. CloseHandle() might be enough in Windows Sockets, but closesocket() is better because it allows Window Sockets to do its own cleanup.

```
int PASCAL closesocket(SOCKET s);
```

For connection-oriented communications, the server application closes the socket created by accept(), not the one originally returned by socket(). Only when the server goes out of service altogether should it close the listening socket.

Shutting Down

The last thing you have to do is call WSACleanup() to let the Windows Sockets DLL know you are finished using it. Of course, this function is also non-portable.

```
int PASCAL WSACleanup(void);
```

Each call to WSAStartup() must be balanced by a WSACleanup(). You will notice in the code later in this chapter that I call WSAStartup() during DLL_PROCESS_ATTACH handling, but call WSACleanup() in the _WNetShutdown() function. Of course, it makes more sense to call WSACleanup() during DLL_PROCESS_DETACH notification, but this caused strange problems—specifically, the Windows Sockets DLL seemed to have gone away before I got around to calling WSACleanup(). By putting the WSACleanup() in _WNetShutdown(), I know that the Sockets support DLL is still around.

Other Portability Considerations

So far, I have discussed only how Sockets calls behave in blocking mode. Frequently, it is desirable to put a socket into non-blocking mode. In Berkeley Sockets, this is done using the ioctl() function, which is a UNIX system call for configuring an I/O device. There is no ioctl() in the C runtime library for either Windows 3.X or Windows NT, so Windows Sockets provides ioctlsocket().

```
int PASCAL ioctlsocket(SOCKET s, long cmd, u_long *argp);
```

This function plays several roles with respect to sockets. To put a socket into non-blocking mode, pass *cmd* as the constant FIONBIO, and point *argp* to a non-zero variable. On a blocking socket in standard Berkeley usage, the functions accept(), connect(), send(), recv(), sendto(), and recvfrom() do not return until they have completed the requested action. None of these functions includes a timeout parameter, so once they block, you have no control over how long they stay blocked. On a non-blocking socket, on the other hand, they return immediately. You can call the select() function to detect the occurrence of an event—a client connection request, the arrival of a packet, and so on—before you call the relevant function. select() blocks until an event of interest occurs. It also lets you specify a timeout, so it is similar to WaitForMultipleObjects() in that respect.

However, select() is very cumbersome to use, and Windows Sockets offers several useful alternatives. For one thing, you can do overlapped I/O with ReadFile() and WriteFile(), and specify a timeout in your call to WaitForSingleObject(). NT also offers extensions that allow you to set send() and recv() timeouts using setsockopt(). They use the SO_SNDTIMEO and SO_RCVTIMEO socket options, and pass the timeout value in milliseconds. For example:

```
SOCKET s;
int nTimeout = 5000;   // 5-second timeout
s = socket(AF_INET, SOCK_STREAM, 0);
setsockopt(s, SOL_SOCKET, SO_RCVTIMEO, (char *) &nTimeout,
    sizeof (int));
```

Once you have done this, the send() and recv() functions will only block for the amount of time you have specified; they will not block indefinitely. This only works on sockets opened for overlapped I/O.

Finally, Windows Sockets offers the WSAAsyncSelect() function, which puts a socket into non-blocking mode and requests notification of events that occur on it. WSAAsyncSelect() constitutes the bulk of the next section of this chapter, so I defer my discussion until then.

Berkeley to Windows Sockets—A Brief Summary

To summarize, standard Berkeley Sockets calls will port to Windows Sockets, with these exceptions:

- You must call WSAStartup() to initialize the Windows Sockets DLL.
- You must use ioctlsocket() (which is not portable) to configure the socket.
- You can use _read() and _write() to receive and send data, but only after converting the socket descriptor to a file handle by calling _open_ofshandle.
- You must use closesocket() (which is not portable), rather than close() (which is), to close a socket.
- You must call WSACleanup() to shut down the DLL.

The following core functions work the same in both environments, with subtle variations, because a socket is an *unsigned* int in Windows Sockets and an *int* in Berkeley. Therefore, with functions like socket() or accept(), you should test for return values of INVALID_SOCKET (defined as ~0) instead of -1.

- socket()
- bind()
- listen()
- accept()
- connect()
- send()
- recv()
- sendto()
- recvfrom()

The Windows Sockets implementation of select() is syntactically the same as the Berkeley version, but uses arrays of SOCKETs, rather than bit strings.

Windows Sockets Extensions

Windows Sockets has a handful of functions with WSA prefixes that offer asynchronous execution and message-posting. By far the most important of them is WSAAsyncSelect().

WSAAsyncSelect()

WSAAsyncSelect() has two effects: it puts a socket into non-blocking mode, and it asks to have a message posted to a window when certain events occur. Here is its prototype:

```
int PASCAL WSAAsyncSelect(SOCKET s, HWND hWnd, u_int wMsg, long lEvent);
```

What WSAAsyncSelect() says in effect is this: when any of the events described in *lEvent* occur on the socket *s*, post message *wMsg* to window *hWnd*. The possible bit settings for *lEvent*, and the events they represent, are

- FD_READ: Data is available for reading.
- FD_WRITE: The socket can be written to.
- FD_OOB: Urgent data needs to be read.
- FD_ACCEPT: A client request for a connection has arrived.
- FD_CONNECT: A client's attempt to connect to a server has completed.
- FD_CLOSE: The socket has been closed by the partner station.

WSAAsyncSelect() requires that the socket be asynchronous (overlapped). Each call to WSAAsyncSelect() replaces the previous call. Thus, if you want notification of multiple events, as you often do, you must OR the appropriate flags together. Passing *lEvent* as zero cancels notification for the socket.

When the window procedure for the notification window is called, *wParam* contains the socket number. *lParam* contains the event code and any error that may have occurred. The event status can be retrieved using the WSAGETSELECTERROR() macro, as follows:

```
WORD wError;
wError = WSAGETSELECTERROR(lParam);
```

If the error code is zero, the operation was successful. For a list of the possible errors, see Error Codes in the Windows Sockets on-line help. The reference page for each function describes the possible errors more thoroughly. I have found it a helpful practice to print the return value of WSAGetLastError() whenever a problem occurs, perhaps by calling a routine like printfConsole(), which I use all the time. Table 11-1 shows some of the error codes I have encountered and the situations that provoked them.

Table 11-1.   Some Common Windows Sockets Error Codes

Defined Constant	Numeric Value	Situation Where Arose
WSAENOTSOCK	10038	A socket created in one process is used by another process.
WSAEADDRINUSE	10048	Triggered by bind() because a process went down without closing a socket. When you attempt to start the process again, the socket is still bound to the previous socket, and the new bind() fails.
WSAENOBUFS	10055	One of the asynchronous database routines such as WSAGetHostBy Name() was called with an output buffer that was too small.
WSAETIMEDOUT	10060	A client application got bored waiting for connect() to complete.
WSAECONNREFUSED	10061	A client application could not connect to a server because the server backlog was full.
WSAVERNOTSUPPORTED	10092	Calling WSAStartup() and asking for version 1.0.
WSANOTINITIALISED	10093	You didn't call WSAStartup().

The WSAGETSELECTEVENT() macro reports the event.

```
WORD wEvent;
wEvent = WSAGETSELECTEVENT(lParam);
```

It is not necessary to reissue the WSAAsyncSelect(); it is automatically reactivated when you call the enabling function. For FD_READ or FD_OOB events, these are ReadFile(), read(), recv(), and recvfrom(). For FD_ACCEPT, it is accept(). For FD_WRITE, they are WriteFile(), write(), send(), and sendto(). You only need to call WSAAsyncSelect() again when you want notification of different events or when you want to cancel notification altogether.

Use of WSAAsyncSelect() on the Server Side. This is a typical sequence of events in a server application:

1. Create a socket and bind your address to it.
2. Call WSAAsyncSelect(), and request FD_ACCEPT notification.
3. Call listen(), and go on to other tasks.
4. When a connection request comes in, the notification window receives the message and the FD_ACCEPT notification. Respond by calling accept() to complete the connection.
5. Call WSAAsyncSelect () to request FD_READ | FD_OOB | FD_CLOSE notification for the socket created by accept(). This causes notifications to be sent to you when the client sends data or when the client closes the socket it is using.
6. When you receive FD_READ or FD_OOB notification, call ReadFile(), read(), recv(), or recvfrom() to retrieve the data.
7. Respond to FD_CLOSE notification by calling closesocket() with the socket returned by accept().

Use of WSAAsyncSelect() on the Client Side. On the client, a typical scenario might be:

1. Create a socket.
2. Call WSAAsyncSelect() and request FD_CONNECT notification.
3. Call connect(). It returns immediately, and you are free to do something else.
4. When the FD_CONNECT notification comes in telling you that the connection you requested has been established, request FD_READ | FD_OOB | FD_CLOSE notification on the socket (reported in *wParam*).
5. When data from the server arrives, the notification window receives FD_READ or FD_OOB events. You respond by calling ReadFile(), read(), recv(), or recvfrom().

Normally, the client initiates the closing of the connection because the client knows when it no longer needs the services that the server is offering. However, the client should be prepared for an FD_CLOSE notification and close its own socket in response to it.

WSAAsyncSelect() is a very powerful function. Both my Windows Sockets servers (for TCP/IP and NWLink) are built around it. Because of WSAAsyncSelect(), there is no need to multithread a Windows Sockets server; WSAAsyncSelect() provides implicit multithreading. It also removes the need to allocate buffer space before you post an asynchronous receive request. Windows Sockets buffers the data for you, then tells you to come and get it. You can allocate space at the precise moment when you need it. You can find out exactly how much memory to allocate by calling ioctlsocket() with the command code FIONREAD.

```
SOCKET s;
u_long ulBytesAvailable;
LPBYTE lpBuffer;

if ((ioctlsocket(s, FIONREAD, &ulBytesAvailable) == 0) &&
   (ulBytesAvailable > 0))
   {
   lpBuffer = (LPBYTE) VirtualAlloc(NULL, ulBytesAvailable,
                        MEM_COMMIT, PAGE_READWRITE);
   recv(s, lpBuffer, ulBytesAvailable, 0);
   }
```

Miscellaneous WSA Functions

There are several other miscellaneous WSA functions. Most of them are asynchronous versions of functions like gethostbyname() and getservbyname() and are referred to as the WSAAsyncGetXByY() functions. They are provided because some TCP/IP implementations call a Distributed Name Service (DNS) server to do the mappings, so the getXbyY() calls trigger network activity, and can block. The complete set of WSAAsyncGetXByY() functions are listed in Table 11-2.

Table 11-2. WSAAsyncGetXByY() Functions

Function Name	Purpose
WSAAsyncGetServByName	Retrieve service information based on the service name ("telnet", "ftp", "wnetsrvr", and so on)
WSAAsyncGetServByPort	Retrieve service information based on the service's port number
WSAAsyncGetProtoByName	Get protocol information based on the protocol name ("tcp", "udp", and so on)
WSAAsyncGetProtoByNumber	Get protocol information based on the protocol number (IPPROTO_TCP, NSPROTO_SPX, and so on)
WSAAsyncGetHostByName	Get machine's Internet address based on its name
WSAAsyncGetHostByAddr	Get machine information based on its Internet address

WSAGetHostByName(), the asynchronous counterpart to gethostbyname(), is typical.

```
HANDLE PASCAL WSAAsyncGetHostByName(
                HWND    hWnd
                u_int   wMsg,
                LPCSTR  name,
                LPSTR   lpBuffer,
                int     buflen);
```

When invoked, WSAAsyncGetHostByName() returns immediately; its return value is a task handle. When the asynchronous activity completes, the Windows Sockets DLL copies the *hostent* structure to the buffer pointed to by *lpBuffer*, then posts the *wMsg* message to *hWnd*. The *wParam* for the message will be the task handle originally returned by WSAAsyncGetHostByName(). The high word of *lParam* will contain the status of the operation, with zero indicating success. The error code can be extracted with the WSAGETASYNCERROR() macro.

```
WORD wError;
wError = WSAGETASYNCERROR(lParam);
```

If the error code is WSAENOBUFS, *lpBuffer* was not large enough to accommodate all the output information. In this case, the low word of *lParam* tells you how much space you need to allocate. The WSAGETASYNCBUFLEN() macro returns this value:

```
WORD wError;
WORD wBuflen;
wError = WSAGETASYNCERROR(lParam);
if (wError == WSAENOBUFS)
   wBuflen = WSAGETASYNCBUFLEN(lParam);
```

You can cancel the request by calling WSACancelAsyncRequest() with the handle returned by WSAAsyncGetHostByName().

```
int PASCAL WSACancelAsyncRequest(HANDLE hTask);
```

The Level-Zero Windows Sockets DLLs

Because Windows Sockets runs over either TCP/IP or NWLink, there are two level-zero Windows Sockets DLLs: \NTNET\CODE\%Cpu%\ WNETTCP.DLL and \NTNET\CODE\%Cpu%\WNETNW.DLL. They do not differ a great deal from each other; you have already seen what the differences are. Specifically:

- For TCP/IP, the address family is AF_INET. For IPX/SPX, it is either AF_IPX or AF_NS.
- The addresses are layed out differently in memory, so they must be described by different structures. TCP/IP uses the SOCKADDR_IN structure; IPX/SPX uses a SOCKADDR_IPX.
- The calls to socket() for opening a socket are different in the two environments, as shown here.

```
SOCKET sUDP, sIPX;
// Datagram sockets
s = socket(AF_INET, SOCK_DGRAM, 0);                 // TCP/IP
s = socket(AF_NS, SOCK_DGRAM, NSPROTO_IPX);         // IPX/SPX

SOCKET sTCP, sSPX;
// Connection-oriented sockets
s = socket(AF_INET, SOCK_STREAM, 0);                // TCP/IP
s = socket(AF_NS, SOCK_SEQPACKET, NSPROTO_SPX); // IPX/SPX
```

- The biggest difference is the way you translate human-readable machine names to binary addresses. TCP/IP has standardized schemes. One uses Distributed Name Service (DNS) servers; the other is based on database files like hosts and services. IPX/SPX, on the other hand, has never had a host-naming policy. It has relied instead on binary addresses and service advertising. Therefore, I have had to implement a name translation scheme for IPX/SPX. You saw the two versions of my function _WNetGetHostAddress() earlier in this chapter.
- When a station sends a datagram over IPX/SPX, it must first bind to a local address. This is not necessary for TCP/IP. Also, the technique for sending a broadcast datagram is different; each is dependent on the network-specific address format.

Because there is little variation between the two implementations, I use a single set of source code files for most of the routines. Any protocol-specific information is hidden in header files. A master header, WNETWS.H, contains the types, constants, prototypes, and *extern* declarations that apply to both versions. Depending on whether _WINSOCK_TCPIP or _WINSOCK_NWLINK is defined, it includes WNETTCP.H or WNETNW.H. These files define the constants that are dependent on the protocol. Here are the listings for WNETWS.H, WNETTCP.H, and WNETNW.H:

```
/********
 *
 * WNETWS.H
 *
 * Copyright (c) 1994 Ralph P. Davis, All Rights Reserved
 *
 ********/


/*===== Includes =====*/

#ifndef _WNET_INCLUDED
#include "wnet.h"
#endif

#ifdef __cplusplus
extern "C" {
#endif

#define _INC_WINDOWS // Keep WINDOWS.H from being included twice
#ifndef _WINSOCKAPI_
#include <winsock.h>
#endif

#ifdef _WINSOCK_TCPIP
// Building for Windows Sockets over TCP/IP
#include "wnettcp.h"
#else
#ifdef _WINSOCK_NWLINK
// Building for Windows Sockets over NWLink
#include "wnetnw.h"
#endif
#endif


#ifdef __cplusplus

// MAX_LISTEN_REQUESTS is passed as the backlog argument
// to listen()—maximum possible is 5
const short MAX_LISTEN_REQUESTS        = 5;

const int    MAXINT                    =
   (sizeof (int) == 2 ? 0x7FFF : 0x7FFFFFFFL);
const unsigned int MAXUINT             =
   (sizeof (int) == 2 ? 0xFFFF : 0xFFFFFFFFL);

const int RECEIVE_BUFFER_SIZE          = MAXINT;

// MAX_WSA_NAMES is the maximum number of client
```

```
// applications we support
const short MAX_WSA_NAMES              = 128;

// Concurrent connections is the maximum number
// of connections we can have with remote servers—
// it is limited by FD_SETSIZE, a Sockets constant
// that defines the maximum number of available sockets
const short CONCURRENT_CONNECTIONS   = FD_SETSIZE;


#else
#define MAX_LISTEN_REQUESTS      5
#define MAXINT                   (sizeof (int) == 2 ? 0x7FFF : 0x7FFFFFFFL)
#define MAXUINT                  (sizeof (int) == 2 ? 0xFFFF : 0xFFFFFFFFL)
#define RECEIVE_BUFFER_SIZE      MAXINT

#define MAX_WSA_NAMES            128

#define CONCURRENT_CONNECTIONS   FD_SETSIZE

#endif


/*===== Types =====*/

#ifdef __cplusplus
// The CLIENTAPP structure keeps track of the
// sockets belonging to each client application
struct CLIENTAPP
{
    SOCKET sDatagram;
    SOCKET sConnection;
    int    nAccepts;
    SOCKET Sockets[FD_SETSIZE];
    HWND   hWnd;
};

#else
typedef struct tagClientApp
{
    SOCKET sDatagram;
    SOCKET sConnection;
    int    nAccepts;
    SOCKET Sockets[FD_SETSIZE];
    HWND   hWnd;
} CLIENTAPP;
#endif
```

```
/*===== Global Variables =====*/

extern DWORD        dwTLSIndex;
extern HANDLE       hSocketListMutex;
extern HWND         hNotifyWnd;
extern HINSTANCE    hDLLInstance;
extern UINT         WMU_PACKET_RECEIVED;
extern WSADATA      WSAData;
extern CLIENTAPP    *pClientInfo;
extern DWORD        dwBytesTriedToAlloc;
extern DWORD        dwPrecedence;


/*===== Function Prototypes =====*/

BOOL WINAPI _WNetGetHostAddress(LPCSTR lpszHost, LPCSTR lpszService,
                                LPCSTR lpszProto,
                                LPSOCKADDR lpAddr);
LRESULT CALLBACK WinSockWndProc(HWND hWnd, UINT uMessage, WPARAM wParam,
                                LPARAM lParam);
int PASCAL FindNameOfSocket(SOCKET s);
int PASCAL AddToSocketList(int nNameIndex, SOCKET s);
void PASCAL RemoveFromSocketList(int nNameIndex, SOCKET s);

#ifdef __cplusplus
}
#endif


/********
 *
 * WNETTCP.H
 *
 * Copyright (c) 1992-1994 Ralph P. Davis, All Rights Reserved
 *
 ********/


/*===== Includes =====*/

#ifndef _WNET_INCLUDED
#include "wnet.h"
#endif

#ifdef __cplusplus
extern "C" {
#endif
```

```
#ifndef _INC_WINDOWS
#define _INC_WINDOWS // Keep WINDOWS.H from being included twice
#endif

#ifndef _WINSOCKAPI_
#include <winsock.h>
#endif


/*===== Constants =====*/

// MY_ADDRESS_FAMILY will be passed as the first argument
// to socket().
// AF_INET designates Internet (TCP/IP) addressing
#define MY_ADDRESS_FAMILY AF_INET

// DATAGRAM_PROTOCOL_NAME is passed to getservbyname()
// as the protocol associated with datagram service.
// The User Datagram Protocol (UDP) is the one we
// use here
#define DATAGRAM_PROTOCOL_NAME "udp"

// DATAGRAM_PROTOCOL and CONNECTION_PROTOCOL are
// the third argument we pass to
// socket() when we open a socket.
// For TCP/IP, the protocol number is determined
// by the address family and socket type, so
// we pass them as 0
#define DATAGRAM_PROTOCOL        0
#define CONNECTION_PROTOCOL        0

// CONNECTION_PROTOCOL_NAME is the name
// we pass to getservbyname() to bind to our
// connection-oriented port ID.
// We want the Transmission Control Protocol (TCP)
#define CONNECTION_PROTOCOL_NAME "tcp"

// CONNECTION_SOCKET_TYPE is passed as the second
// argument to socket().  For TCP/IP, we open
// a SOCK_STREAM socket.
#define CONNECTION_SOCKET_TYPE    SOCK_STREAM

// This mutex protects the list of sockets open
// by a client app, maintained in the CLIENTAPP
// structure (see WNETWS.H).
#define SOCKET_LIST_MUTEX TEXT("/MUTEX/WNET/SOCKET_LIST_MUTEX")
```

```
// The notify window class is registered so we
// can create an invisible notification window
// to receive WSAAsyncSelect() postings.
#define NOTIFY_WINDOW_CLASS TEXT("WinSockNotify")
#define NOTIFY_WINDOW_TITLE TEXT("Windows Sockets Window")

// The protocol bias is added to the HCONNECTION
// (the socket used by each end to talk to the partner
// station) so we can determine which level-zero
// function to call [see WNETFUNC.CPP-the function
// WNetSend() is a good example].
#define MY_PROTOCOL_BIAS        WINSOCK_BIAS
#define MY_PROTOCOL_PRECEDENCE PROTOCOL_WINSOCK

#ifdef __cplusplus
}
#endif

/********
 *
 * WNETNW.H
 *
 * Copyright (c) 1992-1994 Ralph P. Davis, All Rights Reserved
 *
 ********/


/*===== Includes =====*/

#include "wnet.h"

#ifdef __cplusplus
extern "C" {
#endif

#ifndef _INC_WINDOWS
#define _INC_WINDOWS // Keep WINDOWS.H from being included twice
#endif

#ifndef _WINSOCKAPI_
#include <winsock.h>
#endif

#ifndef _WSIPX_
#include <wsipx.h>
#endif
```

```
/*===== Constants =====*/

// MY_ADDRESS_FAMILY will be passed as the first argument
// to socket().
// AF_NS designates Xerox Network Systems (XNS) addressing
#define MY_ADDRESS_FAMILY AF_NS

// DATAGRAM_PROTOCOL_NAME is passed to getservbyname()
// as the protocol associated with datagram service.
// Here we use Novell's Internet Packet Exchange
// (IPX) protocol
#define DATAGRAM_PROTOCOL_NAME "ipx"

// DATAGRAM_PROTOCOL and CONNECTION_PROTOCOL are
// the third argument we pass to
// socket() when we open a socket.
// For IPX/SPX, unlike TCP/IP, these must be passed
// as the values NSPROTO_IPX and NSPROTO_SPX,
// not as zero
#define DATAGRAM_PROTOCOL        NSPROTO_IPX
#define CONNECTION_PROTOCOL      NSPROTO_SPX

// CONNECTION_PROTOCOL_NAME is the name
// we pass to getservbyname() to bind to our
// connection-oriented port ID.
// We want Novell's Sequenced Packet Exchange (SPX)
// protocol
#define CONNECTION_PROTOCOL_NAME "spx"

// CONNECTION_SOCKET_TYPE is passed as the second
// argument to socket().  For IPX/SPX, we open
// a sequenced packet socket (SOCK_SEQPACKET),
// because it provides better performance than a
// generic SOCK_STREAM socket (though a
// SOCK_STREAM socket is perfectly valid here).
#define CONNECTION_SOCKET_TYPE   SOCK_SEQPACKET

// This mutex protects the list of sockets open
// by a client app, maintained in the CLIENTAPP
// structure (see WNETWS.H).
#define SOCKET_LIST_MUTEX TEXT("/MUTEX/WNET/NWSOCKET_LIST_MUTEX")

// The notify window class is registered so we
// can create an invisible notification window
// to receive WSAAsyncSelect() postings.
#define NOTIFY_WINDOW_CLASS TEXT("NWWinSockNotify")
#define NOTIFY_WINDOW_TITLE TEXT("Windows Sockets Window for NWLink")
```

```
// The protocol bias is added to the HCONNECTION
// (the socket used by each end to talk to the partner
// station) so we can determine which level-zero
// function to call [see WNETFUNC.CPP—the function
// WNetSend() is a good example].
#define MY_PROTOCOL_BIAS NWLINK_BIAS
#define MY_PROTOCOL_PRECEDENCE PROTOCOL_NWLINK

#ifdef __cplusplus

enum
{
   WNET_SPX_SOCKET = 0x5746, // 0x4657 in high-low order
   WNET_IPX_SOCKET = 0x6745  // 0x4567 in high-low order
};

#else

#define WNET_IPX_SOCKET           0x6745
#define WNET_SPX_SOCKET           0x5746

#endif

#ifdef __cplusplus
}
#endif
```

DLL Initialization

The DLL initialization [DllMain()] routine performs four tasks during it DLL_PROCESS_ATTACH processing:

- It allocates a Thread Local Storage index that will be used to remember information about each application using the DLL. The information is stored in a CLIENTAPP structure.

```
struct CLIENTAPP
{
   SOCKET sDatagram;
   SOCKET sConnection;
   int    nAccepts;
   SOCKET Sockets[FD_SETSIZE];
   HWND   hWnd;
};
```

sDatagram and sConnection stay open the whole time the server is running. sDatagram is used to field incoming datagrams, and *sConnection* listens for client connections. The Sockets array tracks the temporary sockets that we create, either when the server side calls accept() or when the client side connects to a server by calling socket() and connect(). *hWnd* is the top-level notification window; it will be the final target of protocol-independent WMU_PACKET_RECEIVED messages.

- Next, DllMain() creates a mutex that guards access to the Sockets array in the CLIENTAPP structure.
- Next, it calls WSAStartup().
- It creates a window to receive WSAAsyncSelect() notifications.

The DLL_THREAD_ATTACH handler initializes the thread's TLS slot to a NULL pointer. The process and thread detach cases clean up resources by freeing memory, destroying the notification window, and closing the mutex handle.

Here is the listing of DllMain(), from \NTNET\CODE\WINSOCK\ _WNETINI.CPP.

```
int WINAPI DllMain(HINSTANCE hInstance,
                   DWORD dwReason,
                   LPVOID lpReserved)
{
    WNDCLASS wndClass;
    CLIENTAPP *lp;

    switch (dwReason)
        {
        case DLL_PROCESS_ATTACH:
            hDLLInstance = hInstance;

            dwTLSIndex = TlsAlloc();

            if (dwTLSIndex == 0xFFFFFFFF)
                return 0;

            // Initialize startup thread's local storage
            TlsSetValue(dwTLSIndex, NULL);

            hSocketListMutex = CreateMutex(NULL, FALSE, SOCKET_LIST_MUTEX);

            // Call WSAStartup(), ask for version 1.1
            // Have to do this for every client process
            if (WSAStartup(0x0101, &WSAData) != 0)
                return 0;
```

```
        wndClass.lpszClassName = NOTIFY_WINDOW_CLASS;
        wndClass.lpfnWndProc = WinSockWndProc;
        wndClass.hInstance   = hInstance;
        wndClass.hCursor     = NULL;
        wndClass.hIcon       = NULL;
        wndClass.hbrBackground = NULL;
        wndClass.lpszMenuName = NULL;
        wndClass.style  = 0;
        wndClass.cbClsExtra = 0;
        wndClass.cbWndExtra = 0;

        if (!RegisterClass(&wndClass))
            return 0;

        hNotifyWnd = CreateWindow(NOTIFY_WINDOW_CLASS,
                                  NOTIFY_WINDOW_TITLE,
                                  WS_OVERLAPPEDWINDOW,
                                  CW_USEDEFAULT,
                                  CW_USEDEFAULT,
                                  CW_USEDEFAULT,
                                  CW_USEDEFAULT,
                                  NULL,
                                  NULL,
                                  hInstance,
                                  NULL);

        return (hNotifyWnd != NULL);
    case DLL_THREAD_ATTACH:
        // Initialize thread local storage
        TlsSetValue(dwTLSIndex, NULL);
        break;
    case DLL_THREAD_DETACH:
        // Make sure memory allocated for thread local storage
        // gets released.
        lp = (CLIENTAPP *) TlsGetValue(dwTLSIndex);
        if (lp != NULL)
            VirtualFree(lp, 0, MEM_RELEASE);
        break;
    case DLL_PROCESS_DETACH:
        CloseHandle(hSocketListMutex);
        DestroyWindow(hNotifyWnd);
        break;
    }
    return 1;
}
```

_WNetInit()

You saw in Chapter 10 that the primary responsibility of _WNetInit() is to set up the registering application as a listening server. What that means for Windows Sockets is:

- Register the WMU_PACKET_RECEIVED message by calling RegisterWindowMessage("WMU_PACKET_RECEIVED"). As noted in Chapters 9 and 10, this is the glue that holds my system together. I'm going to ask WSAAsyncSelect() to post WMU_PACKET_RECEIVED messages to the notification window.
- Create a datagram socket, bind it to the appropriate datagram protocol ("ipx" or "udp"), and listen for datagrams by calling _WNetReceiveDatagram(). Here is the relevant excerpt from the code. Notice how it uses the constants defined in the header files shown above (WNETTCP.H and WNETNW.H).

```
// Open a datagram socket
pClientInfo->sDatagram =
    socket(MY_ADDRESS_FAMILY, SOCK_DGRAM, DATAGRAM_PROTOCOL);
if (pClientInfo->sDatagram == INVALID_SOCKET)
    {
    printfConsole(
        TEXT("\nOpen of datagram socket failed, "
            "WSAGetLastError() = %d"),
        WSAGetLastError());
    return -1;
    }
// Get datagram binding info
if (!_WNetGetHostAddress(szHostName, (LPCSTR) lpEndpoint,
        DATAGRAM_PROTOCOL_NAME, &sa))
    {
    printfConsole(
        TEXT("\n_WNetGetHostAddress() failed, "
            "WSAGetLastError() = %d"),
        WSAGetLastError());
    return -1;
    }
if (bind(pClientInfo->sDatagram, &sa, sizeof (SOCKADDR)) != 0)
    {
    printfConsole(TEXT("\nbind() failed, WSAGetLastError() = %d"),
        WSAGetLastError());
    return -1;
    }
if (!_WNetReceiveDatagram(NULL, 0, nNameIndex, hNotifyWnd))
    {
```

```
   printfConsole(TEXT("\n_WNetReceiveDatagram() failed, "
                       "WSAGetLastError() = %d"),
      WSAGetLastError());
   return -1;
   }
```

- Create a connection-oriented socket to listen for client connections. The code is very much like the code that creates a datagram socket, but the socket types and protocol names change. Also, I call _WNetListen() instead of _WNetReceiveDatagram() to wait for clients to connect. Here is the pertinent section of code.

```
// Open a connection socket
pClientInfo->sConnection =
   socket(MY_ADDRESS_FAMILY, CONNECTION_SOCKET_TYPE,
      CONNECTION_PROTOCOL);
if (pClientInfo->sConnection == INVALID_SOCKET)
   {
   printfConsole(TEXT("\nOpen of connection socket failed, "
                       "WSAGetLastError() = %d"),
      WSAGetLastError());
   return -1;
   }
if (!_WNetGetHostAddress(szHostName, (LPCSTR) lpEndpoint,
      CONNECTION_PROTOCOL_NAME, &sa))
   {
   printfConsole(TEXT("\n_WNetGetHostAddress() failed, "
                       "WSAGetLastError() = %d"),
      WSAGetLastError());
   return -1;
   }
if (bind(pClientInfo->sConnection, &sa, sizeof (SOCKADDR)) != 0)
   {
   printfConsole(TEXT("\nbind() failed, WSAGetLastError() = %d"),
      WSAGetLastError());
   return -1;
   }
if (!_WNetListen(nNameIndex, hNotifyWnd))
   {
   printfConsole(TEXT("\n_WNetListen() failed, "
                       "WSAGetLastError() = %d"),
      WSAGetLastError());
   return -1;
   }
```

- Finally, remember the CLIENTAPP in Thread Local Storage.

An additional consideration—and problem—for _WNetInit() is Unicode. You cannot pass Unicode strings to Windows Sockets; it only understands ANSI. However, in conformance with preferred Windows NT programming practice, I have written my system to be Unicode-compliant. Therefore, I have to check to see if the station and endpoint names are Unicode strings and convert them to ANSI if they are. This is the test I apply: if the size of a character in the current code page is one byte, and the second byte of the station name is a '\0', it's probably a Unicode string, so I convert it by calling WideCharToMultiByte(). Here is the function UnicodeToANSI(), from \NTNET\CODE\WNETMISC.CPP, that performs this conversion:

```
BOOL WINAPI UnicodeToANSI(LPTSTR lpInputString,
                          LPSTR lpszOutputString,
                          int nOutStringLen)
{
#ifndef WIN32S
   CPINFO CodePageInfo;

   GetCPInfo(CP_ACP, &CodePageInfo);

   if (CodePageInfo.MaxCharSize > 1)
      // Only supporting non-Unicode strings
      return FALSE;
   else if (((LPBYTE) lpInputString)[1] == '\0')
      {
      // Looks like unicode, better translate it
      WideCharToMultiByte(CP_ACP, 0, (LPCWSTR) lpInputString, -1,
         lpszOutputString, nOutStringLen, NULL, NULL);
      }
   else
      lstrcpyA(lpszOutputString, (LPSTR) lpInputString);
#else
      lstrcpy(lpszOutputString, (LPSTR) lpInputString);
#endif
   return TRUE;
}
```

Notice that I have to force NT to use the ANSI version of lstrcpy() by calling lstrcpyA() directly. lstrcpy() is actually a macro, defined as lstrcpyW() if UNICODE is defined, and as lstrcpyA() otherwise.

These kinds of conversions are necessary in a lot of places; Unicode, whether it is recommended or not, will cause you a lot of headaches. For example:

- Neither Windows Sockets nor NetBIOS supports it.
- Win32s does not support it, and Chicago isn't going to either.
- NetDDE does not support it.
- On the other hand, the LAN Manager API under Windows NT—a very useful and powerful API—only supports Unicode. The same is true of how Performance Monitoring uses the Registry.

Microsoft recommends the use of Unicode because it is NT's native character set. If you don't use it, NT has to convert all your strings to Unicode, which incurs a performance hit. It is also essential for writing code with the greatest amount of international convertibility. Unfortunately, though, it looks like the Windows world is going to be full of inconsistencies regarding Unicode for some time to come.

_WNetListen() and _WNetReceiveDatagram()

_WNetInit(), as you saw, plugs the application into the network by calling _WNetReceiveDatagram() to listen for datagrams, and _WNetListen() to receive client connections. In Windows Sockets over either protocol, I implement these functions using calls to WSAAsyncSelect(). _WNetListen() requests FD_ACCEPT notification, then calls listen() to put the socket into the listening state. _WNetReceiveDatagram() need only ask for FD_READ events; no other active call is necessary. Here are the complete listings of _WNetListen(), from \NTNET\CODE\WINSOCK_WNETLIS.CPP, and _WNetReceiveDatagram(), from \NTNET\CODE\WINSOCK_-WNETRDG.CPP. Notice how the CLIENTAPP information is pulled from Thread Local Storage by a call to TlsGetValue() at the beginning of the function. This gives us access to the sockets that were created by _WNetInit().

```
/********
*
* _WNETLIS.CPP
*
* Copyright (c) 1992-1994 Ralph P. Davis, All Rights Reserved
*
********/


/*===== Includes =====*/

#include "wnetws.h"
```

```
/*===== Function Definitions =====*/

BOOL WINAPI _WNetListen(int nNameIndex, HWND hWnd)
{
    CLIENTAPP *pTLSData;

    pTLSData = (CLIENTAPP *) TlsGetValue(dwTLSIndex);

    if (pTLSData == NULL)
        pTLSData = pClientInfo;

    // Set the socket into non-blocking mode and
    // ask for FD_ACCEPT notification
    if (WSAAsyncSelect(pTLSData->sConnection, hWnd,
        WMU_PACKET_RECEIVED, FD_ACCEPT) != 0)
        {
        return FALSE;
        }

    // Set him listening
    return (listen(pTLSData->sConnection, MAX_LISTEN_REQUESTS) == 0);
}

/********
 *
 * _WNETRDG.CPP
 *
 * Copyright (c) 1992-1994 Ralph P. Davis, All Rights Reserved
 *
 ********/


/*===== Includes =====*/

#include "wnetws.h"


/*===== Function Definitions =====*/

BOOL WINAPI _WNetReceiveDatagram(LPVOID lpBuffer,
                        WORD wBufferSize,
                        int  nNameIndex,
                        HWND hWnd)
{
    CLIENTAPP *pTLSData;

    pTLSData = (CLIENTAPP *) TlsGetValue(dwTLSIndex);
```

```
if (pTLSData == NULL)
   pTLSData = pClientInfo;

// Buffer argument is irrelevant.  The WinSock DLL does
// all the buffering for us.

// The datagram socket is ready to start accepting datagrams
// Force into non-blocking mode and ask for incoming data
// notification

return (WSAAsyncSelect(pTLSData->sDatagram, hWnd,
        WMU_PACKET_RECEIVED, FD_READ) == 0);
}
```

_WNetReceive()

_WNetReceive() is the other passive operation. It comes in two flavors: blocking and non-blocking. Actually, the caller's preference is indicated by a timeout value, where a value of zero is interpreted as a non-blocking receive.

Non-Blocking Receives. Because _WNetReceive() is used to accept data on a connection-oriented socket, a non-blocking receive calls WSAAsyncSelect() and asks for notification of three events: FD_READ, for the normal arrival of data; FD_OOB, for urgent data; and FD_CLOSE, which indicates that the client station has closed its socket. Here is the code:

```
if (dwTimeout == 0)
    {
    // Request notification for FD_READ, FD_OOB, and FD_CLOSE
    if (WSAAsyncSelect((SOCKET) hConnection, hNotifyWnd,
            WMU_PACKET_RECEIVED,
            FD_READ | FD_OOB | FD_CLOSE) != 0)
      {
      bReturnCode = FALSE;
      }
    }
```

Blocking Receives. To do a blocking receive, it's necessary to turn off asynchronous receives to make sure the data does not sneak in behind your backs. You do this by calling WSAAsyncSelect() with an event code of zero. Once you have done this, the easiest way to receive the data is to call ReadFile(). If it does not immediately produce the data, you can call WaitForSingleObject() and specify a determinate timeout value. The last step

is to reactivate asynchronous notifications by calling WSAAsyncSelect()
once again. Here's how that implementation goes:

```
// Call WSAAsyncSelect() to cancel asynchronous
// notifications
WSAAsyncSelect((SOCKET) hConnection, hNotifyWnd,
               WMU_PACKET_RECEIVED, 0);

// Do Overlapped read
OVERLAPPED ol;
ZeroMemory(&ol, sizeof (OVERLAPPED));
ol.hEvent = CreateEvent(NULL, TRUE, FALSE, NULL);
bReturnCode = ReadFile((HANDLE) hConnection, lpData,
               (DWORD) wDataLength, &dwBytesRead,
               &ol);
if (!bReturnCode && GetLastError() == ERROR_IO_PENDING)
   {
   if (WaitForSingleObject(ol.hEvent, dwTimeout)
      == WAIT_OBJECT_0)
      {
      if (!GetOverlappedResult((HANDLE) hConnection, &ol,
         &dwBytesRead, TRUE))
         {
         bReturnCode = FALSE;
         }
      }
   else
      {
      bReturnCode = FALSE;
      }
   }
CloseHandle(ol.hEvent);
// Turn asynchronous notification on again
if (WSAAsyncSelect((SOCKET) hConnection, hNotifyWnd,
         WMU_PACKET_RECEIVED,
         FD_READ | FD_OOB | FD_CLOSE) != 0)
   {
   bReturnCode = FALSE;
   }
```

Another possibility is to use select(), which behaves very much like
WaitForMultipleObjects()—it puts the calling thread to sleep, but allows you
to specify a timeout. There is some additional complexity in this
implementation. You have to express the timeout value as a *struct timeval*,
which uses seconds and microseconds; you cannot use the Win32
representation (milliseconds). Also, you must add up the number of bytes

you have retrieved—you cannot assume that all your data will come in with a single call to recv(). Here is the above code rewritten to use select() and recv():

```
// Call WSAAsyncSelect() to cancel asynchronous
// notifications
WSAAsyncSelect((SOCKET) hConnection, hNotifyWnd,
               WMU_PACKET_RECEIVED, 0);

fd_set FD_SET;
struct timeval tv, *ptv;

FD_ZERO(&FD_SET);                           // Zero out the set
FD_SET((SOCKET) hConnection, &FD_SET); // Put our socket
                                            // into the set

dwStartTime = GetCurrentTime();

dwWaitTime = dwTimeout;
while ((dwTimeout == INFINITE) ||
       (GetCurrentTime() - dwStartTime) < dwWaitTime)
  {
  if (dwTimeout == INFINITE)
    // Block indefinitely
    ptv = NULL;
  else
    {
    // Scale Win32 timeout to UNIX
    tv.tv_sec = dwWaitTime / 1000;
    // tv_usec is in microseconds
    tv.tv_usec = (dwWaitTime % 1000) * 1000;
    ptv = &tv;
    }
  if (select(1, &FD_SET, NULL, NULL, ptv) == 1)
    {
    // Data is available for reading
    nBytesRead = recv((SOCKET) hConnection,
            (LPSTR) &lpReceiveData[dwBytesRead],
            (int) wDataLength, 0);
    if (nBytesRead == 0 || nBytesRead == SOCKET_ERROR)
      {
      bReturnCode = FALSE;
      break;
      }
    dwBytesRead += (DWORD) nBytesRead;
    // Have we read the amount of data the caller wants?
    if (dwBytesRead < (DWORD) wDataLength)
      {
```

```
                            // No, go pick up some more,
                            // but reduce the amount we ask for
                            // by the amount we've already got
                            wDataLength -= (WORD) dwBytesRead;
                            if (dwTimeout != INFINITE)
                                {
                                // Don't start our whole timeout period
                                // over again—reduce it by the amount
                                // of time we've already been waiting
                                dwWaitTime -= (GetCurrentTime() - dwStartTime);
                                if (dwWaitTime > dwTimeout)  // Wrapped around
                                    {
                                    bReturnCode = FALSE;
                                    break;
                                    }
                                }
                            }
                    else
                        {
                        bReturnCode = TRUE;
                        break;
                        }
                    }
                }
    // Turn asynchronous notification on again
    if (WSAAsyncSelect((SOCKET) hConnection, hNotifyWnd,
                WMU_PACKET_RECEIVED,
                FD_READ | FD_OOB | FD_CLOSE) != 0)
        {
        bReturnCode = FALSE;
        }
```

Here is the complete listing of _WNETRCV.CPP, using ReadFile(). The source code disk also includes _WNETRCV.DPP, which uses select().

```
/********
*
* _WNETRCV.CPP
*
* Copyright (c) 1992-1994 Ralph P. Davis, All Rights Reserved
*
********/


/*===== Includes =====*/

#include "wnetws.h"
```

```
/*===== Function Definitions =====*/

BOOL WINAPI __WNetReceive(HCONNECTION hConnection,
                          LPVOID      lpData,
                          WORD        wDataLength,
                          DWORD       dwTimeout,
                          int         nNameIndex,
                          HWND        hWnd)
{
    DWORD  dwStartTime, dwWaitTime;
    int    nBytesRead;
    DWORD  dwBytesRead = 0L;
    BOOL   bReturnCode = TRUE;
    LPBYTE lpReceiveData = (LPBYTE) lpData;

    if (dwTimeout == 0)
        {
        // Request notification for FD_READ, FD_OOB, and FD_CLOSE
        if (WSAAsyncSelect((SOCKET) hConnection, hNotifyWnd,
                WMU_PACKET_RECEIVED,
                FD_READ | FD_OOB | FD_CLOSE) != 0)
            {
            bReturnCode = FALSE;
            }
        }
    else
        {
        // Call WSAAsyncSelect() to cancel asynchronous
        // notifications
        WSAAsyncSelect((SOCKET) hConnection, hNotifyWnd,
                    WMU_PACKET_RECEIVED, 0);

        // Do Overlapped read
        OVERLAPPED ol;
        ZeroMemory(&ol, sizeof (OVERLAPPED));
        ol.hEvent = CreateEvent(NULL, TRUE, FALSE, NULL);
        bReturnCode = ReadFile((HANDLE) hConnection, lpData,
                    (DWORD) wDataLength, &dwBytesRead,
                    &ol);
        if (!bReturnCode && GetLastError() == ERROR_IO_PENDING)
            {
            if (WaitForSingleObject(ol.hEvent, dwTimeout)
                == WAIT_OBJECT_0)
                {
                if (!GetOverlappedResult((HANDLE) hConnection, &ol,
                    &dwBytesRead, TRUE))
                    {
                    bReturnCode = FALSE;
```

```
            }
          }
      else
          {
        bReturnCode = FALSE;
          }
        }
      }
    CloseHandle(ol.hEvent);
    // Turn asynchronous notification on again
    if (WSAAsyncSelect((SOCKET) hConnection, hNotifyWnd,
          WMU_PACKET_RECEIVED,
          FD_READ | FD_OOB | FD_CLOSE) != 0)
      {
      bReturnCode = FALSE;
      }
    }
  return (bReturnCode);
}
```

The Notification Window Procedure

Once asynchronous requests have been posted, the next event of interest is the awakening of the notification window in response to a network event. There are four events I need to know about:

- FD_ACCEPT indicates that a client application wants to connect to me. The appropriate response is to call accept(). In addition, I do some bookkeeping by adding the new socket to the Sockets array in the CLIENTAPP table and posting a non-blocking _WNetReceive(). As you saw above, this calls WSAAsyncSelect() and asks for FD_READ | FD_OOB | FD_CLOSE notification.

- FD_READ and FD_OOB are treated as the same event—the arrival of data. I call ioctlsocket() with the FIONREAD command to find out how much data is waiting, then call recvfrom(). I use recvfrom() because it will work with either datagram or connection-oriented sockets. Also, it lets me specify the MSG_OOB flag if I'm responding to an FD_OOB event.

  After retrieving the data, I post it upstairs by calling SendMsgFromSharedMem(), discussed in Chapter 9.

- FD_CLOSE lets us know that the client end of the connection has closed its socket. I remove the socket from my internal tables, then call closesocket().

The window procedure, WinSockWndProc(), is defined in \NTNET\CODE\WINSOCK\WSAWND.CPP.

```
/*******
*
*  WSAWND.CPP
*
*  Copyright (c) 1992-1994 Ralph P. Davis, All Rights Reserved
*
********/


/*===== Includes =====*/

#include "wnetws.h"
#include <string.h>


/*===== LOCAL Functions =====*/

void HandleAccept(SOCKET sListen, HWND hWnd);
void HandleRead(SOCKET s, WORD wEvent, HWND hWnd);


/*===== Function Definitions =====*/

LRESULT CALLBACK WinSockWndProc(HWND hWnd, UINT uMessage, WPARAM wParam,
                                LPARAM lParam)
{
    WORD      wEvent, wError;
    int       nNameIndex;

    if (uMessage != WMU_PACKET_RECEIVED)
        return DefWindowProc(hWnd, uMessage, wParam, lParam);

    wError = WSAGETSELECTERROR(lParam);

    if (wError != 0)
        // Problem, can't do any more
        return 0L;

    wEvent = WSAGETSELECTEVENT(lParam);

    switch (wEvent)
        {
        case FD_ACCEPT:
            // Connection request has come in
            HandleAccept((SOCKET) wParam, hWnd);
            break;
        case FD_READ:
        case FD_OOB:
```

```
                HandleRead((SOCKET) wParam, wEvent, hWnd);
                break;
            case FD_CLOSE:
                // Find socket and remove it
                nNameIndex = FindNameOfSocket((SOCKET) wParam);
                RemoveFromSocketList(nNameIndex, (SOCKET) wParam);
                closesocket((SOCKET) wParam);
                break;
            default:
                break;
        }
    return 0L;
}

void HandleAccept(SOCKET sListen, HWND hWnd)
{
    int      nNameLen;
    SOCKET   s;
    SOCKADDR sa;
    int      nNameIndex;

    nNameLen = sizeof (SOCKADDR);
    s = accept(sListen, &sa, &nNameLen);

    if (s != INVALID_SOCKET)
        {
        // Add him to the table
        nNameIndex = FindNameOfSocket(sListen);
        if (nNameIndex == -1)
            {
            closesocket(s);
            return;
            }
        if (AddToSocketList(nNameIndex, s) != 0)
            {
            closesocket(s);
            return;
            }
        if (!__WNetReceive((HCONNECTION) s, NULL, 0L, 0L,
            nNameIndex, hWnd))
            {
            RemoveFromSocketList(nNameIndex, s);
            closesocket(s);
            }
        }
}

void HandleRead(SOCKET s, WORD wEvent, HWND hWnd)
```

```
{
    u_long      ulBytesToRead;
    LPBYTE      lpData;
    int         nNameIndex;
    DWORD       dwBytesRead = 0;
    CLIENTAPP *pTLSData;
    int         nSocketType, nTypeSize = sizeof (int);
    SOCKET      sTransmit;

    // Data is available for reading
    // We'll use recvfrom(), because it will work with both
    // connection and datagram sockets

    if (ioctlsocket(s, FIONREAD, &ulBytesToRead) == 0)
        {
        if (ulBytesToRead > 0L)
            {
            lpData = (LPBYTE) VirtualAlloc(NULL, ulBytesToRead,
                                           MEM_COMMIT,
                                           PAGE_READWRITE);
            if (lpData == NULL)
                {
                dwBytesTriedToAlloc = ulBytesToRead;
                RaiseException(STATUS_NO_MEMORY, 0, 1,
                            &dwBytesTriedToAlloc);
                return;
                }
            if (recvfrom(s, (LPSTR) lpData, (int) ulBytesToRead,
                (wEvent == FD_OOB ? MSG_OOB : 0), NULL, NULL) <= 0)
                {
                // Error
                VirtualFree(lpData, 0, MEM_RELEASE);
                return;
                }
            dwBytesRead += ulBytesToRead;
            }
        nNameIndex = FindNameOfSocket(s);

        if (nNameIndex != -1)
            {
            pTLSData = (CLIENTAPP *) TlsGetValue(dwTLSIndex);

            if (pTLSData == NULL)
                pTLSData = pClientInfo;

            // See if it's a datagram or a stream socket
            // We pass the socket upstairs as zero for
            // datagram sockets
```

```
getsockopt(s, SOL_SOCKET, SO_TYPE,
    (LPSTR) &nSocketType, &nTypeSize);
if (nSocketType == SOCK_DGRAM)
    sTransmit = 0;
else
    sTransmit = (SOCKET) (((DWORD) s) +
        (dwPrecedence * PROTOCOL_BIAS));

SendMsgFromSharedMem(pTLSData->hWnd,
    lpData, (HCONNECTION) sTransmit, dwBytesRead);
    }
  }
}
```

The Active Operations

Call, Send, and Send Datagram are the initiating operations. In Windows Sockets, _WNetCall() and _WNetSendDatagram() both create a socket before calling the appropriate function. _WNetSendDatagram() destroys the socket as soon as it completes. _WNetCall(), since it opens a connection that can be expected to last a little while, remembers the socket in the CLIENTAPP table and keeps it open. _WNetSendDatagram() has another little wrinkle; it must be able to handle broadcast datagrams. My implementation uses the special target station name "WNET_DOMAIN" to indicate that the caller wants a broadcast. This requires some protocol-specific handling, as TCP/IP and IPX/SPX use different broadcasting techniques.

_WNetSend(). I'll start with _WNetSend(), since it is quite brief. The connection is already established; all it has to do is call send() and make sure nothing untoward has occurred. I use send(), rather than _write() or WriteFile(), because it offers the simplest usage.

```
/********
*
*  _WNETSND.CPP
*
*  Copyright (c) 1992-1994 Ralph P. Davis, All Rights Reserved
*
********/


/*===== Includes =====*/
```

```
#include "wnetws.h"


/*===== Function Definitions =====*/

BOOL WINAPI _WNetSend(HCONNECTION hConnection, LPVOID lpData,
                               WORD wDataLength)
{
    int nSent;

    nSent = send((SOCKET) hConnection, (LPCSTR) lpData, wDataLength, 0);

    return (nSent != SOCKET_ERROR && nSent == (int) wDataLength);
}
```

_WNetCall(). _WNetCall() is a little more involved because it has to convert the station name and endpoint from Unicode to ANSI, open a socket, and find out the machine address and service endpoint of the target machine. Once it has done this, it calls connect() and waits to see what it has to say. I'm calling connect() on a blocking socket here. That isn't a problem—it won't block indefinitely if it can't get through. It seems to wait about five seconds for an answer, then fails with a WSAGetLastError() of WSAETIMEDOUT.

Once the connection is established, I enter the connected state by calling WSAAsyncSelect() to request FD_READ | FD_OOB | FD_CLOSE events.

```
/********
*
* _WNETCAL.CPP
*
* Copyright (c) 1992-1994 Ralph P. Davis, All Rights Reserved
*
********/


/*===== Includes =====*/

#include "wnetws.h"


/*===== Function Definitions =====*/

HCONNECTION WINAPI _WNetCall(int nNameIndex,
                               LPVOID lpTargetStation,
                               LPVOID lpEndpoint)
{
```

```
HCONNECTION hConnection;
SOCKADDR RemoteAddress;
SOCKET    s;
char szTargetStation[256];
char szEndpoint[256];

if (lpEndpoint == NULL)
   lpEndpoint = "wnetsrvr";

// Convert station and endpoint to ANSI if they're Unicode
if (!UnicodeToANSI((LPTSTR) lpTargetStation, szTargetStation,
        sizeof (szTargetStation)))
   return 0;

lpTargetStation = szTargetStation;

if (!UnicodeToANSI((LPTSTR) lpEndpoint, szEndpoint,
      sizeof (szEndpoint)))
   return 0;

lpEndpoint = szEndpoint;

if (!_WNetGetHostAddress((LPCSTR) lpTargetStation,
        (LPCSTR) lpEndpoint, CONNECTION_PROTOCOL_NAME,
        &RemoteAddress))
   {
   return 0;
   }

// Open a new socket
s = socket(MY_ADDRESS_FAMILY, CONNECTION_SOCKET_TYPE,
          CONNECTION_PROTOCOL);
if (s == INVALID_SOCKET)
   {
   return 0;
   }

// Don't need to bind the socket

if (connect(s, &RemoteAddress, sizeof (SOCKADDR)) == 0)
   {
   // Ask to be notified of FD_READ, FD_OOB, and FD_CLOSE events
   WSAAsyncSelect(s, hNotifyWnd, WMU_PACKET_RECEIVED,
     FD_READ | FD_OOB | FD_CLOSE);
   hConnection = (HCONNECTION) s;
   }
else
   {
```

```
    closesocket(s);
    hConnection = 0;
    }

if (hConnection != 0)
    AddToSocketList(nNameIndex, s);
return hConnection;
}
```

Again, notice the use of the constants defined in WNETTCP.H and WNETNW.H, which allows use of the same source code for both TCP/IP and IPX/SPX.

_WNetSendDatagram(). The two differences between the TCP/IP and IPX/SPX versions are enough to warrant separate source code files:

- The mechanism for sending a broadcast is different.
- An IPX/SPX station must bind to a local address before it can transmit a datagram.

To send a broadcast datagram, you must target a specific service endpoint—either a UDP port number or an IPX socket. The datagram will then be delivered to all stations where there is a software process with that endpoint open. The TCP/IP version of _WNetSendDatagram() builds a broadcast by first fetching the local station's address; it gets this by calling _WNetGetHostAddress(). This provides the needed port number. The broadcast machine address is INADDR_BROADCAST, defined as 0xFFFFFFFF. The IPX/SPX setting uses a similar technique. It has to retrieve the local station address in order to bind to it. Once it has done this, it replaces the local machine address with the Xerox Network Systems broadcast address. This uses network number 0 and node number 0xFFFFFFFFFFFF (six bytes of 0xFF).

In both cases, notice the following call to setsockopt().

```
BOOL bBroadcast TRUE;
setsockopt(s, SOL_SOCKET,
          SO_BROADCAST, (char FAR *) &bBroadcast, sizeof (BOOL));
```

This is required for the socket to be able to transmit broadcast datagrams.
Here are the listings. First, \NTNET\CODE\WINSOCK\TCPIP\ _WNETSDG.CPP:

```
/********
*
* _WNETSDG.CPP
*
* Copyright (c) 1992-1994 Ralph P. Davis, All Rights Reserved
*
********/


/*===== Includes =====*/

#include "wnetws.h"
#include <string.h>


/*===== Function Definitions =====*/

BOOL WINAPI _WNetSendDatagram(LPVOID lpTargetStation,
                              LPVOID lpEndpoint,
                              LPVOID lpData, WORD wDataLength,
                              int nNameIndex)
{
    SOCKET      s;
    SOCKADDR_IN sin;
    int nSent;
    char szTargetStation[256];
    char szEndpoint[256];

    if (lpEndpoint == NULL)
        lpEndpoint = "wnetsrvr";

    if (wDataLength > (WORD) WSAData.iMaxUdpDg)
        {
        return FALSE;
        }

    // Convert station and endpoint to ANSI if they're Unicode
    if (!UnicodeToANSI((LPTSTR) lpTargetStation, szTargetStation,
            sizeof (szTargetStation)))
        return FALSE;

    lpTargetStation = szTargetStation;

    if (!UnicodeToANSI((LPTSTR) lpEndpoint, szEndpoint,
            sizeof (szEndpoint)))
        return FALSE;
```

```
lpEndpoint = szEndpoint;

s = socket(PF_INET, SOCK_DGRAM, 0);

if (s == INVALID_SOCKET)
   return FALSE;

ZeroMemory(&sin, sizeof (sin));
if (lstrcmpA(szTargetStation, WNET_DOMAINA) == 0)  // Broadcast?
   {
   BOOL bBroadcast = TRUE;
   char szHostName[256];

   if (gethostname(szHostName, sizeof (szHostName)) != 0)
      {
      closesocket(s);
      return FALSE;
      }

   if (!_WNetGetHostAddress(szHostName, (LPCSTR) lpEndpoint, "udp",
         (LPSOCKADDR) &sin))
      {
      closesocket(s);
      return FALSE;
      }
   sin.sin_addr.s_addr = INADDR_BROADCAST;

   // Make sure socket can handle broadcasts

   setsockopt(s, SOL_SOCKET,
      SO_BROADCAST, (char FAR *) &bBroadcast, sizeof (BOOL));
   }
else if (!_WNetGetHostAddress((LPCSTR) lpTargetStation,
                              (LPCSTR) lpEndpoint, "udp",
                              (LPSOCKADDR) &sin))
   {
   closesocket(s);
   return FALSE;
   }

nSent = sendto(s, (LPSTR) lpData, (int) wDataLength,
   0, (LPSOCKADDR) &sin, sizeof (sin));

closesocket(s);

if ((nSent == SOCKET_ERROR) ||
   (nSent != (int) wDataLength))
   {
```

```
      return FALSE;
      }
   return TRUE;
}
```

Next, \NTNET\CODE\WINSOCK\NETWARE_WNETSDG.CPP:

```
/********
 *
 * _WNETSDG.CPP
 *
 * Copyright (c) 1992-1994 Ralph P. Davis, All Rights Reserved
 *
 ********/


/*===== Includes =====*/

#include "wnetws.h"
#include <string.h>


/*===== Function Definitions =====*/

BOOL WINAPI _WNetSendDatagram(LPVOID lpTargetStation,
                        LPVOID lpEndpoint,
                        LPVOID lpData, WORD wDataLength,
                        int nNameIndex)
{
   SOCKET       s;
   SOCKADDR_IPX sipx;
   int nSent;
   char szTargetStation[256];
   char szEndpoint[256];
   char  szHostName[256];

   if (lpEndpoint == NULL)
      lpEndpoint = "wnetsrvr";

   if (wDataLength > (WORD) WSAData.iMaxUdpDg)
      {
      return FALSE;
      }

   gethostname(szHostName, sizeof (szHostName));
   if (!_WNetGetHostAddress((LPCSTR) szHostName,
                            (LPCSTR) "wnetsrvr",
                            "ipx", (LPSOCKADDR) &sipx))
```

```
       return FALSE;

   // Convert station and endpoint to ANSI if they're Unicode
   if (!UnicodeToANSI((LPTSTR) lpTargetStation, szTargetStation,
           sizeof (szTargetStation)))
       return FALSE;

   lpTargetStation = szTargetStation;

   if (!UnicodeToANSI((LPTSTR) lpEndpoint, szEndpoint,
                   sizeof (szEndpoint)))
       return FALSE;
   lpEndpoint = szEndpoint;

   s = socket(AF_NS, SOCK_DGRAM, NSPROTO_IPX);

   if (s == INVALID_SOCKET)
       return FALSE;

   bind(s, (const struct sockaddr *) &sipx, sizeof (SOCKADDR_IPX));

   if (lstrcmpA(szTargetStation, WNET_DOMAINA) == 0)   // Broadcast?
       {
       BOOL bBroadcast = TRUE;

       // Use XNS broadcast address (all 0xFFs)
       FillMemory(sipx.sa_netnum, sizeof (sipx.sa_netnum), '\0');
       FillMemory(sipx.sa_nodenum, sizeof (sipx.sa_nodenum), '\xFF');

       // Make sure socket can handle broadcasts

       setsockopt(s, SOL_SOCKET,
           SO_BROADCAST, (char FAR *) &bBroadcast, sizeof (BOOL));
       }
   else if (!_WNetGetHostAddress((LPCSTR) lpTargetStation,
                               (LPCSTR) lpEndpoint, "ipx",
                               (LPSOCKADDR) &sipx))
       {
       closesocket(s);
       return FALSE;
       }

   nSent = sendto(s, (LPSTR) lpData, (int) wDataLength,
       0, (LPSOCKADDR) &sipx, sizeof (sipx));

   closesocket(s);
```

```
    if ((nSent == SOCKET_ERROR) ||
        (nSent != (int) wDataLength))
        {
        return FALSE;
        }
    return TRUE;
}
```

Hanging Up

_WNetHangup() is as inconsequential in Windows Sockets as in Named Pipes. It is only necessary to close the socket. The only other detail involves bookkeeping: I have to remove the socket from my internal list.

```
/********
 *
 * _WNETHGP.CPP
 *
 * Copyright (c) 1992-1994 Ralph P. Davis, All Rights Reserved
 *
 ********/


/*===== Includes =====*/

#include "wnetws.h"


/*===== Function Definitions =====*/

void WINAPI _WNetHangup(HCONNECTION hConnection)
{
    int nNameIndex;

    closesocket((SOCKET) hConnection);

    nNameIndex = FindNameOfSocket((SOCKET) hConnection);

    if (nNameIndex != -1)
        RemoveFromSocketList(nNameIndex, (SOCKET) hConnection);
}
```

Shutting Down

To shut down:

1. Cancel asynchronous notifications on any open sockets by calling WSAAsyncSelect() with an event mask of zero.
2. Close the sockets.
3. Call WSACleanup().

```cpp
/********
 *
 * _WNETSHD.CPP
 *
 * Copyright (c) 1992-1994 Ralph P. Davis, All Rights Reserved
 *
 ********/


/*===== Includes =====*/

#include "wnetws.h"


/*===== Function Definitions =====*/

void WINAPI _WNetShutdown(int nNameIndex)
{
   int i;
   CLIENTAPP *pTLSData;

   pTLSData = (CLIENTAPP *) TlsGetValue(dwTLSIndex);

   if (pTLSData == NULL)
      // No thread local storage, use global process-wide pointer
      pTLSData = pClientInfo;

   if (pTLSData != NULL)
      {
      // Close all our open sockets
      WSAAsyncSelect(pTLSData->sDatagram, NULL, 0, 0L);
      WSAAsyncSelect(pTLSData->sConnection, NULL, 0, 0L);
      closesocket(pTLSData->sDatagram);
      closesocket(pTLSData->sConnection);

      for (i = 0; i < pTLSData->nAccepts; ++i)
         {
         // We first call WSAAsyncSelect() with the last two arguments
```

```
            // (the message number and the event code) set to zero.
            // This cancels notification for the socket.

            if (pTLSData->Sockets[i] != 0)
               {
               WSAAsyncSelect(pTLSData->Sockets[i],
                  NULL, 0, 0L);
               closesocket(pTLSData->Sockets[i]);
               }
            }
         }
      WSACleanup();
}
```

Windows Sockets Benchmarks

Finally, I'd like to apply the same test to Windows Sockets that I ran with Named Pipes in Chapter 10. Once again, the test has the client transmit data to the server, who sends it right back to the client. The goal is to find out how the two implementations of Windows Sockets compare with each other, and with Named Pipes. Here too a single code bed is used, letting constants define the protocol-specific things. The benchmark server is in \NTNET\CODE\WINSOCK\WNETBNCH.CPP, shown here:

```
/********
*
* WNETBNCH.CPP
*
* Copyright (c) 1993-1994 Ralph P. Davis, All Rights Reserved
*
* Windows Sockets Benchmark Server
*
********/


/*===== Includes =====*/

#include "wnetws.h"
#include <stdio.h>
#include <stdlib.h>


/*===== Global Variables =====*/

char szBuffer[65536];
```

```
/*===== Function Definitions =====*/

void main(int argc, char *argv[])
{
    SOCKET    sListen = INVALID_SOCKET, sAccept = INVALID_SOCKET;
    SOCKADDR  sa;
    WSADATA   WSAData;
    int       nBytes;
    LPSTR     lpServer;

    if (argc > 1)
        lpServer = argv[1];
    else
        lpServer = "NUMBER1";

    try
        {
        if (WSAStartup(0x0101, &WSAData) != 0)
            {
            printf("\nWSAStartup() failed\n");
            ExitProcess(1);
            }

        sListen = socket(MY_ADDRESS_FAMILY, CONNECTION_SOCKET_TYPE,
                    CONNECTION_PROTOCOL);

        if (sListen == INVALID_SOCKET)
            {
            printf("\nUnable to open socket, WSAGetLastError() = %d\n",
                WSAGetLastError());
            ExitProcess(1);
            }

        if (!_WNetGetHostAddress(lpServer, "wnetbnch",
                CONNECTION_PROTOCOL_NAME, &sa))
            {
            printf("\nCan't find local address, WSAGetLastError() = %d\n",
                WSAGetLastError());
            ExitProcess(1);
            }

        if (bind(sListen, &sa, sizeof (SOCKADDR)) != 0)
            {
            printf("\nbind() failed, WSAGetLastError() = %d\n",
                WSAGetLastError());
            ExitProcess(1);
            }
```

```
    printf("\nWaiting for client connections...\n");

while (TRUE)
    {
    listen(sListen, 5);
    sAccept = accept(sListen, NULL, NULL);

    if (sAccept == INVALID_SOCKET)
        {
        printf("\naccept() failed, WSAGetLastError() = %d\n",
            WSAGetLastError());
        }
    else
        {
        BOOL bNoDelay = TRUE;

        setsockopt(sAccept, IPPROTO_TCP, TCP_NODELAY,
            (LPSTR) &bNoDelay, sizeof (BOOL));
        while ((nBytes =
            recv(sAccept, szBuffer, sizeof (szBuffer), 0)) > 0)
            {
            if (send(sAccept, szBuffer, nBytes, 0) <= 0)
                break;
            }
        if (closesocket(sAccept) == SOCKET_ERROR)
            {
            printf("\nclosesocket() failed, "
                    "WSAGetLastError() = %d\n",
                WSAGetLastError());
            }
        }
    }
    }
finally
    {
    if (sAccept != INVALID_SOCKET)
      closesocket(sAccept);
    if (sListen != INVALID_SOCKET)
        closesocket(sListen);
    WSACleanup();
    }
}
```

There is only one client side application, \NTNET\CODE\WINSOCK\ WNETCLI.CPP. Windows Sockets has no equivalent to TransactNamedPipe(). There is also no distinction when communicating with a local Sockets application between calling it by name or using a

nickname such as ".". For local interprocess communication, Windows
Sockets cannot even begin to compete with Named Pipes.

```
/********
*
* WNETCLI.CPP
*
* Copyright (c) 1993-1994 Ralph P. Davis, All Rights Reserved
*
* Client side of Windows Sockets benchmark
*
********/


/*===== Includes =====*/

#include "wnetws.h"
#include <stdio.h>
#include <stdlib.h>


/*===== Global Variables =====*/

char szBuffer[65536];


/*===== Function Definitions =====*/

void main(int argc, char *argv[])
{
   DWORD dwPackets = 100, dwPacketSize = 100;
   SOCKET sCall = INVALID_SOCKET;
   SOCKADDR sa;
   WSADATA  WSAData;
   int      nBytes, nReceived, nTotalReceived = 0;
   DWORD    dwStartTime, dwEndTime;
   DWORD    i;
   DWORD    dwBytesTransmitted = 0;
   DWORD    dwBytesAvailable;
   BOOL     bNoDelay = TRUE;
   LPSTR    lpServer;

   if (argc > 1)
      dwPackets = atoi(argv[1]);

   if (argc > 2)
      dwPacketSize = atoi(argv[2]);
```

```
if (argc > 3)
   lpServer = argv[3];
else
   lpServer = "NUMBER1";

if (WSAStartup(0x0101, &WSAData) != 0)
   {
   printf("\nWSAStartup() failed\n");
   ExitProcess(1);
   }

printf("\nWSAData.iMaxUdpDg = %d\n", WSAData.iMaxUdpDg);

sCall = socket(MY_ADDRESS_FAMILY,
              CONNECTION_SOCKET_TYPE, CONNECTION_PROTOCOL);

if (sCall == INVALID_SOCKET)
   {
   printf("\nUnable to open socket, WSAGetLastError() = %d\n",
       WSAGetLastError());
   ExitProcess(1);
   }

if (!_WNetGetHostAddress(lpServer, "wnetbnch",
       CONNECTION_PROTOCOL_NAME, &sa))
   {
   printf("\nCan't find local address, WSAGetLastError() = %d\n",
       WSAGetLastError());
   ExitProcess(1);
   }

setsockopt(sCall, IPPROTO_TCP, TCP_NODELAY,
   (LPSTR) &bNoDelay, sizeof (BOOL));

if (connect(sCall, &sa, sizeof (SOCKADDR)) != 0)
   {
   printf("\nconnect() failed, WSAGetLastError() = %d\n",
       WSAGetLastError());
   ExitProcess(1);
   }

printf("\nConnected to server\n");
// Do a dummy send() to make sure we're actively
// connected.
// The first send() will block if we're the backlog
// client (i.e., somebody else is connected and
// exchanging data.)
nBytes = send(sCall, szBuffer, 100, 0);
```

```
    for (nTotalReceived = nReceived = 0;
         nBytes != SOCKET_ERROR &&
           nTotalReceived < nBytes;
        )
        {
        nReceived = recv(sCall, szBuffer, nBytes, 0);
        if (nReceived != SOCKET_ERROR)
          nTotalReceived += nReceived;
        }
    for (i = 0, dwStartTime = GetCurrentTime();
         i < dwPackets; ++i)
        {
        if ((nBytes = send(sCall, szBuffer, dwPacketSize, 0))
             != SOCKET_ERROR)
            {
            for (nReceived = 0, nTotalReceived = 0;
                 nTotalReceived < nBytes; )
                {
                if ((nReceived = recv(sCall, szBuffer, nBytes, 0))
                     == SOCKET_ERROR)
                    break;
                nTotalReceived += nReceived;
                }
            dwBytesTransmitted += (DWORD) nTotalReceived;
            }
        }
    dwEndTime = GetCurrentTime();


    if (sCall != INVALID_SOCKET)
        closesocket(sCall);

    WSACleanup();

    printf("\nGetLastError() = %d", GetLastError());
    printf("\n%d packets transmitted in %d milliseconds", i * 2,
        dwEndTime - dwStartTime);
    printf("\nAverage is %d packets per second\n",
        (i * 2000) / (dwEndTime - dwStartTime));

    double dTotalBytes = ((double) dwPacketSize) *
                         ((double) i) * 2000.0;
    double dEndTime = (double) dwEndTime;
    double dStartTime = (double) dwStartTime;

    printf("\nBytes per second = %.2f\n",
        dTotalBytes / (dEndTime - dStartTime));
    ExitProcess(0);
}
```

Notice one subtlety here: the client cannot assume that the recv() call retrieves as many bytes as were transmitted by the send(). TCP/IP may—and, in my experience, does—fragment packets. Thus, a single transmission of 32,768 bytes may be returned in a number of separate packets. For this reason, the client must call recv() in a loop until all the bytes sent have been accounted for.

The first test compares the results of using TransactNamedPipe() in Chapter 10 with Windows Sockets over TCP/IP. The data appears in Table 11-3 and Figure 11-1.

Table 11-3.   Named Pipes versus Windows Sockets over TCP/IP (Remote)

Packet Size	1024	2048	4096	8192	16384	32768
Named Pipes	252527	349488	514249	478364	492085	504200
WinSock-TCP/IP	265629	332467	464926	531085	574071	607039
% Difference	5%	–5%	–10%	11%	17%	20%

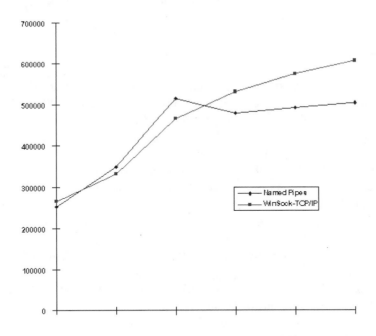

Figure 11-1.   Named Pipes versus Windows Sockets over TCP/IP (Remote)

This data shows that the performance of Windows Sockets over TCP/IP is quite acceptable, in some cases superior to Named Pipes. I invite you to run these tests in your own environments and also to evaluate my benchmark code. The problem with benchmarks is that it is very difficult to eliminate all polluting factors. Let me know your results by contacting me at CompuServe 71161,1060 or phoning me at 703-720-6909. If this data holds up, then clearly the choice of whether to use Windows Sockets over TCP/IP or Named Pipes need not concern itself with performance.

I have not been able to benchmark Windows Sockets over IPX/SPX with NT version 3.5. The NT protocol drivers for IPX/SPX don't work very well in the version that I have. In NT version 3.1, IPX/SPX was only about half as fast as TCP/IP.

Conclusion

Windows Sockets offers a very good programming interface for peer-to-peer communications. It is truly protocol-independent. In the NT environment, it supports connectivity to TCP/IP and NetWare, as we have seen, and also to Macintosh networks. The API is high-level and offers acceptable performance over TCP/IP.

Suggested Readings

AT&T. *UNIX System V Release 4 Programmer's Guide: Networking Interfaces*. Englewood Cliffs, NJ: Prentice-Hall, Inc., 1990.

Allard, J., Keith Moore, and David Treadwell. "Plug into Serious Network Programming with the Windows Sockets API." *Microsoft Systems Journal,* Vol. 8, No. 7, July 1993.

Comer, D. and D. Stevens. *Internetworking with TCP/IP, Volume III: Client-Server Programming and Applications*. Englewood Cliffs, NJ: Prentice Hall, Inc., 1991.

Stevens, W. R. *Unix Network Programming*. Englewood Cliffs, NJ: Prentice Hall, Inc. 1990.

Davis, Ralph. *Windows Network Programming*. Reading, MA: Addison-Wesley Publishing Company, 1993. Chapter 6.

Microsoft Corporation. *Microsoft Knowledge Base for Win32 SDK* articles.
"Supported Versions of Windows Sockets"
"Use WSAAsyncSelect() to Clear Message Queue"
"Writing a Telnet Client"

The Windows Sockets on-line help has a section called References that gives additional sources of information.

## Chapter 12

NetBIOS

Overview

NetBIOS is a well-standardized peer-to-peer programming interface in the PC world. Since it is available on all major network platforms, it offers a high assurance of portability. Due to its wide availability and its generally high-level programming interface, NetBIOS is always a good choice for peer-to-peer applications. You will also see at the end of this chapter that it outperforms Named Pipes and Windows Sockets by a sizable margin. Therefore, although the other APIs are easier to work with, we cannot dismiss NetBIOS lightly.

Probably the worst aspect of working with NetBIOS is that nobody seems to want to document it. Everybody refers you to somebody else's documentation. The definitive reference is IBM's *LAN Technical Reference*, but it is strictly a reference—there is no interpretive material. Microsoft's documentation tells you nothing about programming NetBIOS. Mostly you learn by trial and error, and there is a lot of room for error.

The NetBIOS API

The NetBIOS API under DOS and Windows 3.X is an assembly language interface. You request NetBIOS services by issuing an INT 5CH instruction. You find out that an asynchronous operation has completed through the invocation of a post routine, called at interrupt level with pointers parked in registers. For this reason, the original NetBIOS API cannot go beyond the Intel 80X86 environment.

Because of Microsoft's requirement that NT be portable to non-Intel platforms, they have rewritten the API so that you can use it directly from C and C++, without the intermediary of assembler routines. Instead of issuing an interrupt, you now call the Netbios() function:

```
UCHAR Netbios(PNCB pNCB);
```

This is the only function in the NetBIOS API. *pNCB* points to the NetBIOS data structure, called a **Network Control Block** (NCB). Here is its type definition from \MSTOOLS\H\NB30.H:

```
#define NCBNAMSZ              16
typedef struct _NCB
{
    UCHAR     ncb_command;
    UCHAR     ncb_retcode;
    UCHAR     ncb_lsn;
    UCHAR     ncb_num;
    PUCHAR    ncb_buffer;
    WORD      ncb_length;
    UCHAR     ncb_callname[NCBNAMSZ];
    UCHAR     ncb_name[NCBNAMSZ];
    UCHAR     ncb_rto;
    UCHAR     ncb_sto;
    void (CALLBACK *ncb_post)( struct _NCB * );
    UCHAR     ncb_lana_num;
    UCHAR     ncb_cmd_cplt;
    UCHAR     ncb_reserve[10];
    HANDLE    ncb_event;
} NCB, *PNCB;
```

You request the different NetBIOS services by zeroing the NCB, then populating the necessary fields before calling Netbios(). Notice the *ncb_post* field. This is the NetBIOS post routine, called when an asynchronous operation completes. In DOS and Windows 3.X, this is the routine that gets called at interrupt level, with a pointer to the original NCB in ES:BX. As the prototype shows, NetBIOS now passes you the NCB pointer as a function argument, so the post routine can be written in a high-level language.

NetBIOS Commands

Most NetBIOS commands come in two flavors: wait and no-wait. The wait version blocks until the command completes. The no-wait version returns immediately, and the command continues to be processed in the background.

The standard NetBIOS specification provides only one notification mechanism for asynchronous operations: callback functions. NT still supports callbacks, but adds an additional field to the NCB, shown in the preceding code as *ncb_event*. This is a handle to a Win32 event, which acts just like an event that you use with overlapped file I/O—NT automatically sets it into the nonsignalled state when you call Netbios(), then signals it when the I/O completes.

It is easier to write code that uses callbacks. With event handles, you have to decide how to multithread your application, and it is not always easy to find a clean implementation. However, Microsoft discourages the use of callbacks, saying that they require more system resources than do events. In the level-zero NetBIOS DLL, I go along with their recommendation and use events.

The NetBIOS commands are organized into four groups:

- The Name commands register names with NetBIOS. These names are used as service endpoints on the network.
- The Session commands provide the connection-oriented services.
- The Datagram commands provide the connectionless services.
- The rest of the NetBIOS commands, loosely classified as Miscellaneous, initialize NetBIOS, cancel pending requests, and retrieve status information.

The NetBIOS Name Commands

The Name commands register and unregister network names. The commands and the codes that Microsoft has defined in NB30.H are

- Add a unique name (NCBADDNAME)
- Add a group name (NCBADDGRNAME)
- Delete a name (NCBDELNAME)

NetBIOS 3.0 adds one additional command that locates a station on the network (NCBFINDNAME). I discussed this in connection with Windows Sockets over NWLink in Chapter 11 and will not cover it further in this chapter because it is not a mainstream command (that is, the command is useful, but not essential).

Adding a Unique NetBIOS Name (NCBADDNAME). NetBIOS names are one of the most confusing aspects of NetBIOS because, though they appear to represent stations, they actually identify software processes. Thus, a NetBIOS name is like the combination of a TCP/IP machine address and service port number. Windows NT—all of Microsoft's network operating systems, for that matter—use NetBIOS names to uniquely distinguish machines on a network. When you first start working with NetBIOS, it is tempting to try to recycle the machine name that is already defined. However, this causes all sorts of problems because the operating system uses the machine name for its own purposes. You must come up with some scheme for generating new, unique names.

The way I have handled that problem in the WNet DLLs is to build a NetBIOS name out of a combination between the machine name and the service endpoint name. For the WNet server, for instance, I add the extension ".WNET" to the machine name. On machine NUMBER1, this gives me a NetBIOS name NUMBER1.WNET. For the benchmark tests, the client and server use the names NUMBER1.BCLI and NUMBER1.BSRV. You cannot get too creative because NetBIOS names are limited to 16 (NCBNAMSZ) characters and must be padded on the right with spaces.

Adding a unique name can be a time-consuming operation. If you use the wait version of the command, you may want to spin off a thread to add the name in the background. Because the name is required to be unique, NetBIOS sends a broadcast over the network to see if any other station is using the name, then waits for a response.

To add a unique NetBIOS name:

1. Fill the *ncb_name* field with the name you want to add, and pad it on the right with spaces so it is NCBNAMSZ (16) characters long.
2. If you are using the no-wait command, point the *ncb_post* field to your callback routine, or create an event and put its handle in the *ncb_event* field.
3. Set the *ncb_lana_num* field to the appropriate LAN adapter number (probably zero).
4. Set the *ncb_command* field to NCBADDNAME. If you want the no-wait variety, OR in the ASYNCH flag (defined as 0x80) as well.
5. Call Netbios() and pass it a pointer to the NCB. With blocking commands, Netbios() returns NRC_GOODRET (zero) to indicate success. With non-blocking commands, it immediately returns NRC_GOODRET. *ncb_cmd_cplt* contains NRC_PENDING (0xFF) until the operation completes, at which time *ncb_retcode* reflects the success or failure of the request.

6. If the command is successful, NetBIOS assigns a new name number and returns it in the *ncb_num* field of the NCB.

Adding a Group Name (NCBADDGRNAME). Adding a NetBIOS group name uses the exact same procedure, but the command code is NCBADDGRNAME rather than NCBADDNAME. Also, group names need not be unique on the network (indeed, they are unlikely to be), so it takes much less time to add a group name.

Deleting a Name (NCBDELNAME). To delete a name, set the *ncb_lana_num, ncb_post*, and *ncb_event* fields to the appropriate values. Place the name you want to delete in the *ncb_name field*, and set the *ncb_command* field to NCBDELNAME, ORing in the ASYNCH flag if you want the no-wait command.

The NetBIOS Session Commands

The session commands provide connection-oriented services. The most important commands are Listen (NCBLISTEN), Call (NCBCALL), Send (NCBSEND), Receive (NCBRECV), and Hangup (NCBHANGUP).

Listen (NCBLISTEN). The Listen command allows a server application to receive client requests for service. To issue this command:

1. As always, set the *ncb_lana_num* field to the correct setting, probably zero.
2. Set the *ncb_name* to the name by which client stations will attempt to reach you. This is your service endpoint. It is equivalent to a pipe name or to a TCP/IP host address and port number.
3. Set the *ncb_callname* to the network name from which you are willing to accept requests. This can be a unique NetBIOS name, a group name, or the wildcard character '*' (padded with spaces), which says you will accept requests from anyone.
4. Set the *ncb_post* or *ncb_event* field to a non-zero value if you are doing a no-wait listen.
5. Set *ncb_command* to NCBLISTEN, and OR in the ASYNCH flag if necessary.
6. Call Netbios().

7. When a request for a connection arrives, the *ncb_lsn* field of the NCB will contain the connection ID (or "local session number," in NetBIOS terminology).

8. To continue servicing the connected client, you need to post non-blocking Receive requests.

9. If the Listen command was asynchronous, you will probably want to repost it so that you can continue to accept client connections.

Because listening for client connections is a passive operation, it is intrinsically a background activity. Here are some ways to do a NetBIOS Listen command in the background under NT:

*   Create threads that execute blocking Listen commands. When a request comes in, these threads can create other threads to service the client, then go back to listening.
*   Issue a series of non-blocking Listen requests, then spin off a single thread that waits for the events to signal by calling WaitForMultipleObjects().
*   Issue non-blocking Listen commands using callback functions. This is the simplest way to do things, but the Microsoft documentation states that events are preferable.

Call (NCBCALL). The client-side counterpart to Listen is Call (NCBCALL). This requests a connection with a server application. To post a Call:

1. Fill the *ncb_name* field with your station name, and the *ncb_callname* with the name of the server station.

2. Set the *ncb_post* or *ncb_event* field to a non-zero value if you are doing a no-wait Call.

3. Set the *ncb_command* field to NCBCALL. Include the ASYNCH flag if necessary.

4. Call Netbios(). If it completes successfully, *ncb_lsn* will contain the connection number that NetBIOS has assigned you.

In contrast to the Listen command, the Call command is inherently a synchronous activity. That is, the client application probably needs some data or service from the server application and cannot proceed until it knows it has connected. _WNetCall(), for instance, cannot return until a connection has been established because the connection number is the return value of the function.

Send (NCBSEND). Once a connection is in place, both server and client stations issue Send and Receive commands to exchange data.

To issue a Send command:

1. Point *ncb_buffer* to the data you want to transmit, and set *ncb_length* to the length of the data.
2. Set *ncb_lsn* to the connection number that NetBIOS assigned. This came back in the NCB that you used for the Listen command on the server side, or the Call command on the client.
3. Set *ncb_command* to NCBSEND.
4. For a no-wait operation, set *ncb_post* or *ncb_event*, and OR the ASYNCH bit into the *ncb_command*.
5. Call Netbios().

There are three other variations on the NetBIOS Send command:

- Send No-Ack (NCBSENDNA) reduces the number of data acknowledgments that occur at the NetBIOS level and might therefore be expected to improve performance. This is especially appropriate for a request-response type of exchange, where an acknowledgment is implicit in the nature of the transaction. However, the benchmark data presented later in this chapter shows the gain to be negligible.
- Chain Send (NCBCHAINSEND) concatenates two buffers into a single transmission. It can therefore send twice as much as a normal send. The *ncb_callname* field is used to describe the second buffer. The first two bytes hold the length of the buffer, and the third through sixth bytes point to it. There is no corresponding Chain Receive; the partner station must have multiple Receive NCBs posted in order to accept the data.
- Chain Send No-Ack (NCBCHAINSENDNA) combines Chain Send and Send No-Ack.

Receive (NCBRECV). Receive commands may be synchronous or asynchronous. Because the server application plays a passive role, it is likely to post non-blocking Receive commands as soon as a connection is established so that it can handle any incoming data. The client, on the other hand, normally wants to ask the server some kind of question, so it will probably send some data, then wait for an answer. To post a Receive command:

1. Set *ncb_post* or *ncb_event* if you are doing a no-wait Receive.
2. Set *ncb_lsn* to the connection number assigned by NetBIOS.

3. Point *ncb_buffer* to the buffer where you want to receive the data, and set *ncb_length* to the size of the buffer.
4. Set *ncb_command* to NCBRECV, with the ASYNCH flag if it applies.
5. Call Netbios().

Another kind of Receive is a Receive Any (NCBRECVANY). This accepts data for any connections currently open for the name indicated in the *ncb_num* field. A standard Receive command takes precedence over a Receive Any. So if you have a connection-specific Receive outstanding for a connection, NetBIOS will deliver any data that arrives over that connection to the NCB associated with the Receive, bypassing the Receive Any.

Hangup (NCBHANGUP). A Hangup request terminates a connection. To isse a Hangup command:

1. Set *ncb_lsn* to the number of the connection you want to terminate.
2. Set *ncb_post* and *ncb_event* if you are doing a no-wait Hangup.
3. Set *ncb_command* to NCBHANGUP, ORing in the ASYNCH flag if it is appropriate.
4. Call Netbios().

The NetBIOS Datagram Commands

NetBIOS has four datagram services:

- Send Datagram (NCBDGSEND)
- Receive Datagram (NCBDGRECV)
- Send Broadcast Datagram (NCBDGSENDBC)
- Receive Broadcast Datagram (NCBDGRECVBC)

Send Datagram and Receive Datagram can communicate with single stations using unique names or groups of stations using group names. Send Broadcast Datagram and Receive Broadcast Datagram communicate with all attached stations.

Send Datagram (NCBDGSEND or NCBDGSENDBC). To send a datagram:

1. Set *ncb_num* to the name number assigned when you registered your NetBIOS name.

2. Set *ncb_callname* to the station name you want to communicate with. It can be either a unique name or a group name. The call name is irrelevant for a broadcast datagram, so it is not used.
3. Set *ncb_post* or *ncb_event* if you are doing a no-wait send.
4. Point *ncb_buffer* to the data, and set *ncb_length* to its size.
5. Set *ncb_command* to NCBDGSEND. For broadcast datagrams, the command code is NCBDGSENDBC.
6. Call Netbios().

Receive Datagram (NCBDGRECV or NCBDGRECVBC). To receive a datagram:

1. Set *ncb_num* to the name number corresponding to the name you want to be known by.
2. Point *ncb_buffer* to the buffer where you want to receive the data, and set *ncb_length* to its size.
3. Set *ncb_post* or *ncb_event* for no-wait receives.
4. Set *ncb_command* to NCBDGRECV, or NCBDGRECVBC to receive broadcast datagrams.
5. Call Netbios().

Other NetBIOS Commands

NetBIOS also has some status reporting functions and two miscellaneous operations, Reset (NCBRESET) and Cancel (NCBCANCEL).

Reset (NCBRESET). You have to call Reset before initiating any other NetBIOS operations. It configures NetBIOS for the number of outstanding commands it will support. To request a Reset:

1. Set *ncb_command* to NCBRESET.
2. Set *ncb_num* to the number of outstanding NCBs you want to allow.
3. Call Netbios().

Cancel (NCBCANCEL). There are certain situations in which you must cancel an outstanding request. To do so:

1. Set the *ncb_command* to NCBCANCEL.
2. Point *ncb_buffer* to the NCB that you want to cancel.
3. Call Netbios().

I will have occasion to use both Reset and Cancel in the level-zero NetBIOS DLL. I issue a Reset in the DLL's initialization routine; Cancel terminates a request if a timeout expires before the request completes.

The NetBIOS Level-Zero DLL

Discussion of the NetBIOS level-zero DLL begins in a by-now familiar place: the DLL initialization routine. As usual, I call it DllMain() and place it, along with _WNetInit(), in \NTNET\CODE\NETBIOS_WNETINI.CPP.

DLL Initialization

Before it does anything else, the NetBIOS DllMain() function does a NetBIOS reset by calling a routine I define, NBReset(). This is a required call for any NetBIOS application under Windows NT, like WSAStartup() with Windows Sockets. NBReset() is very brief. Here is its implementation, from \NTNET\CODE\NETBIOS_WNETMIS.CPP:

```
UCHAR NBReset(VOID)
{
   NCB ncbReset;

   ZeroMemory(&ncbReset, sizeof (NCB));
   ncbReset.ncb_command = NCBRESET;
   ncbReset.ncb_num = 64;   // Number of NCBs permitted

   return Netbios(&ncbReset);
}
```

Next, DllMain() allocates a TLS index for future use. The NetBIOS DLL, unlike the other level-zero DLLs, does not use Thread Local Storage. However, because Thread Local Storage is such a handy tool, I assume that I may decide to use it at any moment.

Then, after registering the WMU_PACKET_RECEIVED window message, DllMain() creates a shared memory region for an integer that will count the number of registering applications. I will use this in _WNetShutdown() to decide how extensive a shutdown to carry out.

The DllMain() listing follows.

```
int APIENTRY DllMain(HINSTANCE hInstance,
                     DWORD     dwReason,
                     LPVOID    lpReserved)
   {
```

```
BOOL            bInit;

switch (dwReason)
    {
    case DLL_PROCESS_ATTACH:
        // Do NetBIOS reset for each client application
        if (NBReset() != NRC_GOODRET)
            return 0;

        dwTLSIndex = TlsAlloc();

        if (dwTLSIndex == 0xFFFFFFFF)
            return 0;

        hDLLInstance = hInstance;
        WMU_PACKET_RECEIVED =
          RegisterWindowMessage(TEXT("WMU_PACKET_RECEIVED"));

        // Get shared memory to count client applications
        hRegistrations = CreateFileMapping(
            (HANDLE) 0xFFFFFFFF,
            NULL,
            PAGE_READWRITE,
            0,
            sizeof (int),
            TEXT("/SHARED_MEM/WNET/Registrations"));
        if (hRegistrations == NULL)
            return FALSE;

        bInit = (GetLastError() != ERROR_ALREADY_EXISTS);

        lpnRegistrations = (LPINT) MapViewOfFile(
                hRegistrations,
                FILE_MAP_WRITE,
                0,
                0,
                0);
        if (lpnRegistrations == NULL)
            return FALSE;

        if (bInit)
            *lpnRegistrations = 0;

        break;
    case DLL_PROCESS_DETACH:
        TlsFree(dwTLSIndex);
        UnmapViewOfFile(lpnRegistrations);
```

```
                CloseHandle(hRegistrations);
                break;
        }

    return 1;
}
```

_WNetInit()

In all the level-zero DLLs, _WNetInit() is responsible for setting up the registering application as a server. With NetBIOS, that means:

- Registering a unique NetBIOS name so that it can accept connections
- Registering a NetBIOS group name so that it can receive multicast datagrams
- Posting some Listen requests by calling _WNetListen()
- Listening for datagrams by calling _WNetReceiveDatagram()

With NetBIOS, you must issue a number of Listen and Receive Datagram requests. Later, when a connection is established, I will also spin off several non-blocking Receive requests. NetBIOS does not work like Windows Sockets, where a single call to WSAAsyncSelect() suffices for all the events that may occur. NetBIOS can handle network events only if you give it NCBs; each NCB can handle only one event.

The other work in _WNetInit() involves forcing the station and endpoint names to the ANSI character set (NetBIOS does not support Unicode) and building a NetBIOS name that concatenates them. To emphasize: with NetBIOS, the name that you register is a service endpoint name, not a machine name.

Here is _WNetInit():

```
int WINAPI _WNetInit(HWND hWnd, LPVOID lpStationName,
                     LPVOID lpEndpoint,
                     DWORD  dwDesiredPrecedence)
{
    UCHAR   uNBReturnCode;
    CHAR    szMyName[100];
    int     i;
    DWORD   dwNameLength = NCBNAMSZ;
    int     nNameNumber;
    char    szStationName[256];
    char    szEndpoint[256];

    if (lpStationName == NULL ||
        *((LPSTR) lpStationName) == '\0')
```

```
        {
        GetComputerNameA(szMyName, &dwNameLength);
        lpStationName = szMyName;
        }

    // See if station name is passed as a unicode string
    if (!UnicodeToANSI((LPTSTR) lpStationName, szStationName,
            sizeof (szStationName)))
        return -1;

    lpStationName = szStationName;

    // If called with empty name, build default WNET server name

    if (lpEndpoint == NULL)
        lpEndpoint = ".WNET";

    if (!UnicodeToANSI((LPTSTR) lpEndpoint, szEndpoint,
            sizeof (szEndpoint)))
        return -1;

    lpEndpoint = szEndpoint;

    if (*((LPBYTE) lpEndpoint) != '.')
        lstrcatA(szMyName, ".");
    lstrcatA(szMyName, (LPSTR) lpEndpoint);

    if (*lpnRegistrations == 0) // Only add group name when
                                // first client registers
        {
        if ((uNBReturnCode = NBAddGroupName((LPSTR) WNET_DOMAINA,
                &byGroupNameNumber))
                == NRC_GOODRET)
            {
            // Listen for broadcast datagrams using the
            // group name "WNET_DOMAIN"
            for (i = 0; i < MAX_LISTEN_REQUESTS; ++i)
                {
                if (!_WNetReceiveDatagram(byBroadcastBuffers[i],
                    RECEIVE_BUFFER_SIZE,
                    ((int) byGroupNameNumber) + MAX_NAMES,
                        hWnd))
                    return -1;
                }
            }
        else
            return -1;
        }
```

```
// Pad name with spaces on the right.
while (lstrlenA(szMyName) < NCBNAMSZ)
   lstrcatA(szMyName, " ");

uNBReturnCode = NBAddName(szMyName, &nNameNumber);

if (uNBReturnCode != NRC_GOODRET)
   return -1;

++(*lpnRegistrations);          // Bump usage count

// Post LISTENs and RECEIVE DATAGRAMs.
for (i = 0; i < MAX_LISTEN_REQUESTS; ++i)
   {
   if (!_WNetListen(nNameNumber, hWnd))
      return -1;
   if (!_WNetReceiveDatagram(byDatagramBuffers[i],
         RECEIVE_BUFFER_SIZE, nNameNumber, hWnd))
      return -1;
   }
if (dwDesiredPrecedence == 0xFFFFFFFF)
   dwPrecedence = PROTOCOL_NETBIOS + 1;
else
   dwPrecedence = dwDesiredPrecedence;

return nNameNumber;
}
```

Adding NetBIOS Names

_WNetInit() calls two private routines, NBAddName() and
NBAddGroupName(). As the names suggest, these routines register two new
names with NetBIOS; they are in the source file \NTNET\CODE\
NET-BIOS_WNETNAM.CPP. In both of these routines, I use the *ncb_event*
field of the NCB and execute the no-wait version of the NetBIOS command.
This prevents the routine from entering a suspended state.
WaitForNBNameCommand() calls MsgWaitForMultipleObjects() with an
INFINITE timeout value. Using MsgWaitForMultipleObjects(), enables me
to get any messages that I need to deal with. Notice that I cannot allow a
timeout here—NetBIOS doesn't let you cancel the Name commands, so I
just have to wait until it finishes.

Here are NBAddName(), NBAddGroupName(), and WaitForNBName
Command(). Both NBAddName() and NBAddGroupName() return the
name number that NetBIOS assigns. You will need this for many other
NetBIOS operations.

```c
UCHAR NBAddName(LPSTR lpName, LPINT lpNameNumber)
{
    PNCB     pNcb;
    UCHAR    uNBReturnCode;
    int      nNextNameIndex;
    TCHAR    szUnicodeName[256];

    nNextNameIndex = WNetGetNextNameIndex();
    if (nNextNameIndex == -1)
        return NRC_NORES;

    pNcb = (PNCB) VirtualAlloc(NULL, sizeof (NCB), MEM_COMMIT,
                              PAGE_READWRITE);

    if (pNcb == NULL)
        {
        dwBytesTriedToAlloc = sizeof (NCB);
        RaiseException(STATUS_NO_MEMORY, 0, 1, &dwBytesTriedToAlloc);
        return NRC_NORES;
        }

    pNcb->ncb_event = CreateEvent(NULL, TRUE, FALSE, NULL);
    if (pNcb->ncb_event == NULL)
        return NRC_NORES;

    FillMemory(pNcb->ncb_name, sizeof (pNcb->ncb_name), ' ');
    CopyMemory(pNcb->ncb_name, lpName, lstrlenA(lpName));

    pNcb->ncb_command = NCBADDNAME;

    if (!ISWIN32S())
        pNcb->ncb_command |= ASYNCH;

    Netbios(pNcb);

    if (!ISWIN32S())
        WaitForNBNameCommand(pNcb);

    uNBReturnCode = pNcb->ncb_retcode;

    if (uNBReturnCode == NRC_GOODRET)
        {
        *lpNameNumber = nNextNameIndex;
#ifndef WIN32S
        // We're keeping track of names internally in
        // Unicode format
        MultiByteToWideChar(CP_ACP, 0, (LPCSTR) lpName, -1,
            szUnicodeName, sizeof (szUnicodeName) / sizeof (TCHAR));
```

```
#else
      lstrcpy(szUnicodeName, lpName);
#endif
      WNetSetName(nNextNameIndex, szUnicodeName, NCBNAMSZ + 1);
      nNBNameNumbers[nNextNameIndex] = pNcb->ncb_num;
      }

   VirtualFree(pNcb, 0, MEM_RELEASE);
   return uNBReturnCode;
}

UCHAR NBAddGroupName(LPSTR lpGroupName, LPBYTE lpGroupNameNumber)
{
   PNCB   pNcb;
   UCHAR uNBReturnCode;

   pNcb = (PNCB) VirtualAlloc(NULL, sizeof (NCB), MEM_COMMIT,
                              PAGE_READWRITE);

   if (pNcb == NULL)
      {
      dwBytesTriedToAlloc = sizeof (NCB);
      RaiseException(STATUS_NO_MEMORY, 0, 1, &dwBytesTriedToAlloc);
      return NRC_NORES;
      }

   pNcb->ncb_event = CreateEvent(NULL, TRUE, FALSE, NULL);
   if (pNcb->ncb_event == NULL)
      return NRC_NORES;

   // Add group name, using no-wait option (except for Win32S).

   pNcb->ncb_command = NCBADDGRNAME;

   if (!ISWIN32S())
      pNcb->ncb_command |= ASYNCH;

   FillMemory(pNcb->ncb_name, sizeof (pNcb->ncb_name), ' ');
   CopyMemory(pNcb->ncb_name, lpGroupName,
              lstrlenA(lpGroupName));

   Netbios(pNcb);

   if (!ISWIN32S())
      WaitForNBNameCommand(pNcb);

   uNBReturnCode = pNcb->ncb_retcode;
```

```
    if (uNBReturnCode == NRC_GOODRET)
        *lpGroupNameNumber = pNcb->ncb_num;

    VirtualFree(pNcb, 0, MEM_RELEASE);
    return uNBReturnCode;
}

static void WaitForNBNameCommand(PNCB pNcb)
{
    MSG msg;

    // Note that we can't time out here—if we get a time out,
    // we can't cancel the command (NetBIOS won't let you
    // cancel any of the name commands).

    // However, we also won't be able to free the memory, because
    // the command will still be outstanding.

    switch (MsgWaitForMultipleObjects(1, &pNcb->ncb_event, FALSE,
                INFINITE, QS_ALLEVENTS))
        {
        case WAIT_OBJECT_0:
            // Command completed
            break;
        case 1:
            // Got a message
            if (PeekMessage(&msg, NULL, 0, 0, PM_REMOVE))
                {
                if (msg.message == WM_QUIT)
                    PostMessage(msg.hwnd, WM_QUIT, msg.wParam, msg.lParam);
                else
                    {
                    TranslateMessage(&msg);
                    DispatchMessage(&msg);
                    }
                }
            break;
        default:
            // What?  How'd that happen?
            break;
        }
}
```

Listening for Connections

_WNetInit() also calls _WNetListen() to make the registering application available for clients to connect to. In _WNetListen(), you see the first use of a background thread to wait for the operation to complete. Listen requests are inherently open-ended; you have no idea when they are going to complete. I want _WNetListen() to return quickly, so whatever residual activity it is going to carry out must execute in the background. _WNetListen() calls ThreadWait(), which starts the thread, whose entry point is NetBIOSPollingThread(). It blocks on the *ncb_event* of the NCB by calling WaitForSingleObject(). When it wakes up, it calls the NetBIOS post routine, NBWndProc(), just as if NetBIOS had called it directly. The name NBWndProc() is historical; in *Windows Network Programming*, it is a true window procedure.

_WNetListen() uses a data structure that is a subclass of the NCB, which I call an XNCB (eXtended Network Control Block). This includes two additional fields that are necessary for proper handling of asynchronous events when they complete:

- The original size of the buffer. When an asynchronous Receive or Receive Datagram completes, NetBIOS sets the *ncb_length* field to indicate how much data has arrived. When recycling the NCB, you must reset *ncb_length* to the originally allocated buffer size. Otherwise, the buffer space keeps shrinking and shrinking.
- The handle of the top-level application window that is the ultimate recipient of WMU_PACKET_RECEIVED messages.

Here is the type definition, from \NTNET\CODE\NETBIOS\ WNETNB.H:

```
struct XNCB
{
   NCB   ncbBase;
   HWND  hWnd;
   WORD  wOriginalDataLength;
};            // Extended NCB
```

And here is the listing of \NTNET\CODE\NETBIOS_WNETLIS.CPP:

```
/********
*
*  _WNETLIS.CPP
*
*  Copyright (c) 1992-1994 Ralph P. Davis, All Rights Reserved
*
********
```

```
/*===== Includes =====*/

#include "wnetnb.h"
#include <string.h>


/*===== Function Definitions =====*/

BOOL WINAPI _WNetListen(int nNameIndex, HWND hWnd)
{
    LPXNCB lpXNCB;
    UCHAR  uNBReturnCode;
    BOOL   bReturnCode = TRUE;

    lpXNCB = (LPXNCB) VirtualAlloc(NULL, sizeof (XNCB),
                                   MEM_COMMIT,
                                   PAGE_READWRITE);

    if (lpXNCB == NULL)
        {
        dwBytesTriedToAlloc = sizeof (XNCB);
        RaiseException(STATUS_NO_MEMORY, 0, 1, &dwBytesTriedToAlloc);
        return FALSE;
        }

    FillMemory(lpXNCB->ncbBase.ncb_callname,
               sizeof (lpXNCB->ncbBase.ncb_callname), ' ');

    lpXNCB->ncbBase.ncb_callname[0] = '*';  // Anybody

    FillMemory(lpXNCB->ncbBase.ncb_name,
               sizeof (lpXNCB->ncbBase.ncb_name),
               ' ');

#ifndef WIN32S
    WideCharToMultiByte(CP_ACP, 0, WNetGetName(nNameIndex),
        WNetGetNameLength(nNameIndex), (LPSTR) lpXNCB->ncbBase.ncb_name,
        sizeof (lpXNCB->ncbBase.ncb_name), NULL, NULL);
#else
    CopyMemory(lpXNCB->ncbBase.ncb_name, WNetGetName(nNameIndex),
        WNetGetNameLength(nNameIndex));
#endif

    lpXNCB->hWnd = hWnd;

    lpXNCB->ncbBase.ncb_command = NCBLISTEN | ASYNCH;

    if (!ISWIN32S())
```

```
    // Use an unnamed auto-reset event
    lpXNCB->ncbBase.ncb_event = CreateEvent(NULL, TRUE, FALSE, NULL);
else
    lpXNCB->ncbBase.ncb_event = NULL;

// If CreateEvent() fails, use callback
if (lpXNCB->ncbBase.ncb_event == NULL)
    lpXNCB->ncbBase.ncb_post = NBWndProc;

uNBReturnCode = Netbios((PNCB) lpXNCB);

if (uNBReturnCode == NRC_GOODRET)
    {
    // Non-blocking—spin off thread to poll status of event
    if (lpXNCB->ncbBase.ncb_event != NULL)
        {
        bReturnCode = ThreadWait((PNCB) lpXNCB);
        }
    }
else
    {
    bReturnCode = FALSE;
    }
return bReturnCode;
}
```

Here are ThreadWait() and NetBIOSPollingThread(), from \NTNET\CODE\NETBIOS_WNETRCV.CPP:

```
BOOL ThreadWait(PNCB pNCB)
{
    HANDLE hThread;
    DWORD  dwThreadID;
    DWORD  dwError;

    // Non-blocking—spin off thread to poll status of event
    hThread = CreateThread(NULL, 0, NetBIOSPollingThread,
        pNCB, 0, &dwThreadID);
    if (hThread == NULL)
        {
        dwError = GetLastError();
        CloseHandle(pNCB->ncb_event);
        NBCancel(pNCB);
        return FALSE;
        }
    CloseHandle(hThread);
    return TRUE;
}
```

```
DWORD WINAPI NetBIOSPollingThread(LPVOID lpParameter)
{
    LPXNCB lpXNCB = (LPXNCB) lpParameter;

    WaitForSingleObject(lpXNCB->ncbBase.ncb_event, INFINITE);

    // The event handle gets closed in NBWndProc()
    NBWndProc((PNCB) lpXNCB);

    ExitThread(0);
    return 0;   // Humor the compiler
}
```

Listening for Datagrams

Besides listening for connection requests, the server module must also be prepared to receive datagrams. Therefore, _WNetInit() calls _WNetReceiveDatagram() to make buffer space available. The juggling at the beginning of the routine is checking the input name index to see if it is greater than the constant MAX_NAMES, defined as 256. This bias is added to indicate that the name number identifies the NetBIOS group name that was added, rather than a unique name. _WNetInit() asks to receive datagrams directed to this name so that it can get multicast datagrams. It also listens using the name number of the unique name so that it can receive datagrams directed specifically to it.

```
/********
*
*  _WNETRDG.CPP
*
* Copyright (c) 1992-1994 Ralph P. Davis, All Rights Reserved
*
********/


/*===== Includes =====*/

#include "wnetnb.h"


/*===== Function Definitions =====*/

BOOL WINAPI _WNetReceiveDatagram(LPVOID lpBuffer,
                      WORD wBufferSize,
                      int  nNameIndex,
                      HWND hWnd)
```

```
{
    LPXNCB  lpXNCB;
    UCHAR   uNBReturnCode;

    if (wBufferSize > RECEIVE_BUFFER_SIZE)
        return FALSE;

    lpXNCB = (LPXNCB) VirtualAlloc(NULL, sizeof (XNCB),
                                    MEM_COMMIT,
                                    PAGE_READWRITE);

    if (lpXNCB == NULL)
        {
        dwBytesTriedToAlloc = sizeof (XNCB);
        RaiseException(STATUS_NO_MEMORY, 0, 1, &dwBytesTriedToAlloc);
        return FALSE;
        }

    lpXNCB->ncbBase.ncb_command = NCBDGRECV | ASYNCH;

    if (nNameIndex > MAX_NAMES)  // Flag that this is a NetBIOS group
        lpXNCB->ncbBase.ncb_num = (BYTE) (nNameIndex - MAX_NAMES);
    else
        lpXNCB->ncbBase.ncb_num = (BYTE) nNBNameNumbers[nNameIndex];

    lpXNCB->ncbBase.ncb_buffer = (LPBYTE) lpBuffer;
    lpXNCB->wOriginalDataLength =
        lpXNCB->ncbBase.ncb_length = wBufferSize;

    if (!ISWIN32S())
        lpXNCB->ncbBase.ncb_event = CreateEvent(NULL, TRUE, FALSE, NULL);
    else
        lpXNCB->ncbBase.ncb_event = NULL;

    if (lpXNCB->ncbBase.ncb_event == NULL)
        lpXNCB->ncbBase.ncb_post = NBWndProc;
    lpXNCB->hWnd = hWnd;

    uNBReturnCode = Netbios((PNCB) lpXNCB);

    if (uNBReturnCode != NRC_GOODRET)
        {
        VirtualFree(lpXNCB, 0, MEM_RELEASE);
        return FALSE;
        }
    else if (lpXNCB->ncbBase.ncb_event != NULL)
        {
```

```
    return ThreadWait((PNCB) lpXNCB);
    }
else
    return TRUE;
}
```

The NetBIOS Post Routine—NBWndProc()

The NetBIOSPollingRoutine() listed earlier calls NBWndProc() directly when WaitForSingleObject() releases. NBWndProc() is also passed to Netbios() as the post routine if for any reason I am unable to create an event. The name "NBWndProc()" comes from the fact that in the Windows 3.X code presented in *Windows Network Programming* this function is invoked by a PostMessage() from the assembler post routine. In the NT version, it is not a true window procedure.

NBWndProc() is the most complex routine on the server side. It has to take care of many things, and it can make a lot of mistakes. First, keep in mind that NBWndProc() is responsible for processing asynchronous requests when they complete. In order to keep the server alive, you have to repost requests. However, there are many error conditions that preclude reposting the NCB—doing so results in an infinite cycle; as soon as you reissue the command, it fails with the same error that you just finished dealing with. The nested *switch* statement at the top of NBWndProc() evaluates the NCB to see if it can be reposted. Notice that only passive requests—Listen, Receive, Receive Any, Receive Datagram, and Receive Broadcast Datagram—are recycled. It makes no sense to recycle one of the active requests, like Call, Send, Send Datagram, or Hangup. These are one-time operations, whereas the passive operations need to maintain a continuous flow.

```
void CALLBACK NBWndProc(PNCB pNCB)
{
    LPXNCB lpXNCB = (LPXNCB) pNCB;
    WPARAM wOutParam;
    BOOL   bRepost;

    switch (lpXNCB->ncbBase.ncb_command & (~ASYNCH))
        {
        case NCBRECV:
        case NCBRECVANY:
            // See if command completed with some kind of error
            // that prevents reposting the NCB
            switch (lpXNCB->ncbBase.ncb_retcode)
                {
                case NRC_SCLOSED:
```

```
            case NRC_SABORT:
            case NRC_ILLNN:
            case NRC_NAMERR:
            case NRC_SNUMOUT:
                VirtualFree(lpXNCB->ncbBase.ncb_buffer, 0,
                            MEM_RELEASE);
                bRepost = FALSE;
                break;
            default:
                bRepost = TRUE;
                break;
            }
        break;
    case NCBDGRECV:
    case NCBLISTEN:
    case NCBDGRECVBC:
        switch (lpXNCB->ncbBase.ncb_retcode)
            {
            case NRC_SCLOSED:
            case NRC_SNUMOUT:
            case NRC_ILLNN:
            case NRC_NAMERR:
                bRepost = FALSE;
                break;
            default:
                bRepost = TRUE;
                break;
            }
        break;
    default:
        bRepost = FALSE;
        break;
    }
```

Following is a second *switch* statement, which decides what to do next. If the NCB represents a successful Listen command, then a connection has been established. The appropriate response is to post connection-specific Receive commands, which is done by calling _WNetReceive(). If the NCB is some other connection-oriented operation, like a Receive or Receive Any command, I capture the NetBIOS local session number (the *ncb_lsn* field of the NCB). When I post the WMU_PACKET_RECEIVED message upstairs, the *wParam* contains the HCONNECTION, which for NetBIOS is the LSN. The *default* for the *switch* statement handles NCBs that come from datagram actions, like Receive Datagram or Receive Broadcast Datagram. In this case, I pass the HCONNECTION as zero.

```
switch (lpXNCB->ncbBase.ncb_command & (~ASYNCH))
    {
    case NCBLISTEN:
        // Connect request has arrived—post asynchronous
        // listens by calling _WNetReceive()
        if (lpXNCB->ncbBase.ncb_retcode == NRC_GOODRET)
            {
            int i;
            LPBYTE lpBuffer;

            for (i = 0; i < MAX_LISTEN_REQUESTS; ++i)
                {
                lpBuffer = (LPBYTE) VirtualAlloc(NULL,
                                    MAX_SEND_BUFFER_SIZE,
                                    MEM_COMMIT,
                                    PAGE_READWRITE);
                if (lpBuffer != NULL)
                    {
                    _WNetReceive(
                    (HCONNECTION) lpXNCB->ncbBase.ncb_lsn,
                    lpBuffer, MAX_SEND_BUFFER_SIZE,
                    0, 0, lpXNCB->hWnd);
                    }
                else
                    {
                    dwBytesTriedToAlloc = MAX_SEND_BUFFER_SIZE;
                    RaiseException(STATUS_NO_MEMORY, 0, 1,
                        &dwBytesTriedToAlloc);
                    }
                }
            }
        break;
    case NCBCALL:
    case NCBSEND:
    case NCBRECV:
    case NCBHANGUP:
    case NCBRECVANY:
    case NCBCHAINSEND:
        // Connection-oriented exchange of data
        // The connection number appears in the ncb_lsn
        // field of the NCB
        wOutParam = (WPARAM) lpXNCB->ncbBase.ncb_lsn;
        break;
    default:
        wOutParam = 0;
        break;
    }
```

Next, I pass the data along to SendMsgFromSharedMem(), which puts it into shared memory and calls the notification window.

```
// Make sure packet was not received in error.
if (lpXNCB->hWnd != NULL &&
   lpXNCB->ncbBase.ncb_retcode == NRC_GOODRET)
   {
// Post message and data to originating window

   if (lpXNCB->ncbBase.ncb_length != 0)
      {
      // Post WMU_PACKET_RECEIVED message to
      // originating window

      // Copy the data into shared memory
      if (wOutParam != 0)
         wOutParam += (dwPrecedence * PROTOCOL_BIAS);
      SendMsgFromSharedMem(lpXNCB->hWnd, lpXNCB->ncbBase.ncb_buffer,
         (HCONNECTION) wOutParam,
         lpXNCB->ncbBase.ncb_length);
      }
   }
```

Finally, I repost the request if it is appropriate to do so, after first restoring the *ncb_length* field to its original value. The *wOriginalDataLength* field of the XNCB remembers this information. If I am not recycling the NCB, I close the event handle and release the memory allocated for the XNCB.

```
   if (bRepost)      // Recycle original passive request
      {
      // Reset receive buffer length in NCB to
      // size of original buffer (remembered in the
      // extended NCB)
      lpXNCB->ncbBase.ncb_length =
         lpXNCB->wOriginalDataLength;
      Netbios((PNCB) lpXNCB);
      if (lpXNCB->ncbBase.ncb_event != NULL)
         {
         ThreadWait((PNCB) lpXNCB);
         }
      }
   if (!bRepost)
      {
      if (lpXNCB->ncbBase.ncb_event != NULL)
         CloseHandle(lpXNCB->ncbBase.ncb_event);
      VirtualFree(lpXNCB, 0, MEM_RELEASE);
      }
```

Connection-Oriented Receives

NBWndProc() calls _WNetReceive() when a Listen completes successfully. This function provides buffer space for NetBIOS to receive incoming packets on the newly established connection.

A request for a blocking receive is treated in a pseudo-blocking manner. I still execute a no-wait Receive, but use MsgWaitForMultipleObjects() in a timeout loop so that I don't freeze the application. The command issued is NCBRECV, unless the HCONNECTION is passed in as zero. In this case, I cannot do a connection-specific receive, so I use NCBRECVANY.

```
/*******
 *
 *  _WNETRCV.CPP
 *
 * Copyright (c) 1992-1994 Ralph P. Davis, All Rights Reserved
 *
 *******/


/*===== Includes =====*/

#include "wnetnb.h"


/*===== Function Definitions =====*/

BOOL WINAPI _WNetReceive(HCONNECTION hConnection,
                         LPVOID      lpData,
                         WORD        wDataLength,
                         DWORD       dwTimeout,
                         int         nNameIndex,
                         HWND        hWnd)
{
    LPXNCB lpXNCB;
    UCHAR  uNBReturnCode;
    BOOL   bReturnCode = TRUE;
    LPBYTE lpQueuedPacket;
    DWORD  dwStartTime, dwWaitTime;
    MSG    msg;

    if (dwTimeout == 0)
        {
        lpQueuedPacket = WNetGetNextQueuedPacket(hConnection);
        if (lpQueuedPacket != NULL)
            {
            WNetCopyQueuedPacket(lpQueuedPacket, (LPBYTE) lpData,
```

```
            wDataLength);
        return TRUE;
        }
    }

lpXNCB = (LPXNCB) VirtualAlloc(NULL, sizeof (XNCB),
                                MEM_COMMIT,
                                PAGE_READWRITE);
if (lpXNCB == NULL)
    {
    dwBytesTriedToAlloc = sizeof (XNCB);
    RaiseException(STATUS_NO_MEMORY, 0, 1, &dwBytesTriedToAlloc);
    return FALSE;
    }

// Get Win32 event
if (!ISWIN32S())
    lpXNCB->ncbBase.ncb_event = CreateEvent(NULL, TRUE, FALSE, NULL);
else
    lpXNCB->ncbBase.ncb_event = NULL;

if (dwTimeout > 0)
    {
    // We have to have the event for a blocking receive,
    // so we can control the arrival of data
    if (lpXNCB->ncbBase.ncb_event == NULL)
        {
        VirtualFree(lpXNCB, 0, MEM_RELEASE);
        return FALSE;
        }
    lpXNCB->ncbBase.ncb_command = NCBRECV | ASYNCH;
    }
else
    {
    // For non-blocking receives, we can just use a
    // callback if we couldn't create an event
    if (lpXNCB->ncbBase.ncb_event == NULL)
        lpXNCB->ncbBase.ncb_post = NBWndProc;
    lpXNCB->hWnd = hWnd;
    if (hConnection == 0)
        lpXNCB->ncbBase.ncb_command = NCBRECVANY | ASYNCH;
    else
        lpXNCB->ncbBase.ncb_command = NCBRECV | ASYNCH;
    lpXNCB->ncbBase.ncb_num = (BYTE) nNBNameNumbers[nNameIndex];
    }

lpXNCB->ncbBase.ncb_lsn = (BYTE) hConnection;
lpXNCB->ncbBase.ncb_buffer = (LPBYTE) lpData;
```

```
lpXNCB->ncbBase.ncb_length = wDataLength;

// Remember original size of the buffer so we can
// repost the request with the correct value
lpXNCB->wOriginalDataLength =
    lpXNCB->ncbBase.ncb_length;

// Invoke NetBIOS
uNBReturnCode = Netbios((PNCB) lpXNCB);

if (uNBReturnCode != NRC_GOODRET)
    {
    bReturnCode = FALSE;
    }
if (dwTimeout > 0 && bReturnCode)
    {
    // Blocking request, wait for event to signal
    // Wait requested timeout period, but pick up
    // any messages that come in by using MsgWaitForMultipleObjects()
    for (bReturnCode = FALSE, dwStartTime = GetCurrentTime(),
         dwWaitTime = dwTimeout;
         GetCurrentTime() - dwStartTime < dwTimeout;)
        {
        switch (MsgWaitForMultipleObjects(1,
                &lpXNCB->ncbBase.ncb_event, FALSE, dwWaitTime,
                QS_ALLEVENTS))
            {
            case WAIT_OBJECT_0:
                // Event completed
                dwStartTime -= dwTimeout;  // Kill the loop
                bReturnCode = TRUE;
                break;
            case 1:
                // A message came in—get it
                if (PeekMessage(&msg, NULL, 0, 0, PM_REMOVE))
                    {
                    if (msg.message == WM_QUIT)
                        {
                        // Force exit from loop
                        dwStartTime = GetCurrentTime() - (dwTimeout + 1);
                        PostMessage(msg.hwnd, WM_QUIT,
                                    msg.wParam, msg.lParam);
                        }
                    else
                        {
                        TranslateMessage(&msg);
                        DispatchMessage(&msg);
                        }
```

```
                    }
                 dwWaitTime -= (GetCurrentTime() - dwStartTime);
                 break;
              default:
                 // Event timed out—see if packet arrived
                 // asynchronously
                 lpQueuedPacket = WNetGetNextQueuedPacket(hConnection);
                 if (lpQueuedPacket != NULL)
                    {
                    // Yes, packet came in behind the scenes—retrieve it
                    WNetCopyQueuedPacket(lpQueuedPacket,
                       (LPBYTE) lpData, wDataLength);
                    bReturnCode = TRUE;
                    }
                 break;
              }
           }
        }
  else if (dwTimeout == 0)
     {
     bReturnCode = ThreadWait((PNCB) lpXNCB);
     }

  if (dwTimeout > 0)
     {
     if (lpXNCB->ncbBase.ncb_retcode == NRC_PENDING)
        NBCancel((PNCB) lpXNCB);

     CloseHandle(lpXNCB->ncbBase.ncb_event);
     VirtualFree(lpXNCB, 0, MEM_RELEASE);
     }
  return bReturnCode;
}
```

If the request times out, I have to cancel it so that stray NCBs won't be lying around. To do this, I call NBCancel() near the end of _WNetReceive(). NBCancel() is defined along with NBReset() in \NTNET\CODE\NETBIOS\ _WNETMIS.CPP. With Cancel, the *ncb_buffer* field of the NCB points to the NCB that you want to kill.

```
void NBCancel(PNCB pNCB)
{
NCB ncbCancel;

// You can't cancel a request unless it's
// currently pending
if (pNCB->ncb_cmd_cplt != NRC_PENDING)
```

```
                    return;

                ZeroMemory(&ncbCancel, sizeof (NCB));
                ncbCancel.ncb_command = NCBCANCEL;
                ncbCancel.ncb_buffer = (PUCHAR) pNCB;

                Netbios(&ncbCancel);
            }
```

Establishing a Connection

_WNetCall() issues a NetBIOS Call command. Most of the complexity of the function comes from setting up the name fields of the NCB. They must be converted from Unicode to ANSI and padded on the right with spaces. Also, the *lpEndpoint* argument, which identifies the service endpoint on the target machine, must be concatenated with the station name. (This is required only by my implementation, not by NetBIOS.) The NetBIOS name, as I have said, is not an actual machine name. Rather, it is a process identifier, used by NetBIOS to target the specific server application.

```
/********
 *
 * _WNETCAL.CPP
 *
 * Copyright (c) 1992-1994 Ralph P. Davis, All Rights Reserved
 *
 ********/


/*===== Includes =====*/

#include "wnetnb.h"
#include <string.h>


/*===== Function Definitions =====*/

HCONNECTION WINAPI _WNetCall(int nNameIndex,
                             LPVOID lpTargetStation,
                             LPVOID lpEndpoint)
{
    HCONNECTION hConnection;
    PNCB        pNCB;
    UCHAR       uNBReturnCode;
    char        szTargetStation[256];
    char        szEndpoint[256];
```

```
   if (lpEndpoint == NULL)
      lpEndpoint = ".WNET";

   // Convert station and endpoint to ANSI if they're Unicode
   if (!UnicodeToANSI((LPTSTR) lpTargetStation, szTargetStation,
         sizeof (szTargetStation)))
      return 0;

   lpTargetStation = szTargetStation;

   if (!UnicodeToANSI((LPTSTR) lpEndpoint, szEndpoint,
                     sizeof (szEndpoint)))
      return 0;

   lpEndpoint = szEndpoint;

   pNCB = (PNCB) VirtualAlloc(NULL, sizeof (NCB),
                             MEM_COMMIT,
                             PAGE_READWRITE);

   if (pNCB == NULL)
      {
      dwBytesTriedToAlloc = sizeof (NCB);
      RaiseException(STATUS_NO_MEMORY, 0, 1, &dwBytesTriedToAlloc);
      return 0;
      }

   FillMemory(pNCB->ncb_name, sizeof (pNCB->ncb_name), ' ');
#ifndef WIN32S
   WideCharToMultiByte(CP_ACP, 0, WNetGetName(nNameIndex),
      WNetGetNameLength(nNameIndex), (LPSTR) pNCB->ncb_name,
      sizeof (pNCB->ncb_name), NULL, NULL);
#else
   CopyMemory(pNCB->ncb_name, WNetGetName(nNameIndex),
      WNetGetNameLength(nNameIndex));
#endif

   FillMemory(pNCB->ncb_callname, sizeof (pNCB->ncb_callname), ' ');
   CopyMemory(pNCB->ncb_callname, lpTargetStation,
      lstrlenA((LPCSTR) lpTargetStation));
   CopyMemory(pNCB->ncb_callname + lstrlenA((LPCSTR) lpTargetStation),
      lpEndpoint, lstrlenA((LPCSTR) lpEndpoint));

   pNCB->ncb_command = NCBCALL;

   uNBReturnCode = Netbios(pNCB);

   if (uNBReturnCode == NRC_GOODRET)
```

```
      hConnection = (HCONNECTION) pNCB->ncb_lsn;
   else
      hConnection = 0;

   VirtualFree(pNCB, 0, MEM_RELEASE);
   return hConnection;
}
```

Connection-Oriented Sends

In _WNetSend(), I again implement an operation that appears to block, but does not actually do so. I submit a no-wait Send, then go into a timeout loop built around MsgWaitForMultipleObjects(). Here too, if the command times out, I have to cancel it.

```
/********
 *
 *  _WNETSND.CPP
 *
 * Copyright (c) 1992-1994 Ralph P. Davis, All Rights Reserved
 *
 ********/


/*===== Includes =====*/

#include "wnetnb.h"


/*===== Function Definitions =====*/

BOOL WINAPI _WNetSend(HCONNECTION hConnection, LPVOID lpData,
                      WORD wDataLength)
{
   PNCB    pNCB;
   DWORD   dwStartTime, dwWaitTime;
   MSG     msg;
   BOOL    bReturnCode = TRUE;
   UCHAR   uNBReturnCode;

   pNCB = (PNCB) VirtualAlloc(NULL, sizeof (NCB), MEM_COMMIT,
                              PAGE_READWRITE);

   if (pNCB == NULL)
      {
      dwBytesTriedToAlloc = sizeof (NCB);
      RaiseException(STATUS_NO_MEMORY, 0, 1, &dwBytesTriedToAlloc);
```

```
      return FALSE;
      }

pNCB->ncb_lsn = (BYTE) hConnection;
pNCB->ncb_command = NCBSEND;

if (!ISWIN32S())
   pNCB->ncb_event = CreateEvent(NULL, TRUE, FALSE, NULL);
else
   pNCB->ncb_event = NULL;

// If event was not successfully created, we'll do this
// as a blocking operation
if (pNCB->ncb_event != NULL)
   pNCB->ncb_command |= ASYNCH;
pNCB->ncb_buffer = (LPBYTE) lpData;

pNCB->ncb_length = wDataLength;

try
   {
   uNBReturnCode = Netbios(pNCB);
   if (pNCB->ncb_event != NULL)
      {
      // Use a five-second timeout
      for (dwStartTime = GetCurrentTime(), dwWaitTime = 5000;
          GetCurrentTime() - dwStartTime < 5000;)
         {
         switch (MsgWaitForMultipleObjects(1,
                &pNCB->ncb_event, FALSE, dwWaitTime,
                QS_ALLEVENTS))
            {
            case WAIT_OBJECT_0:
               // Event completed
               dwStartTime -= 5000;  // Kill the loop
               bReturnCode = (pNCB->ncb_retcode == NRC_GOODRET);
               break;
            case 1:
               // A message came in—get it
               if (PeekMessage(&msg, NULL, 0, 0, PM_REMOVE))
                  {
                  if (msg.message == WM_QUIT)
                     {
                     // Force exit from loop
                     dwStartTime = GetCurrentTime() - 5001;
                     PostMessage(msg.hwnd, WM_QUIT, msg.wParam,
                            msg.lParam);
                     }
```

```
            else
                {
                TranslateMessage(&msg);
                DispatchMessage(&msg);
                }
            }
        dwWaitTime -= (GetCurrentTime() - dwStartTime);
        break;
    default:
        // Send timed out
        bReturnCode = FALSE;
        NBCancel(pNCB);
        break;
        }
        }
        }
    }
except (EXCEPTION_EXECUTE_HANDLER)
    {
    uNBReturnCode = 0xFF;
    bReturnCode = FALSE;
    }
if (pNCB->ncb_event != NULL)
    CloseHandle(pNCB->ncb_event);
VirtualFree(pNCB, 0, MEM_RELEASE);
return bReturnCode;
}
```

Sending a Datagram

The NetBIOS version of _WNetSendDatagram() is probably the longest.
Most of the code just involves setting up the names and the other fields of
the NCB. There is one interesting aspect I'd like to call your attention to. I
send a broadcast datagram by specifying a target station of
"WNET_DOMAIN". For the other APIs you have looked at, I had to
interpret the name and translate it into the appropriate address. With
NetBIOS, though, I just send the datagram to "WNET_DOMAIN". That is
the group name that _WNetInit() registers when it calls
NBAddGroupName(). I am actually doing a multicast, not a broadcast, so I
use the standard Send Datagram command code, NCBDGSEND, rather than
the Send Broadcast Datagram code, NCBDGSENDBC.

```
/********
*
* _WNETSDG.CPP
*
* Copyright (c) 1992-1994 Ralph P. Davis, All Rights Reserved
*
********/


/*===== Includes =====*/

#include "wnetnb.h"
#include <string.h>


/*===== Functions Definitions =====*/

BOOL WINAPI _WNetSendDatagram(LPVOID lpTargetStation,
                             LPVOID lpEndpoint,
                             LPVOID lpData, WORD wDataLength,
                             int nNameIndex)
{
    LPXNCB  lpXNCB;
    TCHAR   szTarget[NCBNAMSZ + 1];
    UCHAR   uNBReturnCode;
    char    szTargetStation[256];
    char    szEndpoint[256];


    // Convert station and endpoint to ANSI if they're Unicode
    if (!UnicodeToANSI((LPTSTR) lpTargetStation, szTargetStation,
            sizeof (szTargetStation)))
       return FALSE;

    lpTargetStation = szTargetStation;

    if (lpEndpoint == NULL)
       lpEndpoint = ".WNET";

    if (!UnicodeToANSI((LPTSTR) lpEndpoint, szEndpoint,
                       sizeof (szEndpoint)))
       return FALSE;

    lpEndpoint = szEndpoint;

    if (lstrcmpA((LPSTR) lpTargetStation, WNET_DOMAINA) == 0)
       lpEndpoint = NULL;
```

```
// Datagrams limited to 512 bytes.
if (wDataLength > RECEIVE_BUFFER_SIZE)
   return FALSE;

lpXNCB = (LPXNCB) VirtualAlloc(NULL, sizeof (XNCB),
                               MEM_COMMIT,
                               PAGE_READWRITE);

if (lpXNCB == NULL)
   {
   dwBytesTriedToAlloc = sizeof (XNCB);
   RaiseException(STATUS_NO_MEMORY, 0, 1, &dwBytesTriedToAlloc);
   return FALSE;
   }

lpXNCB->ncbBase.ncb_command = NCBDGSEND | ASYNCH;

FillMemory(szTarget, sizeof (szTarget) - 1, ' ');
szTarget[sizeof (szTarget) - 1] = '\0';

CopyMemory(szTarget, lpTargetStation,
           lstrlenA((LPCSTR) lpTargetStation));

if (lpEndpoint != NULL)
   CopyMemory(szTarget + lstrlenA((LPCSTR) lpTargetStation),
              lpEndpoint, lstrlenA((LPCSTR) lpEndpoint));

if (!ISWIN32S())
   lpXNCB->ncbBase.ncb_event = CreateEvent(NULL, TRUE, FALSE, NULL);
else
   lpXNCB->ncbBase.ncb_event = NULL;

if (lpXNCB->ncbBase.ncb_event == NULL)
   lpXNCB->ncbBase.ncb_post = NBWndProc;

lpXNCB->ncbBase.ncb_num = (BYTE) nNBNameNumbers[nNameIndex];
CopyMemory(lpXNCB->ncbBase.ncb_callname, szTarget,
           sizeof (lpXNCB->ncbBase.ncb_callname));
lpXNCB->ncbBase.ncb_buffer = (LPBYTE) lpData;
lpXNCB->ncbBase.ncb_length = wDataLength;

uNBReturnCode = Netbios((PNCB) lpXNCB);

if (uNBReturnCode != NRC_GOODRET)
   return FALSE;
else if (lpXNCB->ncbBase.ncb_event != NULL)
   {
   return ThreadWait((PNCB) lpXNCB);
```

```
        }
    else
        return TRUE;
}
```

Hanging Up and Shutting Down

The Hangup command terminates a connection. All _WNetHangup() has to do is set the *ncb_lsn* field to the HCONNECTION passed to it, set the *ncb_command* to NCBHANGUP, then call Netbios().

```
/********
*
* _WNETHGP.CPP
*
* Copyright (c) 1992-1994 Ralph P. Davis, All Rights Reserved
*
********/


/*===== Includes =====*/

#include "wnetnb.h"


/*===== Function Definitions =====*/

void WINAPI _WNetHangup(HCONNECTION hConnection)
{
    PNCB         pNcb;

    pNcb = (PNCB) VirtualAlloc(NULL, sizeof (NCB),
                               MEM_COMMIT,
                               PAGE_READWRITE);
    if (pNcb == NULL)
        {
        dwBytesTriedToAlloc = sizeof (NCB);
        RaiseException(STATUS_NO_MEMORY, 0, 1, &dwBytesTriedToAlloc);
        ExitThread(0);
        return;
        }
    pNcb->ncb_lsn     = (BYTE) hConnection;
    pNcb->ncb_command = NCBHANGUP;

    Netbios(pNcb);
    VirtualFree(pNcb, 0, MEM_RELEASE);
}
```

In NetBIOS, shutting down involves removing the names you have registered from the NetBIOS name table. _WNetShutdown() deletes the unique name that _WNetInit() registered. If this is the last application using the DLL, it also deletes the group name ("WNET_DOMAIN").

```
/********
*
* _WNETSHD.CPP
*
* Copyright (c) 1992-1994 Ralph P. Davis, All Rights Reserved
*
********/


/*===== Includes =====*/

#include "wnetnb.h"


/*===== Function Definitions =====*/
void WINAPI _WNetShutdown(int nNameIndex)
{
    TCHAR szDropName[256];
    char  szDropNameA[256];

    if (nNameIndex >= 0 && nNameIndex < MAX_NAMES)
        {
        lstrcpy(szDropName, WNetGetName(nNameIndex));
#ifndef WIN32S
        WideCharToMultiByte(CP_ACP, 0, szDropName, -1,
            szDropNameA, sizeof (szDropNameA), NULL, NULL);
#else
        lstrcpy(szDropNameA, szDropName);
#endif
        NBDropName(szDropNameA, nNameIndex);
        }

    if ((-(*lpnRegistrations)) <= 0)
        {
        NBDropName((LPSTR) WNET_DOMAINA, ((int) byGroupNameNumber + 255));
        }
}
```

NetBIOS Benchmarks

In this section, I discuss how NetBIOS performs compared to Named Pipes and Windows Sockets. I provide two versions of the client. One version (WNETCLI.EXE) uses NCBSEND to transmit packets; the other (WNETCLI2.EXE) uses NCBSENDNA—Send without acknowledgments. You will notice that the code is much less complicated that what you have seen in the level-zero DLL. That is because all the calls here are synchronous. Managing asynchronous calls is the most difficult aspect of programming NetBIOS and generally requires more code than either Named Pipes or Windows Sockets.

I will anticipate a bit, and tell you that I got some big surprises when I wrote this section. I started this book intending to marginalize NetBIOS, but the benchmark data slapped me right in the face.

Here is the server (\NTNET\CODE\NETBIOS\WNETBNCH.CPP):

```
/********
 *
 * WNETBNCH.CPP
 *
 * Copyright (c) 1994 Ralph P. Davis, All Rights Reserved
 *
 * NetBIOS benchmark server
 *
 ********/

/*===== Includes =====*/

#include <windows.h>
#include <nb30.h>
#include <stdio.h>
#include <string.h>


/*===== Global Variables =====*/

BYTE *byBuffer;


/*===== Function Definitions =====*/

void main(int argc, char *argv[])
{
   DWORD   dwBytes;
   char szMyName[MAX_COMPUTERNAME_LENGTH + 1];
   DWORD dwNameLength = MAX_COMPUTERNAME_LENGTH;
```

```
UCHAR  uReturnCode;
NCB    ListenNCB, ReceiveNCB, SendNCB;
NCB    AddNameNCB, HangupNCB, DropNameNCB;
NCB    NCBReset;

ZeroMemory(&NCBReset, sizeof (NCB));
NCBReset.ncb_command = NCBRESET;
NCBReset.ncb_num = 64;  // Number of outstanding NCBs permitted

Netbios(&NCBReset);

if (argc > 1)
   strcpy(szMyName, argv[1]);
else
   GetComputerName(szMyName, &dwNameLength);

strcat(szMyName, ".BSRV");

while (strlen(szMyName) < NCBNAMSZ)
   strcat(szMyName, " ");

ZeroMemory(&HangupNCB, sizeof (NCB));
HangupNCB.ncb_command = NCBHANGUP;

ZeroMemory(&DropNameNCB, sizeof (NCB));
DropNameNCB.ncb_command = NCBDELNAME;
CopyMemory(DropNameNCB.ncb_name, szMyName, NCBNAMSZ);

ZeroMemory(&AddNameNCB, sizeof (NCB));
CopyMemory(AddNameNCB.ncb_name, szMyName, NCBNAMSZ);
AddNameNCB.ncb_command = NCBADDNAME;
if ((uReturnCode = Netbios(&AddNameNCB)) != NRC_GOODRET)
   {
   printf("\nAdd of name %s failed, return code = %x", szMyName,
      uReturnCode);
   ExitProcess(1);
   }

byBuffer = (BYTE *) VirtualAlloc(NULL, (1024 * 1024), MEM_COMMIT,
            PAGE_READWRITE);

if (byBuffer == NULL)
   {
   printf("\nMemory allocation error");
   ExitProcess(1);
   }
printf("\nWaiting for client connections...\n");
```

```
    try
        {
      while (TRUE)
          {
          ZeroMemory(&ListenNCB, sizeof (NCB));
          CopyMemory(ListenNCB.ncb_name, szMyName, NCBNAMSZ);
          FillMemory(ListenNCB.ncb_callname, NCBNAMSZ, ' ');
          ListenNCB.ncb_callname[0] = '*';
          ListenNCB.ncb_command = NCBLISTEN;

          if (Netbios(&ListenNCB) != NRC_GOODRET)
             break;
          ZeroMemory(&ReceiveNCB, sizeof (NCB));
          ZeroMemory(&SendNCB, sizeof (NCB));

          ReceiveNCB.ncb_lsn = SendNCB.ncb_lsn = ListenNCB.ncb_lsn;
          ReceiveNCB.ncb_buffer = byBuffer;
          ReceiveNCB.ncb_length = 60000;
          ReceiveNCB.ncb_command = NCBRECV;

          SendNCB.ncb_buffer = byBuffer;
          SendNCB.ncb_command = NCBSEND;

          while (Netbios(&ReceiveNCB) == NRC_GOODRET)
              {
              SendNCB.ncb_length = ReceiveNCB.ncb_length;
              ReceiveNCB.ncb_length = 60000;

              if (Netbios(&SendNCB) != NRC_GOODRET)
                 break;
              }
          HangupNCB.ncb_lsn = SendNCB.ncb_lsn;
          }
        }
    finally
        {
      Netbios(&DropNameNCB);
      printf("\nNetBIOS Server terminating\n");
      VirtualFree(byBuffer, 0, MEM_RELEASE);
        }
    ExitProcess(0);
}
```

Here is WNETCLI.CPP, which uses NCBSEND. WNETCLI2.CPP differs only in the use of NCBSENDNA instead of NCBSEND, so I do not list it.

```
/********
*
* WNETCLI.CPP
*
* Copyright (c) 1994 Ralph P. Davis, All Rights Reserved
*
* NetBIOS benchmark client
*
********/

/*===== Includes =====*/

#include <windows.h>
#include <nb30.h>
#include <stdio.h>
#include <stdlib.h>
#include <string.h>


/*===== Global Variables =====*/

BYTE byBuffer[60000];


/*===== Function Definitions =====*/

void main(int argc, char *argv[])
{
    DWORD   dwBytes;
    DWORD   dwStartTime, dwEndTime;
    DWORD   dwPackets;
    DWORD   dwPacketSize = sizeof (byBuffer);
    char    szMyName[MAX_COMPUTERNAME_LENGTH + 1];
    char    szServerName[MAX_COMPUTERNAME_LENGTH + 1];
    DWORD   dwNameLength = MAX_COMPUTERNAME_LENGTH;
    UCHAR   uLSN;
    NCB     CallNCB, ReceiveNCB, SendNCB;
    NCB     AddNameNCB, HangupNCB, DropNameNCB;
    DWORD   i;
    NCB     NCBReset;

    ZeroMemory(&NCBReset, sizeof (NCB));
    NCBReset.ncb_command = NCBRESET;
    NCBReset.ncb_num = 64;  // Number of outstanding NCBs permitted

    Netbios(&NCBReset);

    if (argc > 1)
```

```
      dwPackets = atoi(argv[1]);
   else
      dwPackets = 250;

   if (argc > 2)
      dwPacketSize = atoi(argv[2]);

   if (argc > 3)
      // Last argument is server name
      strcpy(szServerName, argv[3]);
   else
      strcpy(szServerName, "NUMBER1");

   GetComputerName(szMyName, &dwNameLength);

   strcat(szMyName, ".BCLI");

   while (strlen(szMyName) < NCBNAMSZ)
      strcat(szMyName, " ");

   strcat(szServerName, ".BSRV");
   while (strlen(szServerName) < NCBNAMSZ)
      strcat(szServerName, " ");

   ZeroMemory(&HangupNCB, sizeof (NCB));
   HangupNCB.ncb_command = NCBHANGUP;

   ZeroMemory(&DropNameNCB, sizeof (NCB));
   DropNameNCB.ncb_command = NCBDELNAME;
   CopyMemory(DropNameNCB.ncb_name, szMyName, NCBNAMSZ);

   ZeroMemory(&AddNameNCB, sizeof (NCB));
   CopyMemory(AddNameNCB.ncb_name, szMyName, NCBNAMSZ);
   AddNameNCB.ncb_command = NCBADDNAME;
   if (Netbios(&AddNameNCB) != NRC_GOODRET)
      {
      printf("\nAdd of name %s failed", szMyName);
      ExitProcess(1);
      }

   ZeroMemory(&CallNCB, sizeof (NCB));
   CopyMemory(CallNCB.ncb_name, szMyName, NCBNAMSZ);
   CopyMemory(CallNCB.ncb_callname, szServerName, NCBNAMSZ);
   CallNCB.ncb_command = NCBCALL;
   if (Netbios(&CallNCB) != NRC_GOODRET)
      {
```

```
      printf("\nCouldn't connect to server %s",
          szServerName);
      Netbios(&DropNameNCB);
      ExitProcess(1);
      }
  printf("\nConnected to server %s", szServerName);

  ZeroMemory(&ReceiveNCB, sizeof (NCB));
  ZeroMemory(&SendNCB, sizeof (NCB));

  ReceiveNCB.ncb_lsn = SendNCB.ncb_lsn = CallNCB.ncb_lsn;
  ReceiveNCB.ncb_buffer = byBuffer;
  ReceiveNCB.ncb_length = SendNCB.ncb_length = (WORD) dwPacketSize;
  ReceiveNCB.ncb_command = NCBRECV;

  SendNCB.ncb_buffer = byBuffer;
  SendNCB.ncb_command = NCBSEND;

  for (i = 0, dwStartTime = GetCurrentTime(); i < dwPackets; ++i)
      {
      if (Netbios(&SendNCB) != NRC_GOODRET)
          break;
      if (Netbios(&ReceiveNCB) != NRC_GOODRET)
        break;
      }
  dwEndTime = GetCurrentTime();

  printf("\nGetLastError() = %d", GetLastError());
  printf("\n%d packets transmitted in %d milliseconds", i * 2,
      dwEndTime - dwStartTime);
  printf("\nAverage is %d packets per second\n",
      (i * 2000) / (dwEndTime - dwStartTime));
  double dTotalBytes = ((double) dwPacketSize) *
                        ((double) i) * 2000.0;
  double dEndTime = (double) dwEndTime;
  double dStartTime = (double) dwStartTime;

  printf("\nBytes per second = %.2f\n",
   dTotalBytes / (dEndTime - dStartTime));

  HangupNCB.ncb_lsn = SendNCB.ncb_lsn;
  Netbios(&HangupNCB);
  Netbios(&DropNameNCB);

  ExitProcess(0);
}
```

Now let's take a look at some data. Table 12-1 shows how the two client applications stack up against each other.

Table 12-1. NetBIOS Benchmark Statistics

Packet Size	1024	2048	4096	8192	16384	32768
NetBIOS-Send	200567	274530	430478	687536	690288	738600
NetBIOS-Send No-Ack	198449	276383	419457	690143	688837	739433
% Difference	-1%	1%	-3%	0%	0%	0%

There is virtually no difference between them.

Table 12-2 collects the statistics gathered over the last several chapters. Specifically, it shows the numbers for:

- Named Pipes using TransactNamedPipe()
- Windows Sockets over TCP/IP
- NetBIOS using Send

Table 12-2. Comparison of All Evaluated APIs and Protocols

Packet Size	1024	2048	4096	8192	16384	32768
Named Pipes-TransactNamedPipe()	252527	349488	514249	478364	492085	504200
WinSock-TCP/IP	265629	332467	464926	531085	574071	607039
NetBIOS-Send	200567	274530	430478	687536	690288	738600

Figure 12-1 gives a graphic presentation of the data, which should give you a pretty clear sense of how the APIs and protocols compare with each other. By the way, Figure 12-1 is the reason you are reading Chapter 12 rather than Appendix A.

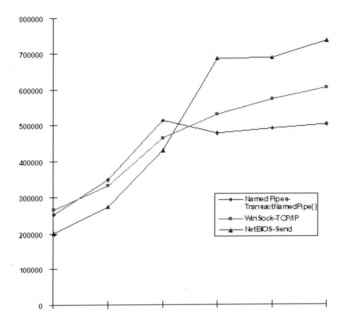

Figure 12-1.   Comparison of All Evaluated APIs and Protocols.

Conclusion

The NetBIOS API is more cumbersome that either Windows Sockets or
Named Pipes, principally because it is much more difficult to process
asynchronous I/O requests. NetBIOS is well established in the PC world and
supported on a wide variety of network platforms. Were it not for its superior
performance with packet sizes of 8K and up, there would be little reason to
use it. Indeed, it was my original intention to relegate NetBIOS to an
appendix. The results of my benchmark tests make it clear that, whatever
failings it may have, NetBIOS cannot be ignored in the Windows NT
environment.

Having shown you my attempt to hide the details of these APIs and
protocols, I now take you to another way of concealing them—Remote
Procedure Calls. RPC is almost the API I'm looking for. It makes exactly the
kinds of decisions I've talked about in the last several chapters—like what
protocol to use to talk to a given host, and even what host to ask for the
answer to a given question.

Suggested Readings

Christian, Kaare. *The Microsoft Guide to C++ Programming*, Chapter 5. Redmond, WA: Microsoft Press, 1992. This is not a book on network programming, but Christian's Chapter 5 does an excellent job of encapsulating the NetBIOS API in a C++ class hierarchy.

Davis, Ralph. *Windows Network Programming*. Chapter 3 and Chapter 14, pages 428–437. Reading, MA. Addison-Wesley Publishing Company, 1993.

IBM Corporation. *Local Area Network Technical Reference*, Part Number SC30-3383-03.

## Chapter 13

Remote Procedure Calls (RPC) and NT Services

Overview of RPC

RPC is a programming interface designed to provide interoperability among heterogeneous hosts on a network. It is intended to be hardware- and operating system-independent. RPC is a strategic element in Microsoft's distributed application architecture; much of NT itself is built around RPC.

Microsoft RPC is based on the RPC defined by the Open Software Foundation (OSF) as part of their Distributed Computing Environment (DCE). The gospels of OSF RPC are *OSF DCE Application Development Guide* and *OSF DCE Application Development Reference*.

One important purpose of RPC is to shield applications from the complexities of networks. Communications, error handling, and data-type conversion are handled automatically. We have seen that there are seven basic peer-to-peer operations. RPC makes them invisible.

- Listen sets a server up so that clients can connect to it.
- Call attempts to establish a connection from a client to a server.
- Send transmits data over a connection.
- Receive waits for data to arrive over a connection.
- Hangup terminates a connection between a client and a server.
- Send Datagram sends a packet of data using connectionless service.
- Receive Datagram looks for datagrams to arrive.

As seen in the previous three chapters, Named Pipes, Windows Sockets, and NetBIOS provide a handful of functions or commands to implement these operations. Ironically, RPC, which is supposed to simplify things, provides a suite of around 100 functions. However, most of the work is done by only a few of them.

RPC gives you the equivalent of the Call, Listen, and Hangup operations that were discussed in Chapter 9. The concepts of sending and receiving lose some of their meaning; once a client and server have established a connection (called a **binding** in RPC parlance), the data exchange takes place through the medium of remote procedure calls. The client application issues function calls just as if they were implemented as part of its own code. What the client actually calls, however, is a stub routine that is generated by the RPC compiler. The stub packages the function arguments, ships them to the host, waits for its answer, and returns the results to the client application. On the server side, the function call is received by the RPC server stub, which dispatches the remote procedure call to the local function responsible for processing it.

Microsoft RPC Compliance with OSF/DCE

Microsoft RPC is an implementation of the OSF/DCE specification for remote procedure calls. It differs from OSF RPC in several ways:

- Functions in the RPC runtime libraries are renamed according to Microsoft conventions. rpc_string_binding_compose(), for instance, becomes RpcStringBindingCompose().
- Functions report status information through their return values. In OSF, they do this through an output variable.
- Data types are given new names, using all capital letters and *typedefs* for structure types. For example, the OSF type *handle_t* becomes an RPC_BINDING_HANDLE in Microsoft RPC, though the OSF type is also supported.
- Some functions have additional NT-specific arguments, like security descriptors.
- Additional functions and macros provide features like structured exception handling.

Structure of RPC

RPC consists of several components:

- The Interface Definition Language (IDL) compiler. Microsoft's version is called MIDL, for the Microsoft Interface Definition Language. The IDL compiler takes a mandatory Interface Definition Language (.IDL) file and an optional Attribute Configuration (.ACF) file as input and generates C source code for the client and server stubs. These stubs are then submitted to the C compiler and linked with the client- and server-side applications.

By the way, the Microsoft RPC documentation erroneously says that ACF stands for Application Configuration File. However, the OSF documents, which must be considered the authoritative ones, use the term Attribute Configuration File. I will use the OSF term throughout this chapter.

- The RPC runtime library, used primarily by server applications to advertise their services, and by clients to locate and connect to servers.
- The actual remote procedure calls. To the client application, these appear to be local function calls. The RPC runtime takes care of passing the data to the server, calling the correct server function, and passing any return data back to the client.

The Interface Definition Language (IDL) File

The code in this chapter centers around the WNet RPC Server, a component of my WNet software system that runs as an RPC-based NT service. The .IDL file for the WNet RPC server, \NTNET\CODE\WNRPC.IDL, defines five functions. The client side of four of these functions is built into the DLL \NTNET\CODE\%Cpu%\WNETRPC.DLL. Here is a brief description of them:

- _RpcGetRemoteUser() returns the name of the user logged in on a machine. The server module retrieves this when it starts up by calling GetUserName().
- The Windows Network Manager calls _RpcSetLocalUser() when it loads. This is because the WNet RPC Server is started automatically by the operating system and will report that the logged-in user is SYSTEM unless you tell it otherwise. This function provides an example of using the Local Procedure Call (LPC) facility.
- _RpcWinExec() runs a program on a remote machine.
- _RpcIsWNetServerRunning() checks to see if a window belonging to the WNet server window class ("WNETMASTER") exists. The Windows Network Manager uses this to determine whether to enable the WNetMessageBox() button on the View Stations dialog box.
- Because RPC runs on top of the native NT protocols, you would expect there to be a performance penalty for using it, and indeed there is. _RpcBenchmark() does the server end of the benchmark tests that were

run in the last three chapters, so you can get an idea just how great that penalty is. The benchmark client runs as a standalone application.

The IDL listing for the WNet RPC Server follows.

```
/********
 *
 * WNRPC.IDL
 *
 * Copyright (c) 1993-1994 Ralph P. Davis, All Rights Reserved
 *
 * Defines interface for WNet RPC Server
 *
 ********/

[ uuid (9534E4E0-1BD6-101A-80FA-00001B3EF36B),
  version(1.0),
  pointer_default(unique)]
interface wnrpc
{
#ifdef UNICODE
void _RpcGetRemoteUser([out, string] wchar_t szString[255],
                [in, out] unsigned long *plLen);
void _RpcSetLocalUser([in, string] wchar_t szUser[255]);
unsigned long _RpcWinExec([in, string] wchar_t szProgram[255],
                [in] unsigned long nCmdShow);
#else
void _RpcGetRemoteUser([out, string] unsigned char szString[255],
                [in, out] unsigned long *plLen);
void _RpcSetLocalUser([in, string] unsigned char szUser[255]);
unsigned long _RpcWinExec([in, string] unsigned char szProgram[255],
                [in] unsigned long nCmdShow);
#endif
unsigned long _RpcIsWNetServerRunning(void);
void _RpcBenchmark(handle_t hServer,
                unsigned long dwLength,
                [in, size_is(32768), length_is(dwLength)]
                unsigned char *pcInBuffer,
                [out, size_is(32768), length_is(dwLength)]
                unsigned char *pcOutBuffer);
}
```

There are several parts to the IDL file. The interface name (in this case, *wnrpc*) is used to generate global variables. One is used as the binding handle for RPCs that work with implicit handles, and is called *<interface name>_IfHandle*. There are two variables generated to represent the client's and server's view of the interface. In Windows NT 3.1, they were named

<interface name>_ClientIfHandle and *<interface name>_ServerIfHandle*. NT 3.5 also embeds the version number in the variable names. Thus, for version 1.0 of an interface, it creates the names *<interface name>_v1_0_c_ifspec* and *<interface name>_v1_0_s_ifspec*. The variables spawned by my IDL file are *wnrpc_IfHandle, wnrpc_v1_0_c_ifspec,* and *wnrpc_v1_0_s_ifspec*. You can force MIDL to use the 3.1-style names with the */oldnames* command-line switch.

MIDL also creates the C files *<interface name>_c.c, <interface name>_s.c, <interface name>_x.c,* and *<interface name>_y.c,* and the header file *<interface name>.h*. Here, it makes the files *wnrpc_c.c, wnrpc_s.c, wnrpc_x.c, wnrpc_y.c,* and *wnrpc.h. wnrpc_c.c* and *wnrpc_x.c* are compiled and linked with the client application. *wnrpc_s.c* and *wnrpc_y.c* become part of the server (\NTNET\CODE\%Cpu%\WNRPC.EXE).

The *uuid* clause at the beginning of the file provides a unique identifier for the interface. UUID is an OSF acronym for Universal Unique Identifier. UUIDs are 16-byte binary numbers. You generate them with the utility *uuidgen*, which resides in \MSTOOLS\BIN. *uuidgen* will create a skeletal .IDL file for you if you run it like this:

```
uuidgen -i -o<.IDL file name>
```

You can also create new UUIDs in software by calling the UuidCreate() function.

The interface UUID enables clients to find exactly the RPC server they want. The MIDL compiler incorporates the interface UUID into the C code that it emits, and the RPC runtime uses it to match RPC calls to servers that support them. This way, the name of the function you are calling remotely does not have to be unique, which would be a very difficult and restrictive requirement. Because they use the UUID to dispatch the remote procedure call, the RPC runtime modules do not get confused if two servers implement an RPC with the same name.

You can use UUIDs to define an even more precise matching between client and server. In addition to the interface UUID, you can also create object UUIDs. You then pass arrays of these UUIDs to the relevant RPC functions. The RPC runtime modules will use the combination of interface UUID and object UUIDs to find the precise server to service a remote procedure call. However, this is a more esoteric usage that is not necessary for many (if not most) RPC applications. I do not consider it further in this chapter, and I pass all relevant arguments as NULL.

The version number (given here as 1.0) provides for more precise version-specific client-server matching. This allows for the possibility that more than one copy of the same server application might be offering the same interface (as identified by its UUID), but in different versions.

The body of the .IDL file, contained between the curly braces, contains the prototypes of the remote procedure calls that the interface embodies. The prototypes look like standard C prototypes, but include additional information that tells the compiler whether a given argument is for input (*[in]*), output (*[out]*), or both (*[in, out]*). In the prototype for _RpcBenchmark(), you also see specifiers that tell MIDL how big an array is and how many arguments to actually transmit. The first argument, *dwLength*, is the number of array elements that we want to be transmitted on a given call. The *size_is(32768)* specifiers says that 32768 is the biggest the array will ever get, and the *length_is(dwLength)* says to consult *dwLength* to determine how many array elements to transmit. The *string* specifier says that argument is a null-terminated string.

The Attribute Configuration (.ACF) File

Here is the attribute configuration (.ACF) file for the WNet RPC server, \NTNET\CODE\WNRPC.ACF:

```
/********
 *
 * WNRPC.ACF
 *
 * Attribute Configuration file for WNet RPC Server
 *
 ********/

[implicit_handle(handle_t wnrpc_IfHandle)]
interface wnrpc
{

}
```

The .ACF file specifies the type of binding handles you will use. Binding handles are the program variables used to establish client-server connections. They have the data type *handle_t* in OSF spelling, RPC_BINDING_HANDLE by Microsoft conventions. This is the RPC equivalent of the WNet HCONNECTION. Possible types are:

- Explicit handles (*explicit_handle*). In this case, each remote procedure call includes a binding handle as its first argument, by OSF convention. Explicit handles allow a client application to target multiple RPC servers. You use explicit handles by declaring variables of the appropriate type and including a binding handle as one of the arguments to your remote procedure calls. _RpcBenchmark() has an explicit handle as its first argument.

```
void _RpcBenchmark(handle_t hServer,
                   unsigned long dwLength,
                   [in,  size_is(32768), length_is(dwLength)]
                   unsigned char *pcInBuffer,
                   [out, size_is(32768), length_is(dwLength)]
                   unsigned char *pcOutBuffer);
```

This allows the benchmark client to query the RPC Name Service database for all the machines running the WNet RPC Server and to do the benchmark test in a round-robin fashion.

- Implicit handles (*implicit_handle*). Here, the binding handle is a global variable—the one specified in parentheses—that is not included in the function parameter lists. The header file that MIDL generates has an *extern* reference to it, and the actual variable is declared in the client-side stub (*wnrpc_c.c*, in this case).
- Auto handles (*auto_handle*). This imposes the least burden on client applications; they need know nothing whatsoever about RPC. The client stub that MIDL creates uses the RPC Name Service database to locate and bind to a server. Auto handles are suitable when you do not care which server handles a remote procedure call. Here is the syntax I would use if I wanted to request auto handles instead of implicit handles.

```
[auto_handle] interface wnrpc
{
}
```

If you neither provide an .ACF file nor specify handle types, MIDL will use auto handles for any remote procedure calls that do not pass a binding handle explicitly.

Implicit handles strike a good balance between client RPC awareness and flexibility in the choice of servers.

The RPC Runtime Library (Server Side)

Most of the RPC sample applications that ship with the Win32 SDK use implicit handles and the same few functions on the client and server ends of the conversation. There are three functions that initialize the server and set it up to receive incoming RPCs:

- RpcServerUseProtseqEp() says that the server wants to support a certain communications protocol, using a known endpoint (like a named pipe or a TCP port).
- RpcServerRegisterIf() lets the RPC runtime modules know about the server's interface UUID.
- RpcServerListen() completes the process by putting the server into the listening state, ready to service arriving RPC requests.

Declaring Communications Protocols. RpcServerUseProtseqEp() tells the RPC runtime that the server understands a given communications protocol and will be listening for incoming calls on a well-known endpoint (a pipe name, a socket, or whatever term the protocol uses). The prototype in the on-line help is only half right. It implies that there is only an ANSI version of the function. However, like most Win32 functions, RpcServerUseProtseqEp() exists in both ANSI and Unicode versions. Here's a more accurate prototype:

```
typedef long RPC_STATUS;
#define RPC_ENTRY __stdcall

RPC_STATUS RPC_ENTRY RpcServerUseProtseqEp(
                        LPTSTR       lpProtseq,
                        unsigned int nMaxCalls,
                        LPTSTR       lpEndpoint,
                        LPVOID       lpSecurityDescriptor);
```

lpProtseq is the protocol sequence that you want to register. It is passed as a string. Table 13-1 shows some of the protocols that Microsoft RPC v1.0 supports.

Table 13-1. Microsoft RPC Protocol Sequences

Protocol Sequence String	Protocol
ncacn_np	Named Pipes (Microsoft extension to OSF)
ncacn_ip_tcp	Connection-oriented service using TCP
ncacn_dnet_nsp	Connection-oriented service using DECnet
ncacn_spx	Connection-oriented service using Novell's SPX (Microsoft extension)
ncalrpc	Local RPC (Microsoft extension)
ncacn_nb_nb	NetBIOS over NetBEUI (Microsoft extension)
ncacn_nb_ipx	NetBIOS over Novell's IPX (an undocumented Microsoft extension)
ncacn_nb_tcp	NetBIOS over TCP/IP (Microsoft extension)

For each protocol sequence, endpoints have a specific format. For *ncacn_np*, the endpoint is a pipe name, in the format \PIPE\<rest of pipe name>. For *ncacn_ip_tcp*, the endpoint is a string representation of a TCP port, like "25000". For *ncacn_nb_nb* and *ncacn_nb_tcp*, the endpoint is a string representation of a number between 32 and 255, for instance, "127". (Endpoints below 32 are reserved for system use.) For *ncacn_spx*, the endpoint is an SPX socket between 1 and 65535, also passed as a string. For *ncalrpc*, the endpoint is some kind of string that uniquely identifies the RPC server, like "WNET_RPC_SERVER".

The different protocol sequences also have different ways of representing host names. This is not an issue with server-side calls, but does become important on the client side. Most of the protocols just use the machine name, like NUMBER1. However, *ncacn_np* adds \\ to the front of the name. *ncacn_spx* uses the IPX address formatted as a string. For instance, the address of my NT Advanced Server machine is "0000000100C0D1800E65".

Additional information on the formatting of host names and endpoints is available in the Win32 on-line help. You can find each protocol sequence ("ncacn_np", "ncacn_ip_tcp", for example) in the Search dialog box. The reference page has the complete details.

The *nMaxCalls* argument tells the RPC runtime what you estimate is the maximum number of concurrent requests you will receive. This is not a ceiling; RPC can accept more requests if the number exceeds this amount. This may be something like the number of threads RPC spins off initially to service client RPCs. You can request the default number by passing this as RPC_C_PROTSEQ_MAX_REQS_DEFAULT, which is defined as 10. (Many of the RPC constants, like RPC_C_PROTSEQ_MAX_REQS_DEFAULT, will challenge your typing abilities.)

The SECURITY_DESCRIPTOR argument (*lpSecurityDescriptor*) demands some attention. You saw in Chapter 10 that you must supply a security descriptor when you create a named pipe. The same applies to RpcServerUseProtseqEp() when you register *ncacn_np*. Interestingly enough, the security descriptor is also meaningful for the *ncacn_ip_tcp*, *ncacn_spx*, and *ncalrpc* protocol sequences, in spite of the fact that, at least with *ncacn_ip_tcp* and *ncacn_spx*, the underlying API makes no provision for security descriptors. However, with the NetBIOS protocols, *ncacn_nb_nb*, *ncacn_nb_tcp*, and *ncacn_nb_ipx*, you **must** pass *lpSecurityDescriptor* as NULL. If you do not, RpcServerUseProtseqEp() or RpcServerUseProtseq() fails, returning ERROR_INVALID_PARAMETER. Presumably, this is a bug that wil eventually disappear; it makes no sense.

Here is a call to RpcServerUseProtseqEp() that registers the Named Pipes protocol and the endpoint \PIPE\WNET\WNRPC. I also show you again how to set up a SECURITY_DESCRIPTOR to allow unlimited access, by tying a NULL discretionary access control list to it.

```
RPC_STATUS RpcStatus;
SECURITY_DESCRIPTOR SecurityDescriptor;
InitializeSecurityDescriptor(&SecurityDescriptor,
   SECURITY_DESCRIPTOR_REVISION);
SetSecurityDescriptorDacl(&SecurityDescriptor, TRUE, NULL, FALSE);

RpcStatus = RpcServerUseProtseqEp(
            TEXT("ncacn_np"),
            RPC_C_PROTSEQ_MAX_REQS_DEFAULT,
            TEXT("\\PIPE\\WNET\\WNRPC"),
            &SecurityDescriptor);
if (RpcStatus != RPC_S_OK)
   // Something's wrong here
```

The server can call RpcServerUseProtseqEp() to register as many protocol sequences as it wants to. If the server expects to be called by clients on the same machine, it is a good idea to register the *ncalrpc* protocol. This allows you to use the Local Procedure Call (LPC) version of RPC, which is considerably faster than just using one of the standard protocols locally. The benchmark data at the end of this chapter makes this dramatically clear.

Additional Security Considerations. An extra layer of security protection is provided by RPC client impersonation. You saw in Chapter 10 that the Named Pipes API provides the ImpersonateNamedPipeClient() function. Similarly, Microsoft RPC offers RpcImpersonateClient().

```
RPC_STATUS RPC_ENTRY RpcImpersonateClient(
                     RPC_BINDING_HANDLE hServerIf);
```

Just as with ImpersonateNamedPipeClient(), RpcImpersonateClient() allows the server-side RPC to take on the security characteristics of the client that it is servicing. *hServerIf* is the server-side interface handle—the global variable in the format *<interface name>_vl_o_s_if spec* that MIDL generates. You can pass it as zero to indicate the client that the current thread is servicing, which is normally what you want. RpcImpersonateClient() does not require that the underlying protocol be Named Pipes, even though Named Pipes is the only networked API to provide an explicit call for client impersonation.

The RPC _RpcWinExec(), which allows for remote program execution, impersonates its client so that it does not allow back-door entry into its host machine. Normally, the WNet RPC Server runs as the operating system itself; allowing unrestricted execution of programs could be quite risky. Here is the function:

```
unsigned long _RpcWinExec(TCHAR szProgram[255],
                          unsigned long uCmdShow)
{
   unsigned long uRetcode;
   CHAR szProgramA[255];

#ifdef UNICODE
   WideCharToMultiByte(CP_ACP, 0, szProgram, -1,
      szProgramA, sizeof (szProgramA), NULL, NULL);
#else
   lstrcpy(szProgramA, szProgram);
#endif
   RpcImpersonateClient(wnrpc_ServerIfHandle);
   uRetcode = (unsigned long) WinExec(szProgramA, uCmdShow);
   RpcRevertToSelf();
   return uRetcode;
}
```

RpcRevertToSelf() returns the server to its own security context.

Dynamic Endpoints. RpcServerUseProtseqEp() registers well-known endpoints—endpoints whose names or numbers you know when you write your application. Most of the time, this should be the case. However, you can also ask RPC to improvise dynamic endpoints for you by just registering the protocol sequence, without a specific endpoint. The RpcServerUseProtseq() and RpcServerUseAllProtseqs() functions accomplish this.

```
RPC_STATUS RPC_ENTRY RpcServerUseProtseq(
                      LPTSTR       lpProtseq,
                      unsigned int nMaxCalls,
                      LPVOID       lpSecurityDescriptor);

RPC_STATUS RPC_ENTRY RpcServerUseAllProtseqs(
                      unsigned int nMaxCalls,
                      LPVOID       lpSecurityDescriptor);
```

The arguments are the same as for RpcServerUseProtseqEp(), but RpcServerUseProtseq() omits the endpoint, and RpcServerUseAllProtseqs() drops the protocol sequence and the endpoint.

At first, it may seem tempting to use dynamic endpoints because you are
assured of having a unique service address and you don't have to know
how a given protocol sequence formats its endpoints. I found
RpcServerUseAllProtseqs() especially alluring because of its promise of
universal connectivity. However, as you will see, dynamic endpoints present
some serious disadvantages for client applications, at least under Microsoft
RPC v1.0.

Registering the Server's Interface.   The next step for the server is to
register its interface by calling RpcServerRegisterIf(). This takes the server
interface handle that was produced by the MIDL compiler and makes the
RPC runtime aware of its corresponding UUID. If you look at the stub files
that MIDL generates, you will see that the client and server interface handles
both incorporate the UUID. Here's how the WNet RPC Server calls
RpcServerRegisterIf().

```
if (RpcServerRegisterIf(wnrpc_v1_0_s_ifspec,
                        NULL,
                        NULL) != RPC_S_OK)
    // Trouble!        .
```

The second and third arguments to RpcServerRegisterIf() are NULL if the
server implements the functions exactly as they are named in the .IDL file.
This is the most common usage. If the server requires a higher level of
virtualization, the third argument points to a function table containing
pointers to the functions that implement the published interface. They can be
named anything you want. You can also provide more than one function
table for each interface by setting the second argument to a non-NULL
value. However, this is quite esoteric; passing both arguments as NULL
usually suffices.

Listening for Remote Procedure Calls.   At this point, the server is properly
initialized and can start listening for RPC requests. The function that opens
the incoming channel is RpcServerListen(). Here again is an excerpt from
the WNet RPC Server:

```
if (RpcServerListen(1, 40, FALSE) != RPC_S_OK)
    // Server couldn't enter the listening state,
    // we have to bail out
```

The arguments to RpcServerListen() state the minimum number of threads
to spin off, the recommended maximum number, and a flag saying whether

RpcServerListen() should return immediately (TRUE) or block (FALSE). As with RpcServerUseProtseq(), RpcServerUseProtseqEp(), and RpcServerUseAllProtseqs(), the maximum number is just a suggestion. If you need more resources than this, the RPC runtime will provide them automatically. If you pass the last argument as FALSE, RpcServerListen() does not return until another thread in the server application leaves the listening state by calling RpcMgmtStopServerListening(). Passing it as TRUE, on the other hand, allows the server to do other processing. The actual remote procedure calls are handled in the background by RPC worker threads. Eventually, the server must call RpcMgmtWaitServerListen(), which, like RpcServerListen(), blocks until someone calls RpcMgmtStopServerListening(). RpcMgmtWaitServerListen() takes no arguments.

Server Shutdown. The server withdraws from the listening state by calling RpcMgmtStopServerListening().

```
RPC_STATUS RPC_ENTRY RpcMgmtStopServerListening(
                   RPC_BINDING_HANDLE hBinding);
```

You pass *hBinding* as NULL to shut down your own server application. You can shut down a remote server by passing the handle that represents your binding to that server.

The other steps in cleanup make sure clients don't try to connect to you after you've gone away. This can put them to sleep for quite a while, and there is little they can do to control the timeout. The only required call (besides RpcMgmtStopServerListening(), that is) is RpcServerUnregisterIf(), which reverses the action of RpcServerRegisterIf(). Here is a typical shutdown sequence:

```
RpcMgmtStopServerListening(NULL);
RpcServerUnregisterIf(wnrpc_v1_0_s_ifspec, NULL, TRUE);
```

The third argument to RpcServerUnregisterIf() says whether to wait for all current RPCs to complete (TRUE), or to panic and shutdown immediately (FALSE). Ordinarily, you want to give all RPCs a chance to complete. The second argument is used only if you passed the second argument of RpcServerRegisterIf() as a non-NULL value, which is, as I stated previously, a much more esoteric usage. See the RPC on-line manuals if you are interested in how this works.

Registering with the RPC Name Service and Endpoint Mapper Databases. The RPC runtime suite includes two very important components that permit client applications to browse the network for compatible servers. The Name Service lists servers and the machines where they reside. Using it, clients can find servers that support an RPC interface they are interested in. My observation suggests that full server browsing is only supported on an NT Advanced Server domain.

The Endpoint Mapper is responsible for routing incoming RPC requests to the correct server process. It is consulted when a client submits a partially bound handle. This can happen for two reasons:

- The server is using dynamically assigned endpoints, so the client has no way of knowing what they are in advance.
- The server is using well-known endpoints, but the client, for some reason, does not know the endpoints.

When an RPC with a partially bound handle arrives, the Endpoint Mapper tries to locate a server on the local machine that offers the interface embodied in the handle (as identified by its UUID). If it succeeds in finding one, it fills in the data structure represented by the handle with the additional information. At this point, the handle is fully bound, and subsequent requests using it go directly to the server application without passing through the Endpoint Mapper.

The server must tell the Name Service and Endpoint Mapper of its existence. To do so, it first calls RpcServerInqBindings() to find out about the endpoints that RPC has created for it. This function takes a single argument, a pointer to a pointer to an RPC_BINDING_VECTOR. This is a structure containing an array of the binding handles (RPC_BINDING_HANDLE) that RPC has created for you. The server does not need to know anything about the contents of the array; its only further responsibility is to free the memory by calling RpcBindingVectorFree() when it is through with the array.

```
RPC_STATUS RPC_ENTRY RpcServerInqBindings(
                RPC_BINDING_VECTOR **lplpBindingVector);
```

RpcServerInqBindings() allocates the memory and returns the array of binding handles in *lplpBindingVector*. The server then passes this information to the functions that register with the RPC databases, RpcNsBindingExport() and RpcEpRegister().

```
RPC_STATUS RPC_ENTRY RpcEpRegister(
                    RPC_IF_HANDLE        hInterface,
                    RPC_BINDING_VECTOR  *lpBindingVector,
                    UUID_VECTOR         *lpUuidVector,
                    LPTSTR               lpComment);
```

RpcEpRegister() takes the server interface handle and the binding vector returned by RpcServerInqBindings(). The third argument can be an array of object UUIDs, or NULL if you are not using objects. The last is a comment string that only has meaning for your application; it is not interpreted by RPC in any way.

Here are the calls to RpcServerInqBindings() and RpcEpRegister() from the WNet RPC Server.

```
RPC_STATUS RpcStatus;
RPC_BINDING_VECTOR pBindingVector;
// Find out how RPC bound our endpoints
if ((RpcStatus = RpcServerInqBindings(&pBindingVector)) != RPC_S_OK)
    {
    WNetReportEvent(RpcStatus,
        TEXT("RpcServerInqBindings()"),
        FALSE);
    }
else
    {
    // Give the RPC Endpoint Mapper the
    // binding information it needs
    RpcStatus = RpcEpRegister(wnrpc_v1_0_s_ifspec,
                pBindingVector,
                NULL,
                NULL);
    if (RpcStatus != RPC_S_OK)
        {
        WNetReportEvent(RpcStatus,
            TEXT("RpcEpRegister()"),
            FALSE);
        }
    }
```

RpcNsBindingExport() is a little more complicated because it must include a entry name as the primary key for your entry in the database. Here is the prototype:

```
RPC_STATUS RPC_ENTRY RpcNsBindingExport(
                            unsigned long        dwSyntax,
                            LPTSTR               lpszEntryName,
                            RPC_IF_HANDLE        hInterface,
                            RPC_BINDING_VECTOR  *lpBindingVector,
                            UUID_VECTOR         *lpUUIDVector);
```

dwSyntax defines the format of the name. The constant RPC_C_NS_ SYNTAX_DEFAULT says to use the default syntax for Microsoft RPC. This is stored in the Registry under HKEY_LOCAL_MACHINE\Software\ Microsoft\Rpc\NameService\DefaultSyntax. The default syntax is RPC_C_NS_SYNTAX_DCE, standard OSF/DCE name syntax. In this format, the name begins with "/.:/" to designate the local domain, followed by the rest of the name. A Microsoft extension is supposed to allow you to use the format "/.../<Windows NT domain name>/<rest of name>". However, I have had little success using names in anything but standard OSF/DCE format.

hInterface is the server interface handle, and *lpBindingVector* is the RPC_BINDING_VECTOR that was populated by RpcServerInqBindings().

RpcServerInqBindings(), RpcEpRegister(), and RpcNsBindingExport() have their corresponding cleanup functions. RpcBindingVectorFree() releases the memory allocated by RpcServerInqBindings(). RpcEpUnregister() tells the RPC Endpoint Mapper that you are no longer in service. RpcNsBindingUnexport() removes your entry name from the Name Service database. Their syntax is similar to their partner functions; rather than show their prototypes, I just list the function WNetStartRPCServer() from the WNet RPC server. This is the routine that does all the RPC initialization and cleanup. It is found in the source file \NTNET\CODE\RPCSERV\WNRPC.CPP.

```
DWORD WINAPI WNetStartRPCServer(LPVOID lpv)
{
    RPC_STATUS           RpcStatus;
    RPC_BINDING_VECTOR  *pBindingVector = NULL;
    SECURITY_DESCRIPTOR  SecurityDescriptor;
    BOOL bIfRegistered = FALSE, bNsExported = FALSE,
        bEpRegistered = FALSE;
    DWORD dwError;

    UNREFERENCED_PARAMETER(lpv);

    // We have to tie a security descriptor to some of the
    // protocol sequences we register, or else we won't
    // be able to do RPC from remote stations.
```

```
InitializeSecurityDescriptor(&SecurityDescriptor,
                          SECURITY_DESCRIPTOR_REVISION);
SetSecurityDescriptorDacl(&SecurityDescriptor,
              TRUE, NULL, FALSE);

// Register Local Procedure Call protocol
// using a dynamic endpoint
if ((RpcStatus = RpcServerUseProtseqEp(TEXT("ncalrpc"),
      5,
      TEXT("WNET_RPC_SERVER"),
      &SecurityDescriptor))
   != RPC_S_OK)
   {
   WNetStopRPCServer(RpcStatus,
      TEXT("RpcServerUseProtseq(\"ncalrpc\")"));
   ExitThread(RpcStatus);
   }

// Register named pipes protocol
// Endpoint is the named pipe \\PIPE\\WNET\\WNRPC
if ((RpcStatus = RpcServerUseProtseqEp(TEXT("ncacn_np"),
        5,
        TEXT("\\PIPE\\WNET\\WNRPC"), &SecurityDescriptor))
   != RPC_S_OK)
   {
   WNetStopRPCServer(RpcStatus,
      TEXT("RpcServerUseProtseqEp(\"ncacn_np\")"));
   ExitThread(RpcStatus);
   }

// Register TCP/IP protocol
// Endpoint is TCP socket number 35000
if ((RpcStatus = RpcServerUseProtseqEp(TEXT("ncacn_ip_tcp"),
        5,
        TEXT("35000"),
        &SecurityDescriptor))
   != RPC_S_OK)
   {
   WNetStopRPCServer(RpcStatus,
      TEXT("RpcServerUseProtseqEp(\"ncacn_ip_tcp\")"));
   ExitThread(RpcStatus);
   }

// Register SPX protocol
// Endpoint is IPX socket number 20480
if ((RpcStatus = RpcServerUseProtseqEp(TEXT("ncacn_spx"),
        5,
        TEXT("20480"),
```

```
            &SecurityDescriptor))
      != RPC_S_OK)
      {
      WNetReportEvent(RpcStatus,
        TEXT("RpcServerUseProtseqEp(\"ncacn_spx\")"),
        FALSE);
      }


// For the three flavors of NetBIOS (ncacn_nb_nb, ncacn_nb_tcp,
// and ncacn_nb_ipx) I use dynamic endpoints to show how
// it's done

// Register NetBIOS over NetBEUI
// Notice the NULL pointers for the SECURITY_DESCRIPTOR
// If you try to pass a security descriptor here,
// RpcServerUseProtseq() fails with a return code
// of ERROR_INVALID_PARAMETER

if ((RpcStatus = RpcServerUseProtseq(TEXT("ncacn_nb_nb"),
        5,
        NULL))
      != RPC_S_OK)
      {
      WNetReportEvent(RpcStatus,
        TEXT("RpcServerUseProtseq(\"ncacn_nb_nb\")"),
        FALSE);
      }


// Register NetBIOS over TCP/IP

if ((RpcStatus = RpcServerUseProtseq(TEXT("ncacn_nb_tcp"),
        5,
        NULL))
      != RPC_S_OK)
      {
      WNetReportEvent(RpcStatus,
        TEXT("RpcServerUseProtseq(\"ncacn_nb_tcp\")"),
        FALSE);
      }


// Register NetBIOS over IPX

if ((RpcStatus = RpcServerUseProtseq(TEXT("ncacn_nb_ipx"),
        5,
        NULL))
      != RPC_S_OK)
      {
      WNetReportEvent(RpcStatus,
```

```
            TEXT("RpcServerUseProtseq(\"ncacn_nb_ipx\")"),
            FALSE);
    }


// Register the server interface, represented by the global
// variable wnrpc_v1_0_S_ifspec, which was generated by
// the MIDL compiler
if ((RpcStatus = RpcServerRegisterIf(wnrpc_v1_0_S_ifspec,
                        NULL,
                        NULL)) != RPC_S_OK)
    {
    WNetStopRPCServer(RpcStatus,
        TEXT("RpcServerRegisterIf()"));
    ExitThread(RpcStatus);
    }

bIfRegistered = TRUE;

try
    {
    // Find out how RPC bound our endpoints
    if ((RpcStatus = RpcServerInqBindings(&pBindingVector)) !=
            RPC_S_OK)
        {
        WNetReportEvent(RpcStatus,
            TEXT("RpcServerInqBindings()"),
            FALSE);
        }
    else
        {
        // Tell Name Service database we're alive
        if ((RpcStatus = RpcNsBindingExport(RPC_C_NS_SYNTAX_DEFAULT,
                        TEXT("/.:/WNET_RPC_SERVER"),
                        wnrpc_ServerIfHandle,
                        pBindingVector,
                        NULL)) != RPC_S_OK)
            {
            WNetReportEvent(RpcStatus,
                TEXT("RpcNsBindingExport()"),
                FALSE);
            }
        else
            bNsExported = TRUE;

        // Give the RPC Endpoint Mapper the
        // binding information it needs
        RpcStatus = RpcEpRegister(wnrpc_v1_0_s_ifspec,
                        pBindingVector,
```

```
                              NULL,
                              NULL);
             if (RpcStatus != RPC_S_OK)
                 {
                 WNetReportEvent(RpcStatus,
                    TEXT("RpcEpRegister()"),
                    FALSE);
                 }
             else
                 bEpRegistered = TRUE;
             }
         if ((RpcStatus = RpcServerListen(1, 40, FALSE)) != RPC_S_OK)
             {
             WNetStopRPCServer(RpcStatus,
                 TEXT("RpcServerListen()"));
             leave;
             }
         }
     finally
         {
         if (bEpRegistered)
             // Get us out of the Endpoint Mapper
             // database so nobody thinks we're still on-line
             RpcEpUnregister(wnrpc_v1_0_s_ifspec, pBindingVector,
                             NULL);

         if (bNsExported)
             // Pull us out of the Name Service database also
             RpcNsBindingUnexport(RPC_C_NS_SYNTAX_DEFAULT,
                                  TEXT("/.:/WNET_RPC_SERVER"),
                                  wnrpc_ServerIfHandle,
                                  NULL);
         if (pBindingVector != NULL)
             RpcBindingVectorFree(&pBindingVector);

         // Unregister our interface if RpcServerRegisterIf()
         // was successful
         if (bIfRegistered)
             RpcServerUnregisterIf(wnrpc_v1_0_s_ifspec, NULL, TRUE);
         }

     ExitThread(dwError = GetLastError());

     return dwError;
     }
```

MIDL_user_allocate() and MIDL_user_free(). RPC applications need to provide callback functions for memory allocation; they must be named MIDL_user_allocate() and MIDL_user_free(). (Actually, you can also call them midl_user_allocate() and midl_user_free(), as the RPC headers provide macros for those spellings.) The stub routines that MIDL creates call these functions when they need to allocate memory. My implementation uses single-step operations with VirtualAlloc() and VirtualFree().

```
void __RPC_FAR * __RPC_API MIDL_user_allocate(size_t len)
{
    return(VirtualAlloc(NULL, len, MEM_COMMIT,
                    PAGE_READWRITE));
}

void __RPC_API MIDL_user_free(void __RPC_FAR * ptr)
{
    VirtualFree(ptr, 0, MEM_RELEASE);
}
```

You will know if you need to provide these functions; your RPC application will not be able to link if the stubs that MIDL generates call them.

A Typical Remote Procedure Call on the Server. The function on the server side that handles a remote procedure call does not differ in any way from a normal local function. Here is the function _RpcGetRemoteUser(), which I use to report the user logged in on the host machine. The client end, WNetGetRemoteUser(), appears in the next section of this chapter.

```
void _RpcGetRemoteUser(TCHAR szString[255], unsigned long *plLen)
{
    DWORD dwLength;

    dwLength = GetEnvironmentVariable(TEXT("USERNAME"), szString,
                *plLen);

    if (dwLength == 0)
        {
        lstrcpy(szString, szUserName);
        *plLen = lstrlen(szUserName);
        }
    else
        *plLen = dwLength;
}
```

Using RPC Function Calls (Client Side)

If the server uses well-known endpoints, and the client knows what they are, then two functions suffice to establish the client-server link: RpcStringBindingCompose() and RpcBindingFromStringBinding(). RpcStringBindingCompose() takes separate arguments representing the target machine, the protocol sequence, and the endpoint to use, and combines them into a specially formatted string. RpcBindingFromStringBinding() parses this string and connects to the host and endpoint that it indicates.

Here is the listing of the function SetupRPCBinding(). This resides in the WNet RPC support DLL, \NTNET\CODE\%Cpu%\WNETRPC.DLL; you can find the source code in \NTNET\CODE\WNETGUSR.CPP. To demonstrate the flexibility that RPC gives you, it alternates between using Named Pipes and TCP/IP. Notice several things:

- The protocol sequence *ncacn_np* (Named Pipes) requires a prefix of "\\\\" for the target station. TCP/IP (*ncacn_ip_tcp*), on the other hand, uses the unadorned machine name.
- Both protocols use well-known endpoints: the named pipe \PIPE\WNET\WNRPC and TCP port number 35000.
- Of the global variables generated by MIDL (*wnrpc_v1_0_s_ifspec*, *wnrpc_v1_0_s_ifspec*, and *wnrpc_IfHandle*), it is the third one that captures the handle representing our link to the server. You pass RpcBindingFromStringBinding() a pointer to it, along with the string binding created by RpcStringBindingCompose().
- RpcStringBindingCompose() allocates memory for you; you must free it by calling RpcStringFree().

```
BOOL SetupRPCBinding(LPTSTR lpszStation, TCHAR **pszStringBinding)
{
    TCHAR   szStation[MAX_COMPUTERNAME_LENGTH + 1];
    static BOOL bUseStationPrefix = TRUE;
    TCHAR *lpszProtocol;
    TCHAR *lpszEndpoint;

    if (bUseStationPrefix)
        {
        lstrcpy(szStation, TEXT("\\\\"));
        lstrcat(szStation, lpszStation);
        lpszProtocol = TEXT("ncacn_np");
        lpszEndpoint = TEXT("\\PIPE\\WNET\\WNRPC");
        }
    else
        {
```

```
      lstrcpy(szStation, lpszStation);
      lpszProtocol = TEXT("ncacn_ip_tcp");
      lpszEndpoint = TEXT("35000");
      }
bUseStationPrefix = !bUseStationPrefix;

if (RpcStringBindingCompose(NULL,    // If non-NULL, specifies
                                     // an object UUID that the
                                     // server has registered.
                                     // Otherwise, tells RPC to
                                     // match client and server
                                     // on the basis of the
                                     // interface UUID
                            lpszProtocol,
                            szStation,
                            lpszEndpoint,
                            NULL,
                            pszStringBinding))
      return FALSE;

if (RpcBindingFromStringBinding(*pszStringBinding,
      &wnrpc_IfHandle) != RPC_S_OK)
      {
      RpcStringFree(pszStringBinding);
      return FALSE;
      }
   return TRUE;
}
```

Once the server binding is in place, you can make remote procedure calls to the server. Here is WNetGetRemoteUser(), from the same source file as SetupRPCBinding(). After calling SetupRPCBinding(), it issues the remote procedure call _RpcGetRemoteUser(). Notice the use of the RpcTryExcept, RpcExcept, and RpcEndExcept macros. Under Windows NT, these map to the Structured Exception Handling macros *try* and *except*. (RpcEndExcept inserts the closing curly brace.) The client must issue its remote procedure calls in a *try* block because the RPC client stub reports errors by raising exceptions, not with function return codes. This makes sense; the client/server interface is using function return codes for its own purposes, and the RPC stub cannot interpose its own return codes.

The call to RpcBindingFree() at the end of WNetGetRemoteUser() is the RPC Hangup operation. It closes the binding between the client and the server.

```
DWORD WINAPI WNetGetRemoteUser(LPTSTR   lpszStation,
                              LPTSTR   lpszUserName,
                              LPDWORD  lpdwNameLength)
{
    DWORD dwRetcode = NO_ERROR;
    TCHAR *pszStringBinding;

#ifdef WIN32S
    *lpszUserName = '\0';
    *lpdwNameLength = 0;
    return NO_ERROR;
#else
    if (!SetupRPCBinding(lpszStation, &pszStringBinding))
        {
        return (DWORD) -1;
        }

    RpcTryExcept
        {
        _RpcGetRemoteUser(lpszUserName, lpdwNameLength);
        }
    RpcExcept(1)
        {
        dwRetcode = ((DWORD) -1);
        }
    RpcEndExcept

    RpcBindingFree(&wnrpc_IfHandle);
    RpcStringFree(&pszStringBinding);

    return dwRetcode;
#endif
}
```

Handling Dynamic Endpoints on the Client Side. Dynamic endpoints do not impose any additional burden on the client. It can go through the exact same sequence of steps as shown in SetupRPCBinding() and WNetGetRemoteUser(). Instead of passing specific endpoints like "\\PIPE\\WNET\\WNRPC" and "35000", you simply pass NULL pointers. The request will reach the Endpoint Mapper on the host, and it will complete the binding by filling in the correct endpoint. From that time on, there is no need for the services of the Endpoint Mapper, so subsequent RPCs go directly to the server.

There is, however, a serious disadvantage with dynamic endpoints. If the server application is not running, the client enters a profound state of quiescence and does not leave it for quite a while. Nowhere in any of the functions we have discussed is there a provision for a timeout, and the default timeout seems to be very long. You can control it a little bit by calling RpcMgmtSetComTimeout(), but this does not let you set an absolute timeout, only a relative one, and the waiting period still seems interminable. In the interim, you can do nothing to your application, except kill it with Task Manager. For this reason, I have given up using dynamic endpoints, though I use them with the NetBIOS protocols in the WNet RPC Server just to show you how it's done.

Using the Name Service Database to Browse for Compatible Servers. The purpose of the Name Service database in the OSF/DCE specification is to allow servers and clients to discover each other. You saw earlier in this chapter how the server reports its presence by calling RpcNsBindingExport(). Similarly, the client can enumerate RPC servers by calling RpcNsBindingImportBegin(), RpcNsBindingImportNext(), and RpcNsBindingImportDone(). RpcNsBindingImportBegin() opens an enumeration handle that then serves as an input argument to the other two functions. RpcNsBindingImportNext() returns a binding to one of the servers whose interface UUID matches the one passed by the client in its call to RpcNsBindingImportBegin(). Finally, RpcNsBindingImportDone() closes the handle.

I use this technique in the RPC benchmark client application to compare the performance of the different protocol sequences. The client enumerates all compatible servers and performs the same send and receive operation that our other benchmarks have done. The server function, _RpcBenchmark(), just copies an input buffer to an output buffer; here is the code.

```
void _RpcBenchmark(handle_t hServer,
                   unsigned long dwLength,
                   unsigned char *pcInBuffer,
                   unsigned char *pcOutBuffer)
{
    // Send it back to the client
    CopyMemory(pcOutBuffer, pcInBuffer, dwLength);
}
```

Here is the listing of the benchmark client. Notice that it converts a partial binding to a complete one by calling RpcEpResolveBinding(). Another way to do this is to call _RpcBenchmark() before starting the timer. If you call _RpcBenchmark() with a partial binding and the clock is running, you penalize yourself for the services of the Endpoint Mapper.

```
/********
*
* WNETCLI.CPP
*
* Copyright (c) 1994 Ralph P. Davis, All Rights Reserved
*
* RPC benchmark client
*
********/

/*===== Includes =====*/

#ifdef __cplusplus
extern "C" {
#endif

#include <windows.h>
#include "wnrpc.h"
#include <math.h>
#include <stdio.h>
#include <stdlib.h>
#include <string.h>


/*===== Global Variables =====*/

BYTE byInBuffer[60000];
BYTE byOutBuffer[60000];


/*===== Function Definitions =====*/

void main(int argc, char *argv[])
{
    DWORD   dwStartTime, dwEndTime;
    DWORD   dwPackets;
    DWORD   dwPacketSize = 1024;
    DWORD   i;
    DWORD   dwError;
    RPC_NS_HANDLE hnsBenchmark;
    RPC_BINDING_HANDLE hBenchmark;
    RPC_STATUS RpcStatus;
    LPTSTR pszNewBinding;

    if (argc > 1)
        dwPackets = atoi(argv[1]);
    else
        dwPackets = 250;
```

```
if (argc > 2)
   dwPacketSize = atoi(argv[2]);

RpcTryExcept
   {
   RpcStatus = RpcNsBindingImportBegin(
                  RPC_C_NS_SYNTAX_DEFAULT,
                  TEXT("/.:/WNET_RPC_SERVER"),
                  wnrpc_v1_0_c_ifspec, // This is a global
                                       // variable generated
                                       // by the MIDL compiler
                  NULL,
                  &hnsBenchmark);
   }
RpcExcept (1)
   {
   RpcStatus = RpcExceptionCode();
   }
RpcEndExcept

if (RpcStatus != RPC_S_OK)
   {
   wprintf(TEXT("\nRpcNsBindingImportBegin() failed, "
              "error code = %d"),
      RpcStatus);
   ExitProcess(RpcStatus);
   }

do
   {
   RpcTryExcept
      {
      RpcStatus = RpcNsBindingImportNext(hnsBenchmark,
                                         &hBenchmark);
      }
   RpcExcept (1)
      {
      RpcStatus = RpcExceptionCode();
      }
   RpcEndExcept

   if (RpcStatus == RPC_S_NO_MORE_BINDINGS)
      break;
   if (RpcStatus != RPC_S_OK)
      continue;

   RpcStatus = RpcEpResolveBinding(hBenchmark, wnrpc_v1_0_c_ifspec);
```

```
    if (RpcStatus == RPC_S_OK)
        {
        RpcStatus =
            RpcBindingToStringBinding(hBenchmark, &pszNewBinding);
        if (RpcStatus == RPC_S_OK)
            {
            wprintf(TEXT("\n=============================="));
            wprintf(TEXT("\nBinding string is %s"), pszNewBinding);
            RpcStringFree(&pszNewBinding);
            }
        }
    if (RpcStatus != RPC_S_OK)
        {
        wprintf(TEXT("\nUnable to resolve binding, RpcStatus = %d"),
            RpcStatus);
        }

    RpcStatus = ERROR_SUCCESS;
    for (i = 0, dwStartTime = GetCurrentTime(); i < dwPackets; ++i)
        {
        RpcTryExcept
            {
            _RpcBenchmark(hBenchmark,
                dwPacketSize, (LPBYTE) byInBuffer, (LPBYTE) byOutBuffer);
            }
        RpcExcept (1)
            {
            RpcStatus = RpcExceptionCode();
            }
        RpcEndExcept
        }
    dwEndTime = GetCurrentTime();

    wprintf(TEXT("\nGetLastError() = %d"), RpcStatus);
    wprintf(TEXT("\n%d packets transmitted in %d milliseconds"), i,
        dwEndTime - dwStartTime);
    if ((dwEndTime - dwStartTime) > 0)
        {
        wprintf(TEXT("\nAverage is %d packets per second\n"),
            (i * 2000) / (dwEndTime - dwStartTime));

        double dTotalBytes = ((double) dwPacketSize) *
                             ((double) i) * 2000.0;
        double dEndTime = (double) dwEndTime;
        double dStartTime = (double) dwStartTime;

        wprintf(TEXT("\nBytes per second = %.2f\n"),
            (dTotalBytes / (dEndTime - dStartTime)));
        }
```

```
    wprintf(TEXT("\n===============================\n\n"));

    RpcBindingFree(&hBenchmark);
    } while (TRUE);

    RpcNsBindingImportDone(&hnsBenchmark);

    wprintf(TEXT("\n\n\n"));
    fflush(stdout);
    ExitProcess(0);
}


#ifdef __cplusplus
}
#endif
```

I have discovered one limitation with the RPC Name Service, which may be a reasonable one: It permits browsing of remote machines only on an NT Advanced Server domain. If you have a workgroup consisting of nothing but NT workstations, the Name Service calls only enumerate servers running on the same machine as the client.

RPC Benchmark Data

My purpose in running the benchmark tests with RPC is to assess the performance penalty that RPC entails. Some slowdown is to be expected. After all, RPC does a lot for you. So the question is not, "Is there a slowdown?" but rather, "Is the higher level of service worth the price you pay?"

Local Data Transfer with RPC

The first test compares the performance of seven RPC protocols when both the client and server are running on the same machine. That machine is a 100 MHz MIPS NT Advanced Server host. One of my questions was how much of an optimization Local RPC (the *ncalrpc* protocol sequence) provides. Table 13-2 tabulates the results, and Figure 13-1 presents them in graphic format.

You can see that *ncalrpc* far outstrips all the other protocol sequences. Remember, though, that native Named Pipes were extremely fast. Table 13-3 shows the numbers for *ncalrpc* versus those for Named Pipes with a target machine of ".". They are charted in Figure 13-2.

Table 13-2.   RPC Protocols and Local Data Transfer

Packet Size	1024	2048	4096	8192	16384	32768
ncalrpc	853333	1462857	2275555	2730666	3062429	3105971
ncacn_nb_nb	310302	561094	930908	325078	327680	654050
ncacn_nb_ipx	206868	301176	426666	391700	105668	168084
ncacn_nb_tcp	220214	325078	499512	487618	541618	552580
ncacn_spx	238138	330322	493492	494984	533680	538504
ncacn_ip_tcp	288450	405544	549798	587240	607940	628944
ncacn_np	455110	803136	1342950	1187246	1430916	1443524

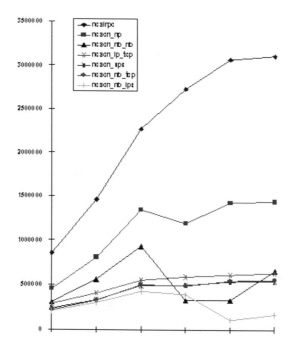

Figure 13-1. Graph of Local RPC Results

Table 13-3. Local Named Pipes vs. Local RPC

Packet Size	1024	2048	4096	8192	16384	32768
ncalrpc	853333	1642857	2275555	2730666	3062429	3105971
Local Named Pipes	2560000	4096000	6301538	6826666	6971914	6362718
% Difference	200%	149%	176%	150%	127%	104%

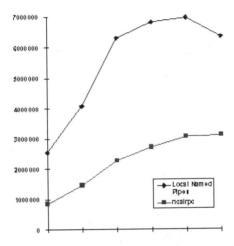

Figure 13-2.   Graph of Local Named Pipes versus Local RPC

From this data, it is safe to conclude that, although *ncalrpc* is quite fast, native Named Pipes are considerably faster.

Remote Data Transfer with RPC

In this test, a 66 MHz 486 NT workstation sent packets to a 100 MHz MIPS-based NT Advanced Server. Table 13-4 shows how the different protocols compare with each other, and the results are graphed in Figure 13-3. I omit the IPX/SPX protocol sequences because I could not test them under NT version 3.5. They are slow in 3.1.

Table 13-4. Performance of RPC Protocols with Remote Data Transfer

Packet Size	1024	2048	4096	8192	16384	32768
ncacn_nb_nb	191223	282093	421616	325920	325887	435976
ncacn_nb_tcp	164895	237724	357105	357261	390467	399293
ncacn_ip_tcp	182694	249300	375263	395176	424400	428004
ncacn_np	176399	265629	404943	323347	323315	326407

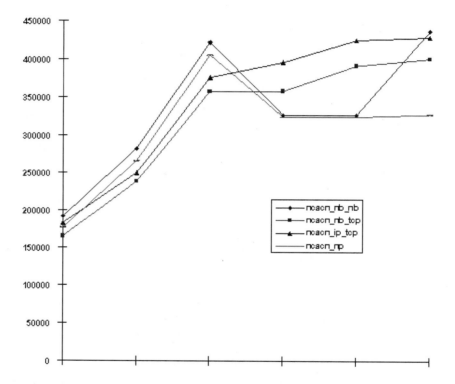

Figure 13-3.   Performance of RPC Protocols with Remote Data Transfer

The numbers show that NetBIOS performs quite well over both NetBEUI (*ncacn_nb_nb*) and TCP/IP (*ncacn_nb_tcp*). The fastest transfer rate is 435,976 bytes per seconds, achieved by *ncacn_nb_nb* at a packet size of 32,768. Named Pipes (*ncacn_np*) gets almost this high at packet size 4,096, then tapers off to a more modest, but still acceptable, transfer rate. TCP/IP (*ncacn_ip_tcp*) is always at or near the top.

The data is consistent with that presented in Chapter 12 for the Named Pipes, Windows Sockets, and NetBIOS APIs used directly. Table 13-5 compares *ncacn_np* with Named Pipes, *ncacn_ip_tcp* with Windows Sockets over TCP/IP, and *ncacn_nb_nb* with NetBIOS over NetBEUI.

Table 13-5. Using RPC versus Using Native APIs

Packet Size	1024	2048	4096	8192	16384	32768
ncacn_np	176399	265629	404943	323347	323315	326407
Named Pipes- TransactNamedPipe()	252527	349488	514249	478364	492085	504200
% Difference	43%	32%	27%	48%	52%	54%
ncacn_ip_tcp	182694	249300	375263	395176	424400	428004
WinSock-TCP/IP	265629	332467	464926	531085	574071	607039
% Difference	45%	33%	24%	34%	35%	42%
ncacn_nb_nb	191223	282093	421616	325920	325887	435976
NetBIOS	200567	274530	430478	687536	690288	738600
% Difference	5%	-3%	2%	111%	112%	69%

These numbers indicate that the performance penalty for using RPC is, unfortunately, not a negligible one. The question whether it is reasonable is one that you will probably have to decide on a case-by-case basis.

Windows NT Services

Windows NT services are the equivalent of UNIX daemons. They are faceless background processes that can be loaded, paused, resumed, and unloaded at runtime. You can also install services so that the operating system loads them at boot time.

Services are console applications that must follow a small set of rules in order to fit into NT's Service Control Manager scheme. These rules enforce an exact structure on NT services, but the structure is simple. Indeed, services can be built from a template. The Win32 SDK includes a sample service, \MSTOOLS\SAMPLES\SERVICE\SIMPLE.C, which has most of the functionality a service normally requires. What gives each service its individual personality are the worker threads you create.

The association between RPC and NT services is a natural one, though it is not compulsory. You can write RPC servers as standard executables, and you can write NT services that do not use RPC. An RPC-based NT service is a powerful vehicle, though, for several reasons:

- The location transparency of RPC allows a service to support client applications anywhere on a network using identical function-call syntax.
- Because services can be configured to start automatically at boot time, you have reasonably high assurance that they will be available when needed.
- The NT Service Control Manager gives the user the flexibility to unload, pause, resume, and reload a service at runtime. If this is undesirable, you can also write a service so that the user cannot unload it.

Much of NT's networking software is implemented as RPC services.

The main() Function in an NT Service

Like all console applications, an NT service is entered through its main() function. main() is very simple: all NT requires it to do is call StartServiceCtrlDispatcher(). This function takes an array of SERVICE_TABLE_ENTRY structures that define the entry points for each of the logical services included in the executable.

```
typedef struct _SERVICE_TABLE_ENTRY
{
    LPTSTR lpszName;
    LPSERVICE_MAIN_FUNCTION lpServiceMain;
} SERVICE_TABLE_ENTRY;
```

Usually, there is only one service per executable. The last element in the array must be NULL.

Here is the main() function from the WNet RPC Server:

```
VOID main(int argc, char *argv[])
{
    SERVICE_TABLE_ENTRY WNetRPCService[] =
        {
          {TEXT("WNet RPC Server"), WNetRPCServiceMain},
          {NULL, NULL}
        };
    DWORD dwUserNameLength = sizeof (szUserName);

    GetUserName(szUserName, &dwUserNameLength);

    UNREFERENCED_PARAMETER(argc);
    UNREFERENCED_PARAMETER(argv);
```

```
// StartServiceCtrlDispatcher() doesn't return until
// the service terminates.

if (!StartServiceCtrlDispatcher(WNetRPCService))
   WNetStopRPCServer(GetLastError(),
      TEXT("StartServiceCtrlDispatcher()"));

ExitProcess(dwLastError);
}
```

As the comment in the code states, if StartServiceCtrlDispatcher() succeeds, it puts the main thread to sleep until the service terminates.

The ServiceMain() Function

Each logical service in the executable has its own entry point, referred to as the ServiceMain() function. You can name the function anything you want to—you tell the Service Control Manager which function to call when you invoke StartServiceCtrlDispatcher(). ServiceMain() has several tasks to accomplish:

1. It registers an additional function (the service control handling function), by calling RegisterServiceCtrlHandler(). This is the function that is called to pause, resume, or stop the service, or to ask it what its current state is.

    ```
    SERVICE_STATUS_HANDLE RegisterServiceCtrlHandler(
                          LPCTSTR lpszService,
                          LPHANDLER_FUNCTION lpHandler);
    ```

    The SERVICE_STATUS_HANDLE is an opaque type that you will use mostly to report your service's status.
2. It calls SetServiceStatus() to inform the Service Control Manager that it is starting up.

    ```
    BOOL SetServiceStatus(
            SERVICE_STATUS_HANDLE hServiceStatus,
            LPSERVICE_STATUS      lpServiceStatus);
    ```

    hServiceStatus was returned by RegisterServiceCtrlHandler(). *lpServiceStatus* points to a SERVICE_STATUS structure. You will look at its fields in the code.
3. It allocates any resources—memory, synchronization objects—the application needs.

4. It starts the worker threads.
5. It calls SetServiceStatus() once again to notify the Service Control Manager that it is running and to let it know what control commands it will accept.
6. It goes to sleep waiting for the worker threads to complete.
7. It cleans up resources—frees memory, closes handles, and so on.
8. It tells the Service Control Manager that it has stopped.

Here is the ServiceMain() function for the WNet RPC Server, called WNetRPCServiceMain(). Comments in the code show where the steps just listed are coded.

```
VOID WNetRPCServiceMain(DWORD dwArgc, LPTSTR *lpArgv)
{
    UNREFERENCED_PARAMETER(dwArgc);
    UNREFERENCED_PARAMETER(lpArgv);
    LPTSTR lpFailedFunction;

    try
        {
        // Step 1. Register the control handler
        if ((hServiceStatus =
            RegisterServiceCtrlHandler(TEXT("WNet RPC Server"),
            WNetRPCServiceCtrlHandler)) == 0)
            {
            lpFailedFunction =
              TEXT("RegisterServiceCtrlHandler()");
            return;
            }

        // Step 2. Tell the Service Control Manager
        // that we're starting up.

        // A dwService type of SERVICE_WIN32_OWN_PROCESS
        // means that only one service is defined
        // as part of this process
        ServiceStatus.dwServiceType            =
            SERVICE_WIN32_OWN_PROCESS;

        // The dwControlsAccepted field indicates
        // what control commands (pause, resume, stop) we're willing to
        // accept
        // We set it to zero to disable control requests during startup
        ServiceStatus.dwControlsAccepted = 0;

        // The dwCurrentState field reports our current status
        // Possible values are:
```

```
//      SERVICE_START_PENDING—initializing
//      SERVICE_RUNNING—in service
//      SERVICE_PAUSE_PENDING—service entering the paused state
//      SERVICE_PAUSED—service has successfully
//                    entered the paused state
//      SERVICE_CONTINUE_PENDING—service is returning from
//                      paused state to running
//      SERVICE_STOP_PENDING—shutting down
//      SERVICE_STOPPED—out of service

// Report status as SERVICE_START_PENDING
ServiceStatus.dwCurrentState      = SERVICE_START_PENDING;

// The dwWin32ExitCode and dwServiceSpecificExitCode fields are
// used to report errors that occur during startup and shutdown
// If the error is defined by Win32 [like a GetLastError() code
// or an RPC error], you use dwWin32ExitCode
// If the error is application-defined, you set dwWin32ExitCode
// to ERROR_SERVICE_SPECIFIC_ERROR, and put your error code
// in dwServiceSpecificExitCode
ServiceStatus.dwWin32ExitCode     = NO_ERROR;
ServiceStatus.dwServiceSpecificExitCode = 0;

// The dwCheckPoint and dwWaitHint fields are used
// to periodically reassure the Service Control Manager
// while you are in one of the pending states
// dwWaitHint is the number of milliseconds you
// expect the operation to take. After that much time,
// the Service Control Manager will ask you how you're
// doing. If it does not receive an updated
// dwCheckPoint by then, it assumes you've failed and gives up.
ServiceStatus.dwCheckPoint        = 1;
ServiceStatus.dwWaitHint          = 5000;  // Milliseconds

if (!SetServiceStatus(hServiceStatus, &ServiceStatus))
    {
    lpFailedFunction = TEXT("SetServiceStatus()");
    return;
    }

// Step 3. No other resources needed

// Step 4. Spin off RPC worker threads (only one here)
// Our worker thread is the WNetStartRPCServer function
// that does our RPC initialization
for (short int i = 0; i < nNumThreads; ++i)
    {
    hThreads[i] = CreateThread(NULL, 0, WNetStartRPCServer, NULL,
```

```
                              0, &dwThreadID[i]);
         if (hThreads[i] == NULL)
            {
            lpFailedFunction =
               TEXT("CreateThread()");
            return;
            }
         }

      // Step 5. Tell NT that we're up and running
      ServiceStatus.dwCurrentState = SERVICE_RUNNING;

      // We'll accept stop and
      // system shutdown control commands.
      // Pause and continue don't make sense, because
      // the only thing we can do is
      // shut down our RPC server startup thread [WNetStartRPCServer()].
      // It's already asleep anyhow, blocked on the call
      // to RpcServerListen()
      // We have no control over the RPC background threads.
      ServiceStatus.dwControlsAccepted =
         SERVICE_ACCEPT_STOP | SERVICE_ACCEPT_SHUTDOWN;
      ServiceStatus.dwWin32ExitCode = NO_ERROR;
      ServiceStatus.dwCheckPoint    = 0;
      ServiceStatus.dwWaitHint      = 0;

      if (!SetServiceStatus(hServiceStatus, &ServiceStatus))
         {
         lpFailedFunction = TEXT("SetServiceStatus()");
         return;
         }

      // Step 6. Block until the server is shutdown by a STOP control
      // (or system shutdown)

      // Wait until all worker threads complete
      WaitForMultipleObjects(nNumThreads, hThreads, TRUE, INFINITE);
      }
   finally
      {
      // We're done—do cleanup
      // Service was already stopped in response to
      // the control command (unless we had a problem
      // during initialization)

      // Step 7. Cleanup resources

      // AbnormalTermination() indicates that something in our
      // initialization failed. Write a message to the event log
```

```
    if (AbnormalTermination())
        WNetStopRPCServer(GetLastError(),
            lpFailedFunction);

    // Close the thread handles
    for (short int i = 0; i < nNumThreads; ++i)
        {
        if (hThreads[i] != NULL)
            {
            CloseHandle(hThreads[i]);
            hThreads[i] = NULL;
            }
        }

    // Step 8. Tell Service Control Manager that we're
    // done.
    // But check to make sure that we are currently either
    // in the SERVICE_STOP_PENDING or SERVICE_RUNNING
    // state.
    if (ServiceStatus.dwCurrentState == SERVICE_RUNNING ||
        ServiceStatus.dwCurrentState == SERVICE_STOP_PENDING)
        {
        ServiceStatus.dwCurrentState  = SERVICE_STOPPED;
        ServiceStatus.dwWin32ExitCode = dwLastError;
        ServiceStatus.dwCheckPoint    = 0;
        ServiceStatus.dwWaitHint      = 0;

        SetServiceStatus(hServiceStatus, &ServiceStatus);
        }
    }
    return;
}
```

The Service Control-Handling Function

The service control-handling function receives control commands from the Service Control Manager (or from any application that makes the appropriate API calls). The commands SERVICE_CONTROL_PAUSE and SERVICE_CONTROL_CONTINUE tell the service to suspend and resume its operations. They can often be implemented by calling SuspendThread() and ResumeThread() with the handles of the worker threads. SERVICE_CONTROL_INTERROGATE asks the service to report its current status. The control command SERVICE_CONTROL_SHUTDOWN indicates that the operating system is shutting down. SERVICE_CONTROL_STOP instructs the service to bring itself out of service. This normally involves at least these steps:

1. Calling SetServiceStatus() to notify the Service Control Manager that you are shutting down.
2. Doing application-specific cleanup.
3. Calling SetServiceStatus() once more to tell the Service Control Manager that you are out of service.

No matter what control command it receives, the control handler is required to report its current status when it exits.

The service control handler for the WNet RPC Server is WNetRPCServiceCtrlHandler(). It responds to SERVICE_CONTROL_STOP and SERVICE_CONTROL_SHUTDOWN commands. SERVICE_CONTROL_PAUSE and SERVICE_CONTROL_RESUME are probably irrelevant here because the only worker thread is already asleep, blocked on its call to RpcServerListen(). Incoming RPCs are being serviced by threads that the RPC runtime has created. You have no idea what their handles are, and no control over them.

```
VOID WNetRPCServiceCtrlHandler(DWORD dwCommand)
{
    // We don't accept Pause and Continue, because
    // they don't make sense

    // Our server thread spins off background threads that
    // do the listens, so suspending our server thread
    // has no effect

    switch (dwCommand)
        {
        case SERVICE_CONTROL_STOP:
        case SERVICE_CONTROL_SHUTDOWN:
            // Tell Service Control Manager that we're coming down
            ServiceStatus.dwCurrentState  = SERVICE_STOP_PENDING;
            ServiceStatus.dwWin32ExitCode = NO_ERROR;
            ServiceStatus.dwCheckPoint    = 1;
            ServiceStatus.dwWaitHint      = 3000;

            SetServiceStatus(hServiceStatus, &ServiceStatus);

            WNetStopRPCServer(0, NULL);

            ++ServiceStatus.dwCheckPoint;
            break;
        case SERVICE_CONTROL_INTERROGATE:
            // Tell me what shape you're in.
            // If checkpoint is greater than zero, bump it
            if (ServiceStatus.dwCheckPoint > 0)
```

```
            ++ServiceStatus.dwCheckPoint;
         break;
      default:
         break;
      }
   SetServiceStatus(hServiceStatus, &ServiceStatus);
   return;
}
```

Additional Service-Related Functions

Win32 also provides a set of functions for service management. The first argument to all these functions is the machine name, so they can be used to control services across a network, as well as locally. The REGINST program that I present in Chapter 15 uses almost all of them to install the WNet RPC Server. The actual installation is accomplished by a call to CreateService(), but it will fail if the server already exists. I detect its existence by calling OpenService() to get a handle to it (typed as an SC_HANDLE). If OpenService() returns a non-NULL value, I have to delete the service by calling DeleteService(). However, in order to do this, I have to make sure it isn't currently running; if it is, I have to shut it down. To find out if it's running, I use the ControlService() function to send it a SERVICE_CONTROL_STOP command. If it succeeds, I know the service is currently running, but I have to wait for it to go completely off-line. I do this by calling QueryServiceStatus() in a loop until the service reports its status as SERVICE_STOPPED. Finally, after creating the service, I complete the cycle by starting it up, using the function StartService(). Here are the appropriate lines of code.

```
SC_HANDLE hService, hServiceControlManager;
TCHAR     szServiceExecutable[MAX_PATH + 1];

// Install the WNet RPC Server in the Service Control
// Manager's database
hServiceControlManager = OpenSCManager(
                          NULL,
                          TEXT("ServicesActive"),
                          SC_MANAGER_ALL_ACCESS);
if (hServiceControlManager != NULL)
   {
   ExpandEnvironmentStrings(
      TEXT("%HOMEDRIVE%\\NTNET\\CODE\\%Cpu%\\WNRPC.EXE"),
      szServiceExecutable,
      sizeof (szServiceExecutable));
```

```
// First, try to open service
// If it already exists, we'll stop it,
// then delete it.
hService = OpenService(hServiceControlManager,
                        TEXT("WNet RPC Server"),
                        SERVICE_ALL_ACCESS);
if (hService != NULL)
    {
    SERVICE_STATUS ServiceStatus;
    DWORD          dwCheckPoint = 0xFFFFFFFF;
    DWORD          dwStartTime = GetCurrentTime();

    // Stop it by sending it a STOP command
    if (ControlService(hService, SERVICE_CONTROL_STOP,
                    &ServiceStatus))
        {
        while ((ServiceStatus.dwCurrentState != SERVICE_STOPPED) &&
                ((GetCurrentTime() - dwStartTime) < 10000))
            {
            if (dwCheckPoint == ServiceStatus.dwCheckPoint)
                // Give up—check point hasn't been incremented
                break;
            dwCheckPoint = ServiceStatus.dwCheckPoint;
            Sleep(ServiceStatus.dwWaitHint);
            QueryServiceStatus(hService, &ServiceStatus);
            }
        if (ServiceStatus.dwCurrentState == SERVICE_STOPPED)
            DeleteService(hService);
        }
    else
        DeleteService(hService);
    CloseServiceHandle(hService);
    }

hService = CreateService(
                hServiceControlManager,
                TEXT("WNet RPC Server"),
                TEXT("WNet RPC Server"),
                SERVICE_ALL_ACCESS,
                SERVICE_WIN32_OWN_PROCESS,
                SERVICE_AUTO_START,
                SERVICE_ERROR_NORMAL,
                szServiceExecutable,
                NULL,
                NULL,
                NULL,
                NULL,
                NULL);
```

```
   if (hService != NULL)
       {
       // Start it running
       StartService(hService, 0, NULL);
       CloseServiceHandle(hService);
       wprintf(TEXT("\nWNet RPC Server successfully installed\n"));
       }
   else
       {
       wprintf(TEXT("\nUnable to install WNet RPC Server, ")
               TEXT("GetLastError() = %d\n"),
           GetLastError());
       }
   CloseServiceHandle(hServiceControlManager);
   }
else
   {
   wprintf(TEXT("\nUnable to access Service Control Manager, ")
           TEXT("GetLastError() = %d\n"),
       GetLastError());
   }
```

Event Logging

Services have no front end. Thus, they cannot display messages, either by calling printf(), as console applications normally can, or with MessageBox(). (Actually, they do have limited access to MessageBox(). See the Knowledge Base article "Access to Display from Win32 Services.") If a service wants to report some condition, its best option is to record an event in the event log. The administrator can then view the information with the Event Viewer.

There are three functions you need to call to log an event. RegisterEventSource() obtains a handle to the log file, ReportEvent() deposits a record in the log, and DeregisterEventSource() closes the handle and terminates the log file interaction. If you have message files that are private to your application, you can add an entry to the Registry, telling NT where to find them. The Registry key that stores this information is HKEY_LOCAL_MACHINE\SYSTEM\CurrentControlSet\Services\Event Log\Application. Under this key, you add one naming your service. (See Chapter 15 for details.)

You can use the event log even if you do not register your application. However, doing so allows you to use multi-language message files, as shown in Chapter 7. This is the strategy that the WNet RPC Server uses. It has only a single message in the message file (\NTNET\CODE\WNETMSGS.MC). Here is the header portion of the file and the definition of the message. As you saw in Chapter 7, this file is processed by the Windows NT Message Compiler and eventually produces the DLL \NTNET\CODE\ WNETMSGS.DLL.

```
;/********
;*
;* WNETMSGS.MC
;*
;*********/

SeverityNames=(Success=0x0:STATUS_SEVERITY_SUCCESS
               Informational=0x1:STATUS_SEVERITY_INFORMATIONAL
               Warning=0x2:STATUS_SEVERITY_WARNING
               Error=0x3:STATUS_SEVERITY_ERROR
               )

LanguageNames=(English=0x0009:MSG00001
               French=0x000c:MSG00002
               Spanish=0x000a:MSG00003
               )
MessageID=
Severity=Error
SymbolicName=MSG_RPC_SERVER_FAILED
Language=English
%1!s! failed. %2!s!
.
Language=French
%1!s! a manqué. %2!s!
.
Language=Spanish
%1!s! fracasó. %2!s!
.
```

The message has two insertion sequences, designated by *%1!s!* and *%2!s!*. These codes say "Substitute the first and second insertion sequences that I pass you, and expect null-terminated strings." The WNet RPC Server calls its own routine WNetReportEvent() when it encounters a problem. The problem may be merely a warning, or it can be an error that is sufficiently serious to warrant closing the service. The first insertion string is passed to WNetReportEvent() and indicates the function that failed. The second one is built by calling FormatMessage() with the error code represented by the *dwErrorCode* argument. Here is the code for WNetReportEvent():

```
VOID WNetReportEvent(DWORD dwErrorCode, LPTSTR lpszErrorMsg,
             BOOL bError)
{
```

```
// Services don't have a user interface, so the
// only way for them to report error conditions
// is to use the event-logging facility
// that NT provides.

// To do this, you call RegisterEventSource() to
// get a handle, then call ReportEvent() to
// log the error

// Finally, you call DeregisterEventSource() to
// release the handle
HANDLE hSource;
TCHAR szLastErrorMsg[1024];
LPTSTR lpszMessageStrings[2];

// Look up message string for system error.
FormatMessage(FORMAT_MESSAGE_FROM_SYSTEM,
              NULL,
              dwErrorCode,
              LANG_USER_DEFAULT,
              szLastErrorMsg,
              sizeof (szLastErrorMsg),
              NULL);

// RegisterEventSource() takes two arguments—the machine name
// (NULL means the local machine)
// and the name of the application logging the event
hSource = RegisterEventSource(NULL, TEXT("WNet RPC Server"));

if (hSource != NULL)
    {
    // The lpszMessageStrings array that we pass
    // to ReportEvent() has the insertion sequences
    // for our message.
    lpszMessageStrings[0] = lpszErrorMsg;
    lpszMessageStrings[1] = szLastErrorMsg;

    ReportEvent(hSource,
          bError ? EVENTLOG_ERROR_TYPE :    // Level of severity
                EVENTLOG_WARNING_TYPE,
          0,                                // Category—we're not
                                            //    using it
          MSG_RPC_SERVER_FAILED,            // Message identifier
          NULL,                             // User security ID (SID)—
                                            //    not using it
          2,                                // Number of insertion
                                            //    strings in
                                            //    lpszMessageStrings
```

```
                                               //    array
        0,                                     // Number of bytes of
                                               //    binary data to include
        (LPCTSTR *) lpszMessageStrings,        // Messages to log
        NULL);                                 // Binary data to log—
                                               //    we're not using any

    DeregisterEventSource(hSource);
    }
}
```

Because I have added information about the WNet RPC Server to the Registry—specifically, which DLL contains its messages—I can pass my own error code to ReportEvent(), and it maps them to the correct message. Figure 13-4 shows how Event Viewer reports an error that I purposely triggered, by registering the OSF RPC protocol sequence "ncadg_ip_udp", representing the User Datagram Protocol (UDP).

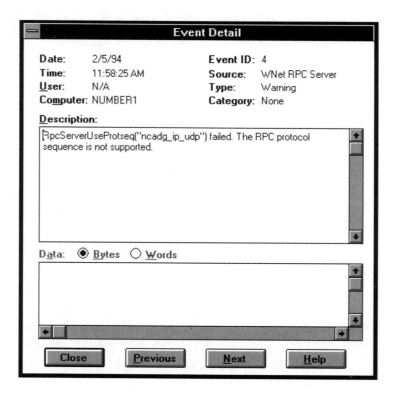

Figure 13-4.   Event Viewer Screen for WNet RPC Server

Conclusion

Remote Procedure Calls are a powerful paradigm for distributed applications. They hide many of the details of client-server communications and allow developers to concentrate on writing their applications. RPCs can access servers either locally or remotely. When talking to a server process on a local machine, the Microsoft protocol *ncalrpc* allows you to take advantage of NT's optimized Local Procedure Call (LPC) facility. For remote communications, Microsoft RPC supports a wide range of protocols that permit connectivity to NT, UNIX, NetWare, and DECNet networks.

Windows NT services are background processes that you can configure to load when the operating system boots. They are often written as RPC server applications. The combination of RPC and Windows NT services is a powerful one. It allows you to place server applications anywhere on a network and have a high level of confidence in their availability. Though users can load and unload services at runtime if they want to, you can also write services so they cannot be unloaded, thereby protecting their availability.

As you would expect, RPC is slower than just coding directly to the underlying API. However, RPC gives the kind of flexibility I discussed in Chapter 9 because it frees you from having to decide which protocols to use. The data presented here quantifies the performance penalty (see Table 13-5). Unfortunately, it is not insignificant, so you need to carefully consider the tradeoffs.

Microsoft seems to be positioning RPC as a cornerstone in its distributed applications strategy. RPC libraries are available for DOS and Windows 3.X. Since none are available for Win32S you have to provide your own 32-bit to 16-bit translation layer, called a "Universal Thunk" in Win32S jargon.

Suggested Readings

Open Software Foundation. *OSF/DCE Application Development Guide*. Englewood Cliffs, NJ: Prentice-Hall, Inc., 1993.

Open Software Foundation. *OSF/DCE Application Development Reference*. Englewood Cliffs, NJ: Prentice-Hall, Inc., 1993.

Microsoft RPC v1.0 in the Win32 On-Line Reference.

RPC Manuals supplied on the Win32 SDK CD-ROM, in the DOC\RPC directory:

Chapter 1, "Introduction to RPC"

Chapter 2, "A Tutorial Introduction"

Chapter 3, "Data and Attributes"

Chapter 4, "Arrays and Pointers"
Chapter 5, "Binding and Handles"
Chapter 6, "The IDL and ACF Files"
Chapter 7, "Run-Time API Functions"
Chapter 8, "Memory Management"
Chapter 9, "Building RPC Applications"
Chapter 10, "MIDL Language Reference"
Chapter 11, "MIDL Command-Line Reference"
Chapter 12, "RPC Data Types and Structures"
Chapter 13, "API Function Reference"
Chapter 14, "Installing RPC"
Appendix A, "Error Codes"
Appendix B, "MIDL Compiler Errors and Warnings"
Appendix C, "RPC Routines"
Appendix D, "RPC Version 1.0 MIDL Grammar"
Appendix E, "RPC Version 1.0 ACF Grammar"
Appendix F, "RPC Redistributable Run-Time Components"

Services Overview in the Win32 on-line help. Published as Chapter 58 in *Win32 Programmer's Reference, Volume 2.*

Event Logging Overview in the on-line help. Published as Chapter 65 in *Win32 Programmer's Reference, Volume 2.*

Eddon, Guy."Windows NT Remote Procedure Calls." *Windows/DOS Developer's Journal*, Vol. 4, No. 9, September 1993.

Microsoft Knowledge Base for Win32 articles:
"Access to Display from Win32 Services"
"Sharing Win32 Services"
"Distributed Computing Environment (DCE) Compliance"
"Determing Whether App Is Running as Service or .EXE"
"Using RPC Callback Functions"

Part 4 Other APIs of Interest

## Chapter 14

The Win32 Security API

Overview

The Win32 Security API is austere, intimidating, and one of the most difficult API sets that you will have to contend with in your work with Windows NT. However, let me at once present two mitigating factors: You probably won't have to use it that much, and it's child's play next to OLE 2.

To make my discussion as succinct as possible, I depart from my normal procedure in this chapter. Rather than integrating the Security API into my WNet DLLs, I present a series of vignettes—small applets that don't do a great deal of useful work, but do illustrate the points I want to emphasize.

The Windows NT Security Model

Security is a pervasive element in the Windows NT environment. Many of the key building blocks of NT applications are NT objects of one sort or another. Files, pipes, threads, processes, synchronization objects, shared memory, and windows are some of the most important.

Security Attributes

In previous chapters, you saw that the functions that create these objects (with the exception of windows) include one argument that points to a SECURITY_ATTRIBUTES structure. This structure is the highest-level entry point into the NT security system and governs two aspects of an object: its inheritability and its accessibility. Here's how it's typed:

```
typedef struct _SECURITY_ATTRIBUTES
{
   DWORD  nLength;
   LPVOID lpSecurityDescriptor;
   BOOL   bInheritHandle;
} SECURITY_ATTRIBUTES;
```

You will set *nLength* to *sizeof (SECURITY_ATTRIBUTES);* presumably this field is for version control. *lpSecurityDescriptor* points to a SECURITY_DESCRIPTOR. Setting it to NULL is the same as passing the SECURITY_ATTRIBUTES themselves as NULL. It causes the affected object to acquire security characteristics by default mechanisms that I examine in this chapter. *bInheritHandle*, if set to TRUE, allows child processes to inherit the handle of the object you are creating.

Table 14-1 lists some of the functions that take a SECURITY_ ATTRIBUTES pointer and refers you to the relevant chapters in this book.

Table 14-1.   Functions That Take SECURITY_ATTRIBUTES

Function Name	Where Discussed in This Book
CreateFile	Chapter 7—Win32 File I/O
	Chapter 10—Named Pipes and Mailslots
CreateMailslot	Chapter 10—Named Pipes and Mailslots
CreateProcess	Not discussed
CreateConsoleScreenBuffer	Not discussed
CreateDirectory	Chapter 7—Win32 File I/O
CreateEvent	Chapter 6—Synchronization Objects
CreateFileMapping	Chapter 8—Dynamic Link Libraries
CreateMutex	Chapter 6—Synchronization Objects
CreateNamedPipe	Chapter 10—Named Pipes and Mailslots
CreatePipe	Not discussed
CreateRemoteThread	Not discussed
CreateSemaphore	Chapter 6—Synchronization Objects
CreateThread	Chapter 5—Multithreading
RegCreateKeyEx	Chapter 15—The Registry and Performance Monitoring
RegSaveKey	Chapter 15—The Registry and Performance Monitoring

Other functions involve an implicit attachment of security properties. Perhaps one of the most surprising is CreateWindow(). There are no SECURITY_ATTRIBUTES as such involved, but windows in NT belong to a hierarchy of screen-based objects. The top of the hierarchy is the process window station, created when you start a process. The threads spawned by that process get their own desktops, and these in turn create windows. Window handles—the familiar HWNDs—do not play a direct role in any Win32 security APIs, but you can control the security characteristics of window stations and desktops. Then, when you call CreateWindow(), the resultant HWND inherits the security settings from the window station and its thread desktop.

Figure 14-1 shows a process window station with desktops for two threads. The first thread has created two windows, and the second owns one.

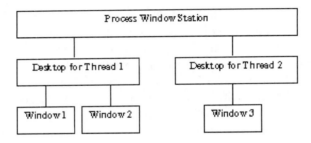

Figure 14-1.   Hierarchy of Screen-Based Object Classes

In many of the code examples in previous chapters, I ignored the SECURITY_ATTRIBUTES by passing it as a NULL pointer. However, as I hinted on several occasions, this is not an empty action. You will see that it has a very specific meaning that may not always be what you intend. Another use of the SECURITY_ATTRIBUTES is to create a handle that can be inherited by child processes. In this case, you often set the *bInheritHandle* field to TRUE, and *lpSecurityDescriptor* to NULL. This too is a significant action.

There are no functions that manipulate SECURITY_ATTRIBUTES. The format of the structure is exposed, and you can set and read the fields directly.

Security Descriptors

The most important field in the SECURITY_ATTRIBUTES is *lpSecurityDescriptor*, which points to a SECURITY_DESCRIPTOR. Unlike the SECURITY_ATTRIBUTES, the internal layout of this structure is not documented. You can think of a SECURITY_DESCRIPTOR as a single record in the security database. For each protected object, there exists at most one SECURITY_DESCRIPTOR. It carries the information needed to regulate attempts to use the object. Each item in the SECURITY_ DESCRIPTOR has two corresponding functions—one to read it and one to write it.

Information Stored in a Security Descriptor. These are the data items and the functions you use to manipulate them:

- The object's owner (GetSecurityDescriptorOwner() and SetSecurity DescriptorOwner()). This is represented by the Security Identifier (SID) of the owner. I will discuss SIDs in more detail shortly.
- The primary group to which the owner belongs (GetSecurity DescriptorGroup() and SetSecurityDescriptorGroup)). This is the group to which NT automatically assigns you when your account is first created. It is also identified by its SID.
- The discretionary access control list (DACL), which determines who may do what with the object (GetSecurityDescriptorDacl() and SetSecurityDescriptorDacl()).
- The system access control list (SACL), which specifies how you want to audit the use of the object (GetSecurityDescriptorSacl() and SetSecurityDescriptorSacl()).

Because the security database represents users and groups in the same way, the owner- and group-related functions have identical syntax. Similarly, because the last two groups of functions work with access control lists, they are syntactically the same. Of all these functions, the most important are GetSecurityDescriptorDacl() and SetSecurityDescriptorDacl(); they allow you to control who can use an object. They are discussed extensively through the rest of the chapter, so I will only show the syntax for the owner-related functions here.

```
BOOL GetSecurityDescriptorOwner(
        PSECURITY_DESCRIPTOR lpSecurityDescriptor,
        PSID                 *ppSID,
        LPBOOL                lpbOwnerDefaulted);
```

A pointer to the security identifier (SID) of the object's owner is returned in **ppSID*, and **lpbOwnerDefaulted* reports whether the owner was determined by some default mechanism or set explicitly. The pointer returned in **ppSID* is not allocated; it is an address within the security descriptor. If GetSecurityDescriptorOwner() or any function in the Security API returns FALSE, consult GetLastError() to find out what the exact problem is.

```
BOOL SetSecurityDescriptorOwner(
        PSECURITY_DESCRIPTOR lpSecurityDescriptor,
        PSID                 pSID,
        BOOL                 bOwnerDefaulted);
```

The owner of the object is changed to the object to whose SID *pSID* points. SIDs are binary data; you will see shortly how you match human-readable names to their underlying SIDs, and vice-versa.

Initializing a Security Descriptor. When creating a new object, you assemble its security descriptor from scratch. In this case, the first function you call is InitializeSecurityDescriptor(). This takes a pointer to the security descriptor and a constant specifying the security descriptor revision:

```
BOOL InitializeSecurityDescriptor(
        PSECURITY_DESCRIPTOR lpSecurityDescriptor,
        DWORD                dwRevision);
```

It is suggested that you pass *dwRevision* as SECURITY_DESCRIPTOR_ REVISION, currently defined as 1. Presumably, if Microsoft comes out with a new SECURITY_DESCRIPTOR layout, the constant will be redefined, but existing code that uses existing objects will not break because both are version-stamped.

Self-relative versus Absolute Security Descriptors. Security descriptors may be in either self-relative or absolute format. In self-relative format, the individual fields are represented as offsets from the beginning of the SECURITY_DESCRIPTOR. In absolute format, they are actual pointers. The self-relative format is useful for putting security descriptors into places where pointers have no meaning, like on disk or in a network packet. Certain types of securable objects are permanent, that is, they continue to exist even when NT is shut down. These include file objects, Registry keys, and NT services, and may also include private objects. It therefore stands to reason that when you retrieve a security descriptor, you get it in self-relative format. However, if you alter the contents of a security descriptor, you do so by passing pointers to your own program variables. The security descriptor incorporates the information you are putting into it by adding your pointers. Therefore, with functions like SetSecurityDescriptorDacl() or SetSecurityDescriptorSacl(), the security descriptor must be in absolute format. InitializeSecurityDescriptor() creates an absolute descriptor.

For example, if you want to read the SECURITY_DESCRIPTOR of a file in order to grant rights to someone, you have to convert the security descriptor from self-relative to absolute format. Win32 provides functions for making these conversions, MakeAbsoluteSD() and MakeSelfRelativeSD(). MakeSelfRelativeSD() is simple, but MakeAbsoluteSD() is cumbersome. Because you have to provide locations for all of the pieces of the security descriptor, it requires eleven arguments (so it's tied with CreateWindow()).

Let's take a closer look at discretionary access control lists and the functions that manage them.

Access-Control Lists (ACLs) and Access Control Entries (ACEs)

Access-control lists are the most important data structure in the security API because they determine who can and cannot use an object, and the precise manner in which they can use it. They are made up in turn of access-control entries (ACEs), one for each user being granted or denied access. The ACL structure type defines an access control list.

```
typedef struct _ACL
{
    BYTE AclRevision;   // Set this to the constant ACL_REVISION
    BYTE Sbz1;
    WORD AclSize;
    WORD AceCount;
    WORD Sbz2;
} ACL;
```

This is obviously just a header. AclSize is the byte size of the entire list, including all the access-control entries. AceCount is the number of ACEs following the ACL. The ACEs in turn consist of an ACE_HEADER followed by the access-control information.

```
typedef struct _ACE_HEADER
{
    BYTE AceType;
```

```
    BYTE AceFlags;
    WORD AceSize;
} ACE_HEADER;
```

The AceType indicates what this ACE is doing—allowing access, denying it, or requesting an audit trail. The appropriate constants are ACCESS_ALLOWED_ACE_TYPE, ACCESS_DENIED_ACE_TYPE, and SYSTEM_AUDIT_ACE_TYPE. A fourth type, SYSTEM_ALARM_ACE_TYPE, is not supported yet. AceSize is the size of the ACE, including the ACE_HEADER. This is necessary because security identifiers are of variable length.

The rest of the ACE contains two pieces of information: the rights being conferred, withheld, or audited, and the security identifier of the user or group in question. Here is the type definition of an ACCESS_ALLOWED_ACE, which is typical:

```
typedef struct _ACCESS_ALLOWED_ACE
{
    ACE_HEADER Header;
    ACCESS_MASK Mask;
    DWORD SidStart;
} ACCESS_ALLOWED_ACE;
```

The ACCESS_MASK is a DWORD whose bits represent the appropriate permissions. Because of the large number of object types, there can be a wide difference in meaning. For this reason, Win32 provides generic masks that you can pass; it then takes care of translating them to the specific rights that are relevant for a given object. These masks are GENERIC_READ, GENERIC_WRITE, GENERIC_EXECUTE, and GENERIC_ALL, and they occupy the high four bits of the ACCESS_MASK. You will see how these get translated when you examine some actual DACLs.

Security Identifiers (SID)

The atomic unit of representation in the Windows NT security database is the security identifier, or SID. This is a binary number, whose format can be rather complex. It is intended to be an opaque data type, which applications are not supposed to access directly.

SID Representation in Memory. The following *typedef* for a SID appears in WINNT.H.

```
#define ANYSIZE_ARRAY 1
typedef struct _SID_IDENTIFIER_AUTHORITY
{
   BYTE Value[6];
} SID_IDENTIFIER_AUTHORITY, *PSID_IDENTIFIER_AUTHORITY;

typedef struct _SID
{
   BYTE Revision;
   BYTE SubAuthorityCount;
   SID_IDENTIFIER_AUTHORITY IdentifierAuthority;
   DWORD SubAuthority[ANYSIZE_ARRAY];
} SID;
```

The subject of how SIDs are represented is complex and esoteric, and unlikely to affect your life as a programmer. If you are interested, there are good discussions elsewhere in the literature. The *Security Overview* in the on-line help, also published as Chapter 49 of *Win32 Programmer's Reference, Volume 2*, is helpful. Look for the section called *Security Identifiers*. Two articles by Rob Reichel in the April and May 1993 issues of *Windows/DOS Developer's Journal* clarified a lot of things for me. I'll punt, so we can get on to the details of working with SIDs.

Converting SIDs to Names and Names to SIDs. Users, of course, have little patience with binary network addresses, binary security identifiers—binary anythings, really, nor should they. They want to see user and group names that make sense to them. However, NT, as operating systems are wont to do, likes dealing with compact, symbolic representations like SIDs. We developers are caught in the middle, and have to please both of them. Fortunately, Win32 provides two very useful functions that map names to SIDs and SIDs to names: LookupAccountName() and LookupAccountSid(). LookupAccountName() takes a name in user-readable format, like the group "Everyone" or user "ralphd" and returns the corresponding SID. Every legitimate name will have a SID that the system knows about. LookupAccountSid() takes a SID and returns its name. This is useful for dumping ACLs to the user, for instance. The access-control entries consist of rights masks and SIDs, so you need to convert the SIDs to human-readable format to display them. It may surprise you to learn that not all SIDs have a matching name. When you logon to NT, it assigns you a **logon SID**, which is used for the duration of your NT session, and has no name to go with it. It is this SID that receives rights to the process window station and the thread desktop and, through them, to all windows created by processes that the user runs.

I will make considerable use of LookupAccountName() and LookupAccountSid() in the code examples here. Here are their prototypes:

```
BOOL LookupAccountName(
        LPCTSTR lpszMachineName,
        LPCTSTR lpszAccountName,
        PSID    pSID,
        LPDWORD lpdwSIDSize,
        LPTSTR  lpszReferencedDomain,
        LPDWORD lpdwReferencedDomain,
        PSID_NAME_USE pSidNameUse);

BOOL LookupAccountSid(
        LPCTSTR lpszMachineName,
        PSID    pSID,
        LPCTSTR lpszAccountName,
        LPDWORD lpdwAccountSize,
        LPTSTR  lpszReferencedDomain,
        LPDWORD lpdwReferencedDomain,
        PSID_NAME_USE pSidNameUse);
```

The *lpszMachineName* argument may tip you off to the fact that these functions can be executed on remote computers. If you pass it as NULL, the function queries the local database. *lpszAccountName* and *pSID* are the input or output data, depending on the function, and *lpdwSIDSize* is used to report the length of the SID. The other arguments are of less interest, but you have to supply them—the functions won't accept NULL pointers. *pSidNameUse* points to a variable of the enumerated type SID_NAME_USE, which gives you an idea of the types of objects NT supports.

```
typedef enum tagSID_NAME_USE
{
    SidTypeUser = 1,
    SidTypeGroup,
    SidTypeDomain,
    SidTypeAlias,
    SidTypeWellKnownGroup,
    SidTypeDeletedAccount,
    SidTypeInvalid,
    SidTypeUnknown
} SID_NAME_USE;
```

Using the Win32 Security Functions

In this section, you will look closely at how you use the Win32 Security API for various tasks. You will also find out how the functions mentioned in Table 14-1 behave. I have divided the code samples into groups according to the kind of object they work with. NT recognizes these categories of securable objects and provides different functions for manipulating their security descriptors:

- File objects include standard disk files, named pipes, and mailslots (GetFileSecurity() and SetFileSecurity()).
- Kernel objects consist primarily of synchronization objects, file-mapping objects, and process and thread handles (GetKernelObjectSecurity() and SetKernelObjectSecurity()).
- Private objects are objects known only to your application. You can use them to protect server applications where no built-in security exists. The functions are CreatePrivateObjectSecurity(), GetPrivateObjectSecurity(), SetPrivateObjectSecurity(), and DestroyPrivateObjectSecurity().
- User objects are process window stations, thread desktops, and the windows and menus that are their descendants. The relevant functions are GetUserObjectSecurity() and SetUserObjectSecurity().
- Registry keys are records in the NT configuration database. The functions that manipulate their security descriptors are RegGetKeySecurity() and RegSetKeySecurity(), which are discussed in Chapter 15.
- Shares are directories and print queues that you are making available for remote users. The relevant functions are NetShareGetInfo() and NetShareSetInfo(). They are part of the LAN Manager API, which is presented in Chapter 16.
- NetDDE shares are aliases for DDEML service and topic pairs. They are used by the NetDDE communications protocol. The functions that read and write their security descriptors are NDdeGetShareSecurity() and NDdeSetShareSecurity(). NetDDE is presented in Chapter 17.
- Service objects are the services known to the Service Control Manager, which you looked at in Chapter 13. With their DACLs, you can control who is allowed to start, stop, pause, and configure a service, or query its status. The functions, which are documented in the Services group, are QueryServiceObjectSecurity() and SetServiceObjectSecurity(). Because they are more narrowly specialized than the others, I do not discuss them further.

File Objects—Named Pipes

File objects are a very important topic for this book. First of all, one of the things you most need to do in a network environment is control who can access files stored on a server. Second, because Named Pipes and Mailslots are file systems, they are treated as file objects for security purposes. When writing a server application, you need to be able to control access to your service endpoints. With Named Pipes and Mailslots, this protection is built in. You may never need to control the security properties of a disk file in a program, since the NT File Manager allows you to do this interactively. However, there is no analogous tool for Pipes and Mailslots; because they are invisible program objects, you must use the Security API to regulate their use.

If you don't add security descriptors to file objects, NT adds them for you. You will see exactly how it does that in the sample applications.

Creating a Named Pipe with NULL Security Attributes. The first sample, SECUTST1, creates a named pipe, \\.\PIPE\WNET\SECUTST1, passing a NULL SECURITY_ATTRIBUTES pointer to CreateNamedPipe(). It then dumps the pipe's DACL to see who has been assigned rights to it. Here is what it finds if you're logged on as *administrator*:

```
Access allowed ace
Access rights 001F01FF granted to Administrators on
   \\.\PIPE\WNET\SECUTEST
Access allowed ace
Access rights 001F01FF granted to SYSTEM on \\.\PIPE\WNET\SECUTEST
```

As you can see, you did not get a pipe with unrestricted access. Rather, both the group Administrators and the user SYSTEM (denoting the operating system itself) have access rights 0x001F01FF. Let's see what this rights mask means and how it got there.

If you browse through \MSTOOLS\H\WINNT.H, you will find this definition for FILE_ALL_ACCESS:

```
#define FILE_ALL_ACCESS (STANDARD_RIGHTS_REQUIRED | SYNCHRONIZE | 0x1FF)
```

The 0x1FF in this definition accounts for the low 16 bits of the access rights requested above. It corresponds to the constants FILE_GENERIC_READ | FILE_GENERIC_WRITE | FILE_GENERIC_EXECUTE, which confer all possible rights to the file itself.

Later in the file, STANDARD_RIGHTS_REQUIRED is defined as
0x000F0000L, and SYNCHRONIZE is 0x00100000L. SYNCHRONIZE
access, which was discussed in Chapter 6, gives you permission to use the
object's handle for synchronization purposes. STANDARD_
RIGHTS_REQUIRED is a combination of other bits that grant DELETE,
READ_CONTROL, WRITE_DAC, and WRITE_OWNER access.
DELETE lets you delete an object. READ_CONTROL permits you to read
its security descriptor. WRITE_DAC lets you change the discretionary
access control list in the security descriptor. WRITE_OWNER allows you to
change the object's owner.

That accounts for all the bits in the access mask. You now know that all
members of the group Administrators, and the special user SYSTEM, have
all possible rights to the named pipe. Let's look at the code that tells us that,
then see how they got the rights.

The first part of main() creates the pipe and calls the routine RunTests().

```
void main(int argc, char *argv[])
{
    HANDLE hFile;
    SECURITY_INFORMATION SecurityInformation;

    // Create pipe using NULL SECURITY_ATTRIBUTES
    hFile = CreateNamedPipe("\\\\.\\PIPE\\WNET\\SECUTEST",
                    PIPE_ACCESS_DUPLEX,
                    PIPE_TYPE_MESSAGE |
                    PIPE_READMODE_BYTE |
                    PIPE_WAIT,
                    1, 0, 0, 0,
                    NULL);
    if (hFile == INVALID_HANDLE_VALUE)
    {
        printf("\nUnable to create pipe, GetLastError() = %d\n",
            GetLastError());
        ExitProcess(1);
    }

    SecurityInformation = DACL_SECURITY_INFORMATION;
    RunTests("\\\\.\\PIPE\\WNET\\SECUTEST",
        &SecurityInformation);

    CloseHandle(hFile);
```

Getting a File Object's Security Descriptor. The variable *Security Information* that is passed to RunTests() is set to indicate that you want to read the discretionary access control list (DACL) of the object. RunTests() calls GetFileSecurity() to read the pipe's security descriptor.

```
BOOL GetFileSecurity(LPTSTR lpFileName,
                     SECURITY_INFORMATION SecurityInformation,
                     PSECURITY_DESCRIPTOR lpSecurityDescriptor,
                     DWORD                dwSecDescSize,
                     LPDWORD              lpdwSecDescActualSize);
```

To read a file's security descriptor, you pass the file name *(lpFileName)*, rather than a handle to an open file. *SecurityInformation* includes bits that tell GetFileSecurity() how much information we need. By setting it to DACL_SECURITY_INFORMATION, you say that you want only the discretionary access control list. *dwSecDescSize* is the size of the buffer at *lpSecurityDescriptor*. If this is merely *sizeof* (SECURITY_DESCRIPTOR), the function is likely to fail. SECURITY_DESCRIPTORs are variable-length structures because they contain access control lists and SIDs, both of which are structures containing open-ended arrays. If *dwSecDescSize* is too small to hold all the output information, GetFileSecurity() returns FALSE, and GetLastError() reports ERROR_INSUFFICIENT_BUFFER. In this case, **lpdwSecDescActualSize* tells you exactly how much memory you need. This is the cleanest way to retrieve a security descriptor, but for the sake of brevity, I just create a large output buffer (8192 bytes) on the stack.

Here is RunTests().

```
VOID RunTests(LPTSTR lpName, SECURITY_INFORMATION *pSecurityInfo)
{
   BYTE    bySDBuffer[8192];
   PSECURITY_DESCRIPTOR lpSecurityDescriptor =
      (PSECURITY_DESCRIPTOR) bySDBuffer;
   DWORD   dwSDSize;

   dwSDSize = sizeof (bySDBuffer);

   if (!GetFileSecurity(lpName, *pSecurityInfo,
      lpSecurityDescriptor, dwSDSize, &dwSDSize))
      {
      printf("\nGetFileSecurity() failed, GetLastError() = %d",
         GetLastError());
      return;
      }

   DumpDACL(lpName, lpSecurityDescriptor);
}
```

Reading the Discretionary Access Control List. Once RunTests() has fetched the security descriptor, it passes it to DumpDACL(), which prints all the entries in the discretionary access control list. DumpDACL(), like RunTests(), calls one Win32 function, GetSecurityDescriptorDacl(), and one local function, DumpACEs(). GetSecurityDescriptorDacl() returns a pointer to the DACL. This pointer is not allocated; it points to the actual location of the DACL in the security descriptor.

```
BOOL GetSecurityDescriptorDacl(
        PSECURITY_DESCRIPTOR lpSecurityDescriptor,
        LPBOOL              lpbDaclPresent,
        PACL               *ppDACL,
        LPBOOL              lpbDaclDefaulted);
```

ppDACL points to a PACL pointer that GetSecurityDescriptorDacl() fills in with the address of the DACL. When the function completes, *lpbDaclPresent* will be set to TRUE if a DACL is present. If it's FALSE, *ppDACL* does not contain a valid address.

Here is the listing of DumpDACL(). Along with other auxiliary functions, it is contained in \NTNET\CODE\SECURITY\SECUHLPR.CPP.

```
VOID DumpDACL(LPTSTR lpFileName, PSECURITY_DESCRIPTOR pSD)

{
    PACL pACL = NULL;
    BOOL bDACLPresent;
    BOOL bDACLDefaulted;

    if (!GetSecurityDescriptorDacl(pSD, &bDACLPresent,
        &pACL, &bDACLDefaulted))
        {
        printf("\nGetSecurityDescriptorDacl() failed, "
            "GetlastError() = %d",
          GetLastError());
        return;
        }

    if (bDACLPresent)
       printf("\nDACL is present\n");
    else
       printf("\nNo DACL is present\n");

    if (bDACLDefaulted)
       printf("\nDACL provided by default mechanism\n");
    else
```

```
        printf("\nDACL explicitly assigned\n");

    if (pACL != NULL)
        DumpACEs(pACL, lpFileName);
    else
        printf("\n%s has a NULL DACL", lpFileName);
    printf("\n");
}
```

Walking the Discretionary Access Control List. DumpACEs() examines each access control entry in the DACL and displays its type, the user or group name, and the rights mask. Because you do not know the format of the access control list in advance, you have to declare it as a raw BYTE array, then parse it based on the information you find in the headers. The list header is contained in the ACL structure that begins the list; each ACE has its own ACE_HEADER.

DumpACEs() uses two Win32 functions: GetAclInformation() and GetAce(). Among other things, GetAclInformation() reports the number of ACEs in the list.

```
BOOL GetAclInformation(PACL    pACL,
                       LPVOID  lpOutputBuffer,
                       DWORD   dwOutputSize,
                       ACL_INFORMATION_CLASS ACLInfo);
```

ACL_INFORMATION_CLASS is an enumeration type whose two possible values are AclRevisionInformation and AclSizeInformation. If you ask it for the size information, which is what you're interested in here, it fills *lpOutputBuffer* with an ACL_SIZE_INFORMATION structure.

```
typedef struct _ACL_SIZE_INFORMATION
{
    DWORD    AceCount;
    DWORD    AclBytesInUse;
    DWORD    AclBytesFree;
} ACL_SIZE_INFORMATION;
```

AceCount is the number of ACEs comprising the list. For each of these, DumpACEs() calls GetAce() to get a pointer to its contents.

```
BOOL GetAce(PACL    pACL,
            DWORD   dwIndex,
            LPVOID *lpACE);
```

dwIndex says which element in the list you want, starting with zero. *lpACE* points to a VOID pointer; on output, it will contain the address of the requested ACE. Just as with GetSecurityDescriptorDacl(), this pointer is not allocated; it is the address of the ACE within the DACL.

With a pointer to the ACE in hand, DumpACEs() looks at the ACE_HEADER to determine what kind of ACE it's looking at, then skips past the header to examine the access mask and the SID. It calls a local routine, DumpSID(), to convert the SID in the ACE to a user-readable account name.

Here's the full code for DumpACEs(), also from \NTNET\CODE\ SECURITY\SECUHLPR.CPP.

```
VOID DumpACEs(PACL pACL, LPTSTR lpFileName)
{
    BYTE byBuffer[1024];
    ACL_SIZE_INFORMATION *pACLSize =
        (ACL_SIZE_INFORMATION *) byBuffer;
    LPVOID pACE;
    ACE_HEADER *pACEHeader;
    LPBYTE lpTemp;
    TCHAR   szSIDName[256];
    TCHAR   szNameType[256];
    DWORD   dwAccessMask;
    PSID    pSID;
    LPTSTR  lpVerb;

    if (pACL == NULL)
        {
        printf("\nDumpACEs() passed a NULL ACL pointer");
        return;
        }

    if (!GetAclInformation(pACL, byBuffer, sizeof (byBuffer),
        AclSizeInformation))
        {
        printf("\nGetAclInformation() failed, GetLastError() = %d",
            GetLastError());
        return;
        }
    for (DWORD i = 0; i < pACLSize->AceCount; ++i)
        {
        if (!GetAce(pACL, i, &pACE))
            {
            printf("\nGetAce() failed, GetLastError() = %d",
                GetLastError());
            continue;
```

```
        }
    pACEHeader = (ACE_HEADER *) pACE;
    lpTemp = (LPBYTE) pACE;

    lpTemp += sizeof (ACE_HEADER);
    dwAccessMask = *(ACCESS_MASK *) lpTemp;
    lpTemp += sizeof (ACCESS_MASK);
    pSID = (PSID) lpTemp;

    switch (pACEHeader->AceType)
        {
        case ACCESS_ALLOWED_ACE_TYPE:
            printf("\nAccess allowed ace");
            lpVerb = "granted to";
            break;
        case ACCESS_DENIED_ACE_TYPE:
            printf("\nAccess denied ace");
            lpVerb = "denied to";
            break;
        case SYSTEM_AUDIT_ACE_TYPE:
            printf("\nSystem audit ace");
            lpVerb = "being audited for";
            break;
        case SYSTEM_ALARM_ACE_TYPE:
            printf("\nSystem alarm ace");
            lpVerb = "being audited for";
            break;
        }
    if (DumpSID(pSID, szSIDName, szNameType))
        {
        printf("\nAccess rights %08X %s %s on %s",
            dwAccessMask, lpVerb,
            szSIDName, lpFileName);
        }
    }
```

Mapping a SID to an Account Name.   DumpSID() calls
LookupAccountSid() to translate the SID passed to it into a readable name.

```
BOOL DumpSID(PSID pSID, LPTSTR lpSIDName, LPTSTR lpNameType)
{
    TCHAR szAccount[256];
    DWORD dwAccountSize = sizeof (szAccount);
    TCHAR szDomain[256];
    DWORD dwDomainSize = sizeof (szDomain);
    SID_NAME_USE SidNameUse;
```

```
    if (!LookupAccountSid(NULL, pSID, szAccount,&dwAccountSize,
        szDomain, &dwDomainSize, &SidNameUse))
    {
    printf("\nLookupAccountSid() failed, GetLastError() = %d",
        GetLastError());
    return FALSE;
    }
    sprintf(lpSIDName, "%s", szAccount);
    if (lpNameType != NULL)
        sprintf(lpNameType, "%s", SidNames[SidNameUse]);
    return TRUE;
}
```

Default Assignment of Security Descriptors. So far you have seen that a named pipe created by the administrator with NULL SECURITY_ATTRIBUTES ends up with all access granted to Administrators and SYSTEM. You also looked at the code that determines that. How did Administrators and SYSTEM get assigned rights to this pipe?

When you logon to Windows NT, it generates a logon SID for you, then creates an access token that gets attached to every process you run. This token contains all the security-related information NT needs to judge your requests to use protected objects. These include your user SID, your primary group, and any other groups you belong to. Another piece of information the token carries is called the default discretionary access control list. Now, the documentation for CreateNamedPipe() is a little vague on what happens if you pass a NULL SECURITY_ATTRIBUTES: "If *lpSecurityAttributes* is NULL, the pipe is created with a default security descriptor." However, it is reasonable to surmise that there is a connection between the default DACL in the token and the DACL that eventually gets assigned. The second test that SECUTST1.EXE performs, in the last half of main(), checks this hypothesis. To do so, it reads the process token by calling GetTokenInformation() and asking for the default DACL.

```
BOOL GetTokenInformation(
        HANDLE                  hToken,
        TOKEN_INFORMATION_CLASS TokenInfo,
        LPVOID                  lpOutputBuffer,
        DWORD                   dwOutputSize,
        PDWORD                  lpdwActualOutputSize);
```

The token handle is retrieved by calling OpenProcessToken() as follows.

```
HANDLE hToken;
OpenProcessToken(GetCurrentProcess(),
                 TOKEN_ALL_ACCESS,
                 &hToken);
```

TOKEN_INFORMATION_CLASS is an enumerated type. The value that asks for the default DACL is TokenDefaultDacl. The information is returned in a TOKEN_DEFAULT_DACL structure, typed as follows.

```
typedef struct _TOKEN_DEFAULT_DACL
{
    PACL DefaultDacl;
} TOKEN_DEFAULT_DACL;
```

After obtaining this information, SECUTST1 calls DumpACEs() again to display the contents of the token's default DACL.

```
/*=======================================================*/
  // Part II.
  // Let's get the default DACL for our process' token
  // This is where the DACL came from that got
  // tied to the named pipe we created

  HANDLE hToken = NULL;
  OpenProcessToken(GetCurrentProcess(),
                   TOKEN_ALL_ACCESS,
                   &hToken);

  if (hToken != NULL)
      {
      BYTE   byACLBuffer[4096];
      DWORD  dwACLSize = sizeof (byACLBuffer);
      TOKEN_DEFAULT_DACL *pTokenDefaultDACL =
         (TOKEN_DEFAULT_DACL *) byACLBuffer;

      // Get the DACL for the token and dump it.
      if (!GetTokenInformation(hToken, TokenDefaultDacl,
         byACLBuffer, dwACLSize, &dwACLSize))
         {
         printf("\nGetTokenInformation() failed, "
                "GetLastError() = %d",
                GetLastError());
         }
      else
```

```
                 {
                 DumpACEs(pTokenDefaultDACL->DefaultDacl,
                    "Process token default DACL");
                 }
             }
         fflush(stdout);
         ExitProcess(0);
     }
```

This is what DumpACEs() tells us:

```
Access allowed ace
Access rights 10000000 granted to Administrators on Process token
   default DACL
Access allowed ace
Access rights 10000000 granted to SYSTEM on Process token default DACL
```

This looks very much like the information that results from dumping the file's DACL. Indeed, the only difference is the rights mask. Here, you see 0x10000000; before, you saw 0x001F01FF. The fact that only one bit is set in the rights mask might lead you to suspect that a single *#define* describes it. This is exactly right. Here is the relevant line from \MSTOOLS\H\WINNT.H:

```
#define GENERIC_ALL   (0x10000000L)
```

My interpretation of what happened is this: the default DACL in the token represents the rights using their generic description because the DACL may be applied to more than one type of object. When the process owning the token creates a named pipe without specifying a security descriptor, NT allocates one and copies the token's default DACL into it. At this time, it maps the generic rights in the token to the specific rights for the object. Here, GENERIC_ALL (0x10000000L) becomes FILE_ALL_ACCESS (0x001F01FFL).

Here's the significance of this discovery: if you create a named pipe with a NULL security descriptor, only users belonging to your primary group (and the system itself) will be able to connect to it.

Creating a File Object with Unrestricted Access. The solution to this was presented in Chapter 10: assign the pipe a security descriptor with a NULL DACL. Here's how you do this:

```
SECURITY_ATTRIBUTES SecurityAttributes;
SECURITY_DESCRIPTOR SecurityDescriptor;

InitializeSecurityDescriptor(&SecurityDescriptor,
   SECURITY_DESCRIPTOR_REVISION);
SetSecurityDescriptorDacl(&SecurityDescriptor,
                          TRUE,
                          NULL,    // No DACL
                          FALSE);
SecurityAttributes.lpSecurityDescriptor = &SecurityDescriptor;
```

This makes the pipe available to anyone. The server can still protect itself by calling ImpersonateNamedPipeClient() when a connection is established. This assures that the server will run in the security context of the client for the duration of their interaction. When the client disconnects, the server can return to its own security environment by calling RevertToSelf(). Both ImpersonateNamedPipeClient() and RevertToSelf() are used in the code presented in Chapter 10. See the routine NamedPipesThread() in \NTNET\CODE\NMPIPE_WNETINI.CPP.

The next sample application shows how to create a more precisely crafted DACL for the pipe, denying access to some users while allowing it to others.

Controlling Access to a Named Pipe. Next, you are going to specifically grant rights to the named pipe when creating it. Let's say you want to allow broad access to all users except those belonging to the Guests group. You simply add an ACE that denies GENERIC_ALL access to Guests, and follow it with one that gives Everyone GENERIC_ALL access. Even though members of Guests also belong to Everyone, they will be denied access to the pipe because we explicitly forbid them to use it.

Once again, you will use InitializeSecurityDescriptor() to create an empty security descriptor as shown in the preceding code block. But before calling SetSecurityDescriptorDacl(), you will invoke InitializeAcl(), AddAccessDeniedAce(), and AddAccessAllowedAce(). These functions create the necessary access control list. InitializeAcl() requires a pointer to the buffer that it will convert to an ACL; it needs to know the size of the buffer; and it needs the ACL revision number. The last item is represented by the Win32 constant ACL_REVISION. Here is the call to InitializeAcl() from \NTNET\CODE\SECURITY\SECUTST2.CPP:

```
InitializeAcl((PACL) byACLBuffer, sizeof (byACLBuffer),
   ACL_REVISION);
```

AddAccessDeniedAce() and AddAccessAllowedAce() have the same argument lists, which include a pointer to the ACL, the ACL revision, the rights you are granting or denying, and the SID of the affected account. Here is how I call AddAccessDeniedAce():

```
// Add access denied ACE first, by convention
// Get SID for "Guests"
if (NameToSID("Guests", (PSID) bySIDBuffer, &dwSIDSize))
    {
    AddAccessDeniedAce((PACL) byACLBuffer, ACL_REVISION,
        GENERIC_ALL, bySIDBuffer);
    }
```

Here is the main() function from SECUTST2.CPP. RunTests() is the same as in SECUTST1.CPP, and is shown earlier in this chapter. It calls GetFileSecurity() to collect the DACL of the pipe, then calls DumpDACL().

```
void main(int argc, char *argv[])
{
   HANDLE hFile;
   SECURITY_INFORMATION SecurityInformation;
   BYTE    byACLBuffer[4096];
   DWORD   dwACLSize = sizeof (byACLBuffer);
   SECURITY_DESCRIPTOR SecurityDescriptor;
   SECURITY_ATTRIBUTES SecurityAttributes;
   BYTE    bySIDBuffer[1024];
   DWORD   dwSIDSize = sizeof (bySIDBuffer);

   SecurityInformation = DACL_SECURITY_INFORMATION;

   InitializeSecurityDescriptor(&SecurityDescriptor,
      SECURITY_DESCRIPTOR_REVISION);

   // Set up ACL with two ACEs
   InitializeAcl((PACL) byACLBuffer, sizeof (byACLBuffer),
      ACL_REVISION);

   // Add access denied ACE first, by convention
   // Get SID for "Guests"
   if (NameToSID("Guests", (PSID) bySIDBuffer, &dwSIDSize))
      {
      AddAccessDeniedAce((PACL) byACLBuffer, ACL_REVISION,
         GENERIC_ALL, bySIDBuffer);
      }

   dwSIDSize = sizeof (bySIDBuffer);
   // Now add access allowed ACE for "Everyone"
```

```
    if (NameToSID("Everyone", (PSID) bySIDBuffer, &dwSIDSize))
        {
        AddAccessAllowedAce((PACL) byACLBuffer, ACL_REVISION,
            GENERIC_ALL, bySIDBuffer);
        }

    // Insert the DACL into the SECURITY_DESCRIPTOR
    if (!SetSecurityDescriptorDacl(&SecurityDescriptor,
        TRUE, (PACL) byACLBuffer, FALSE))
        printf("\nSetSecurityDescriptorDacl() failed, "
            "GetLastError() = %d",
            GetLastError());

    // Create pipe using non-NULL SECURITY_ATTRIBUTES
    SecurityAttributes.nLength = sizeof (SECURITY_ATTRIBUTES);
    SecurityAttributes.lpSecurityDescriptor =
        &SecurityDescriptor;
    SecurityAttributes.bInheritHandle = FALSE;

    hFile = CreateNamedPipe("\\\\.\\PIPE\\WNET\\SECUTEST",
                            PIPE_ACCESS_DUPLEX,
                            PIPE_TYPE_MESSAGE |
                            PIPE_READMODE_BYTE |
                            PIPE_WAIT,
                            1, 0, 0, 0,
                            &SecurityAttributes);

    if (hFile == INVALID_HANDLE_VALUE)
        {
        printf("\nUnable to create pipe, GetLastError() = %d\n",
            GetLastError());
        ExitProcess(1);
        }
    RunTests("\\\\.\\PIPE\\WNET\\SECUTEST",
        &SecurityInformation);

    CloseHandle(hFile);

    ExitProcess(0);
}
```

Here is the output from SECUTST2.EXE:

```
Access denied ace
Access rights 001F01FF denied to Guests on \\.\PIPE\WNET\SECUTEST
Access allowed ace
Access rights 001F01FF granted to Everyone on \\.\PIPE\WNET\SECUTEST
```

The rights explicitly assigned have superseded the default DACL from the process token. Notice that the GENERIC_ALL (0x10000000L) rights mask that was passed to AddAccessDeniedAce() and AddAccessAllowedAce() has again been translated to FILE_ALL_ACCESS (0x001F01FF).

Mapping an Account Name to a SID. Building the ACEs requires finding out the SIDs for Guests and Everyone. NameToSID() is another helper routine in \NTNET\CODE\SECURITY\SECUHLPR.CPP. It uses LookupAccountName() to perform the conversion.

```
BOOL NameToSID(LPTSTR lpName, PSID pSID, LPDWORD lpdwSIDSize)
{
   TCHAR szDomain[256];
   DWORD dwDomainSize = sizeof (szDomain);
   SID_NAME_USE SidNameUse;

   if (!LookupAccountName(NULL, lpName, pSID, lpdwSIDSize,
         szDomain, &dwDomainSize, &SidNameUse))
      {
      printf("\nLookupAccountName() failed, GetLastError() = %d",
         GetLastError());
      return FALSE;
      }
   return TRUE;
}
```

File Objects—Standard Disk Files

Disk files behave very much like named pipes. The next sample application, SECUTST3.EXE, explores what happens when you create a disk file without SECURITY_ATTRIBUTES. SECUTST3 differs very little from SECUTST1. Instead of calling CreateNamedPipe(), it calls CreateFile(), after first getting a temporary file name from GetTempFileName(). Here is main() from \NTNET\CODE\SECURITY\SECUTST3.CPP:

```
void main(int argc, char *argv[])
{
   HANDLE hFile;
   SECURITY_INFORMATION SecurityInformation =
      DACL_SECURITY_INFORMATION;
   TCHAR  szTempFileName[MAX_PATH + 1];

   GetTempFileName("\\NTNET\\CODE",
                  "WNET",
                  0,
                  szTempFileName);
```

```
    // Open temporary file with NULL SECURITY_ATTRIBUTES
    printf("\nCreating file %s", szTempFileName);
    hFile = CreateFile(szTempFileName,
                GENERIC_ALL,
                0,
                NULL,
                OPEN_EXISTING,  // GetTempFileName() creates it
                FILE_ATTRIBUTE_NORMAL,
                NULL);
    if (hFile == INVALID_HANDLE_VALUE)
        {
        printf("\nUnable to create file %s, GetLastError() = %d\n",
            szTempFileName, GetLastError());
        ExitProcess(1);
        }
    RunTests(szTempFileName, &SecurityInformation);

    CloseHandle(hFile);
    DeleteFile(szTempFileName);
    fflush(stdout);
    ExitProcess(0);
}
```

RunTests() is the same as for SECUTST1 and SECUTST2; see the listing earlier in this chapter. Here is the program's output.

```
Creating file \NTNET\CODE\WNE2E.tmp
DACL is present

DACL explicitly assigned

Access allowed ace
Access rights 001F01FF granted to Administrators on
   \NTNET\CODE\WNE2E.tmp

Access allowed ace
Access rights 001301BF granted to Everyone on \NTNET\CODE\WNE2E.tmp

Access allowed ace
Access rights 001F01FF granted to Administrators on
   \NTNET\CODE\WNE2E.tmp

Access allowed ace
Access rights 001301BF granted to Server Operators on
   \NTNET\CODE\WNE2E.tmp

Access allowed ace
Access rights 001F01FF granted to SYSTEM on \NTNET\CODE\WNE2E.tmp
```

You have more entries than you did when creating a named pipe. Administrators and SYSTEM are both still there, with FILE_ALL_ACCESS rights. You also have entries for Everyone and Server Operators, and an extra ACE for Administrators. As you might expect, the additional ACEs are inherited from the file's parent directory. Figure 14-2 shows the File Manager permissions screen for \NTNET\CODE, the directory in which I ran this test.

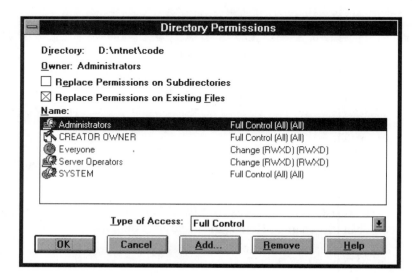

Figure 14-2.   File Manager Permissions Screen for \NTNET\CODE

The only one of the trusted users that did not propagate to the temporary file is CREATOR OWNER. However, you can see in Figure 14-2 that the directory's owner is none other than Administrators.

This is concrete evidence of how the NT File System handles inheritance of rights, and it's an important part of operating system policy; system administrators don't want to assign rights to every single file that every user on their systems create. Therefore, in the absence of any other restrictions—which, in our context, means when you pass NULL SECURITY_ ATTRIBUTES to CreateFile()—the DACL of the parent directory propagates to newly created files and directories. Actually, a walk of the directory's DACL reveals that, in addition to the ACEs that grant rights to the directory itself, there are others flagged as INHERIT_ONLY_ACEs (in the AceFlags field of the ACE_HEADER). These describe the rights that contained objects inherit.

Kernel Objects

The next sample application, SECUTST4, demonstrates that things are a little different with kernel objects. It creates four kernel objects—a mutex, an event, a shared-memory object, and a thread—with NULL SECURITY_ATTRIBUTES, then dumps their DACLs. Here is main() from \NTNET\CODE\SECURITY\SECUTST4.CPP.

```cpp
void main(int argc, char *argv[])
{
    HANDLE hMutex;
    SECURITY_INFORMATION SecurityInformation;

    hMutex = CreateMutex(NULL, FALSE,
        "/MUTEX/WNET/NICE_LITTLE_MUTEX");
    if (hMutex == NULL)
        {
        printf("\nUnable to create mutex, GetLastError() = %d\n",
            GetLastError());
        ExitProcess(1);
        }
    RunTests(hMutex, &SecurityInformation, "Mutex");

    CloseHandle(hMutex);

/*========================================*/
    // Test with an event
    HANDLE hEvent;

    hEvent = CreateEvent(NULL, TRUE, FALSE,
        "/EVENT/WNET/NICE_LITTLE_EVENT");

    if (hEvent == NULL)
        {
        printf("\nUnable to create event, GetLastError() = %d\n",
            GetLastError());
        ExitProcess(1);
        }
    RunTests(hEvent, &SecurityInformation, "Event");

    CloseHandle(hEvent);

/*========================================*/
    // Test with shared memory
    HANDLE hSharedMemory;

    hSharedMemory =
```

```
        CreateFileMapping((HANDLE) 0xFFFFFFFF,
                          NULL,
                          PAGE_READWRITE,
                          0,
                          4096,
                          "/SHARED_MEM/WNET/NICE_SHARED_MEMORY");
    RunTests(hSharedMemory, &SecurityInformation,
        "Shared Memory");

    CloseHandle(hSharedMemory);

/*==========================================*/
    // Test with a thread
    HANDLE hThread;
    DWORD  dwThreadID;

    hThread = CreateThread(NULL, 0, TestThread, NULL, 0, &dwThreadID);
    if (hThread == NULL)
        {
        printf("\nUnable to create thread, GetLastError() = %d\n",
            GetLastError());
        ExitProcess(1);
        }
    RunTests(hThread, &SecurityInformation, "Thread");

    CloseHandle(hThread);

    ExitProcess(0);
}
```

RunTests() differs from previous versions in that it calls GetKernelObjectSecurity() instead of GetFileSecurity(). GetKernelObjectSecurity() takes an object HANDLE as its first argument, instead of the file name that GetFileSecurity() wants.

```
        BOOL GetKernelObjectSecurity(
                HANDLE               hObject,
                SECURITY_INFORMATION SecurityInformation,
                PSECURITY_DESCRIPTOR lpSecurityDescriptor,
                DWORD                dwOutBufferSize,
                LPDWORD              lpdwOutBufferActualSize);
```

This is RunTests() as SECUTST4.CPP implements it.

```
VOID RunTests(HANDLE hObject, SECURITY_INFORMATION *pSecurityInfo,
            LPTSTR lpObjectType)
{
```

```
BYTE    bySDBuffer[8192];
PSECURITY_DESCRIPTOR lpSecurityDescriptor =
    (PSECURITY_DESCRIPTOR) bySDBuffer;
DWORD   dwSDSize;

dwSDSize = sizeof (bySDBuffer);

if (!GetKernelObjectSecurity(hObject, *pSecurityInfo,
    lpSecurityDescriptor, dwSDSize, &dwSDSize))
    {
    printf("\nGetKernelObjectSecurity() failed, "
            "GetLastError() = %d",
        GetLastError());
    return;
    }

DumpDACL(lpObjectType, lpSecurityDescriptor);
}
```

The output generated by SECUTST4 is sparse.

```
No DACL is present

DACL explicitly assigned

Mutex has a NULL DACL

No DACL is present

DACL explicitly assigned

Event has a NULL DACL

No DACL is present

DACL explicitly assigned

Shared Memory has a NULL DACL

No DACL is present

DACL explicitly assigned

Thread has a NULL DACL
```

So kernel objects behave differently from file objects. When you create one with NULL SECURITY_ATTRIBUTES, you actually get an object with no security restrictions.

Private Objects

Private objects are a more sophisticated use of the Win32 Security API. They allow you to implement protection in situations where NT itself does not provide it, by building objects from scratch. One use for this might be to protect Windows Sockets or NetBIOS endpoints, as the underlying API has no built-in security.

With private objects, there are two additional functions: CreatePrivateObjectSecurity() and DestroyPrivateObjectSecurity(). The first generates a new SECURITY_DESCRIPTOR that can take its initial characteristics from several sources:

- The object's parent, if the concept has meaning for the object
- A template SECURITY_DESCRIPTOR that you provide to CreatePrivateObjectSecurity()
- The default DACL of the process's token, if neither of the other sources exist

SECUTST5 demonstrates the last, SECUTST6 the second, and SECUTST7 the first.

Defining How Generic Rights Map to Object-Specific Rights. When you create a private object, you must define how generic rights translate into specific rights. You do this by setting the fields of a GENERIC_MAPPING structure.

```
typedef struct _GENERIC_MAPPING
{
    ACCESS_MASK GenericRead;     // What does GENERIC_READ mean?
    ACCESS_MASK GenericWrite;    // How about GENERIC_WRITE?
    ACCESS_MASK GenericExecute;  // GENERIC_EXECUTE?
    ACCESS_MASK GenericAll;      // GENERIC_ALL?
} GENERIC_MAPPING;
```

You populate each field with the specific rights that correspond to the generic constant. In SECUTST5 and SECUTST6, I use the rights appropriate for file objects. After all, NT has no preconceptions about the object, so it lets me create the object any way I want to. Here are the lines from \NTNET\CODE\SECURITY\SECUTST5.CPP, including the call to CreatePrivateObjectSecurity():

```
GenericMapping.GenericRead    = FILE_GENERIC_READ;
GenericMapping.GenericWrite   = FILE_GENERIC_WRITE;
```

```
GenericMapping.GenericExecute = FILE_GENERIC_EXECUTE;
GenericMapping.GenericAll     = FILE_ALL_ACCESS;

if (!CreatePrivateObjectSecurity(NULL, NULL,
        &pSecurityDescriptor, FALSE, hToken, &GenericMapping))
    {
    printf("\nCreatePrivateObjectSecurity() failed, "
            "GetLastError() = %d",
            GetLastError());
    ExitProcess(GetLastError());
    }
```

Creating a Private Object with Default Security. The first two arguments
to CreatePrivateObjectSecurity() are the parent and template security
descriptors. The third points to a pointer to a SECURITY_DESCRIPTOR
for which CreatePrivateObjectSecurity() allocates memory. Passing the first
two parameters as NULL is the same as creating a file with no
SECURITY_ATTRIBUTES. Notice that you must also pass a HANDLE to
your process's token. Here is the complete listing of the first part of main(),
up to the point where it calls RunTests():

```
void main(int argc, char *argv[])
{
    SECURITY_INFORMATION SecurityInformation;
    PSECURITY_DESCRIPTOR pSecurityDescriptor;
    GENERIC_MAPPING GenericMapping;
    HANDLE hToken;

    SecurityInformation = DACL_SECURITY_INFORMATION;

    hToken = GetProcessToken();
    if (hToken == NULL)
        {
        ExitProcess(GetLastError());
        }

    GenericMapping.GenericRead    = FILE_GENERIC_READ;
    GenericMapping.GenericWrite   = FILE_GENERIC_WRITE;
    GenericMapping.GenericExecute = FILE_GENERIC_EXECUTE;
    GenericMapping.GenericAll     = FILE_ALL_ACCESS;

    if (!CreatePrivateObjectSecurity(NULL, NULL,
            &pSecurityDescriptor, FALSE, hToken, &GenericMapping))
        {
        printf("\nCreatePrivateObjectSecurity() failed, "
                "GetLastError() = %d",
```

```
                        GetLastError());
                    ExitProcess(GetLastError());
                    }
                RunTests(pSecurityDescriptor,
                    &SecurityInformation);
```

RunTests() retrieves the object's security descriptor by calling GetPrivateObjectSecurity(). Just as you pass GetFileSecurity() the file name and GetKernelObjectSecurity() the object HANDLE, you give GetPrivateObjectSecurity() the SECURITY_DESCRIPTOR generated by CreatePrivateObjectSecurity().

```
VOID RunTests(PSECURITY_DESCRIPTOR pSecurityDescriptor,
             SECURITY_INFORMATION *pSecurityInfo)
{
   BYTE    bySDBuffer[8192];
   PSECURITY_DESCRIPTOR lpSecurityDescriptor =
      (PSECURITY_DESCRIPTOR) bySDBuffer;
   DWORD   dwSDSize;

   dwSDSize = sizeof (bySDBuffer);

   if (!GetPrivateObjectSecurity(pSecurityDescriptor, *pSecurityInfo,
      lpSecurityDescriptor, dwSDSize, &dwSDSize))
      {
      printf("\nGetPrivateObjectSecurity() failed, "
            "GetLastError() = %d, dwSDSize = %d",
         GetLastError(), dwSDSize);
      return;
      }

   DumpDACL("Private Object", lpSecurityDescriptor);
}
```

The output from SECUTST5 follows.

```
Access allowed ace
Access rights 001F01FF granted to Administrators on Private Object
Access allowed ace
Access rights 001F01FF granted to SYSTEM on Private Object
```

This is exactly what you saw with a named pipe created with no security attributes. The private object inherits the default DACL of the process's token. The rights that have been granted are also the same (0x001F01FF, corresponding to FILE_ALL_ACCESS). This is because the custom mapping uses the same scheme as file objects.

Creating a Standalone Private Object with Explicit Security. In SECUTST6, I create a private object from a security descriptor template and assign the template the same DACL used previously—one that denies GENERIC_ALL access to Guests and grants it to Everyone. main() has a little more work to do because it must initialize the security descriptor and populate its DACL. By the way, instead of calling NameToSID() to get the SIDs for Guests and Everyone, I build their SIDs from scratch by calling AllocateAndInitializeSid(). The *Security Overview* section in the on-line help tells you how to do this. From the Overview screen, click the *Security Identifiers* topic. It explains how SIDs are constructed.

```c
void main(int argc, char *argv[])
{
    SECURITY_INFORMATION SecurityInformation;
    SECURITY_DESCRIPTOR  SecurityDescriptor;
    PSECURITY_DESCRIPTOR pSecurityDescriptor;
    GENERIC_MAPPING GenericMapping;
    HANDLE hToken;
    BYTE   byACLBuffer[1024];

    hToken = GetProcessToken();

    if (hToken == NULL)
        ExitProcess(GetLastError());

    SecurityInformation = DACL_SECURITY_INFORMATION;

    // With a standalone private object, we first create a
    // template SECURITY_DESCRIPTOR that has
    // the characteristics we want.
    // In this case, we'll use it to build
    // a DACL that denies access to "Guests"
    // and permits it to "Everyone"
    InitializeSecurityDescriptor(&SecurityDescriptor,
        SECURITY_DESCRIPTOR_REVISION);

    // Set up ACL with two ACEs
    InitializeAcl((PACL) byACLBuffer, sizeof (byACLBuffer),
        ACL_REVISION);

    // Add access denied ACE first, by convention
    // This time, we'll build the SIDs from scratch

    // Create the SID for "Guests". This is NT authority, the built-in
    // domain, and the Guests alias
    SID_IDENTIFIER_AUTHORITY SIAWindowsNT =
```

```
   SECURITY_NT_AUTHORITY;

PSID pGuestSID;

if (!AllocateAndInitializeSid(&SIAWindowsNT,
                              2,    // 2 subauthorities
                              SECURITY_BUILTIN_DOMAIN_RID,
                              DOMAIN_ALIAS_RID_GUESTS,
                              0, 0, 0, 0, 0, 0,
                              &pGuestSID))
   {
   printf("\nAllocateAndInitializeSid() failed, "
          "GetLastError() = %d",
       GetLastError());
   ExitProcess(GetLastError());
   }

AddAccessDeniedAce((PACL) byACLBuffer, ACL_REVISION,
   GENERIC_ALL, pGuestSID);

FreeSid(pGuestSID);

// Create the SID for "Everyone". This uses world
// authority, rather than NT authority
SID_IDENTIFIER_AUTHORITY SIAWorld =
   SECURITY_WORLD_SID_AUTHORITY;
PSID pEveryoneSID;

if (!AllocateAndInitializeSid(&SIAWorld,
                              1,    // 1 subauthority
                              SECURITY_WORLD_RID,
                              0, 0, 0, 0, 0, 0, 0,
                              &pEveryoneSID))
   {
   printf("\nAllocateAndInitializeSid() failed, "
          "GetLastError() = %d",
       GetLastError());
   ExitProcess(GetLastError());
   }

// Now add access allowed ACE for "Everyone"
AddAccessAllowedAce((PACL) byACLBuffer, ACL_REVISION,
   GENERIC_ALL, pEveryoneSID);

FreeSid(pEveryoneSID);

// Insert the DACL into the SECURITY_DESCRIPTOR
if (!SetSecurityDescriptorDacl(&SecurityDescriptor,
```

```
        TRUE, (PACL) byACLBuffer, FALSE))
    printf("\nSetSecurityDescriptorDacl() failed, "
            "GetLastError() = %d",
        GetLastError());

    // Set generic-to-specific access mapping as if
    // this object were a file
    GenericMapping.GenericRead    = FILE_GENERIC_READ;
    GenericMapping.GenericWrite   = FILE_GENERIC_WRITE;
    GenericMapping.GenericExecute = FILE_GENERIC_EXECUTE;
    GenericMapping.GenericAll     = FILE_ALL_ACCESS;

    // Now when we call CreatePrivateObjectSecurity(),
    // we pass the second argument as a pointer to
    // our template security descriptor, instead of
    // as a NULL pointer.
    if (!CreatePrivateObjectSecurity(NULL,
        &SecurityDescriptor,
        &pSecurityDescriptor, FALSE, hToken, &GenericMapping))
        {
        printf("\nCreatePrivateObjectSecurity() failed, "
                "GetLastError() = %d",
            GetLastError());
        ExitProcess(GetLastError());
        }

    RunTests(pSecurityDescriptor,
        &SecurityInformation);
```

The program's output reflects the new DACL that we have created.

```
Access denied ace
Access rights 001F01FF denied to Guests on Private Object
Access allowed ace
Access rights 001F01FF granted to Everyone on Private Object
```

Creating a Contained Private Object with Inherited Security. To create a private object that is a descendant of another object, you pass the security descriptor of the parent as the first argument of CreatePrivateObjectSecurity(). SECUTST7 makes its object a child of the \NTNET\CODE directory, getting its security descriptor by invoking GetFileSecurity() as follows:

```
    // We'll create this object as a child of the
    // directory \NTNET\CODE.
    BYTE byParentSecurityDescriptor[1024];
```

```
DWORD dwParentSDSize =
   sizeof (byParentSecurityDescriptor);

GetFileSecurity("\\NTNET\\CODE",
                DACL_SECURITY_INFORMATION,
                byParentSecurityDescriptor,
                dwParentSDSize,
                &dwParentSDSize);
```

The call to CreatePrivateObjectSecurity() changes accordingly.

```
// Now when we call CreatePrivateObjectSecurity(),
// we pass the first argument as a pointer to
// the parent object's security descriptor, instead of
// as a NULL pointer. The second argument becomes
// NULL.
PSECURITY_DESCRIPTOR pSecurityDescriptor;

if (!CreatePrivateObjectSecurity(
    (PSECURITY_DESCRIPTOR) byParentSecurityDescriptor,
    NULL,
    &pSecurityDescriptor, FALSE, hToken, &GenericMapping))
```

So does the program's output.

```
DACL is present

DACL explicitly assigned

Access allowed ace
Access rights 001F01FF granted to Administrators on Private Object
Access allowed ace
Access rights 001301BF granted to Everyone on Private Object
Access allowed ace
Access rights 001F01FF granted to Administrators on Private Object
Access allowed ace
Access rights 001301BF granted to Server Operators on Private Object
Access allowed ace
Access rights 001F01FF granted to SYSTEM on Private Object
```

Checking a Request to Access a Private Object. To demonstrate how to validate an attempt to access a private object, I added code at the end of main() in SECUTST5, SECUTST6, and SECUTST7. This code calls the AccessCheck() function, which compares the DACL in a security descriptor with a token and a requested access mask. Here is the excerpt from SECUTST5.CPP:

```
if (!AccessCheck(pSecurityDescriptor,    // Has DACL of interest
        hNewToken,                        // Contains user and group info
        dwAccessRequested,                // Must have been translated
                                          // so it contains no generic
                                          // rights
        &GenericMapping,                  // Tells NT how to map any
                                          // generic rights it encounters
        (PPRIVILEGE_SET) byPrivilegeSet,  // Throwaway arguments,
        &dwPrivilegeSetSize,              // but they're required
        &dwAccessGranted,                 // Returns granted rights
        &bStatus))                        // Returns yes or no
    {
    // Function failed
    }
    else
    {
    // Function succeeded, bStatus says yes or no
    if (bStatus)
        {
        // You're OK, dwAccessGranted says what rights
        // you have
        }
    else
        {
        // Get lost—but ask GetLastError() why you were rejected
        }
    }
```

Things get a little esoteric with AccessCheck(). Notice the argument that I call *hNewToken*. The name may tip you off to the fact that this is not the process's token; it is an impersonation token that the current thread is using. AccessCheck() requires an impersonation token. This makes it particularly useful in implementing a network server application—you pass it a token representing a client application, and it tells you whether the security descriptor allows access by that client.

To get an impersonation token in this situation, you have to impersonate yourself. I came up with the technique that I implement here mostly by trial and error; I do not claim to have any deep understanding of security impersonation in Windows NT.

To impersonate yourself:

1. Call ImpersonateSelf() to begin the impersonation.
2. Call OpenThreadToken() to get a HANDLE to the impersonation token. You must use OpenThreadToken() because OpenProcessToken() returns the original token of the process.

3. Do whatever you need to with the token. In this particular case, that involves a call to AccessCheck().

4. Call RevertToSelf() to end the impersonation.

All of this is done within the main thread of the application; I have not spun off any secondary threads. I suspect that what happens here is that the call to ImpersonateSelf() generates a new token and attaches it to the current thread. However, the original process token is still in existence. The only difference between the new token and the old is that the old one is a primary token and the new one is an impersonation token.

User Objects

User objects are the windows that the user actually sees on the screen. Windows themselves cannot be protected directly. There are no security hooks in the functions that create or manipulate windows; if you pass a window handle to GetUserObjectSecurity() or SetUserObjectSecurity(), the function fails. The securable objects are the parent and grandparent classes of visible windows—the thread desktop and the process window station.

The thread desktop is represented by an object of type HDESK. You can find out its handle by passing the current thread ID to GetThreadDesktop().

```
HDESK hDesktop =
    GetThreadDesktop(GetCurrentThreadId());
```

GetProcessWindowStation() tells you the handle of your process's window station, typed as an HWINSTA.

```
HWINSTA hWindowStation = GetProcessWindowStation();
```

These are the handles that you pass to GetUserObjectSecurity() and SetUserObjectSecurity() as their first argument. The other arguments are the same as for GetFileSecurity(), GetKernelObjectSecurity(), and GetPrivateObjectSecurity(), except that the second argument, the SECURITY_INFORMATION that says what part of the security descriptor you are interested in, is passed as a pointer instead of by value.

SECUTST8, the application that demonstrates user object security, is the only one of this suite of applications that runs in a window. This is not required—you get the same results with a console application. However, because you are dealing with user objects, I wanted to create the most germane environment.

I will not list WinMain(), as it presents the usual litany of calls—register your window class, create a window, run your message loop, and exit. The window procedure, MainWndProc(), starts the tests in response to either a main menu selection or a WM_PAINT message.

```
LRESULT CALLBACK MainWndProc(HWND hWnd, UINT uMessage,
                            WPARAM wParam, LPARAM lParam)
{
   static SECURITY_INFORMATION SecurityInformation =
      DACL_SECURITY_INFORMATION;
   HDC hDC;
   TEXTMETRIC tm;
   PAINTSTRUCT ps;

   switch (uMessage)
      {
      case WM_CREATE:
         hDC = GetDC(hWnd);
         GetTextMetrics(hDC, &tm);
         lFontHeight = tm.tmHeight + tm.tmExternalLeading;
         ReleaseDC(hWnd, hDC);

         break;
      case WM_COMMAND:
         switch (LOWORD(wParam))
            {
            case IDM_RUNTESTS:
               hDC = GetDC(hWnd);
               RunTests(hDC, &SecurityInformation);
               ReleaseDC(hWnd, hDC);
               break;
            case IDM_EXIT:
               PostMessage(hWnd, WM_CLOSE, 0, 0);
               break;
            }
         break;
      case WM_PAINT:
         hDC = BeginPaint(hWnd, &ps);
         RunTests(hDC, &SecurityInformation);
         EndPaint(hWnd, &ps);
         break;
      case WM_DESTROY:
         PostQuitMessage(0);
         break;
      default:
         return DefWindowProc(hWnd, uMessage, wParam, lParam);
      }
```

```
          return 0;
      }
```

RunTests() does two cycles of tests, one with the thread desktop and one with the process window station. For both objects, it calls GetUserObjectSecurity() to get the security descriptor, then a private version of DumpDACL() that writes its findings to the window. Here is RunTests():

```
VOID RunTests(HDC hDC,
              SECURITY_INFORMATION *pSecurityInfo)
{
   BYTE    bySDBuffer[8192];
   PSECURITY_DESCRIPTOR lpSecurityDescriptor =
      (PSECURITY_DESCRIPTOR) bySDBuffer;
   DWORD   dwSDSize;
   HDESK   hDesktop;
   HWINSTA hWindowStation;

   nYPosition = 0;
   hCurrentDC = hDC;
   hDesktop = GetThreadDesktop(GetCurrentThreadId());
   dwSDSize = sizeof (bySDBuffer);

   if (!GetUserObjectSecurity((HANDLE) hDesktop, pSecurityInfo,
      lpSecurityDescriptor, dwSDSize, &dwSDSize))
      {
      printfConsole("GetUserObjectSecurity() failed, "
                  "GetLastError() = %d",
         GetLastError());
      return;
      }

   DumpDACL("Thread Desktop", lpSecurityDescriptor);

   hWindowStation = GetProcessWindowStation();
   dwSDSize = sizeof (bySDBuffer);

   if (!GetUserObjectSecurity((HANDLE) hWindowStation, pSecurityInfo,
      lpSecurityDescriptor, dwSDSize, &dwSDSize))
      {
      printfConsole("GetUserObjectSecurity() failed, "
                  "GetLastError() = %d",
         GetLastError());
      return;
      }

   DumpDACL("Window Station", lpSecurityDescriptor);
}
```

Let's look at what this produces. SECUTST8 displays the information somewhat differently from the other samples because you can't convert one of the SIDs in the DACL to a name. So SECUTST8 dumps the SIDs in addition to the user name, as you can see in Figure 14-3.

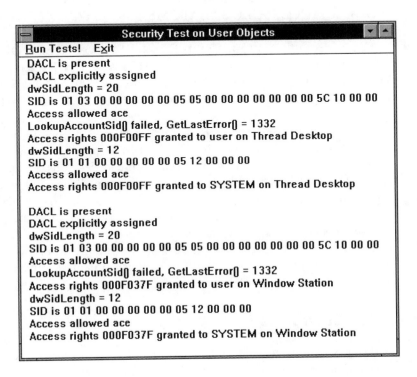

```
─                   Security Test on User Objects                ▼ ▲
Run Tests!   Exit
DACL is present
DACL explicitly assigned
dwSidLength = 20
SID is 01 03 00 00 00 00 00 05 05 00 00 00 00 00 00 00 5C 10 00 00
Access allowed ace
LookupAccountSid() failed, GetLastError() = 1332
Access rights 000F00FF granted to user on Thread Desktop
dwSidLength = 12
SID is 01 01 00 00 00 00 00 05 12 00 00 00
Access allowed ace
Access rights 000F00FF granted to SYSTEM on Thread Desktop

DACL is present
DACL explicitly assigned
dwSidLength = 20
SID is 01 03 00 00 00 00 00 05 05 00 00 00 00 00 00 00 5C 10 00 00
Access allowed ace
LookupAccountSid() failed, GetLastError() = 1332
Access rights 000F037F granted to user on Window Station
dwSidLength = 12
SID is 01 01 00 00 00 00 00 05 12 00 00 00
Access allowed ace
Access rights 000F037F granted to SYSTEM on Window Station
```

Figure 14-3.   DACL Dump for User Objects

Window stations and thread desktops are unusual objects because no functions create them. They are created for you when you start up a process or thread, and the security descriptor is created at that time. The first SID found in the DACL is the logon SID, generated when you logon. This SID does not correspond to any account name in the security database; when you call LookupAccountSid(), it has nothing to give you and produces the error message shown in Figure 14-3.

The high 16 bits of the rights masks are just STANDARD_ RIGHTS_REQUIRED, that is, WRITE_DAC | READ_CONTROL | WRITE_OWNER | DELETE, described in more detail earlier in this chapter. The low 16 bits differ from what you have seen before. The documentation is vague on their precise significance, but the constant definitions are readily available. They appear in WINUSER.H, rather than WINNT.H.

For a process window station, 0x037F is WINSTA_ENUMDESKTOPS | WINSTA_READATTRIBUTES | WINSTA_ACCESSCLIPBOARD | WINSTA_CREATEDESKTOP | WINSTA_WRITEATTRIBUTES | WINSTA_ACCESSGLOBALATOMS | WINSTA_EXITWINDOWS | WINSTA_ENUMERATE | WINSTA_READSCREEN.

For a thread desktop, 0x00FF is DESKTOP_READOBJECTS | DESKTOP_CREATEWINDOW | DESKTOP_CREATEMENU | DESKTOP_HOOKCONTROL | DESKTOP_JOURNALRECORD | DESKTOP_JOURNALPLAYBACK | DESKTOP_ENUMERATE | DESKTOP_WRITEOBJECTS.

Some of these constants seem self-explanatory. I decline to discuss them further, because I am not entirely clear on their precise significance.

Windows and menus are subclasses of thread desktops and inherit their security properties. The only rights currently defined for window and menu objects are the standard ones—those contained in bits 16–19 of the access mask. There are no window- and menu-specific rights at this time.

User object security is all handled behind the scenes. You can alter the DACL of either the process window station or the thread desktop, but playing with the security properties of these objects seems like a risky enterprise, so I have not experimented further.

System Access Control Lists

Although system access control lists (SACLs) are not as important as DACLs, no serious discussion of the Win32 Security API can ignore them altogether. By tying an SACL to an object, you generate audit trail messages so that you can determine how objects of yours are being used.

SACLs look very much like DACLs, and the associated functions have the same syntax. To assign an SACL to an object:

1. Enable the SE_SECURITY_NAME privilege for your token by calling AdjustTokenPrivileges(). Administrative users have this privilege, but it is disabled unless you explicitly enable it. Whereas rights confer access to objects, privileges permit you to perform operations.

2. Initialize a security descriptor by calling InitializeSecurity Descriptor().

3. Initialize an ACL by calling InitializeAcl().

4. Instead of adding access allowed and access denied ACEs, you add system audit ACEs. The function that does this is AddSystemAuditAce(). Another type of ACE, the system alarm ACE, is not supported in the current release of Windows NT.

5. To place the SACL into the security descriptor, call SetSecurityDescriptorSacl().

6. For an existing object, call the Set<Object Type>Security() function. If you are creating a new object, put a pointer to the new security descriptor into a SECURITY_ATTRIBUTES structure and call the Create<Object>() function.

7. To restore the previous state of the environment, call AdjustTokenPrivileges() once again to return your privileges to their former setting.

In the remainder of this section, I present a sample application, SECUTST9, that adds an SACL to a file or dumps its SACL. This is the only sample with command-line arguments. You run it as follows:

```
secutst9 <file name> [<dump SACL>]
```

SECUTST9 does not care what the second argument is. If there is more than one argument, it reports the current SACL but does not change it.

Enabling Token Privileges

SECUHLPR.CPP contains a routine called TurnPrivilegeOn(), which enables a requested privilege. It calls LookupPrivilegeValue() to convert the string name of the privilege into its binary value, called its Locally Unique ID (LUID). Then, after obtaining a HANDLE to the process's token, it calls AdjustTokenPrivileges(). For some reason, you are cautioned not to test the return value of AdjustTokenPrivileges() but to immediately ask GetLastError() how things went. That is the reason for the fancy footwork at the end of the listing.

```
BOOL TurnPrivilegeOn(LPTSTR lpPrivilegeName,
                     PTOKEN_PRIVILEGES pCurrentPrivileges)
{
   HANDLE hToken;

   hToken = GetProcessToken();

   if (hToken == NULL)
      return FALSE;
```

```
        LUID PrivilegeValue;

        // Get value of privilege name
        if (!LookupPrivilegeValue(
                NULL,
                lpPrivilegeName,
                &PrivilegeValue))
          {
          printf("\nLookupPrivilegeValue() failed, "
                 "GetLastError() = %d",
                 GetLastError());
          return FALSE;
          }

        // Set TOKEN_PRIVILEGES structure
        // to enable the requested privilege
        TOKEN_PRIVILEGES NewPrivilegeSet;
        NewPrivilegeSet.PrivilegeCount = 1;
        NewPrivilegeSet.Privileges[0].Luid = PrivilegeValue;
        NewPrivilegeSet.Privileges[0].Attributes =
          SE_PRIVILEGE_ENABLED;

        DWORD dwOutLength;

        AdjustTokenPrivileges(hToken, FALSE,
          &NewPrivilegeSet, sizeof (TOKEN_PRIVILEGES),
          pCurrentPrivileges, &dwOutLength);
        return (GetLastError() == NO_ERROR);
}
```

Steps 2 and 3, in which you initialize a security descriptor and an ACL, are no different from how these tasks were done earlier in this chapter.

Adding a System Audit ACE

AddAuditAccessAce() adds a new access control entry to the SACL. Its first four arguments are the same as for AddAccessAllowedAce() and AddAccessDeniedAce(). They identify the buffer where you are assembling the ACL, the ACL revision, the kinds of access you want to audit, and the SID. AddAuditAccessAce() takes two additional arguments, boolean flags that state whether to audit successful accesses, failed accesses, or both. Notice that the access mask includes the flag ACCESS_SYSTEM_ SECURITY. The documentation on this bit is not clear, but the effect certainly is: SACLs don't work if you don't set them.

Here are the pertinent lines of code from SECUTST9.CPP:

```
// Add a system audit ACE for "Everyone"
// Audit all successful and unsuccessful access attempts.

if (NameToSID("Everyone", (PSID) bySIDBuffer, &dwSIDSize))
    {
    if (!AddAuditAccessAce((PACL) byACLBuffer, ACL_REVISION,
        ACCESS_SYSTEM_SECURITY | GENERIC_READ |
        GENERIC_WRITE | GENERIC_EXECUTE |
        STANDARD_RIGHTS_REQUIRED,
        bySIDBuffer, TRUE, TRUE))
        {
        printf("\nAddAuditAccessAce() failed, "
            "GetLastError() = %d",
            GetLastError());
        }
    }
```

The combination ACCESS_SYSTEM_SECURITY | GENERIC_READ | GENERIC_WRITE | GENERIC_EXECUTE | STANDARD_RIGHTS_ REQUIRED produces the same access mask that File Manager gives you if you check all the check boxes in Figure 14-4.

Here is the output from SECUTST9 when I ask it to dump the SACL that File Manager produces:

```
SACL is present

SACL explicitly assigned

System audit ace
Access rights 011F01BF being audited for Everyone on secutst6.out
```

I get the exact same output when I tell SECUTST9 to create a new SACL. In the access mask, GENERIC_READ, GENERIC_WRITE, and GENERIC_EXECUTE have been mapped to FILE_GENERIC_READ, FILE_GENERIC_WRITE, and FILE_GENERIC_EXECUTE.

Here is the main() function from \NTNET\CODE\SECUTST9.CPP:

```
void main(int argc, char *argv[])
{
    SECURITY_INFORMATION SecurityInformation =
        SACL_SECURITY_INFORMATION;
    BYTE   byACLBuffer[4096];
    DWORD  dwACLSize = sizeof (byACLBuffer);
    SECURITY_DESCRIPTOR SecurityDescriptor;
```

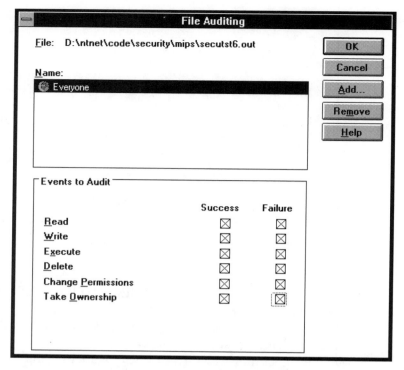

Figure 14-4.　File Manager Audit Trail Dialog Box

```
BYTE    bySIDBuffer[1024];
DWORD   dwSIDSize = sizeof (bySIDBuffer);

if (argc == 1)
    {
    printf("\nUsage:  secutst8 <filename>");
    ExitProcess(1);
    }

// We have to enable the SE_SECURITY_NAME
// privilege in order to play with SACLs
TOKEN_PRIVILEGES CurrentPrivileges;

TurnPrivilegeOn(SE_SECURITY_NAME, &CurrentPrivileges);

SecurityInformation = SACL_SECURITY_INFORMATION;

// The presence of a second command-line argument says to read the
// SACL, not alter it
if (argc <= 2)
    {
```

```
   InitializeSecurityDescriptor(&SecurityDescriptor,
      SECURITY_DESCRIPTOR_REVISION);

   // Set up ACL with one ACE
   InitializeAcl((PACL) byACLBuffer, sizeof (byACLBuffer),
      ACL_REVISION);

   dwSIDSize = sizeof (bySIDBuffer);

   // Add a system audit ACE for "Everyone"
   // Audit all successful and unsuccessful access attempts.

   if (NameToSID("Everyone", (PSID) bySIDBuffer, &dwSIDSize))
      {
      if (!AddAuditAccessAce((PACL) byACLBuffer, ACL_REVISION,
            ACCESS_SYSTEM_SECURITY | GENERIC_READ |
            GENERIC_WRITE | GENERIC_EXECUTE |
            STANDARD_RIGHTS_REQUIRED,
            bySIDBuffer, TRUE, TRUE))
         {
         printf("\nAddAuditAccessAce() failed, "
               "GetLastError() = %d",
               GetLastError());
         }
      }

   // Insert the SACL into the SECURITY_DESCRIPTOR
   if (!SetSecurityDescriptorSacl(&SecurityDescriptor,
      TRUE, (PACL) byACLBuffer, FALSE))
      printf("\nSetSecurityDescriptorSacl() failed, "
            "GetLastError() = %d",
            GetLastError());

   // Tie the SACL to the file
   if (!SetFileSecurity(argv[1], SecurityInformation,
      &SecurityDescriptor))
      {
      printf("\nSetFileSecurity() failed, "
            "GetLastError() = %d",
            GetLastError());
      }
   }
RunTests(argv[1], &SecurityInformation);

RestorePrivileges(&CurrentPrivileges);

fflush(stdout);
ExitProcess(0);
}
```

Conclusion

The Win32 Security API is very powerful, but very complex. It is somewhat thinly documented, so you are often on your own to figure out how things really work. Nevertheless, correct addition of security features to server applications can greatly enhance their value. They can protect their service endpoints from unauthorized access and audit the usage of sensitive objects.

Part of my purpose in this chapter has been to see what happens when you pass NULL pointers for SECURITY_ATTRIBUTES or SECURITY_ DESCRIPTOR arguments. Here is what I discovered:

- File objects and registry keys inherit the security characteristics of the directory or containing key where they reside. More precisely, a new DACL is built for them containing all the inheritable ACEs in the DACL of the owner.
- Although a named pipe is a file object (because Named Pipes are an NT file system), a named pipe takes on the default DACL of the access token belonging to the process that calls CreateNamedPipe(). Presumably, this is because the concept of owning directory has no meaning for a named pipe.
- Kernel objects created with NULL security attributes are unprotected. Some important objects in this category are mutexes, events, semaphores, threads, processes, and file mappings.
- Private objects—those whose meaning is known only to your application—can inherit a parent's security, can take on the security of the process's token, or can be created with a brand new set of security characteristics.
- User objects—windows and menus—inherit security from the process windowstation and the thread desktop. There is rarely ever a reason to set explicit security restrictions here.

I hope the vignettes I presented here have helped clarify this often confusing subject for you.

Suggested Readings

Security Overview in the Win32 API on-line help. Also published as Chapter 58 in *Win32 Programmer's Reference, Volume 2*.

Microsoft Corporation. *Windows NT Resource Kit, Volume 1*. Chapter 2. Microsoft Press, 1993.

Reichel, Rob. "Inside Windows NT Security, Part 1." *Windows/DOS Developer's Journal*, Vol. 4, No. 4, April 1993.

Reichel, Rob. "Inside Windows NT Security, Part 2." *Windows/DOS Developer's Journal*, Vol. 4, No. 5, May 1993.

Microsoft Knowledge Base for Win32 SDK articles:
"Precautions When Passing Security Attributes"
"Security and Screen Savers"
"Impersonation Provided by ImpersonateNamedPipeClient()"
"Gaining Access to ACLs"
"Administrator Access to Files"
"Passing Security Information to SetFileSecurity()"
"Extracting the SID from an ACE"
"How to Add an Access-Allowed ACE to a File"
"Computing the Size of a New ACL"
"Validating User Accounts (Impersonation)"
"FILE_READ_EA and FILE_WRITE_EA Specific Types"
"System GENERIC_MAPPING Structures"
"Validating User Account Password under Windows NT"
"Setting File Permissions"
"Definition of a Protected Server" and
"Security Attributes on Named Pipes"

## Chapter 15

The Registry and Performance Monitoring

Historical Overview

The Registry was introduced in Windows 3.1 as a means for OLE clients and servers to discover each other. Its focus was quite narrow, and you could spend your entire professional life writing Windows programs without finding out about it. In Windows NT, the Registry and its significance have expanded greatly. It is now a general-purpose configuration database that keeps track of everything Windows NT needs to know about your hardware, software, and user environment. In the process, it has become a critical cornerstone of the operating system.

The Registry in Windows 3.1 recognizes only a single data type, null-terminated strings. Under NT, a wide variety of types exist. To support the added functionality, there are new functions, having the same name as their 3.1 counterparts and an Ex() suffix. In this chapter, I will cover and use only the new versions.

The Registry as a Hierarchical Database

Two types of entities are stored in the Registry: keys and values. Keys identify the individual database records, and values are the attributes (or fields) of those records. Keys exist in a hierarchical framework, very much like a directory tree. There are two trees, each with its own responsibilities:

- One tree keeps track of user profiles, which are the WIN.INI settings for all of the users known on the current machine. It is rooted at the key HKEY_USERS. The special key HKEY_CURRENT_USER points to the branch of HKEY_USERS that stores the profile of the currently logged-in user.

- The other tree keeps track of the hardware and software configuration of your machine and contains the security database. It is rooted in the key HKEY_LOCAL_MACHINE. The special key HKEY_CLASSES_ROOT, provided for compatibility with the Windows 3.1 Registry, is an alias for HKEY_LOCAL_MACHINE\Software\Classes, which maps filename extensions to the applications that process them and stores OLE object information.

The Registry Editor (%SystemRoot%\SYSTEM32\REGEDT32.EXE) is handy for familiarizing yourself with the structure of the Registry. Use REGEDT32 with caution—if you delete the wrong keys, you can wreck NT so thoroughly that your only remedy is to reinstall it. The Options popup on the main menu has an item that lets you set REGEDT32 to read-only mode. Turning this on is a good idea if you are browsing the contents of the Registry and want to keep yourself from accidentally deleting information.

Figure 15-1 and Figure 15-2 show the Registry Editor screens for the level of detail immediately beneath HKEY_LOCAL_MACHINE and HKEY_USERS. In Figure 15-1, SAM and SECURITY contain the security database; they are off limits, even to administrators. In Figure 15-2, there are two entries—one a default user profile, and the other specific to administrator, and identified by his SID.

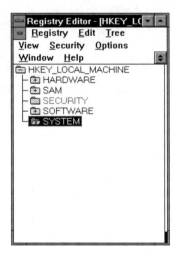

Figure 15-1.   The HKEY_LOCAL_MACHINE Registry Node

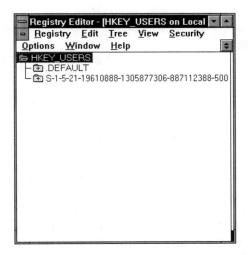

Figure 15-2. The HKEY_USERS Registry Node

The trees branch out very quickly, so you don't have to go very far down before the Registry Editor display won't fit on a single screen. Our primary interest will be HKEY_LOCAL_MACHINE\SOFTWARE. The convention is that, under this key, vendors add a key designating their company, and under it, keys for each software product. Finally, under the software product key, there is a CurrentVersion key that contains all configuration information on the current version. The key that contains much of NT's configuration is HKEY_LOCAL_MACHINE\SOFTWARE\Microsoft\Windows NT\ CurrentVersion. I will be writing directly to a couple of the keys underneath this, and also storing some information under HKEY_LOCAL_MACHINE\SYSTEM\CurrentControlSet\Services, which records information on installed services.

The Win32 Registry API

Table 15-1 lists the Win32 Registry functions.

Because the Registry is a database, many of these functions perform the standard database management operations—add, update, query, and delete.

Table 15-1. Win32 Registry Functions

Function Name	Description
RegCloseKey	Closes a registry key when you are finished using it
RegConnectRegistry	Connects to the Registry on a remote machine
RegCreateKeyEx	Adds a new record to the Registry
RegDeleteKey	Deletes an existing record
RegDeleteValue	Deletes an attribute (value) of a record (key)
RegEnumKeyEx	Enumerates the keys that are immediate children of a given key
RegEnumValue	Enumerates the values belonging to a given key
RegFlushKey	Forces write of an open key to disk
RegGetKeySecurity	Retrieves the security descriptor of a registry key
RegLoadKey	Restores a branch of the Registry tree from a backup file created by RegSaveKey
RegNotifyChangeKeyValue	Requests notification of changes in the Registry
RegOpenKeyEx	Opens an existing key in the Registry
RegQueryInfoKey	Gets all information about a key, including what subkeys it has, what values it possesses, its security descriptor, and when it was last modified
RegQueryValueEx	Reads a specific attribute of an open key.
RegReplaceKey	Changes the file that backs up a branch of the Registry
RegRestoreKey	Overwrites the contents of an existing key with information saved in a Registry backup file (created by RegSaveKey)
RegSaveKey	Saves a branch of the Registry to a file
RegSetKeySecurity	Provides a new security descriptor for a Registry key
RegSetValueEx	Adds or modifies an attribute of an existing key
RegUnLoadKey	Unloads a Registry branch that was installed by calling RegLoadKey

Adding a Record

To add a record to the Registry, you create a new key relative to either an existing, open key, or to one of the predefined keys (HKEY_LOCAL_ MACHINE, HKEY_USERS, HKEY_CURRENT_USER, or HKEY_ CLASSES_ROOT), which are always open. The function that does this is RegCreateKeyEx().

```
LONG RegCreateKeyEx(
        HKEY                    hTopLevelKey,
        LPCTSTR                 lpszNewKeyName,
        DWORD                   dwReserved,        // Has to be zero
        LPTSTR                  lpszKeyClass,
        DWORD                   dwOptions,
        REGSAM                  SAMDesiredAccess,
        LPSECURITY_ATTRIBUTES   lpSecurityAttributes,
        PHKEY                   phNewKey,
        LPDWORD                 lpdwDisposition);
```

hTopLevelKey is the already existing key from which the new key will be descended. *lpszNewKeyName* specifies the path to the new key and may contain several components. For instance, if you are creating the key HKEY_LOCAL_MACHINE\SOFTWARE\My Company\My Software\ CurrentVersion, you do not have to create My Company, then My Software, then CurrentVersion. A single call installs the entire Registry branch.

lpszKeyClass specifies the class of data that the key embodies and is a string representation of one of the Registry types. The most common types are:

- "REG_SZ": a null-terminated string. The Registry stores all strings in Unicode.
- "REG_MULTI_SZ": An array of null-terminated strings, itself terminated by a Unicode NULL.
- "REG_EXPAND_SZ": A null-terminated string containing environment variables, like "%SystemRoot%\system32".
- "REG_DWORD": A 32-bit data item.
- "REG_BINARY": Raw binary data, whose format is interpreted by the application that uses the data. For instance, security identifiers are stored in this format.

dwOptions states whether the information stored in the key is volatile (REG_OPTION_VOLATILE) or non-volatile (REG_OPTION_NON_ VOLATILE). Volatile keys are destroyed when you shut down the system and are not restored at startup. On the other hand, NT calls RegSaveKey() to save non-volatile keys to a file when you shut down, then rebuilds the Registry from the file at startup. All the keys describing your hardware configuration are volatile, and are regenerated when you restart your system.

SAMDesiredAccess states what kind of access you want to the key handle. Registry keys are protected objects, so your access request must be consistent with the security attributes of the key. RegCreateKeyEx() can be used to open existing keys, as well as for creating new ones. Possible values are KEY_ALL_ACCESS, KEY_CREATE_LINK, KEY_CREATE_ SUB_KEY, KEY_ENUMERATE_SUB_KEYS, KEY_EXECUTE, KEY_NOTIFY, KEY_QUERY_VALUE, KEY_READ, KEY_SET_ VALUE, and KEY_WRITE. As always, you get better performance by requesting only the level of access you actually need. The on-line documentation tells you what rights you need to perform what operations; out of laziness, I frequently just say KEY_ALL_ACCESS.

lpSecurityAttributes allows you to control the inheritability and accessibility of the key handle. To limit access, you build a security descriptor using the techniques discussed in Chapter 14 and point the *lpSecurityDescriptor* field of the SECURITY_ATTRIBUTES to it. If you pass the security attributes as NULL, the new key inherits the security restrictions of the key under which it is added.

Finally, the variable pointed to by *phNewKey* will return the new key handle, and *lpdwDisposition* will tell you whether a new key was created (REG_CREATED_NEW_KEY) or an existing one was opened (REG_OPENED_EXISTING_KEY).

In a departure from normal Win32 usage (where a return value of TRUE or FALSE indicates success or failure, and GetLastError() reports specific error conditions) RegCreateKeyEx()—and all the Registry functions—return the actual error code if they fail or ERROR_SUCCESS if they succeed.

Opening an Existing Record

RegCreateKeyEx() can be used to open existing keys and to create new ones. You can also call RegOpenKeyEx() to open a key.

```
LONG RegOpenKeyEx(
      HKEY     hAncestorKey,
      LPCTSTR  lpszKeyPath,
      DWORD    dwReserved,  // Must be zero
      REGSAM   SAMDesiredAccess,
      PHKEY    phOpenedKey);
```

The arguments are the same as for RegCreateKeyEx(), with the omission of those that do not apply.

Updating a Record

In Registry terms, updating a record means setting the values associated with a key. Figure 15-3 shows the Registry entry describing File manager extensions. The full key is HKEY_LOCAL_MACHINE\SOFTWARE\

Microsoft\Windows NT\CurrentVersion\File Manager\AddOns. The right-hand side of the screen indicates that this key has one value, "Mail File Manager Extension," whose type is REG_SZ. The data stored in that value is "SendFI32.dll." For me, it helps clarify the issue to refer to values as attributes, using the more common terminology from database theory.

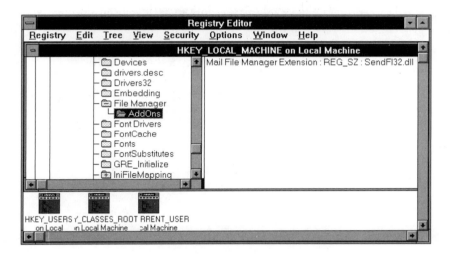

Figure 15-3. A Registry Key and Its Value

RegSetValueEx() changes the data stored in a key's value and creates the value if it does not already exist.

```
LONG RegSetValueEx(
        HKEY        hOpenKey,
        LPCTSTR     lpszValueName,
        DWORD       dwReserved,      // Must be zero
        DWORD       dwType,
        CONST BYTE *lpbyData,
        DWORD       dwDataSize);
```

hOpenKey will have been generated by RegCreateKeyEx() or RegOpenKeyEx(). *lpszValueName* is the name of the value whose associated data you want to change. *dwType* is the Registry type of the data. Again, this is most commonly REG_SZ, REG_MULTI_SZ, REG_EXPAND_SZ, REG_DWORD, or REG_BINARY. *lpbyData* points to the data, and *dwDataSize* tells NT how much data is there. If *lpbyData* points to a

Unicode string, as it often will, *dwDataSize* must be ((lstrlen((LPCTSTR) lpbyData) + 1) * sizeof (TCHAR)).

Querying a Record

The functions you will use most often to retrieve Registry key data are RegEnumKeyEx(), which reports all the keys that are children of a given key, and RegQueryValueEx(), which retrieves the data associated with an attribute. If you know nothing about the structure of a branch, you can call RegQueryInfoKey() to find out how many subkeys and values a key has, and RegEnumValue() to enumerate a key's values. In this chapter, RegEnumKeyEx() and RegQueryValueEx() are sufficient to my purpose—finding out what level-zero WNet DLLs are available, and where to find them.

```
LONG RegEnumKeyEx(
        HKEY      hParentKey,
        DWORD     dwIndex,
        LPTSTR    lpszKeyName,
        LPDWORD   lpdwKeyNameSize,
        LPDWORD   lpdwReserved,    // Must be NULL
        LPTSTR    lpszClassName,
        LPDWORD   lpdwClassNameSize,
        PFILETIME pLastWriteTime);
```

dwIndex is used to iterate over all the subkeys belonging to *hParentKey*. The first time you call RegEnumKeyEx(), pass it as zero, then increment it for each subsequent call. (It is not bumped automatically.) *lpszKeyName* returns the name of the key. *lpdwKeyNameSize* points to a DWORD that has the length of the buffer at *lpszKeyName* on input and the actual length of the key name on output. You have to reset it each time you call RegEnumKeyEx(). *lpszKeyName* will report only the subkey component, not the full Registry path name. *lpszClassName* and *lpdwClassNameSize* tell you the class that the subkey belongs to, and *pLastWriteTime* tells you when it was last modified. The last three may be passed as NULL. As long as RegEnumKeyEx() returns ERROR_SUCCESS, you can keep asking it for more information. When there are no more subkeys to enumerate, it returns ERROR_NO_MORE_ITEMS.

RegQueryValueEx() fetches the data associated with a key value.

```
LONG RegQueryValueEx(
        HKEY        hTargetKey,
        LPTSTR      lpszValueName,
```

```
        LPDWORD     lpdwReserved,    // Must be NULL
        LPDWORD     lpdwDataType,
        LPBYTE      lpbyData,
        LPDWORD     lpdwDataSize);
```

hTargetKey is the key whose value *lpszValueName* you want to read. The variable pointed to by *lpdwDataType* returns the type of the data as a numeric code (most often REG_SZ, REG_MULTI_SZ, REG_EXPAND_SZ, REG_DWORD, or REG_BINARY). *lpbyData* renders the data, and *lpdwDataSize* reports the number of bytes in the data, if the data type does not imply it.

You will see later in this chapter that RegQueryValueEx() IS the Performance Monitoring API.

Closing and Deleting a Key

When you are done with your Registry operations, you close the key you have been using by passing RegCloseKey() its handle. You can also delete keys from the Registry by calling RegDeleteKey().

```
LONG RegDeleteKey(
        HKEY    hTopLevelKey,
        LPCTSTR lpszKeyPath);
```

To remove a value that you have associated with a key, call RegDeleteValue().

```
LONG RegDeleteValue(
        HKEY   hTargetKey,
        LPTSTR lpszValueName);
```

Connecting to the Registry on a Remote Machine

You can open Registry keys across a network by calling RegConnectRegistry().

```
LONG RegConnectRegistry(
        LPTSTR    lpszComputerName,
        HKEY      hRootKey,     // Must be HKEY_LOCAL_MACHINE
                                // or HKEY_USERS
        PHKEY     phAssignedKey);
```

From this point on, you perform your Registry manipulations using the handle returned through *phAssignedKey*. This is a powerful capability; it allows you to write distributed configuration management systems.

Security and the Registry

Because the Registry is of such crucial importance, it must be protected. For this reason, Windows NT attaches security descriptors to Registry keys when you create them. If you call RegCreateKeyEx() with either a NULL SECURITY_ATTRIBUTES or a SECURITY_ATTRIBUTES containing a NULL *lpSecurityDescriptor*, the new key inherits the security characteristics of its containing key. RegGetKeySecurity() and RegSetKeySecurity() retrieve and change a Registry key's security descriptor.

```
LONG RegGetKeySecurity(
        HKEY                 hKeyOfInterest,
        SECURITY_INFORMATION SecurityInfo,
        PSECURITY_DESCRIPTOR lpSecurityDescriptor,
        LPDWORD              lpDescriptorSize);

LONG RegSetKeySecurity(
        HKEY                 hKeyOfInterest,
        SECURITY_INFORMATION SecurityInfo,
        PSECURITY_DESCRIPTOR lpSecurityDescriptor);
```

The arguments to RegGetKeySecurity() are the same as for the other functions explored in Chapter 14 (GetFileSecurity(), GetKernelObject Security(), GetPrivateObjectSecurity(), and GetUserObjectSecurity()), except that the first is the handle of the key you are interested in. Notice again that the return values follow Registry API usage, rather than normal Win32 convention, because they return the Win32 error code, rather than TRUE or FALSE.

Using the Registry

The purposes to which the Registry can be applied are innumerable. In this section, I will discuss some of the things I have found the Registry useful for and show you the corresponding code. Besides Performance Monitoring, which is covered in the final section of the chapter, I have used the Registry for:

- Initialization-file mapping
- Providing a flexible scheme for plugging level-zero DLLs into my WNet system;
- Registering applications for intelligent event logging

Initialization-File Mapping

When all users run their own copy of Windows 3.1, it is acceptable for their personal preferences to be stored in .INI files, either on their local hard disks or in personal network directories. However, with a protected, multiuser operating system like Windows NT, this invites problems. Therefore, the NT Registry provides a key that you can use to map .INI file references to the Registry, HKEY_LOCAL_MACHINE\SOFTWARE\Microsoft\Windows NT\CurrentVersion\IniFileMapping. This key in turn contains subkeys named for the .INI files they replace. Figure 15-4 shows the IniFileMapping node on my machine.

Figure 15-4. IniFileMapping Registry Node

This is how .INI files are formatted.

```
[network]
NETDLL=C:\NTNET\CODE\MIPS\WNETTCP.DLL
```

network is called the **section**, and NETDLL the **key**. Under the Registry keys representing the .INI files, there are keys for each section in the file. For instance, my .INI files have one section, the *network* section just shown. Figure 15-5 shows the explosion of the WNETPIPE.INI key.

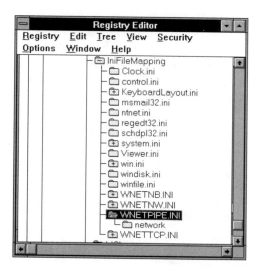

Figure 15-5.   Explosion of the WNETPIPE.INI Key

For each section key, the .INI-file keys themselves are stored as values. The values, though, do not contain the actual information. Instead, they point to another location in the Registry where the information resides. NETDLL is the key for my .INI files. The string is too long to appear on the REGEDT32 screen; it is shown as

```
NETDLL : REG_SZ : SYS:Microsoft\Windows NT\CurrentVersion\
Windows Network Manager\NamedPipes
```

The SYS: that you see here is an alias for HKEY_LOCAL_ MACHINE\SOFTWARE\.

So that the reference in my .INI-file mapping can be resolved, I add a single key under HKEY_LOCAL_MACHINE\Microsoft\Windows NT\CurrentVersion called Windows Network Manager. For each level-zero DLL, I add keys under it—NamedPipes, NetBIOS, NWLink, and WindowsSockets. If you run INSTALME.CMD on the disk that comes with this book, you will have these keys too. Figure 15-6 shows the Windows Network Manager Registry node.

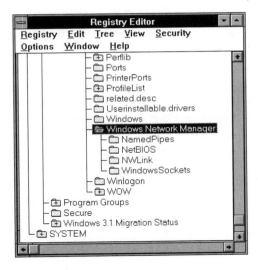

Figure 15-6. **Windows Network Manager Registry Node**

Each of these keys has a NETDLL value, and this is where the name of the actual DLL is finally found. Figure 15-7 shows the breakout for NamedPipes. (The PRECEDENCE value is used to determine usage priority, as you will see.)

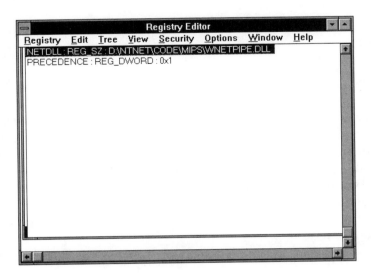

Figure 15-7. **Named Pipes Registry Values**

Once you have mapped an .INI file, all function calls that refer to that file are actually directed to the Registry, unbeknown to you. Thus, you can continue to store and retrieve the information using calls like WritePrivateProfileString() and GetPrivateProfileString(), and NT will automatically go to the Registry on your behalf. Here is an excerpt from the code in WNetInit() that asks the respective .INI files (WNETPIPE.INI, WNETTCP.INI, WNETNW.INI, and WNETNB.INI) where their DLLs are.

```
TCHAR           szAPI[MAX_PATH + 1];
DWORD           dwAPISize = sizeof (szAPI);
HINSTANCE       hNetLib;
int             i;
static          TCHAR *szDLLNames[MAX_PROTOCOLS] = {TEXT("WNETPIPE.DLL"),
                                                    TEXT("WNETTCP.DLL"),
                                                    TEXT("WNETNB.DLL"),
                                                    TEXT("WNETNW.DLL"),
                                                    NULL};
static          TCHAR *szININames[MAX_PROTOCOLS] = {TEXT("WNETPIPE.INI"),
                                                    TEXT("WNETTCP.INI"),
                                                    TEXT("WNETNB.INI"),
                                                    TEXT("WNETNW.INI"),
                                                    NULL};
for (i = 0; i < MAX_PROTOCOLS && szDLLNames[i] != NULL; ++i)
   {
   // Get full path name of DLL to load from the Registry
   GetPrivateProfileString(TEXT("NETWORK"),
      TEXT("NETDLL"), szDLLNames[i],
      szAPI, sizeof (szAPI), szININames[i]);

   hNetLib = LoadLibrary(szAPI);
   // Etc.
   }
```

There is a serious limitation with this approach. Suppose I want to add a new level-zero DLL, or maybe someone else develops one to support a protocol I don't know anything about. In order for this new DLL to be loaded, I have to go in and change WNetInit() so that it knows to ask for it. Why should WNetInit() have to have so much knowledge about what's plugged in underneath it? If keys describing all the level-zero DLLs are already in the Registry, why can't you just enumerate all the subkeys of Windows Network Manager?

Enumerating Subkeys

Here is a second implementation of WNetInit(). It does a RegEnumKeyEx() to find out all the keys contained under Windows Network Manager, then calls RegOpenKeyEx() to open them. For each key it successfully opens, it calls RegQueryValueEx() to read the NETDLL and PRECEDENCE value. PRECEDENCE is necessary for prioritizing the level-zero APIs. I cannot assume the order that the Registry keys will be returned in, so PRECEDENCE tells me where each DLL fits in the loading scheme. Here is the new code, whose source is in \NTNET\CODE\REGISTRY\ WNETINIT.CPP:

```
TCHAR        szAPI[MAX_PATH + 1];
DWORD        dwAPISize = sizeof (szAPI);
HINSTANCE    hNetLib;
HKEY         hRegistryKey = NULL, hSubkey = NULL;
DWORD        dwPrecedence;
DWORD        dwPrecedenceSize = sizeof (DWORD);
TCHAR        szKeyName[1024];
DWORD        dwKeyNameSize = sizeof (szKeyName);

try
    {
    // Open registry key where Windows Network Manager
    // level-zero information is kept
    if (RegOpenKeyEx(HKEY_LOCAL_MACHINE,
        TEXT("Software\\Microsoft\\Windows NT\\CurrentVersion\\")
        TEXT("Windows Network Manager"),
        0,
        KEY_ALL_ACCESS,
        &hRegistryKey) != ERROR_SUCCESS)
        {
        bClientIDOK = FALSE;
        leave;
        }

    for (i = 0; i < MAX_PROTOCOLS; ++i)
        {
        // Get full path name of DLL to load from the Registry
        dwKeyNameSize = sizeof (szKeyName);
        if (RegEnumKeyEx(hRegistryKey, i, szKeyName,
            &dwKeyNameSize, NULL, NULL, NULL, NULL) !=
            ERROR_SUCCESS)
            leave;

        // Open the subkey
        if (RegOpenKeyEx(hRegistryKey, szKeyName,
```

```
        0, KEY_ALL_ACCESS, &hSubkey) != ERROR_SUCCESS)
        leave;

    // Now get the values for "NETDLL" and "PRECEDENCE"
    dwAPISize = sizeof (szAPI);
    if (RegQueryValueEx(hSubkey,
         TEXT("NETDLL"), NULL,
         NULL, (LPBYTE) szAPI, &dwAPISize) != ERROR_SUCCESS)
        leave;

    if (RegQueryValueEx(hSubkey,
           TEXT("PRECEDENCE"), NULL,
           NULL, (LPBYTE) &dwPrecedence,
           &dwPrecedenceSize)
         != ERROR_SUCCESS)
        dwPrecedence = (i + 1);

    RegCloseKey(hSubkey);
    hSubkey = NULL;  // So finally block doesn't try to close it

    hNetLib = LoadLibrary(szAPI);
    // Et cetera
    }
finally
    {
    if (hSubkey != NULL)
        RegCloseKey(hSubkey);
    if (hRegistryKey != NULL)
        RegCloseKey(hRegistryKey);
    }
```

Other users adding a DLL need only tell the Registry about it by adding a key under Windows Network Manager. No .INI-file mapping is necessary, and it doesn't matter what you call the key. RegEnumKeyEx() will find it.

Adding Information to the Registry

When you install the source code disk, a program called REGINST.EXE adds the necessary entries to the Registry. main() calls a local function AddIniFileToRegistry() to accomplish this. Here's how main() installs Named Pipes:

```
ExpandEnvironmentStrings(
    TEXT("%HOMEDRIVE%\\NTNET\\CODE\\%Cpu%\\WNETPIPE.DLL"),
    szDLLName,
    sizeof (szDLLName));
```

```
AddIniFileToRegistry(TEXT("NamedPipes"),
    TEXT("WNETPIPE.INI"),
    TEXT("\\NTNET\\WNETPIPE.INI"),
    &bNamedPipes, szDLLName, 1);
```

ExpandEnvironmentStrings() produces a string with the environment variable names %HOMEDRIVE% and %Cpu% replaced with their values. AddIniFileToRegistry() makes the required Registry calls. Specifically:

1. It calls RegCreateKeyEx() to add the key HKEY_LOCAL_ MACHINE\SOFTWARE\Microsoft\Windows Nt\CurrentVersion\ Windows Network Manager\%s, where %s is replaced with the *lpszKeyName* argument ("NamedPipes", "NetBIOS", "NWLink", or "WindowsSockets").

2. It calls RegSetValueEx() to set the NETDLL and PRECEDENCE values.

3. It creates a key to perform .INI-file mapping. This key is HKEY_LOCAL_MACHINE\SOFTWARE\Microsoft\Windows NT\- CurrentVersion\IniFileMapping\%s\network. The %s is replaced with the name of the .INI file ("WNETPIPE.INI", "WNETTCP.INI", "WNETNB.INI", "WNETNW.INI").

4. It adds the value NETDLL for this key and sets it to point to the key/value pair we added in steps 1 and 2.

```
void AddIniFileToRegistry(LPTSTR lpszKeyName,
        LPTSTR lpszIniFileName,
        LPTSTR lpszIniFileFullName,
        BOOL  *pbReturnValue,
        LPTSTR lpszDLLName,
        DWORD dwPrecedence)
{
    HKEY  hNewKey;
    DWORD dwDisposition;
    TCHAR szKeyName[1024], szIniFileKeyName[1024];

    swprintf(szKeyName,
        TEXT("SOFTWARE\\Microsoft\\Windows NT\\CurrentVersion\\")
        TEXT("Windows Network Manager\\%s"), lpszKeyName);

    // Step 1. Create key representing the level-zero API
    if (RegCreateKeyEx(HKEY_LOCAL_MACHINE,
        szKeyName, 0, TEXT("REG_SZ"),
        REG_OPTION_NON_VOLATILE,
        KEY_ALL_ACCESS, NULL,
        &hNewKey, &dwDisposition)
```

```
            != ERROR_SUCCESS)
        DisplayError(GetLastError(), lpszIniFileName,
            lpszIniFileFullName, pbReturnValue);
    else
        {
        // Step 2. Set NETDLL and PRECEDENCE values
        if (RegSetValueEx(hNewKey, TEXT("NETDLL"), 0, REG_SZ,
            (LPBYTE) lpszDLLName,
                ((lstrlen(lpszDLLName) + 1) * sizeof (TCHAR)))
            != ERROR_SUCCESS)
            DisplayError(GetLastError(), lpszIniFileName,
                lpszIniFileFullName, pbReturnValue);
        if (RegSetValueEx(hNewKey, TEXT("PRECEDENCE"),
            0, REG_DWORD,
            (LPBYTE) &dwPrecedence, sizeof (DWORD)))
            DisplayError2(GetLastError(), TEXT("PRECEDENCE"),
                szKeyName, pbReturnValue);
        RegCloseKey(hNewKey);
        }

    swprintf(szIniFileKeyName,
        TEXT("SOFTWARE\\Microsoft\\Windows NT\\CurrentVersion\\")
        TEXT("IniFileMapping\\%s\\network"), lpszIniFileName);

    // Step 3. Create IniFileMapping key for this .INI file
    if (*pbReturnValue && (RegCreateKeyEx(HKEY_LOCAL_MACHINE,
        szIniFileKeyName, 0, TEXT("REG_SZ"),
        REG_OPTION_NON_VOLATILE,
        KEY_ALL_ACCESS, NULL, &hNewKey, &dwDisposition) ==
        ERROR_SUCCESS))
        {
        swprintf(szKeyName,
            TEXT("SYS:Microsoft\\Windows NT\\CurrentVersion\\")
            TEXT("Windows Network Manager\\%s"), lpszKeyName);

        // Step 4. Add NETDLL value, pointing to the key/value
        //          pair we added in steps 1 and 2.
        if (RegSetValueEx(hNewKey, TEXT("NETDLL"), 0, REG_SZ,
            (LPBYTE) szKeyName,
            ((lstrlen(szKeyName) + 1) * sizeof (TCHAR)))
            != ERROR_SUCCESS)
            {
            RegDeleteKey(HKEY_LOCAL_MACHINE,
                szIniFileKeyName);
            *(wcsrchr(szIniFileKeyName, '\\')) = '\0';
            RegDeleteKey(HKEY_LOCAL_MACHINE,
                szIniFileKeyName);
            DisplayError(GetLastError(), lpszIniFileName,
```

```
                lpszIniFileFullName, pbReturnValue);
        }
    RegCloseKey(hNewKey);
    }
  else if (*pbReturnValue)
    DisplayError(GetLastError(), lpszIniFileName,
        lpszIniFileFullName, pbReturnValue);
}
```

Registering an Application for Event Logging

In Chapter 13, you examined the use of Event Logging in NT Services. When a service (or, indeed, any NT application) encounters a condition it wants to report in a permanent log, it can do so by calling RegisterEventSource(), ReportEvent(), and DeregisterEventSource(). You saw that, by telling the Event Logger about your application, you can have it place formatted error messages into the log file for you, reading them from a message DLL that you provide. You do this by adding a Registry entry under the key HKEY_LOCAL_MACHINE\SYSTEM\CurrentControlSet\Services\ EventLog\Application. The key that you add names your service or application and tells the Event Logger where to find your messages. Then you call RegisterEventSource(), passing it the name you added to the Registry. ReportEvent() will now accept your error codes and translate them into the corresponding messages, adding insertion sequences as appropriate. Here is the WNetReportEvent() from Chapter 13, shown again here for ease of reference:

```
VOID WNetReportEvent(DWORD dwErrorCode, LPTSTR lpszErrorMsg,
                     BOOL bError)
{
    // Services don't have a user interface, so the
    // only way for them to report error conditions
    // is to use the event-logging facility
    // that NT provides.

    // To do this, you call RegisterEventSource() to
    // get a handle, then call ReportEvent() to
    // log the error

    // Finally, you call DeregisterEventSource() to
    // release the handle
    HANDLE hSource;
    TCHAR szLastErrorMsg[1024];
    LPTSTR lpszMessageStrings[2];
```

```
// Look up message string for system error.
FormatMessage(FORMAT_MESSAGE_FROM_SYSTEM,
              NULL,
              dwErrorCode,
              LANG_USER_DEFAULT,
              szLastErrorMsg,
              sizeof (szLastErrorMsg),
              NULL);

// RegisterEventSource() takes two arguments—the machine name
// (NULL means the local machine)
// and the name of the application logging the event
hSource = RegisterEventSource(NULL, TEXT("WNet RPC Server"));

if (hSource != NULL)
    {
    // The lpszMessageStrings array that we pass
    // to ReportEvent() has the insertion sequences
    // for our message.
    lpszMessageStrings[0] = lpszErrorMsg;
    lpszMessageStrings[1] = szLastErrorMsg;

    ReportEvent(hSource,
          bError ? EVENTLOG_ERROR_TYPE :    // Level of severity
                   EVENTLOG_WARNING_TYPE,
          0,                                // Category—we're not
                                            //   using it
          MSG_RPC_SERVER_FAILED,            // Message identifier
                                            // Defined in WNETMSGS.MC
                                            // and the header file
                                            // WNETMSGS.H that the
                                            // Message Compiler
                                            // generates
          NULL,                             // User security ID (SID)—
                                            //   not using it
          2,                                // Number of insertion
                                            //   strings in
                                            //   lpszMessageStrings
                                            //   array
          0,                                // Number of bytes of
                                            //   binary data to include
          (LPCTSTR *) lpszMessageStrings,   // Messages to log
          NULL);                            // Binary data to log—
                                            //   we're not using any

    DeregisterEventSource(hSource);
    }
}
```

Figure 15-8 shows the Event Logger Application node. You can see that there is an entry for WNet RPC Server, which is also the second argument that WNetReportEvent() passes to RegisterEventSource().

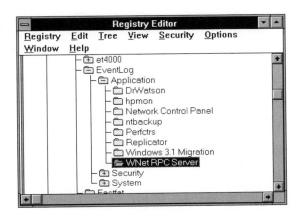

Figure 15-8. Event Logger Application Registry Node

The registered applications have well-known values that enable Event Logger to map their error codes. The WNet RPC Server uses two of them: EventMessageFile and TypesSupported. EventMessageFile describes the path to our message DLL, and TypesSupported indicates the kinds of messages we will be inserting. The WNet RPC Server has only two kinds: warning and error messages.

I add these entries to the Registry in the main() function in REGINST.EXE. Because the EventMessageFile entry (%HOMEDRIVE%\ NTNET\CODE\%Cpu%\WNETMSGS.DLL) contains environment variables, I specify its type as REG_EXPAND_SZ.

```
// Next, add an Event Log entry for the WNet RPC Server
// so we can use event logging the right way
HKEY      hRegistryKey;
TCHAR     szMessageFile[MAX_PATH + 100];  // Leave lots of room
DWORD     dwEventTypes =
          EVENTLOG_ERROR_TYPE | EVENTLOG_WARNING_TYPE;
DWORD dwDisposition;

RegDeleteKey(HKEY_LOCAL_MACHINE,
     TEXT("SYSTEM\\CurrentControlSet\\Services\\EventLog")
     TEXT("\\Application\\WNet RPC Server"));
if (RegCreateKeyEx(HKEY_LOCAL_MACHINE,
```

```
   TEXT("SYSTEM\\CurrentControlSet\\Services\\EventLog")
   TEXT("\\Application\\WNet RPC Server"),
   0,
   TEXT("REG_EXPAND_SZ"),
   REG_OPTION_NON_VOLATILE,
   KEY_ALL_ACCESS,
   NULL,
   &hRegistryKey,
   &dwDisposition) == ERROR_SUCCESS)
{
lstrcpy(szMessageFile,
   TEXT("%HOMEDRIVE%\\NTNET\\CODE\\%Cpu%\\WNETMSGS.DLL"));
RegSetValueEx(hRegistryKey,
   TEXT("EventMessageFile"),
   0,
   REG_EXPAND_SZ,
   (LPBYTE) szMessageFile,
   ((lstrlen(szMessageFile) + 1) * sizeof (TCHAR)));
RegSetValueEx(hRegistryKey,
   TEXT("TypesSupported"),
   0,
   REG_DWORD,
   (LPBYTE) &dwEventTypes,
   sizeof (DWORD));
RegCloseKey(hRegistryKey);
}
```

All accesses to WNETMSGS.DLL will be indirect. You saw in Chapter 7 that you can call LoadLibrary() to load the library, then pass FormatMessage() its handle and the message identifier for any string in the DLL. WNetReportEvent() shows how you retrieve a string for Event Logging—you never actually mention the DLL, except to install it in the Registry. RegisterEventSource() looks up your application name in the Registry and knows from the EventMessageFile value which DLL to load. Your call to ReportEvent() then extracts the appropriate string.

Performance Monitoring

Performance Monitoring is a capability built into Windows NT that allows you to keep track of system usage so that you can identify problems and bottlenecks and correct them before they turn into crises. It is of particular interest to network programming and administration because you can obtain a great deal of information about your network. Table 15-2 shows the Windows NT objects related to network management that you can monitor and their descriptions, which are stored in the Registry.

Table 15-2.   Performance Monitoring Objects Related to Network Management

Object Name	Description
ICMP	The ICMP Object Type includes those counters that describe the rates that ICMP Messages are received and sent by a certain entity using the ICMP protocol. It also describes various error counts for the ICMP protocol.
IP	The IP Object Type includes those counters that describe the rates that IP datagrams are received and sent by a certain computer using the IP protocol. It also describes various error counts for the IP protocol.
NBT Connection	The NBT Connection Object Type includes those counters that describe the rates that bytes are received and sent over a single NBT connection connecting the local computer with some remote computer. The connection is identified by the name of the remote computer.
NetBEUI	The NetBEUI protocol handles data transmission for that network activity which follows the NetBIOS End User Interface standard.
NetBEUI Resource	The NetBEUI Resource object tracks the use of resources (i.e., buffers) by the NetBEUI protocol.
Network Interface	The Network Interface Object Type includes those counters that describe the rates that bytes and packets are received and sent over a Network TCP/IP connection. It also describes various error counts for the same connection.
NWLink IPX	The NWLink IPX transport handles datagram transmission to and from computers using the IPX protocol.
NWLink NetBIOS	The NWLink NetBIOS protocol layer handles the interface to applications communicating over the IPX transport.
NWLink SPX	The NWLink SPX transport handles data transmission and session connections for computers using the SPX protocol.
Redirector	The Redirector is the object that manages network connections to other computers that originate from your own computer.
Server	Server - is the process that interfaces the services from the local computer to the network services.
TCP	The TCP Object Type includes those counters that describe the rates that TCP Segments are received and sent by a certain entity using the TCP protocol. In addition, it describes the number of TCP connections that are in each of the possible TCP connection states.
UDP	The UDP Object Type includes those counters that describe the rates that UDP datagrams are received and sent by a certain entity using the UDP protocol. It also describes various error counts for the UDP protocol.

Another excellent source of information on the use of Performance Monitoring for network management is Chapter 7 of Russ Blake's *Optimizing Windows NT*, published as Volume 3 of the *Windows NT Resource Kit*.

In this section, I am going to use Performance Monitoring to check the validity of the benchmark data I collected in Chapter 10. My hypothesis is that if my results are not concordant with those reported by Performance Monitoring, I am doing something wrong. This will not help me identify polluting factors in my benchmark environment. First of all, pollution cannot be avoided; it can only be minimized. Second, if my benchmark data is polluted, then the Performance Monitoring results will be polluted by the same factors.

The Performance Monitoring API

There is no Performance Monitoring API as such. A single call to RegQueryValueEx(), with the special key HKEY_PERFORMANCE_DATA, collects the data you request. The tricks here are knowing what to ask for and what to do with the information you get. Then, I will first show you how you request data, then how you analyze it.

Objects and Counters

The Registry does not actually store any performance data. The call to RegQueryValueEx() for HKEY_PERFORMANCE_DATA causes NT to collect the data from the management agents. The Registry actually stores information on what types of objects can be monitored as well as the data items, called **counters**, that track a specific aspect of the object's behavior. These are stored as REG_MULTI_SZ strings—arrays of null-terminated Unicode strings—in whatever languages are supported on the host machine. They reside under the key HKEY_LOCAL_MACHINE\SOFTWARE\ Microsoft\Windows NT\CurrentVersion\Perflib. Each supported language is represented by an additional subkey, named for the code identifying the language. For English, this is 009. You don't need to hard-code language values into a program; you can get this value by asking for LOWORD(GetUserDefaultLangID()). The language-specific key has two REG_MULTI_SZ values: Counters and Help, as shown in Figure 15-9.

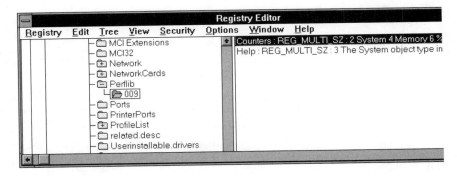

Figure 15-9.   The Perflib Registry Key for the English Language

Counters stores the names of all the objects and counter types and their numeric identifiers. The layout is

```
<ID>\0<name>\0<ID>\0<name>\0 ... <ID>\0<name>\0\0
```

Figure 15-10 shows the dialog box that appears when you double click on the Counters value. I have scrolled down into the listbox to show you the NetBEUI object.

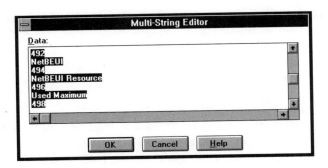

Figure 15-10.   The Counters Value

In Figure 15-10, 492 is the identifier for NetBEUI, 494 for NetBEUI Resource, and so on. Both NetBEUI and NetBEUI Resource are objects, while Used Maximum is a counter.

Explain Text

The second named value in Figure 15-9 is Help. This stores text that provides a brief description of what each of the objects and counters represents, referred to as "Explain text." Like the object and counter names, it is stored as a contiguous array of null-terminated Unicode strings. Here, too, you have identifier/text pairs. Most of the identifiers are one more than the object identifier. For instance, the identifier for the NetBEUI explain text is 493. The text reads as follows: "The NetBEUI protocol handles data transmission for that network activity which follows the NetBIOS End User Interface standard."

Retrieving Performance Data

When calling RegQueryValueEx() to get performance data, several choices are available for the value name that you request:

- TEXT("Global") asks for all data, except that which the system considers costly to retrieve.
- A string in the format TEXT("nnn xx yy"), where *nnn*, *xx*, and *yy* are identifiers for objects that you want, retrieves performance data for those objects and any related objects. For example, threads cannot exist without processes, so if you ask for information on threads, you will also find out about the processes that own them.
- TEXT("Foreign ssss") requests performance data for a remote machine, designated by ssss.
- TEXT("Foreign ssss nnn xx yy") asks for object-specific statistics on machine ssss.
- Finally, TEXT("Costly") says you want the data for objects that are considered expensive.

The data is returned in a rather complex arrangement. The structures are well documented in several places. The *Performance Monitoring Overview* in the Win32 on-line help is quite good and includes sample programs that you can copy to disk, compile, and run. Another excellent source is *Optimizing Windows NT*, the third volume of the *Windows NT Resource Kit*. Chapter 12 discusses the topic "Writing a Custom Windows NT Performance Monitor." The book's author, Russ Blake, is the person who wrote the Performance Monitor, an excellent management tool provided with Windows NT, and he knows what he's talking about. The source code to Performance Monitor itself comes with the Win32 SDK, in \MSTOOLS\SAMPLES\SDKTOOLS\PERFMON. Finally, the header file

\MSTOOLS\H\WINPERF.H is extensively commented and offers some of the best explanations of the data structures you will find.

Not only is there a large amount of data available; there is considerable variation in the types of data reported. Because one of the goals of Performance Monitoring is to be system-independent, the data describes itself. That is, it tells you how big the data items are, where to find them, what their data types are, and how to interpret and present the information. This is the most daunting aspect of writing code that uses Performance Monitoring. I found the functions in the on-line help to be very helpful in figuring out what exactly is going on (not to mention numerous sessions with WINDBG).

Data Structures Returned by the System

The first structure in the data returned by RegQueryValueEx() is a PERF_DATA_BLOCK.

```
typedef struct _PERF_DATA_BLOCK
{
    WCHAR           Signature[4];   // Unicode "PERF"
    DWORD           LittleEndian;
    DWORD           Version;
    DWORD           Revision;
    DWORD           TotalByteLength;
    DWORD           HeaderLength;
    DWORD           NumObjectTypes;
    DWORD           DefaultObject;
    SYSTEMTIME      SystemTime;
    LARGE_INTEGER   PerfTime;
    LARGE_INTEGER   PerfFreq;
    LARGE_INTEGER   PerfTime100nSec;
    DWORD           SystemNameLength;
    DWORD           SystemNameOffset;
} PERF_DATA_BLOCK;
```

Five fields are of particular interest:

- *TotalByteLength* is the size of the entire block returned by RegQueryValueEx().
- *HeaderLength* is the offset to the next portion of the block, which contains an array of object descriptions.
- *NumObjectTypes* is the number of elements in the array that follows the PERF_DATA_BLOCK.

- *SystemTime* is a SYSTEMTIME structure that reports the time the sample is taken.
- *PerfTime* is the value of the high-resolution counter at the time of the sample. Not all machines have such a counter, though, which is why the SYSTEMTIME is also provided. When you retrieve a counter value, its type tells you which value to use in computing elapsed time.

The Object Description Array. Following the PERF_DATA_BLOCK is an array that describes all the pertinent objects, their counters and the current values of the counters. The first structure you find is a PERF_OBJECT_TYPE. Here is how you navigate to it from the PERF_DATA_BLOCK.

```
BYTE byData[100000];                // Buffer that RegQueryValueEx() fills
PPERF_DATA_BLOCK    pPerfData;
PPERF_OBJECT_TYPE   pObjectType;
PBYTE               pTemp;          // For computing byte offsets

pPerfData   = (PPERF_DATA_BLOCK) byData;
pTemp       = byData;
pObjectType = (PPERF_OBJECT_TYPE) (pTemp + pPerfData->HeaderLength);
```

The block of data headed by the PERF_OBJECT_TYPE structure contains information on the object, followed by descriptions of its counters, then followed by the counter data. If the object supports multiple instances (like threads and processes), the counter data is presented on a per-instance basis, along with structures describing the object instance. Let's look at the PERF_OBJECT_TYPE structure first, then consider the simplest case, an object that does not support instances.

```
typedef struct _PERF_OBJECT_TYPE
{
    DWORD   TotalByteLength;
    DWORD   DefinitionLength;
    DWORD   HeaderLength;
    DWORD   ObjectNameTitleIndex;
    LPWSTR  ObjectNameTitle;
    DWORD   ObjectHelpTitleIndex;
    LPWSTR  ObjectHelpTitle;
    DWORD   DetailLevel;
    DWORD   NumCounters;
    DWORD   DefaultCounter;
    DWORD   NumInstances;
    DWORD   CodePage;
    LARGE_INTEGER PerfTime;
```

```
         LARGE_INTEGER PerfFreq;
    } PERF_OBJECT_TYPE;
```

The following fields are of greatest interest:

- *TotalByteLength* is the size of this complete object description. The next object description in the array is at this offset.
- *DefinitionLength* is the size of the PERF_OBJECT_TYPE structure and all the counter definitions that follow it. It is therefore the offset to the actual counter data for an object that cannot have multiple instances or to the array of object instance descriptors.
- *HeaderLength* is the size of the PERF_OBJECT_TYPE structure, so it is the offset to the counter definitions that follow.
- *ObjectNameTitleIndex* is the numeric identifier for this object. This is the value associated with the object name in Figure 15-10. This field is important because when you are looking for information on a single object, you have to scan the object descriptions for the correct *ObjectNameTitleIndex*. It also lets you find printable text in the user's native language.
- *NumCounters* tells you the number of counters describing this object.
- *NumInstances* is the number of instances of the object, with -1 indicating that the object cannot have multiple instances.

Here is a *for* loop that steps through the array of object descriptions. I use a simple BYTE pointer (*pTemp*), because it eliminates the necessity for a lot of type casting, which is both hard to read and easy to do wrong.

```
BYTE byData[100000];              // Buffer that RegQueryValueEx() fills
PPERF_DATA_BLOCK  pPerfData;
PPERF_OBJECT_TYPE pObjectType;
PBYTE             pTemp;          // For computing byte offsets

pPerfData   = (PPERF_DATA_BLOCK) byData;
pTemp       = byData;
pObjectType = (PPERF_OBJECT_TYPE) (pTemp + pPerfData->HeaderLength);
pTemp       = (PBYTE) pObjectType;

for (DWORD i = 0;
     i < pPerfData->NumObjectTypes;
     ++i,
     // Find next object description
     pObjectType = (PPERF_OBJECT_TYPE)
                 (pTemp += pObjectType->TotalByteLength))
    {
    // Process each element
    }
```

The Counter Definitions. Immediately following the PERF_OBJECT_
TYPE is an array of structures describing all the counters for that object. The
structure is typed as a PERF_COUNTER_DEFINITION. This array can be
thought of as the Performance Monitoring database schema for the object.
The data itself is not presented here, but this structure tells you where to find
it, what it looks like, and how big it is.

```
typedef struct _PERF_COUNTER_DEFINITION
{
    DWORD   ByteLength;
    DWORD   CounterNameTitleIndex;
    LPWSTR  CounterNameTitle;
    DWORD   CounterHelpTitleIndex;
    LPWSTR  CounterHelpTitle;
    DWORD   DefaultScale;
    DWORD   DetailLevel;
    DWORD   CounterType;
    DWORD   CounterSize;
    DWORD   CounterOffset;
} PERF_COUNTER_DEFINITION;
```

The most important fields here are

- *ByteLength* is the size of the counter definition structure and the offset
  to the next PERF_COUNTER_DEFINITION in the array.
- *CounterNameTitleIndex* plays the same role as *ObjectNameTitleIndex*
  in the PERF_OBJECT_TYPE structure. It is the identifier associated
  with the counter name as shown in Figure 15-10.
- *CounterType* tells you how to interpret, evaluate, and format the data.
  There are many predefined types. Table 12-4 in Chapter 12 of
  Optimizing Windows NT lists them, and it goes on for four pages.
- *CounterSize* specifies the number of bytes occupied by the counter
  data.
- *CounterOffset* indicates the byte offset of the counter data in the
  counter block structure. If an object does not support instances, this
  follows the counter definition arrays. Otherwise, each object instance
  has its own counter block.

Looking up the Counter Data. For an object without instances, there is
only one more structure to contend with, the PERF_COUNTER_BLOCK. It
has only one field.

```
typedef struct _PERF_COUNTER_BLOCK
{
    DWORD ByteLength;
} PERF_COUNTER_BLOCK;
```

This structure is followed by the counter data. *ByteLength* indicates the total size of the block containing the data. The information for each individual counter can be fetched using the *CounterOffset* information provided in the PERF_COUNTER_DEFINITION. This offset is from the beginning of the PERF_COUNTER_BLOCK. *The CounterSize* field indicates the number of bytes to copy out of the block.

Here is a typical scenario (and the one I will be using). Suppose you want to get the data for one counter belonging to one object type. For instance, to evaluate the Named Pipes benchmark, you need to retrieve the Bytes Total/sec counter (number 388) for the Redirector object (number 262). To do so:

1. Call RegQueryValueEx() to fill the PERF_DATA_BLOCK. RegQueryValueEx() will return ERROR_MORE_DATA if the buffer you provide is not large enough for all the data you could possible retrieve. Even though one of its arguments points to the size of the buffer, it will not set it to reflect the amount of memory it actually needs. You have to either keep trying for more, or allocate a very large buffer, then reallocate it to shrink it. When RegQueryValueEx() finally succeeds, it tells you how much data it actually provided.

2. Use the *HeaderLength* field of the PERF_DATA_BLOCK to find the first PERF_OBJECT_TYPE.

3. Scan through the array of object types for the one whose *ObjectNameTitleIndex* matches the one you want, each time increasing a running pointer by the *TotalByteLength* field of the PERF_OBJECT_TYPE structure.

4. When you find the object you're looking for, remember its address, then go to the array of PERF_COUNTER_DEFINITION structures. This is calculated from the *HeaderLength* field in the PERF_OBJECT_TYPE.

5. Scan the counter definitions for the correct *CounterNameTitleIndex*. Each time through the loop, add the *ByteLength* that you find in the PERF_COUNTER_DEFINITION structure. When you find the one you want, take the PERF_OBJECT_TYPE pointer you remembered in step 4, and add the *DefinitionLength* field of the structure to its base address. This gives you the address of the PERF_ COUNTER_BLOCK containing the data you need.

6. Use the *CounterOffset* and *CounterSize* fields of the PERF_
    COUNTER_DEFINITION to determine where in the counter block
    your data resides, and how many bytes of data you need.

Here is a code fragment that continues the previous one. It implements the
six steps just outlined.

```
BYTE                    byData[100000];  // Buffer that RegQueryValueEx()
                                         // fills
DWORD                   dwDataSize = sizeof (byData);
PPERF_DATA_BLOCK        pPerfData;
PPERF_OBJECT_TYPE       pObjectType;
PBYTE                   pTemp;                 // For computing byte offsets

DWORD                   dwType;

// Step 1. Get performance data from RegQueryValueEx()
RegQueryValueEx(HKEY_PERFORMANCE_DATA,
                TEXT("262"),    // Redirector
                NULL,
                &dwType,
                byData,
                &dwDataSize);

pPerfData   = (PPERF_DATA_BLOCK) byData;
pTemp       = byData;

// Step 2. Find PERF_OBJECT_TYPE array
pObjectType = (PPERF_OBJECT_TYPE) (pTemp + pPerfData->HeaderLength);
pTemp       = (PBYTE) pObjectType;

// Step 3. Scan the array looking for the object we're
//         interested in. The Redirector is object
//         number 262.
for (DWORD i = 0;
     i < pPerfData->NumObjectTypes;
     ++i,
     pObjectType = (PPERF_OBJECT_TYPE)
                   (pTemp += pObjectType->TotalByteLength))
  {
  // Is pObjectType->ObjectNameTitleIndex the one we want?
  // Then look for the counter we need
  if (pObjectType->ObjectNameTitleIndex == 262)
    {
    // Step 4. pObjectType holds the address of the object
    //         Index to PERF_COUNTER_DEFINITIONs
    PPERF_COUNTER_DEFINITION pCounterDefinition;
```

```
        pTemp += pObjectType->HeaderLength;
        pCounter = (PPERF_COUNTER_DEFINITION) pTemp;

        // Step 5. Scan PERF_COUNTER_DEFINITIONs for the
        //         counter we want. For Bytes Total/sec,
        //         we want 388
        for (DWORD j = 0;
             j < pObjectType->NumCounters;
             ++j,
             pCounter = (PPERF_COUNTER_DEFINITION)
                            (pTemp +=  pCounter->ByteLength))
          {
          // Is it the one we're looking for?
          if (pCounter->CounterNameTitleIndex == 388)
              {
              PBYTE pCounterData;

              // Step 6. pCounter->CounterOffset tells us
              //         where the data is,
              //         pCounter->CounterSize tells us
              //         how much of it there is
              pTemp = (PBYTE) pObjectType;
              pCounterData = pTemp +
                            pObjectType->DefinitionLength +
                            pCounter->CounterOffset;

              PBYTE pOutputData =
                  (PBYTE) HeapAlloc(GetProcessHeap(),
                            HEAP_ZERO_MEMORY |
                            HEAP_GENERATE_EXCEPTIONS,
                            pCounter->CounterSize);
              CopyMemory(pOutputData, pCounterData,
                      pCounter->CounterSize);
              return pOutputData;
              }
          }
      }
return NULL;  // Object or counter not found
}
```

Reading Counter Data for an Object Type with Instances. When an object type may have multiple instances, the situation is more complicated. Now, the counter definition array is followed by an array of instance descriptions. Each of these consists of a PERF_INSTANCE_DEFINITION structure and a PERF_COUNTER_BLOCK, containing the counter data for each instance.

```
typedef struct _PERF_INSTANCE_DEFINITION
{
    DWORD ByteLength;
    DWORD ParentObjectTitleIndex;
    DWORD ParentObjectInstance;
    DWORD UniqueID;
    DWORD NameOffset;
    DWORD NameLength;
} PERF_INSTANCE_DEFINITION;
```

The only field of concern is *ByteLength*. This is the offset to the PERF_COUNTER_BLOCK for this instance. To find the next instance in the array, add the *ByteLength* of the PERF_INSTANCE_DEFINITION and the *ByteLength* of the PERF_COUNTER_BLOCK to the address of the current instance definition.

The Revised Benchmark Programs

Before looking at the new benchmark programs, I want to show you the function GetPerformanceCounterData() that encapsulates all the logic discussed in the previous section. It is in the file \NTNET\CODE\ PERFMON\PERFHLPR.CPP. It takes strings representing the object and counter information that the caller needs, a pointer to a pointer that it allocates for the output data, and references to two C++ objects that return the *SystemTime* and the *PerfTime* from the PERF_DATA_BLOCK. The caller then has the option of using either of these. If the machine supports a high-resolution counter, it will use the more precise *SampleTime*.

```
/*******
 *
 * GetPerformanceCounter() reads a requested counter value
 * It allocates an array for the output information
 *
 * Its return value is the number of instances
 * for which the counter is returned.
 *
 ********/

LONG GetPerformanceCounterData(LPWSTR lpwObject,
                               LPWSTR lpwCounter,
                               LPBYTE *lplpOutputData,
                               CSystemTime& SystemTime,
                               CLargeInt&  SampleTime)
{
```

```
WCHAR   szwObjectIndex[100];
WCHAR   szwCounterIndex[100];
LPBYTE  lpOutputData;
LONG    lNumInstances = 0;

// Get performance monitoring data
DWORD   dwType;
LPBYTE  pbyData;
DWORD   dwDataBytes = 163840;

pbyData = (LPBYTE) HeapAlloc(GetProcessHeap(),
                            HEAP_ZERO_MEMORY |
                            HEAP_GENERATE_EXCEPTIONS,
                            dwDataBytes);

while (TRUE)
    {
    DWORD dwError;

    // RegQueryValueEx() will not tell you how
    // much memory you need to allocate if the
    // buffer you initially provide is too small.
    // Therefore, you have to call it in a loop,
    // providing a successively larger buffer until
    // it doesn't return ERROR_MORE_DATA any more.
    if ((dwError = RegQueryValueExW(HKEY_PERFORMANCE_DATA,
        lpwObject,
        NULL,
        &dwType,
        pbyData,
        &dwDataBytes)) == ERROR_MORE_DATA)
        {
        pbyData = (LPBYTE) HeapReAlloc(GetProcessHeap(),
                            HEAP_ZERO_MEMORY,
                            pbyData,
                            dwDataBytes += 4096);
        }
    else if (dwError == ERROR_SUCCESS)
        break;
    else
        return -1;
    }

// Shrink data buffer down
// It looks like RegQueryValueEx() makes you
// pass it a buffer big enough to hold
// all possible output data
pbyData = (LPBYTE) HeapReAlloc(GetProcessHeap(),
```

```
                              HEAP_ZERO_MEMORY,
                              pbyData,
                              dwDataBytes);

   *lplpOutputData = (LPBYTE)
      HeapAlloc(GetProcessHeap(),
                HEAP_ZERO_MEMORY |
                HEAP_GENERATE_EXCEPTIONS,
                dwDataBytes);

   lpOutputData = *lplpOutputData;

   // Look for requested object
   PPERF_DATA_BLOCK pPerfData =
      (PPERF_DATA_BLOCK) pbyData;
   DWORD                    dwThisObject;   // count of objects
   PPERF_OBJECT_TYPE        pThisObject;    // pointer to
                                            // object structure
   PPERF_COUNTER_DEFINITION pThisCounter;
   PBYTE                    pTempObject = pbyData;

   // Remember the sample time as SYSTEMTIME
   // and high-resolution counter time
   SystemTime = pPerfData->SystemTime;
   SampleTime = pPerfData->PerfTime;

   // Beginning of object array is indicated
   // by the HeaderLength field of the PERF_DATA_BLOCK
   pThisObject = (PPERF_OBJECT_TYPE) (pTempObject +
      pPerfData->HeaderLength);

   pTempObject = (PBYTE) pThisObject;

   BOOL   bFound = FALSE;

   // Scan through the object array looking for the
   // one the caller wants.
   // To navigate to each successive element, add
   // the TotalByteLength field of the PERF_OBJECT_TYPE
   // structure to the address of the current
   // PERF_OBJECT_TYPE
   for (dwThisObject = 0;
        !bFound && (dwThisObject < pPerfData->NumObjectTypes);
        dwThisObject++,
           pThisObject = (PPERF_OBJECT_TYPE)
                         (pTempObject +=
                          pThisObject->TotalByteLength))
      {
```

```
swprintf(szwObjectIndex, L"%-d",
   pThisObject->ObjectNameTitleIndex);

// Is this the object we want?
if (CompareStringW(GetUserDefaultLCID(), 0,
    szwObjectIndex, -1, lpwObject, -1) != 2) // Equal strings?
   continue;

// We've found our object, let's find
// the requested counter
DWORD dwThisCounter;
PBYTE pTempCounter;

// The PERF_COUNTER_DEFINITION array starts
// at the address indicated by the HeaderLength
// field of the PERF_OBJECT_TYPE structure
pTempCounter = pTempObject +
              pThisObject->HeaderLength;
pThisCounter =
   (PPERF_COUNTER_DEFINITION) pTempCounter;

// Loop through the counter definitions
// To navigate to the next counter, add the
// ByteLength field of the PERF_COUNTER_DEFINITION
// structure to the address of the current
// PERF_COUNTER_DEFINITION
for (dwThisCounter = 0;
    dwThisCounter < pThisObject->NumCounters;
    dwThisCounter++,
       pThisCounter = (PPERF_COUNTER_DEFINITION)
                     (pTempCounter +=
                      pThisCounter->ByteLength))
  {
  swprintf(szwCounterIndex, L"%-d",
    pThisCounter->CounterNameTitleIndex);

  // Is this the counter we're looking for?
  if (CompareStringW(GetUserDefaultLCID(), 0,
      szwCounterIndex, -1, lpwCounter, -1) == 2) // Equal
                                                 // strings?
    {
    lNumInstances += pThisObject->NumInstances;
    bFound = TRUE;
    break;
    }
  }
```

```
if (bFound && pThisObject->NumInstances >= 0)
    {
    PPERF_INSTANCE_DEFINITION pThisInstance;
    PPERF_COUNTER_BLOCK        pCounterBlock;
    DWORD   dwThisInstance;
    PBYTE   pTempInstance;
    PBYTE   pTempCounterData;

    // This is a multiple-instance object
    // We have to scan the PERF_INSTANCE_DEFINITION
    // array
    // The beginning of the array is found by
    // adding the DefinitionLength field of the
    // PERF_OBJECT_TYPE to the address of the
    // current PERF_OBJECT_TYPE
    pTempInstance = pTempObject +
        pThisObject->DefinitionLength;
    pThisInstance = (PPERF_INSTANCE_DEFINITION)
        pTempInstance;

    for (dwThisInstance = 0;
        dwThisInstance < (DWORD) pThisObject->NumInstances;
        dwThisInstance++)
        {
        // The PERF_COUNTER_BLOCK for this instance
        // is found by adding the ByteLength field of
        // the PERF_INSTANCE_DEFINITION structure to
        // the address of the current
        // PERF_INSTANCE_DEFINITION
        pTempCounterData = pTempInstance +
                            pThisInstance->ByteLength;
        // pTempCounterData now counting to PERF_COUNTER_BLOCK

        pCounterBlock = (PPERF_COUNTER_BLOCK)
            pTempCounterData;

        // Data is at pThisCounter->CounterOffset
        pTempCounterData += pThisCounter->CounterOffset;

        // pThisCounter->CounterSize tells us how many
        // bytes are contained in the data
        CopyMemory(lpOutputData, pTempCounterData,
            pThisCounter->CounterSize);
        lpOutputData += pThisCounter->CounterSize;

        // Move to next element in the instance array.
        // We add the ByteLength field of the
        // PERF_INSTANCE_DEFINITION structure and
```

```
                // the ByteLength field of the
                // PERF_COUNTER_BLOCK to the address of
                // the current PERF_INSTANCE_DEFINITION
                pTempInstance += (pCounterBlock->ByteLength +
                               pThisInstance->ByteLength);
                pThisInstance = (PPERF_INSTANCE_DEFINITION)
                               pTempInstance;
            }
        }
        else if (pThisObject->NumInstances ==
                (PERF_NO_INSTANCES))
        {
        // Object has no instances
        // Counter definition is followed by the counter data
        PBYTE pTempCounterData;
        pTempCounterData = pTempObject +
                           pThisObject->DefinitionLength;
        pTempCounterData += pThisCounter->CounterOffset;
        CopyMemory(lpOutputData, pTempCounterData,
            pThisCounter->CounterSize);
        lpOutputData += pThisCounter->CounterSize;
        lNumInstances = 1;
        }
    }
    return lNumInstances;
}
```

The benchmark client programs call GetPerformanceCounterData() to retrieve Performance Monitoring statistics, then compute the data transfer rate that these statistics indicate. I present a revised version of the Named Pipes benchmark in the following sections. I do not include data for TCP/IP, NetBIOS, or NWLink, because at the time of this writing I could not determine the appropriate counters for Windows NT 3.5. Source code for Named Pipes, TCP/IP, and NetBIOS is included on the disk included with this book.

The Bytes Total/sec Counter

The counter of interest is Bytes Total/sec, with identifier number 388. For Named Pipes, Bytes Total/sec has the type PERF_COUNTER_ BULK_COUNT. This is a composite type, defined as PERF_SIZE_LARGE | PERF_TYPE_COUNTER | PERF_COUNTER_RATE | PERF_TIMER_ TICK | PERF_DELTA_COUNTER | PERF_DISPLAY_PER_SEC. What the other flags mean is that this counter is to be computed by taking successive snapshots and capturing the counter value and the high-resolution performance counter. The value reported is the change in the counter value divided by the change in the timer. The PERF_SIZE_LARGE flag indicates that the counter data is reported as a LARGE_INTEGER, a Win32 type that contains two DWORD parts.

Some Useful C++ Objects

The code that calculates the byte transfer rate uses two C++ classes that I have defined, CLargeInt and CSystemTime. In both cases, the main reason I use a C++ object is so that I can overload the binary minus operator. You cannot perform standard arithmetic on LARGE_INTEGER and SYSTEMTIME structures. I need to subtract LARGE_INTEGER values, because for Named Pipes, the counter is reported that way; if I am using the high-resolution performance counter, its value is also returned as a LARGE_INTEGER. I don't use the CSystemTime class unless there is no high-resolution performance counter on the host machine. In that case, I subtract the end time from the start time by converting the time portion of their SYSTEMTIME structures to milliseconds.

Here are the declarations of these two classes, taken from \NTNET\CODE\PERFMON\PERFHLPR.H. Notice that CLargeInt is not a subclass of LARGE_INTEGER, as CSystemTime is a subclass of SYSTEMTIME. This is because the LARGE_INTEGER type is a union containing a structure, not a simple structure.

```
/*===== Types and Classes =====*/

class CLargeInt
{
    private:
        DWORD LowPart;
        DWORD HighPart;
    public:
        CLargeInt()
            {
            LowPart = 0;
            HighPart = 0;
            }
        CLargeInt(LARGE_INTEGER LargeInt)
            {
            LowPart = LargeInt.LowPart;
            HighPart = LargeInt.HighPart;
            }
        operator DWORD()
            {
```

```
                 return LowPart;
                 }
            CLargeInt operator-(const CLargeInt& nl);
};

class CSystemTime : public _SYSTEMTIME
{
   public:
        CSystemTime();
        CSystemTime(_SYSTEMTIME st);
        double operator-(const CSystemTime& cs);
};
```

Here are the class implementations, from \NTNET\CODE\ PERFMON\PERFHLPR.CPP.

```
/*===== CLargeInt Class =====*/

CLargeInt CLargeInt::operator-(const CLargeInt& nl)
{
   CLargeInt nlResult;

   if (LowPart < nl.LowPart)
      -HighPart;

   nlResult.LowPart = LowPart - nl.LowPart;
   nlResult.HighPart = HighPart - nl.HighPart;
   return nlResult;
}

/*===== CSystemTime Class =====*/

CSystemTime::CSystemTime()
{
   wMilliseconds = wSecond = wMinute = wHour = 0;
   wDay = wDayOfWeek = wMonth = wYear = 0;
}

CSystemTime::CSystemTime(_SYSTEMTIME st)
{
   CopyMemory(this, &st, sizeof (_SYSTEMTIME));
}

double CSystemTime::operator-(const CSystemTime& cs)
{
   // This routine won't work if
   // start time and end time
   // aren't on the same day
```

```
double dStartMilliseconds, dEndMilliseconds;

dStartMilliseconds =
   ((double)  cs.wMilliseconds) +
   (((double) cs.wSecond) * 1000.0) +
   (((double) cs.wMinute) * 1000.0 * 60.0) +
   (((double) cs.wHour) * 1000.0 * 60.0 * 24.0);
dEndMilliseconds =
   ((double)  wMilliseconds) +
   (((double) wSecond) * 1000.0) +
   (((double) wMinute) * 1000.0 * 60.0) +
   (((double) wHour) * 1000.0 * 60.0 * 24.0);

return dEndMilliseconds - dStartMilliseconds;
}
```

Calculating the Byte-Transfer Rate

To calculate the byte-transfer rate using Performance Monitoring statistics, I call GetPerformanceCounterData() just before I start my test, then immediately after I finish it. I then subtract the first counter value from the last one, and the start time from the end time. The QueryPerformanceFrequency() function populates a LARGE_INTEGER with the scale factor for the timer. It reports the number of times a second the high-resolution counter increments.

Here are the relevant code excerpts from \NTNET\CODE\ PERFMON\WNETCLI.CPP, which is my adaptation of the Named Pipes benchmark first presented in Chapter 10. The other two programs, \NTNET\- CODE\PERFMON\WNETCLI2.CPP (NetBIOS) and \NTNET\CODE\WIN- SOCK\WNETCLI2.CPP (Windows Sockets over TCP/IP) are essentially the same.

```
LARGE_INTEGER *lpCounterStart;
LARGE_INTEGER *lpCounterStop;
CLargeInt CounterDelta;
CSystemTime SystemTime[2];
CLargeInt   SampleTime[2];
DWORD  dwTotalBytes = 0;

// [Initialize client and connect to server]

GetPerformanceCounterData(
      REDIRECTOR,                    // Defined as L"262" in PERFHLPR.H
      BYTES_TOTAL_PER_SEC,           // Defined as L"388" in PERFHLPR.H
```

```
            (LPBYTE *) &lpCounterStart,
            SystemTime[0],
            SampleTime[0]);

// [Send data to server and wait for it to come back]

GetPerformanceCounterData(
        REDIRECTOR,
        BYTES_TOTAL_PER_SEC,
        (LPBYTE *) &lpCounterStop,
        SystemTime[1],
        SampleTime[1]);

RegCloseKey(HKEY_PERFORMANCE_DATA);

// [Calculate transfer rate using my own statistics]

// Now present Performance Monitoring data for comparison
printf("\n============================");
printf("\nPerformance monitor stats: ");
CounterDelta = CLargeInt(*lpCounterStop) -
                CLargeInt(*lpCounterStart);

printf("\nBytes transferred = %.0f",
    ((double) ((DWORD) CounterDelta)));

double dMilliSeconds;
LARGE_INTEGER PerformanceFrequency;

if (QueryPerformanceFrequency(&PerformanceFrequency))
    dMilliSeconds =
        ((double) (((DWORD) SampleTime[1]) -
                    ((DWORD) SampleTime[0]))) /
        ((double) (PerformanceFrequency.LowPart))
        * 1000.0;
else
    dMilliSeconds = SystemTime[1] - SystemTime[0];

printf("\nBytes per second = %.2f\n",
    (((double) ((DWORD) CounterDelta)) * 1000.0)
    / dMilliSeconds);
```

Named Pipes

For Named Pipes, the object to query is the Redirector. Named Pipes are an NT file system, and the client opens its end of a connection by passing a UNC filename to CreateFile(). This wakes up the Multiple UNC Provider, who in turns calls on the Redirector. The identifier for the Redirector is 262. Here is its explain text from the Registry:

> The Redirector is the object that manages network connections to other computers that originate from your own computer.

The explain text for the Bytes Total/sec counter is help text number 389:

> Bytes Total/sec is the rate the Redirector is processing data bytes. This includes all application and file data in addition to protocol information such as packet headers.

In the tables and figure that follow, I present the output data. Table 15-3 compares the count of bytes transferred, and Table 15-4 shows the calculated byte-transfer rates. Figure 15-11 graphs the data in Table 15-4. These tests were run at different times from those offered in Chapter 10, so the exact transfer rates are slightly different.

Table 15-3.   Count of Bytes Transferred—Named Pipes

Packet Size	1024	2048	4096	8192	16384	32768
My data	204800	409600	819200	1638400	3276800	6553600
Performance Monitoring data	218800	423600	833200	1667100	3327900	6649500
% Difference	7%	3%	2%	2%	2%	1%

Table 15-4.   Byte-Transfer Rates for Named Pipes

Packet Size	1024	2048	4096	8192	16384	32768
My data	243519	332467	498903	471482	489074	499931
Performance Monitoring data	255694	345559	506577	480170	497132	509493
% Difference	5%	4%	2%	2%	2%	2%

The correspondence between the two sets of data is very close. Figure 15-11 emphasizes the point most dramatically—the Performance Monitoring data strongly corroborates the data I collected.

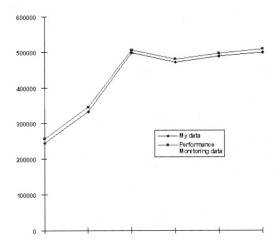

Figure 15-11. Byte-Transfer Rates for Named Pipes

Conclusion

The Windows NT Registry stores a great deal of information on behalf of the operating system and applications that choose to use it. Important uses of the Registry are:

- Mapping initialization-file reads and writes to the Registry so that .INI files, which are problematic in a secure environment, can be eliminated.
- Informing the Event Logger of the existence of your application so that you can use multilingual message files and application-defined events to write entries to the event log.
- Storing information that your program uses directly, thereby allowing it to be reconfigured without any recompilation of code.
- Retrieving Performance Monitoring information.

Performance Monitoring is a powerful, self-correcting capability included in Windows NT. It allows system administrators to precisely diagnose problems and bottlenecks; it also gives developers a hook for obtaining system information for their own purposes. Of special interest for me in the writing of this book are the many objects and counters that pertain to network management.

Suggested Readings

Registry and Initialization Files Overview in the Win32 SDK on-line help. Published as Chapter 52 in *Win32 Programmer's Reference*, Volume 2.

Performance Monitoring Overview in the Win32 SDK on-line help. Published as Chapter 66 in *Win32 Programmer's Reference*, Volume 2.

Event Logging Overview in the Win32 SDK on-line help. Published as Chapter 65 in *Win32 Programmer's Reference*, Volume 2.

Blake, Russ. *Optimizing Windows NT.* Windows NT Resource Kit, Volume 3. Redmond, WA: Microsoft Press, 1993.

Windows NT Resource Guide, Chapters 10–14. *Windows NT Resource Kit.* Volume 1. Redmond, WA: Microsoft Press, 1993.

Microsoft Knowledge Base for Win32 SDK articles:
"Enabling Disk Performance Counters"
"Calculating String Length in Registry"

## Chapter 16

The LAN Manager API for Windows NT

Overview

The LAN Manager API is a rich set of functions for network administration. Among its capabilities are calls that let you add, delete, and enumerate users and groups, associate users with groups, share resources, and determine what machines are attached to your network. Since Windows NT carries forward (or at least superficially appears to) much of the network design of LAN Manager, it is natural that the LAN Manager API should follow it.

Where Does the LAN Manager API Fit In?

Microsoft's position on this API is confusing. The calls are not well documented, though the on-line help and the header files do ship with the Win32 SDK now. The routines themselves reside in NETAPI32.DLL, along with the Netbios() function.

Here's the disclaimer that appears at the top of the on-line help.

The Windows Networking APIs specified in this online help are designed to provide some of the API functionality that was available in LAN Manager 2.x. They are not the base Windows NT networking APIs. Windows NT takes some of the functionality that was previously supplied by the networking software and moves this into the base APIs (such as error and audit logging, printing). Windows NT also provides a network independent set of network APIs (the WNet APIs) that allow network APIs to work across different network vendors' products. If a base API or WNet API exists that could be used by your application, you should convert from the Windows networking API to the public Windows NT equivalent. There are at least three reasons to make the change now:

1. The WNet APIs are network independent, while the Windows networking APIs work only on LAN Manager networks.

2. Some of the Windows networking APIs specified in this document may not be supported in future releases of Windows NT if they have been superseded by base APIs or WNet APIs. (Of course Microsoft does not plan to remove specific Windows networking APIs unless equivalent or better functionality is available from other APIs.)

3. The Windows networking APIs may not be supported on some other future Microsoft platforms, since they are not part of the Win32 API set.

So, now that I've told you why I should **NOT** be writing this chapter, here's why I am:

- The LAN Manager API is excellent and should be available to third-party developers.
- For many of the services that it provides, there is no other way to do it, or at least no documented way. For example, there is no way to add users and groups to the security database, no way to enumerate them, and no way to delete them. These are some of the most important network services.
- The WNet API continues to be of little significance. The only real service it provides is letting you connect to drives and print queues on remote machines.
- In spite of Microsoft's soft-pedaling the LAN Manager API, they have improved and expanded it for Windows NT. The interface to existing functions is better, and there are whole new API categories.

Because of the sheer size of the LAN Manager API, I am not going to try to cover it in its entirety. Ralph Ryan wrote a complete (and very good) book on the OS/2 LAN Manager API, *Microsoft LAN Manager: A Programmer's Guide*. By the way, his book, which was published in 1990, presents benchmark statistics comparing the performance of Named Pipes and NetBIOS. The fastest throughput he recorded was 34K a second. My highest number is over 700K a second! This data underscores the extraordinary pace at which microprocessor technology is advancing.

My approach will be the same one I took in Chapter 11 of *Windows Network Programming*. In that chapter, I concentrated on developing functions that implement the most important network services, which I have already alluded to in this book. Therefore, I have ported the following functions to Windows NT:

- WNetEnumServers() finds out what other servers are attached to the network.
- WNetAddUser() adds a new user to the security database.
- WNetDeleteUser() deletes an existing user.
- WNetEnumUsers() reports all the users currently in the security database.
- WNetAddGroup() creates a new user group.
- WNetDeleteGroup() deletes a group.
- WNetEnumGroups() enumerates the groups.
- WNetAddGroupMember() adds a new member to a group.
- WNetDeleteGroupMember() removes a member from a group.
- WNetEnumGroupMembers() enumerates the members of a group.
- WNetEnumMemberGroups() reports the groups to which a user (or group) belongs.
- WNetIsUserGroupMember() tells whether a given user (or group) belongs to a group.

I have also ported the WNETSVCS sample application from *Windows Network Programming*. It provides dialog boxes that mimic the functionality of the NT User Manager. This will give you a chance to become familiar with the LAN Manager API for Windows NT by seeing how some of the most important functions work.

To give you an idea of the scope of the API, Table 16-1 lists the function categories, along with the functions comprising them and a brief description of their purpose. If a group has been superseded by a Win32 API, I do not list the individual functions.

Table 16-1. LAN Manager API for Windows NT

Category	Component Functions	Purpose	Additional Comments
Access API	<Superseded>	Assigning users permission to files and directories	Replaced by Win32 Security API
Alert API	NetAlertRaise NetAlertRaiseEx	Sending alert messages to network service applications	
Auditing API	<Superseded>	Adding audit trail entries to the system log, reading audit trail	Audit trails are automatically generated by Windows NT when an object has an SACL tied to it, and auditing is enabled. Event Logging API is used to read the logs.

Table 16-1.   LAN Manager API for Windows NT (continued)

Category	Component Functions	Purpose	Additional Comments
Buffer Manipulation API	NetApiBufferAllocate NetApiBufferFree NetApiBufferReallocate NetApiBufferSize	Allocating and releasing memory used for output parameters	New in Windows NT
Configuration API	<Superseded>	Setting machine configuration	Replaced by Registry API
Connection API	<Superseded>	Enumerating connections to remote resources	Replaced by WNetEnumResource()
Domain API	NetGetDCName	Finding out what machine is acting as the domain controller	
Error Logging API	<Superseded>	Reading entries in the system log file	Replaced by Win32 Event Logging API
File API	NetFileEnum NetFileGetInfo NetFileClose	Finding out who currently has files in use, forcing file closing	
Global Group API	NetGroupAdd NetGroupAddUser NetGroupEnum NetGroupGetInfo NetGroupSetInfo NetGroupDel NetGroupDelUser NetGroupGetUsers NetGroupSetUsers	Managing global groups in a domain	Implements the same calls as the LAN Manager Group API, but distinction between local and global groups is new in Windows NT. Global groups only have relevance under Windows NT Advanced Server.
Local Group API	NetLocalGroupAdd NetLocalGroupAddMember NetLocalGroupEnum NetLocalGroupGetInfo NetLocalGroupSetInfo NetLocalGroupDel NetLocalGroupDelMember NetLocalGroupGetMembers NetLocalGroupSetMembers	Managing local groups	New in Windows NT. Functions that manipulate group members use SIDs, not user names.
Message API	NetMessageNameAdd NetMessageNameEnum NetMessageNameGetInfo NetMessageNameDel NetMessageBufferSend	Sending messages to users on the network	

Table 16-1.   LAN Manager API for Windows NT (continued)

Category	Component Functions	Purpose	Additional Comments
Remote Utility API	NetRemoteTOD	Getting current time from a machine on the network	
Replicator API	NetReplGetInfo NetReplSetInfo	Controlling the NT Directory Replicator service	New in Windows NT
Replicator Export Directory API	NetReplExportDirAdd NetReplExportDirDel NetReplExportDirEnum NetReplExportDirGetInfo NetReplExportDirSetInfo NetReplExportDirLock NetReplExportDirUnlock	Setting up directories for export to other machines	New in Windows NT
Replicator Import Directory API	NetReplImportDirAdd NetReplImportDirDel NetReplImportDirEnum NetReplImportDirGetInfo NetReplImportDirSetInfo NetReplImportDirLock NetReplImportDirUnlock	Setting up directories to be imported from other machines	New in Windows NT
Schedule Service API	NetScheduleJobAdd NetScheduleJobDel NetScheduleJobEnum NetScheduleJobGetInfo	Scheduling jobs for local or remote execution at given times	New in Windows NT
Server API	NetServerEnum NetServerGetInfo NetServerSetInfo NetServerDiskEnum	Enumerating and configuring servers, getting operating statistics.	
Service API	<Superseded>	Controlling, starting, and configuring LAN Manager services	Replaced by Win32 Services API
Session API	NetSessionEnum NetSessionGetInfo NetSessionDel	Manipulating sessions, which consist of one or more connections between a resource user and its provider	
Share API	NetShareAdd NetShareEnum NetShareGetInfo NetShareSetInfo NetShareDel NetShareCheck	Managing shared resources	

Table 16-1.   LAN Manager API for Windows NT (continued)

Category	Component Functions	Purpose	Additional Comments
Statistics API	NetStatisticsGet	Retrieving operating statistics for Server and Redirector	Information retrieved is a subset of that available from Performance Monitoring
Transport API	NetServerTransportAdd NetServerTransportDel NetServerTransportEnum NetWkstaTransportAdd NetWkstaTransportDel NetWkstaTransportEnum	Managing bindings between NT Server and Redirector and underlying transport layer	New in Windows NT
Use API	\<Superseded>	Connecting to remote shared resources	Replaced by Win32 WNet API
User API	NetUserAdd NetUserEnum NetUserGetInfo NetUserSetInfo NetUserDel NetUserGetGroups NetUserGetLocalGroups NetUserSetGroups	Managing user accounts	Distinction between global groups and local groups is new in Windows NT
User Modal API	NetUserModalsGet NetUserModalsSet	Controlling user logon settings and restrictions	
Workstation and Workstation User API	NetWkstaGetInfo NetWkstaSetInfo NetWkstaUserGetInfo NetWkstaUserSetInfo NetWkstaUserEnum	Getting and setting workstation and user configuration information, finding out what users are logged in on a workstation	Workstation User API is new in Windows NT

I think you will agree that the API in Table 16-1 does not appear at all obsolescent. In reality, there's a great deal of power available here. I'll stick my neck out and say that this is one of the most significant APIs that NT has to offer.

General Considerations

Before delving into the specifics of the APIs I plan to use, I want to mention a couple of things that apply to the entire LAN Manager API as it is implemented under NT.

Unicode Only

First, only the Unicode character set is supported. For this reason, you will see in my code that I have used the WCHAR and LPWSTR types, which explicitly select Unicode, rather than TCHAR and LPTSTR. I also define the constants UNICODE and _UNICODE, but with these APIs, there can be no question.

Buffer Allocation

Second, the NT implementation corrects one of the most awkward features of the OS/2 LAN Manager API. Previously, when you asked LAN Manager for information, you had to provide a large enough buffer. Otherwise, the function would return ERROR_MORE_DATA. It would also tell you how much memory you needed. In the code in *Windows Network Programming* (Chapter 11), I first pass a zero-length buffer to find out how much memory to allocate, then allocate it and call the function again. The NT LAN Manager API set allocates the output buffer for you. All you have to do is pass it a pointer to a pointer, then call NetApiBufferFree() to release the memory when you're through. This is much more convenient and simplifies coding quite a bit, as you can see by comparing the listings presented here with those in *Windows Network Programming*.

Global Groups and Local Groups

The distinction between global groups and local groups is new to Windows NT. It has been introduced to support the NT Advanced Server notion of trusted domains. Briefly, the difference is that global groups are used to export users from the current domain; local groups, on the other hand, import users into the domain. Local groups can also be used to give domain users rights on individual NT workstations. Local groups may contain global groups (and other local groups) as members. Global groups may only contain users. Permissions can only be granted to local groups.

When you install an NT workstation, NT automatically creates the local groups Administrators, Backup Operators, Guests, Power Users, Replicator, and Users. On an NT Advanced Server, there is no Power Users group, and three additional local groups: Account Operators, Print Operators, and Server Operators. The invisible group Everyone is also created; it contains all users defined in the domain, whether they are administrators, normal users, or guests. The Everyone group is invisible in the sense that you don't see it when you are enumerating groups, and User Manager doesn't show it.

However, as noted in Chapter 14, you can grant and refuse rights to Everyone, and NT normally gives Everyone a default set of rights to files and directories you create. NT workstations have only one global group, called None.

An NT Advanced Server will also have the global groups Domain Users and Domain Admins, and they will automatically be members of the local groups Users and Administrators on all stations in the domain. All NT Advanced Servers in a domain share the same security accounts database. One machine is designated the domain controller; the others become backup controllers so that if the domain controller goes down, the others can fill in for it. The domain controller distributes replicas of the security database to all the backup controllers at periodic intervals.

Figure 16-1 shows the groups on my NT Advanced Server machine. This is a screen shot taken in WNETSVCS. It includes both local and global groups.

Figure 16-2 shows the same screen for an NT workstation.

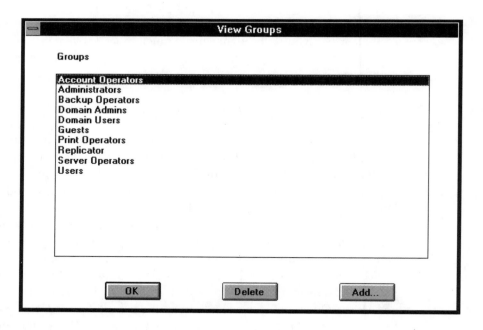

Figure 16-1.   Groups on an NT Advanced Server

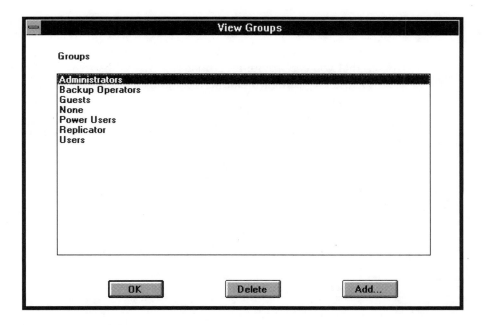

Figure 16-2.   Groups on an NT Workstation

LAN Manager had no concept of global and local groups. For this reason, the old calls now map to operations on global groups, and a new API set, the Local Group category, has been introduced. All the old LAN Manager group functions take user names as arguments (when you add a member, for instance). The NT local group functions take SIDs. The API I implement will take user names and translate them to SIDs by calling LookupAccountName(). User-level applications shouldn't have to deal with SIDs.

Machine Name Arguments

Almost all the LAN Manager functions take the target computer name as their first argument. A NULL pointer indicates the local machine. If the target is remote, the name must be in UNC format: \\<machine name>. I will give the calling application a little leeway; if it doesn't prepend \\ to the computer name, I will. Given the statistics we have seen on the superior performance of local Named Pipes and the *ncalrpc* protocol, I include a check to see if the target computer is the current one, then pass the machine name as NULL if it is.

Levels of Detail

Most of the LAN Manager calls include an argument specifying the level of detail that you are providing, or that you want to be returned. Zero represents the lowest level, often including no more than the object name. Each level corresponds to a structure type named for the object in question and the level of detail. For instance, these are the *typedefs* for the USER_INFO_0 and USER_INFO_1 structures from \MSTOOLS\H\LMACCESS.H.

```
typedef struct _USER_INFO_0
{
    LPWSTR   usri0_name;
} USER_INFO_0, *PUSER_INFO_0, *LPUSER_INFO_0;

typedef struct _USER_INFO_1
{
    LPWSTR   usri1_name;
    LPWSTR   usri1_password;
    DWORD    usri1_password_age;
    DWORD    usri1_priv;
    LPWSTR   usri1_home_dir;
    LPWSTR   usri1_comment;
    DWORD    usri1_flags;
    LPWSTR   usri1_script_path;
} USER_INFO_1, *PUSER_INFO_1, *LPUSER_INFO_1;
```

Include Files and Link Libraries

In any source modules you write that call LAN Manager functions, you need include only LM.H, found in \MSTOOLS\H. Like WINDOWS.H, it is a master header file that includes all the other headers needed to use the LAN Manager API. With OS/2 LAN Manager, you had to define constants before you included the file. These constants influenced which of the secondary headers were included. This is not the case with NT; LM.H includes everybody, no matter what.

All the LAN Manager API is contained in NETAPI32.DLL, so you only need to link with NETAPI32.LIB, which is in \MSTOOLS\LIB, along with most of your other link libraries. This is not done for you by the macros in NTWIN32.MAK; you must specify it in your linker arguments. You can refer to my make file for the WNet LAN Manager DLL (\NTNET\CODE\LANMAN\WNETLM.MAK) to see how to do this.

Finding Out about Servers

NetServerEnum() reports the servers that are present on the network. It also illustrates the standard format for the Windows NT LAN Manager enumeration functions.

```
NET_API_STATUS NET_API_FUNCTION
NetServerEnum (
    LPTSTR      lpszServerName,
    DWORD       dwLevel,
    LPBYTE      *lplpBuffer,
    DWORD       dwPreferredMaxLength,
    LPDWORD     lpdwEntriesRead,
    LPDWORD     lpdwTotalEntries,
    DWORD       dwServerType,
    LPTSTR      lpszDomain,
    LPDWORD     lpdwResumeHandle
    );
```

As always, *lpszServerName* indicates the server where the function is to execute, though with NetServerEnum(), this does not seem that important. The request will be directed to the machine acting as the master browser for the domain. *dwLevel* is the level of information you want returned, and must be 100 or 101. The corresponding structures are a SERVER_INFO_100 and SERVER_INFO_101.

```
typedef struct _SERVER_INFO_100
{
    DWORD           sv100_platform_id;
    LPTSTR          sv100_name;
} SERVER_INFO_100, *PSERVER_INFO_100, *LPSERVER_INFO_100;

typedef struct _SERVER_INFO_101
{
    DWORD           sv101_platform_id;  .
    LPTSTR          sv101_name;
    DWORD           sv101_version_major;
    DWORD           sv101_version_minor;
    DWORD           sv101_type;
    LPTSTR          sv101_comment;
} SERVER_INFO_101, *PSERVER_INFO_101, *LPSERVER_INFO_101;
```

sv101_platform_id can be either SV_PLATFORM_ID_OS2 or SV_PLATFORM_ID_NT, to indicate whether the reported server is running

OS/2 LAN Manager or Windows NT Advanced Server. The fields we mainly want to find out about are *sv101_name*, the server's name, and *sv101_type*, a set of bit flags describing the operating system configuration. These are some of the most common flags:

- SV_TYPE_WORKSTATION (0x00000001): The host is running the Redirector software.
- SV_TYPE_SERVER (0x00000002): The host is running the Server software.
- SV_TYPE_SQLSERVER (0x00000004): The host is running SQL Server.
- SV_TYPE_DOMAIN_CTRL (0x00000008): The host is an NT Advanced Server machine acting as the primary domain controller (the machine that adjudicates logon requests).
- SV_TYPE_DOMAIN_BAKCTRL (0x00000010): The machine is an NT Advanced Server machine serving as a backup domain controller (waiting in the wings to take over should the primary domain controller go down).
- SV_TYPE_AFP (0x00000040): A machine that understands the Apple FileTalk Protocol.
- SV_TYPE_NOVELL (0x00000080): A NetWare server.
- SV_TYPE_SERVER_UNIX (0x00000800): A UNIX machine.
- SV_TYPE_NT (0x00001000): An NT machine, either Advanced Server or standard NT.
- SV_TYPE_WFW (0x00002000): A Windows for Workgroups workstation.
- SV_TYPE_SERVER_OSF (0x00100000): A computer running the OSF operating system.
- SV_TYPE_SERVER_VMS (0x00200000): A VMS host.

You can pass SV_TYPE_ALL (0xFFFFFFFF) to NetServerEnum() to request enumeration of all types of servers.

My machines report the following types:

- NT Advanced Server: SV_TYPE_MASTER_BROWSER | SV_TYPE_NT | SV_TYPE_DOMAIN_CTRL | SV_TYPE_SERVER | SV_TYPE_WORKSTATION.
- NT workstation: SV_TYPE_POTENTIAL_BROWSER | SV_TYPE_BACKUP_BROWSER | SV_TYPE_NT | SV_TYPE_SERVER | SV_TYPE_WORKSTATION.

- Windows for Workgroups station: SV_TYPE_POTENTIAL_ BROWSER | SV_TYPE_WFW | SV_TYPE_SERVER | SV_TYPE_WORKSTATION.

Getting back to the arguments to NetServerEnum(), the *lplpBuffer*, *dwPreferredMaxLength*, *lpdwEntriesRead, lpdwTotalEntries*, and *lpdwResumeHandle* are common to most of the NT LAN Manager enumerators. *lplpBuffer* is a pointer to an LPBYTE, for which NT allocates the requisite amount of memory. On return from NetServerEnum(), it will point to an array of SERVER_INFO_100 or SERVER_INFO_101 structures. *dwPreferred MaxLength* is your preference for the maximum amount of data to be returned, but NT may ignore it. *lpdwEntriesRead* points to a variable that captures the number of elements in the output array. *lpdwTotalEntries* is not significant for NT. OS/2 LAN Manager uses the equivalent argument to tell you how many entries you need to allocate memory for. If *lpdwResumeHandle* is not NULL, it points to a DWORD that you initialize to zero. This permits you to call NetServerEnum() several times in a loop if necessary. After the first call, it is automatically reset.

The *lpszDomain* argument indicates the domain whose servers you want to enumerate, with NULL saying that you want to enumerate all available domains.

WNetEnumServers()

The function I provide, WNetEnumServers(), calls NetServerEnum() and asks it to enumerate the types of servers requested by the caller. It works like a standard Windows enumeration function: for each server it finds, it invokes a callback function, which I type as a SERVERENUMPROC in \NTNET\CODE\WNETAPI.H.

```
typedef BOOL (CALLBACK *SERVERENUMPROC)
              (LPWSTR lpszServerName, DWORD wServerType);
```

The callback is passed the server name and the type mask returned by NetServerEnum().

Here is the listing for \NTNET\CODE\LANMAN\WNETESRV.CPP, containing WNetEnumServers(). Notice the call to NetApiBufferFree() to release the memory allocated by NetServerEnum().

```
/********
*
*  WNETESRV.CPP
*
*  Copyright (c) 1993-1994 Ralph P. Davis, All Rights Reserved
*
********/


/*===== Includes =====*/

#define UNICODE
#define _UNICODE
#include "wnetapi.h"
#include <lm.h>


/*===== Function Definitions =====*/

BOOL WINAPI WNetEnumServers(LPWSTR lpszDomain,
                            DWORD  dwServerType,
                            SERVERENUMPROC lpServerEnumProc)
{
    LPSERVER_INFO_101 lpServerInfo;
    LPWSTR *lpBuffer;
    DWORD dwEntries, dwTotal;
    DWORD i;

    if (NetServerEnum(NULL, 101, (LPBYTE *) &lpBuffer, 65536,
                   &dwEntries, &dwTotal,
                   SV_TYPE_ALL, lpszDomain, NULL) ==
            NERR_Success)
        {
        lpServerInfo = (SERVER_INFO_101 *) lpBuffer;
        for (i = 0; i < dwEntries; ++i)
            {
            if (!lpServerEnumProc(lpServerInfo[i].sv101_name,
                    lpServerInfo[i].sv101_type))
                break;
            }
        }
    NetApiBufferFree(lpBuffer);

    return TRUE;
}
```

WNETSVCS calls WNetEnumServers() with a NULL domain and the type
SV_TYPE_ALL, to request enumeration of all known servers:

```
if (!WNetEnumServers(NULL, SV_TYPE_ALL,
    (SERVERENUMPROC) ServerEnumProc))
```

The callback function, ServerEnumProc(), puts the server names into a listbox and reports the type of the currently selected server in a static text field at the top of the dialog box that you see in Figure 16-3.

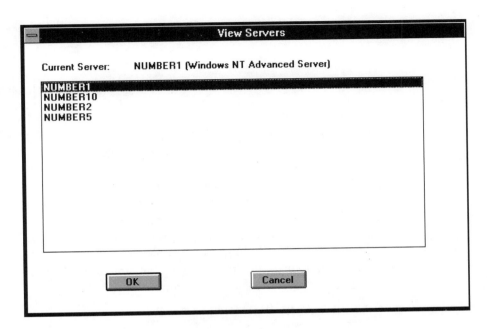

Figure 16-3.   **WNETSVCS View Servers Dialog Box**

Managing Users

A system administrator normally needs to perform three user-related tasks:

- adding new users
- deleting existing users
- listing current users

The LAN Manager API provides a function for each of these: NetUserAdd(), NetUserDel(), and NetUserEnum().

Adding a User

Here is the prototype for NetUserAdd(), also from LMACCESS.H.

```
NET_API_STATUS NET_API_FUNCTION
NetUserAdd (
    LPWSTR      lpszServerName,
    DWORD       dwLevel,
    LPBYTE      lpBuffer,
    LPDWORD     lpdwParameterInError
    );
```

   lpszServerName designates the target machine, with NULL meaning the local computer. As I said above, if it is not NULL, it must be preceded by \\. *dwLevel* indicates the level of detail you are providing. It must be one, two, or three, corresponding to a USER_INFO_1, USER_INFO_2, or USER_INFO_3 structure. Levels two and three provide a great deal of detail describing the user's login profile, but a *dwLevel* of one is sufficient to create a new user. You can use the User Modals API group to tailor the user's profile more precisely. *lpBuffer* points to the structure appropriate to the level of detail you are providing. *lpdwParameterInError* can be useful in tracking mistakes you make. If NetUserAdd() returns ERROR_IN-VALID_PARAMETER (87), the variable pointed to by *lpdwParameter-InError* will tell you which field of the input structure was incorrect. For the USER_INFO_1, the possible values are:

- USER_NAME_PARMNUM (1)
- USER_PASSWORD_PARMNUM (3)
- USER_PASSWORD_AGE_PARMNUM (4)
- USER_PRIV_PARMNUM (5)
- USER_HOME_DIR_PARMNUM (6)
- USER_COMMENT_PARMNUM (7)
- USER_FLAGS_PARMNUM (8)
- USER_SCRIPT_PATH_PARMNUM (9)

WNetAddUser(). Like all the APIs that I present in this chapter, WNetAddUser() is intended to be network-independent. In *Windows Network Programming*, I implement it on top of NetWare, LAN Manager, and Banyan VINES. Here, I provide only an NT version, since it is my policy to not cover third-party software. The code is in \NTNET\CODE\ LANMAN\WNETAUSR.CPP.

```
/********
*
* WNETAUSR.CPP
*
* Copyright (c) 1992-1994 Ralph P. Davis, All Rights Reserved
*
********/


/*===== Includes =====*/

#include "wnetapi.h"


/*===== Function Definitions =====*/

BOOL WINAPI WNetAddUser(LPWSTR lpszServerName,
                        LPWSTR lpszUserName,
                        LPWSTR lpszPassword)
{
   USER_INFO_1 UserInfo;
   NET_API_STATUS dwRetcode;
   DWORD dwErrorParm;
   WCHAR szServerName[MAX_COMPUTERNAME_LENGTH + 1];

   if (IsMyComputerName(lpszServerName))
      lpszServerName = NULL;
   else if (*lpszServerName != L'\\')
      {
      lstrcpy(szServerName, L"\\\\");
      lstrcat(szServerName, lpszServerName);
      lpszServerName = szServerName;
      }

   ZeroMemory(&UserInfo, sizeof (USER_INFO_1));

   UserInfo.usri1_name = lpszUserName;

   UserInfo.usri1_password = lpszPassword;

   UserInfo.usri1_priv =  USER_PRIV_USER;
   UserInfo.usri1_flags = UF_SCRIPT | UF_PASSWD_NOTREQD;

   dwRetcode = NetUserAdd(lpszServerName, 1, (LPBYTE) &UserInfo,
           &dwErrorParm);
   return (dwRetcode == NERR_Success ||
           dwRetcode == NERR_UserExists);
}
```

I fill in the fields of the USER_INFO_1 structure with all the required information. In *Windows Network Programming*, I included an additional argument specifying whether the user was to be given administrative status or not. If so, I set the *usri1_priv* field to USER_PRIV_ADMIN. However, this causes NetUserAdd() to fail in NT. In order to give users administrative status, you have to add them to either the Administrators local group or the Domain Admins global group, which is itself a member of Administrators.

Deleting a User

NetUserDel() is a very simple function.

```
NET_API_STATUS NET_API_FUNCTION
NetUserDel (
    LPWSTR      lpszServerName,
    LPWSTR      lpszUserName
     );
```

It removes user *lpszUserName* from the security accounts database on *lpszServerName*.

WNetDeleteUser(). WNetDeleteUser() reflects the simplicity of NetUserDel(). Most of the code is devoted to normalizing the server name— passing it as NULL if I'm targeting the local machine, and adding two backslashes otherwise.

```
/********
*
*  WNETDUSR.CPP
*
*  Copyright (c) 1992-1994 Ralph P. Davis, All Rights Reserved
*
********/


/*===== Includes =====*/

#include "wnetapi.h"


/*===== Function Definitions =====*/

BOOL WINAPI WNetDeleteUser(LPWSTR lpszServerName,
                           LPWSTR lpszUserName)
```

```
{
    NET_API_STATUS dwRetcode;
    WCHAR szServerName[MAX_COMPUTERNAME_LENGTH + 1];

    if (IsMyComputerName(lpszServerName))
        lpszServerName = NULL;
    else if (*lpszServerName != L'\\')
        {
        lstrcpy(szServerName, L"\\\\");
        lstrcat(szServerName, lpszServerName);
        lpszServerName = szServerName;
        }

    dwRetcode = NetUserDel(lpszServerName, lpszUserName);

    return (dwRetcode == NERR_Success ||
            dwRetcode == NERR_UserNotFound);
}
```

Enumerating Users

NetUserEnum() allocates memory for an array of USER_INFO_X structures, where X represents the level of detail you want.

```
NET_API_STATUS NET_API_FUNCTION
NetUserEnum (
    LPWSTR      lpszServerName,
    DWORD       dwLevel,
    DWORD       dwFilter,
    LPBYTE      *lplpBuffer,
    DWORD       dwPreferredMaxLength,
    LPDWORD     lpdwEntriesRead,
    LPDWORD     lpdwTotalEntries,
    LPDWORD     lpdwResumeHandle
    );
```

There are several levels of detail you can request with *dwLevel*. Level zero returns an array of USER_INFO_0 structures, which contain a single element, a pointer to the user name.

```
typedef struct _USER_INFO_0
{
    LPWSTR    usri0_name;
} USER_INFO_0, *PUSER_INFO_0, *LPUSER_INFO_0;
```

dwFilter can be used to limit the enumeration to certain types of users. Passing it as zero requests all users. However, when you do this on an NT Advanced Server, you get strange-looking user names that are generated from the names of the NT computers in the domain. These are known as **trust accounts**. A workstation trust account is created for each workstation in the domain. These accounts are enumerated if you set *dwFilter* to FILTER_WORKSTATION_TRUST_ACCOUNT. By the same token, a server trust account is created for any NT Advanced Server machine. This corresponds to the filter FILTER_SERVER_TRUST_ACCOUNT. Specifying FILTER_NORMAL_ACCOUNT gives you the same users shown by the NT User Manager, so it is the preferred value to use to avoid startling your users.

lplpBuffer, dwPreferredMaxLength, lpdwEntriesRead, lpdwTotalEntries, and *lpdwResumeHandle* are the standard arguments for the enumeration functions under NT. They behave here just as they do for NetServerEnum(), described earlier in this chapter.

WNetEnumUsers(). My function WNetEnumUsers() calls NetUserEnum() to list users on a given machine. It asks for level zero, as it only needs to report the user names. It passes the filter of FILTER_NORMAL_ ACCOUNT, which lists standard users. The callback function that it invokes is a USERENUMPROC, a type that I define:

```
typedef BOOL (CALLBACK *USERENUMPROC)(LPWSTR lpszServerName,
                                      LPWSTR lpszUserName);
```

Here is the file \NTNET\CODE\LANMAN\WNETEUSR.CPP, with WNetEnumUsers().

```
/********
*
* WNETEUSR.CPP
*
* Copyright (c) 1993-1994 Ralph P. Davis, All Rights Reserved
*
********/


/*===== Includes =====*/

#define UNICODE
#define _UNICODE
#include "wnetapi.h"
```

```
/*===== Function Definitions =====*/

BOOL WINAPI WNetEnumUsers(LPWSTR lpszServerName,
                          USERENUMPROC lpUserEnumProc)
{
    LPUSER_INFO_0 lpBuffer;
    DWORD   dwEntries, dwTotal;
    DWORD   i;
    BOOL    bRetcode = FALSE;
    NET_API_STATUS dwRetcode;
    WCHAR szServerName[MAX_COMPUTERNAME_LENGTH + 1];

    if (IsMyComputerName(lpszServerName))
       lpszServerName = NULL;
    else if (*lpszServerName != L'\\')
       {
       lstrcpy(szServerName, L"\\\\");
       lstrcat(szServerName, lpszServerName);
       lpszServerName = szServerName;
       }

    if ((dwRetcode = NetUserEnum(lpszServerName, 0,
                     FILTER_NORMAL_ACCOUNT,
                     (LPBYTE *) &lpBuffer,
                 65536, &dwEntries,
                 &dwTotal, NULL)) == NERR_Success)
       {
       // lpBuffer contains an array of pointers to
       // USER_INFO_0 structures
       bRetcode = TRUE;
       for (i = 0; i < dwEntries; ++i)
          {
          if (!lpUserEnumProc(lpszServerName, lpBuffer[i].usri0_name))
             break;
          }
       }
    NetApiBufferFree(lpBuffer);
    return bRetcode;
}
```

Figure 16-4 shows you the WNETSVCS View Users Dialog Box listing the users on my Advanced Server machine. WNETSVCS populates the listbox by calling WNetEnumUsers().

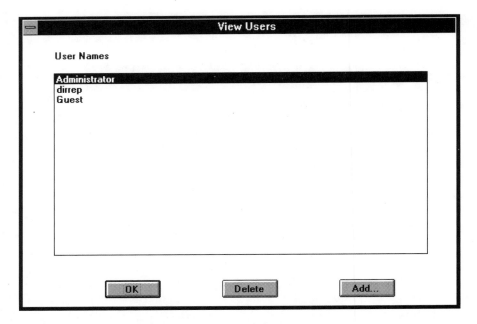

Figure 16-4.   WNETSVCS View Users Dialog Box

Managing Groups

An administrator needs to do the same things with groups as with users:
create them, delete them, and list them. Because NT has two types of groups,
there are two sets of matching functions: NetGroupAdd() and
NetLocalGroupAdd(), NetGroupDel() and NetLocalGroupDel(), and
NetGroupEnum() and NetLocalGroupEnum(). To repeat, the difference
between the two types of groups is that global groups are used to export
users to other domains, and local groups are used to import users and groups
either into the current domain or onto an NT workstation participating in a
domain. Global groups have meaning only in an NT Advanced Server
domain. Permission can be granted only to local groups.

Adding a Group

NetGroupAdd() creates a new global group on the specified server.
NetLocalGroupAdd() has the same syntax as NetGroupAdd(), but creates a
local group instead. By the way, it is not an error to create a global group on
an NT workstation. It is just an empty act because you cannot export the
group anywhere else.

```
NET_API_STATUS NET_API_FUNCTION
NetGroupAdd (
    LPWSTR     lpServerName,
    DWORD      dwLevel,
    LPBYTE     lpBuffer,
    LPDWORD    lpdwParameterInError
    );

NET_API_STATUS NET_API_FUNCTION
NetLocalGroupAdd (
    LPWSTR     lpServerName,
    DWORD      dwLevel,
    LPBYTE     lpBuffer,
    LPDWORD    lpdwParameterInError
    );
```

dwLevel may be from zero to two for NetGroupAdd(), corresponding to a GROUP_INFO_0, GROUP_INFO_1, or GROUP_INFO_2 structure. The level may be only zero or one for NetLocalGroupAdd(). Here, the data types are LOCALGROUP_INFO_0 and LOCALGROUP_INFO_1. Both level-zero structures contain just the group name. Level one adds a descriptive comment. GROUP_INFO_2 contains two additional fields, one for a group ID and one for its attributes. Unfortunately, there is no explanation of what these fields mean.

WNetAddGroup(). WNetAddGroup(), contained in \NTNET\CODE\ LANMAN\WNETAGRP.CPP, calls either NetGroupAdd() or NetLocal-GroupAdd(), depending on the setting of its *bLocal* argument.

```
/********
 *
 * WNETAGRP.CPP
 *
 * Copyright (c) 1992-1994 Ralph P. Davis, All Rights Reserved
 *
 ********/


/*===== Includes =====*/

#include "wnetapi.h"


/*===== Function Definitions =====*/
```

```
BOOL WINAPI WNetAddGroup(LPWSTR lpszServerName,
                         LPWSTR lpszGroupName,
                         BOOL   bLocal)
{
   NET_API_STATUS dwRetcode;
   WCHAR szServerName[MAX_COMPUTERNAME_LENGTH + 1];

   if (IsMyComputerName(lpszServerName))
      lpszServerName = NULL;
   else if (*lpszServerName != L'\\')
      {
      lstrcpy(szServerName, L"\\\\");
      lstrcat(szServerName, lpszServerName);
      lpszServerName = szServerName;
      }

   if (bLocal)
      {
      LOCALGROUP_INFO_0 LocalGroupInfo;

      LocalGroupInfo.lgrpi0_name = lpszGroupName;
      dwRetcode = NetLocalGroupAdd(lpszServerName, 0,
                  (LPBYTE) &LocalGroupInfo, NULL);
      }
   else
      {
      GROUP_INFO_0 GroupInfo;

      GroupInfo.grpi0_name = lpszGroupName;
      dwRetcode = NetGroupAdd(lpszServerName, 0,
                  (LPBYTE) &GroupInfo, NULL);
      }
   return (dwRetcode == NERR_Success ||
           dwRetcode == NERR_GroupExists);
}
```

Deleting Groups

NetGroupDel() and NetLocalGroupDel() are a syntactically identical pair of functions that delete global and local groups, respectively.

```
NET_API_STATUS NET_API_FUNCTION
NetGroupDel (
    LPWSTR    lpszServerName,
    LPWSTR    lpszGroupName
    );
```

```
      NET_API_STATUS NET_API_FUNCTION
      NetLocalGroupDel (
          LPWSTR    lpszServerName,
          LPWSTR    lpszGroupName
          );
```

WNetDeleteGroup().   WNetDeleteGroup() (from \NTNET\CODE\ LANMAN\WNETDGRP.CPP) calls either NetGroupDel() or NetLocal-GroupDel(), again basing its decision on the *bLocal* input parameter.

```
/********
 *
 * WNETDGRP.CPP
 *
 * Copyright (c) 1992-1994 Ralph P. Davis, All Rights Reserved
 *
 ********/


/*===== Includes =====*/

#include "wnetapi.h"


/*===== Function Definitions =====*/

BOOL WINAPI WNetDeleteGroup(LPWSTR lpszServerName,
                            LPWSTR lpszGroupName,
                            BOOL   bLocal)
{
   NET_API_STATUS dwRetcode;
   WCHAR szServerName[MAX_COMPUTERNAME_LENGTH + 1];

   if (IsMyComputerName(lpszServerName))
      lpszServerName = NULL;
   else if (*lpszServerName != L'\\')
      {
      lstrcpy(szServerName, L"\\\\");
      lstrcat(szServerName, lpszServerName);
      lpszServerName = szServerName;
      }

   if (bLocal)
      dwRetcode = NetLocalGroupDel(lpszServerName, lpszGroupName);
   else
      dwRetcode = NetGroupDel(lpszServerName, lpszGroupName);
```

```
    return (dwRetcode == NERR_Success ||
            dwRetcode == NERR_GroupNotFound);
}
```

Enumerating Groups

NetGroupEnum() and NetLocalGroupEnum() are also twin functions that behave exactly like the other enumerators you have already seen, NetServerEnum() and NetUserEnum().

```
NET_API_STATUS NET_API_FUNCTION
NetGroupEnum (
     LPWSTR        lpServerName,
     DWORD         dwLevel,
     LPBYTE        *lplpBuffer,
     DWORD         dwPreferredMaxLength,
     LPDWORD       lpdwEntriesRead,
     LPDWORD       lpdwTotalEntries,
     LPDWORD       lpdwResumeHandle
     );

NET_API_STATUS NET_API_FUNCTION
NetLocalGroupEnum (
     LPWSTR        lpServerName,
     DWORD         dwLevel,
     LPBYTE        *lplpBuffer,
     DWORD         dwPreferredMaxLength,
     LPDWORD       lpdwEntriesRead,
     LPDWORD       lpdwTotalEntries,
     LPDWORD       lpdwResumeHandle
     );
```

Only levels zero and one may be requested here. NetGroupEnum() will return an array of GROUP_INFO_0 or GROUP_INFO_1 structures, and NetLocalGroupEnum() returns LOCALGROUP_INFO_0 and LOCALGROUP_INFO_1.

WNetEnumGroups(). To make sure it enumerates all groups on the target server, WNetEnumGroups() calls one function, then the other. Its callback function is a GROUPENUMPROC.

```
typedef BOOL (CALLBACK *GROUPENUMPROC)(LPWSTR lpszServerName,
                                       LPWSTR lpszGroupName,
                                       BOOL   bLocal);
```

The *bLocal* item passed to the callback tells it what kind of group is being listed. WNETSVCS puts the group name into a listbox and stores the group type (local or global) as listbox item data by sending the listbox an LB_SETITEMDATA message. When WNETSVCS needs to manipulate the group in some way—to delete it, for instance, or to add and remove members—it retrieves the *bLocal* flag by sending LB_GETITEMDATA to the selected item in the listbox.

```cpp
/********
*
* WNETEGRP.CPP
*
* Copyright (c) 1992-1994 Ralph P. Davis, All Rights Reserved
*
********/

/*===== Includes =====*/

#define UNICODE
#include "wnetapi.h"


/*===== Function Definitions =====*/

BOOL WINAPI WNetEnumGroups(LPWSTR lpszServerName,
                           GROUPENUMPROC lpGroupEnumProc)
{
   DWORD dwEntries, dwTotal;
   DWORD i;
   LPLOCALGROUP_INFO_0 lpGroupInfo;
   BOOL  bRetcode = FALSE;
   WCHAR szServerName[MAX_COMPUTERNAME_LENGTH + 1];

   if (IsMyComputerName(lpszServerName))
      lpszServerName = NULL;
   else if (*lpszServerName != L'\\')
      {
      lstrcpy(szServerName, L"\\\\");
      lstrcat(szServerName, lpszServerName);
      lpszServerName = szServerName;
      }

   // First, enumerate local groups
   if (NetLocalGroupEnum(lpszServerName, 0,
                (LPBYTE *) &lpGroupInfo, 65536,
                &dwEntries,
                &dwTotal, NULL) == NERR_Success)
```

```
        {
        bRetcode = TRUE;

        // lpBuffer contains an array of pointers to the
        // Group names
        for (i = 0; i < dwEntries; ++i)
            {
            if (!lpGroupEnumProc(lpszServerName,
                lpGroupInfo[i].lgrpi0_name, TRUE))
                break;
            }
        NetApiBufferFree(lpGroupInfo);
        }

    // Now, enumerate global groups
    if (NetGroupEnum(lpszServerName, 0,
            (LPBYTE *) &lpGroupInfo, 65536,
            &dwEntries,
            &dwTotal, NULL) == NERR_Success)
        {
        bRetcode = TRUE;

        // lpBuffer contains an array of pointers to the
        // Group names
        for (i = 0; i < dwEntries; ++i)
            {
            if (!lpGroupEnumProc(lpszServerName,
                lpGroupInfo[i].lgrpi0_name, FALSE))
                break;
            }
        NetApiBufferFree(lpGroupInfo);
        }

    return bRetcode;
    }
```

Associating Users and Groups

Groups have a major role to play in network administration. They make it much easier to assign permissions to users because you can group many related users into a few groups. Thus, you need to grant permissions only to a handful of groups, rather than to an enormous number of users. Also, if a user's organizational affiliation changes, you don't have to go all over your server trying to find files the user has rights to—you just change the group membership. Therefore, the functions that let you associate users and groups are very important. These functions are:

- NetGroupAddUser() and NetLocalGroupAddMember() add a new member to a group. The difference in the names is not insignificant: NetGroupAddUser() expects a user name, whereas NetLocal-GroupAddMember() requires the new member's SID.
- NetGroupDelUser() and NetLocalGroupDelMember() remove a group member.
- NetGroupGetUsers() and NetLocalGroupGetMembers() return arrays describing the current group members.

I implement the following functions on top of these base calls:

- WNetAddGroupMember()
- WNetDeleteGroupMember()
- WNetEnumGroupMembers()

Two other functions will also come in handy:

- WNetEnumMemberGroups() lists all the groups a given user belongs to.
- WNetIsUserGroupMember() tells us whether user X belongs to group Y.

Adding a User to a Group

NetGroupAddUser() and NetLocalGroupAddMember() are simple functions, as their prototypes show.

```
NET_API_STATUS NET_API_FUNCTION
NetGroupAddUser (
    LPWSTR    lpszServerName,
    LPWSTR    lpszGroupName,
    LPWSTR    lpszUserName
    );

NET_API_STATUS NET_API_FUNCTION
NetLocalGroupAddMember (
    LPWSTR    lpszServerName,
    LPWSTR    lpszGroupName,
    PSID      pMemberSID
    );
```

WNetAddGroupMember(). The only complication here is that NetLocalGroupAddMember() expects the new member's SID, and I want to support human-readable group names in WNetAddGroupMember(). This obliges me to call LookupAccountName() to convert the user's name to its

underlying SID. Once again, a boolean argument determines whether I call
NetGroupAddUser() or NetLocalGroupAddMember().

Here is the listing for \NTNET\CODE\LANMAN\WNETAMBR.CPP.

```
/********
*
* WNETAMBR.CPP
*
* Copyright (c) 1992-1994 Ralph P. Davis, All Rights Reserved
*
********/


/*===== Includes =====*/

#include "wnetapi.h"


/*===== Function Definitions =====*/

BOOL WINAPI WNetAddGroupMember(LPWSTR lpszServerName,
                               LPWSTR lpszGroupName,
                               BOOL   bLocal,
                               LPWSTR lpszUserName)
{
   NET_API_STATUS dwRetcode;
   WCHAR szServerName[MAX_COMPUTERNAME_LENGTH + 1];

   if (IsMyComputerName(lpszServerName))
      lpszServerName = NULL;
   else if (*lpszServerName != L'\\')
      {
      lstrcpy(szServerName, L"\\\\");
      lstrcat(szServerName, lpszServerName);
      lpszServerName = szServerName;
      }

   if (bLocal)
      {
      // Call LookupAccountName() to translate the
      // name to a SID

      BYTE  bySIDBuffer[1024];
      DWORD dwSIDSize = sizeof (bySIDBuffer);
      WCHAR szDomain[256];
      DWORD dwDomainSize = sizeof (szDomain);
      SID_NAME_USE SidNameUse;
```

```
    if (!LookupAccountNameW(lpszServerName,
                            lpszUserName,
                            (PSID) bySIDBuffer,
                            &dwSIDSize,
                            szDomain,
                            &dwDomainSize,
                            &SidNameUse))
        dwRetcode = FALSE;
    else
        dwRetcode = NetLocalGroupAddMember(
                        lpszServerName,
                        lpszGroupName,
                        bySIDBuffer);
    }
else
    {
    dwRetcode = NetGroupAddUser(lpszServerName, lpszGroupName,
                                lpszUserName);
    }

return (dwRetcode == NERR_Success ||
        dwRetcode == NERR_UserInGroup);
}
```

Deleting a Group Member

The delete functions, NetGroupDelUser() and NetLocalGroupDelMember(), are syntactically the same as NetGroupAddUser() and NetLocal-GroupAddMember(), with the latter function also requiring a SID, not a name.

```
NET_API_STATUS NET_API_FUNCTION
NetGroupDelUser (
    LPWSTR    lpszServerName,
    LPWSTR    lpszGroupName,
    LPWSTR    lpszUserName
    );


NET_API_STATUS NET_API_FUNCTION
NetLocalGroupDelMember (
    LPWSTR    lpszServerName,
    LPWSTR    lpszGroupName,
    PSID      pMemberSID
    );
```

WNetDeleteGroupMember(). This function is the mirror image of WNetAddGroupMember(); just use the opposite verb.

```
/********
 *
 * WNETDMBR.CPP
 *
 * Copyright (c) 1992-1994 Ralph P. Davis, All Rights Reserved
 *
 ********/


/*===== Includes =====*/

#include "wnetapi.h"


/*===== Function Definitions =====*/

BOOL WINAPI WNetDeleteGroupMember(LPWSTR lpszServerName,
                                  LPWSTR lpszGroupName,
                                  BOOL   bLocal,
                                  LPWSTR lpszUserName)
{
   NET_API_STATUS dwRetcode;
   BYTE bySIDBuffer[1024];
   DWORD dwSIDSize = sizeof (bySIDBuffer);
   WCHAR szDomain[256];
   DWORD dwDomainSize = sizeof (szDomain);
   SID_NAME_USE SidNameUse;
   WCHAR szServerName[MAX_COMPUTERNAME_LENGTH + 1];

   if (IsMyComputerName(lpszServerName))
      lpszServerName = NULL;
   else if (*lpszServerName != L'\\')
      {
      lstrcpy(szServerName, L"\\\\");
      lstrcat(szServerName, lpszServerName);
      lpszServerName = szServerName;
      }

   if (bLocal)
      {
      if (!LookupAccountNameW(lpszServerName,
                              lpszUserName,
                              (PSID) bySIDBuffer,
                              &dwSIDSize,
                              szDomain,
```

```
                        &dwDomainSize,
                        &SidNameUse))
            return FALSE;

        dwRetcode = NetLocalGroupDelMember(
                        lpszServerName,
                        lpszGroupName,
                        (PSID) bySIDBuffer);
        }
    else
        {
        dwRetcode = NetGroupDelUser(lpszServerName, lpszGroupName,
                                    lpszUserName);
        }
    return (dwRetcode == NERR_Success ||
            dwRetcode == NERR_UserNotInGroup);
}
```

Listing Group Members

Here again, I convert LAN Manager enumerators, where one call returns an
array of objects, to a Windows one, where for each object I invoke a callback
function. The two functions are NetGroupGetUsers() and
NetLocalGroupGetMembers().

NetGroupGetUsers() and NetLocalGroupGetMembers(). Here are the
prototypes for these two functions.

```
NET_API_STATUS NET_API_FUNCTION
NetGroupGetUsers (
    LPWSTR      lpszServerName,
    LPWSTR      lpszGroupName,
    DWORD       dwLevel,
    LPBYTE      *lplpBuffer,
    DWORD       dwPreferredMaxLength,
    LPDWORD     lpdwEntriesRead,
    LPDWORD     lpdwTotalEntries,
    LPDWORD     lpdwResumeHandle
    );

NET_API_STATUS NET_API_FUNCTION
NetLocalGroupGetMembers
    LPWSTR      lpszServerName,
    LPWSTR      lpszGroupName,
    DWORD       dwLevel,
    LPBYTE      *lplpBuffer,
```

```
    DWORD       dwPreferredMaxLength,
    LPDWORD     lpdwEntriesRead,
    LPDWORD     lpdwTotalEntries,
    LPDWORD     lpdwResumeHandle
    );
```

The array returned at **lplpBuffer* consists of GROUP_USERS_INFO_0 or GROUP_USERS_INFO_1 structures for NetGroupGetUsers(), and LOCALGROUP_MEMBERS_INFO_0 or LOCALGROUP_MEMBERS_ INFO_1 for NetLocalGroupGetMembers(). If we ask the latter function for level one, we don't have to worry about converting a SID to a name; the name is supplied in the structure.

```
typedef struct _LOCALGROUP_MEMBERS_INFO_1
{
    PSID          lgrmi1_sid;
    SID_NAME_USE  lgrmi1_sidusage;
    LPWSTR        lgrmi1_name;
} LOCALGROUP_MEMBERS_INFO_1;
```

The level-zero structure has only the SID.

For global groups, the GROUP_USERS_INFO_X structures report the user name. GROUP_USERS_INFO_1 includes attributes, but they are not explained anywhere; I have no idea what they pertain to.

```
typedef struct _GROUP_USERS_INFO_0 {
    LPWSTR  grui0_name;
} GROUP_USERS_INFO_0;

typedef struct _GROUP_USERS_INFO_1 {
    LPWSTR  grui1_name;
    DWORD   grui1_attributes;
} GROUP_USERS_INFO_1;
```

WNetEnumGroupMembers(). WNetEnumGroupMembers() just calls NetGroupGetUsers() or NetLocalGroupGetMembers(), depending on its *bLocal* argument, and reports everyone it encounters. The callback function is a GROUPMEMBERENUMPROC.

```
typedef BOOL (CALLBACK *GROUPMEMBERENUMPROC)(LPWSTR lpszServerName,
                                             LPWSTR lpszGroupName,
                                             LPWSTR lpszUserName);
```

```
/********
*
* WNETEMBR.CPP
*
* Copyright (c) 1992-1994 Ralph P. Davis, All Rights Reserved
*
********/


/*===== Includes =====*/

#include "wnetapi.h"


/*===== Function Definitions =====*/

BOOL WINAPI WNetEnumGroupMembers(LPWSTR lpszServerName,
                                 LPWSTR lpszGroupName,
                                 BOOL   bLocal,
                                 GROUPMEMBERENUMPROC
                                     lpGroupEnumProc)
{
   LPLOCALGROUP_MEMBERS_INFO_1 lpLocalGroupInfo = NULL;
   DWORD          dwEntriesRead = 0, dwTotalAvail = 0;
   DWORD          i;
   BOOL           bRetcode = FALSE;
   WCHAR szServerName[MAX_COMPUTERNAME_LENGTH + 1];

   if (IsMyComputerName(lpszServerName))
      lpszServerName = NULL;
   else if (*lpszServerName != L'\\')
      {
      lstrcpy(szServerName, L"\\\\");
      lstrcat(szServerName, lpszServerName);
      lpszServerName = szServerName;
      }

   if (bLocal)
      {
      bRetcode = TRUE;
      if (NetLocalGroupGetMembers(lpszServerName, lpszGroupName,
                         1,
                         (LPBYTE *) &lpLocalGroupInfo,
                         65536,
                         &dwEntriesRead,
                         &dwTotalAvail,
                         NULL) == NERR_Success)

         {
```

```
          for (i = 0; i < dwEntriesRead; ++i)
             {
              if (!lpGroupEnumProc(lpszServerName, lpszGroupName,
                              lpLocalGroupInfo[i].lgrmi1_name))
                 break;
             }
          NetApiBufferFree(lpLocalGroupInfo);
          }
      }
  else
     {
      LPGROUP_USERS_INFO_0 lpGroupInfo = NULL;

      if (NetGroupGetUsers(lpszServerName, lpszGroupName,
                        0,
                        (LPBYTE *) &lpGroupInfo, 65536,
                        &dwEntriesRead,
                        &dwTotalAvail,
                        NULL) == NERR_Success)
         {
          bRetcode = TRUE;
          for (i = 0; i < dwEntriesRead; ++i)
             {
              if (!lpGroupEnumProc(lpszServerName, lpszGroupName,
                              lpGroupInfo[i].grui0_name))
                 break;
             }
          NetApiBufferFree(lpGroupInfo);
          }
      }
  return bRetcode;
}
```

Determining If a User Belongs to a Group

Before discussing how to enumerate all the groups to which a user belongs, I want to show you how I determine if a user is already in a group or not. The procedure is to call WNetEnumGroupMembers() and have the callback function compare the enumerated users with the user I'm looking for. If it finds a match, it sets a flag and terminates the enumeration. In order to pass information to the callback function in a thread-safe way, I put both the user name that I want to pass to it and its return value into separate Thread Local Storage slots. The code is in \NTNET\CODE\LANMAN\WNETIMBR.CPP.

```
/******
 *
 * WNETIMBR.CPP
 *
 * Copyright (c) 1992-1994 Ralph P. Davis, All Rights Reserved
 *
 *******/


/*===== Includes =====*/

#include "wnetapi.h"


/*===== External Variables =====*/

extern DWORD dwLMTlsIndex[];


/*===== Function Definitions =====*/

BOOL WINAPI WNetIsUserGroupMember(LPWSTR lpszServerName,
                                  LPWSTR lpszGroupName,
                                  BOOL   bLocal,
                                  LPWSTR lpszUserName)
{
    BOOL bRetcode;

    TlsSetValue(dwLMTlsIndex[0], lpszUserName);
    TlsSetValue(dwLMTlsIndex[1], FALSE);

    bRetcode = WNetEnumGroupMembers(lpszServerName,
        lpszGroupName, bLocal,
        (GROUPMEMBERENUMPROC) IsUserGroupMember);

    if (!bRetcode)
        return FALSE;

    bRetcode = (BOOL) TlsGetValue(dwLMTlsIndex[1]);
    TlsSetValue(dwLMTlsIndex[0], NULL);
    TlsSetValue(dwLMTlsIndex[1], NULL);
    return bRetcode;
}

BOOL WINAPI IsUserGroupMember(LPWSTR lpszServer, LPWSTR lpszGroup,
                              LPWSTR lpszUser)
{
    if (lstrcmpiW(lpszUser,
```

```
                    (LPWSTR) TlsGetValue(dwLMTlsIndex[0])) == 0)
        {
      TlsSetValue(dwLMTlsIndex[1], (LPVOID) TRUE);
      return FALSE;          // End enumeration
        }
    else
      return TRUE;
}
```

Incidentally, these routines are built into the DLL WNETLM.DLL. The TLS indices are created when the DLL entry point is called.

Listing Member Groups

The functions of interest here are NetUserGetGroups() and NetUserGetLocalGroups(). These functions are not quite the same.

```
NET_API_STATUS NET_API_FUNCTION
NetUserGetGroups (
      LPWSTR      lpszServerName,
      LPWSTR      lpszUserName,
      DWORD       dwLevel,
      LPBYTE      *lplpBuffer,
      DWORD       dwPreferredMaxLength,
      LPDWORD     lpdwEntriesRead,
      LPDWORD     lpdwTotalEntries
      );

NET_API_STATUS NET_API_FUNCTION
NetUserGetLocalGroups (
      LPWSTR      lpszServerName,
      LPWSTR      lpszUserName,
      DWORD       dwLevel,
      DWORD       dwFlags,
      LPBYTE      *lplpBuffer,
      DWORD       dwPreferredMaxLength,
      LPDWORD     lpdwEntriesRead,
      LPDWORD     lpdwTotalEntries
      );
```

The first function populates an array of GROUP_USERS_INFO_0 or GROUP_USERS_INFO_1 structures. The second generates a LOCALGROUP_MEMBERS_INFO_0 or LOCALGROUP_MEMBERS_INFO_1 array. The *dwFlags* argument that you pass to NetUserGetLocalGroup() says whether to report groups that the user actually belongs to (by passing *dwFlags* as zero), or to also include groups to which she belongs by virtue of being in a group that belongs to it (in which case, you pass *dwFlags* as LG_INCLUDE_INDIRECT).

WNetEnumMemberGroups(). WNetEnumMemberGroups() calls NetUserGetLocalGroups() and NetUserGetGroups() to report the local and global groups to which a user belongs.

```
/********
*
* WNETEMGR.CPP
*
* Copyright (c) 1992-1994 Ralph P. Davis, All Rights Reserved
*
********/


/*===== Includes =====*/

#include "wnetapi.h"


/*===== Function Definitions =====*/
BOOL WINAPI WNetEnumMemberGroups(LPWSTR lpszServerName,
                                 LPWSTR lpszUserName,
                                 MEMBERGROUPENUMPROC
                                      lpGroupEnumProc)
{
   LPLOCALGROUP_USERS_INFO_0 lpLocalGroupInfo = NULL;
   DWORD          dwEntriesRead = 0,
                  dwTotalAvail = 0;
   DWORD          i;
   BOOL           bRetcode = FALSE;
   NET_API_STATUS dwRetcode;
   WCHAR szServerName[MAX_COMPUTERNAME_LENGTH + 1];

   if (IsMyComputerName(lpszServerName))
      lpszServerName = NULL;
   else if (*lpszServerName != L'\\')
      {
      lstrcpy(szServerName, L"\\\\");
      lstrcat(szServerName, lpszServerName);
      lpszServerName = szServerName;
      }

   if ((dwRetcode = NetUserGetLocalGroups(lpszServerName,
                         lpszUserName,
```

```
                                 0, 0,
                                 (LPBYTE *) &lpLocalGroupInfo,
                                 65536,
                                 &dwEntriesRead,
                                 &dwTotalAvail)) == NERR_Success)
        {
        bRetcode = TRUE;
        for (i = 0; i < dwEntriesRead; ++i)
            {
            if (!lpGroupEnumProc(lpszServerName, lpszUserName,
                                 lpLocalGroupInfo[i].lgrui0_name,
                                 TRUE))
                break;
            }
        NetApiBufferFree(lpLocalGroupInfo);
        }

    LPGROUP_INFO_0 lpGroupInfo = NULL;

    if (NetUserGetGroups(lpszServerName, lpszUserName,
                         0,
                         (LPBYTE *) &lpGroupInfo, 65536,
                         &dwEntriesRead,
                         &dwTotalAvail) == NERR_Success)
        {
        bRetcode = TRUE;
        for (i = 0; i < dwEntriesRead; ++i)
            {
            if (!lpGroupEnumProc(lpszServerName, lpszUserName,
                                 lpGroupInfo[i].grpi0_name,
                                 FALSE))
                break;
            }
        NetApiBufferFree(lpGroupInfo);
        }
    return bRetcode;
}
```

Conclusion

In enhancing and expanding the original OS/2 LAN Manager API, Microsoft
has improved it quite a bit. The LAN Manager API for Windows NT is a
rich, large, powerful, and versatile set of functions that deserves to be fully
supported and documented.

Suggested Readings

Ryan, Ralph. *Microsoft LAN Manager—A Programmer's Guide*. Redmond, WA: Microsoft Press, 1990.

Microsoft Corporation. *Microsoft LAN Manager Programmer's Reference*. Redmond, WA: Microsoft Press, 1990.

Microsoft Corporation. "Windows Networking Functions" in the *Win32 Online Help* (Windows NT 3.5). 1994.

Davis, Ralph. *Windows Network Programming*. Reading, MA: Addison-Wesley Publishing Company, 1993. Chapter 11.

Microsoft Corporation. *Microsoft Windows NT Advanced Server Concepts and Planning Guide*. Redmond, WA: Microsoft Corporation, 1993.

## Chapter 17

Additional NT Network APIs

Overview

In this final chapter, I discuss some API sets that are too important to ignore, but that, for one reason or another, do not merit a chapter of their own. The reasons are varied: the API may be of minor importance, but merits my telling you why I think so (for example, the built-in WNet API). The API may be powerful and useful, but waning in importance (for example, NetDDE). Or perhaps, the API is relevant, useful, and maybe even here to stay, but not centrally important (for example, the Messaging API (MAPI)).

Each of these APIs has some code devoted to it in either the Windows Network Manager or the WNETRSC application, included as \NTNET\CODE\WNETRSC\WNETRSC.CPP on the code disk. My plan is to cover these topics only briefly here, show you the relevant code excerpts, and let the APIs speak for themselves as much as possible.

The Built-In WNet Functions

The Windows WNet functions have been around for a long time. They were originally introduced in Windows 3.0 as functions in the network driver, which you could access just by loading the driver or by generating an import library from it. In Windows 3.1, three functions moved into USER.EXE, and joined the documented API—WNetAddConnection(), WNetCancel Connection(), and WNetGetConnection(). In Windows NT, the WNet API is the province of the Multiple Provider Router (MPR), and the functions reside in MPR.DLL. You may remember from Chapter 2 that the MPR takes either requests that use redirected drive letters or calls to the WNet functions and determines which network provider should handle them. This is why Microsoft refers to this API as network-independent; it gives all your installed network providers a chance to respond to function calls. Yes, the WNet API is network-independent, but it is so limited that its network independence does not buy you much.

Connecting to Remote Resources

Here are the Win32 prototypes for WNetAddConnection(), WNetCancel Connection(), and WNetGetConnection():

```
DWORD WNetAddConnection(LPTSTR lpszRemoteName,
                        LPTSTR lpPassword,
                        LPTSTR lpszLocalName);
DWORD WNetCancelConnection(LPTSTR lpszName,
                           BOOL   bForce);
DWORD WNetGetConnection(LPTSTR  lpszLocalName,
                        LPTSTR  lpRemoteName,
                        LPDWORD lpdwBufferSize);
```

WNetAddConnection() maps a local device (such as F:, G:, or LPT1) to a network resource. WNetCancelConnection() restores a mapped device to its local setting. WNetGetConnection() retrieves the network mapping of a local device.

Win32 adds the function WNetAddConnection2(). It provides the same service as WNetAddConnection(), but has some syntactic differences:

- The local and remote resource names are passed in a NETRESOURCE structure.
- An argument is added to specify a different user name than the one under which you are logged in.
- You can specify that the new connection is to be remembered for the user, and restored every time he or she logs on.

```
DWORD WNetAddConnection2(LPNETRESOURCE ResourceInformation,
                         LPTSTR        lpszPassword,
                         LPTSTR        lpszNewUserName,
                         DWORD         dwFlags);
```

The NETRESOURCE structure is typed as follows

```
typedef struct _NETRESOURCE
{
    DWORD   dwScope;
    DWORD   dwType;
    DWORD   dwDisplayType;
    DWORD   dwUsage;
    LPTSTR  lpLocalName;
    LPTSTR  lpRemoteName;
    LPTSTR  lpComment;
    LPTSTR  lpProvider;
} NETRESOURCE;
```

The *lpLocalName* and *lpRemoteName* fields of the NETRESOURCE structure specify the local device and the remote resource. *dwType* can specify RESOURCETYPE_DISK, RESOURCETYPE_PRINT, or RESOURCETYPE_ANY. You can pass *lpProvider* as a non-NULL pointer if you know the name of the network where the resource resides, but usually it is advisable to pass *lpProvider* as NULL. When you do so, the Multiple Provider Router (MPR) takes care of locating the correct network provider.

lpszNewUserName will be passed as non-NULL only when you use a name that differs from the one you used when you logged in.

The *dwFlags* argument can take on one non-zero value, CONNECT_UPDATE_PROFILE, which will cause the new connection to be remembered.

Breaking a Connection to a Remote Resource

Win32 also adds WNetCancelConnection2() for disconnecting from a remote resource. It has one more argument than WNetCancelConnection(), specifying whether the connection should be dropped from the user's list of persistent connections (those that NT automatically restores when the user logs in).

```
DWORD WNetCancelConnection2(
        LPTSTR  lpszLocalOrRemoteName,
        DWORD   dwFlags,
        BOOL    bForce);
```

lpszLocalOrRemoteName can be passed as either the redirected local device or as the remote resource it is connected to. If the latter, all the user's connections to the resource are terminated. If *dwFlags* is passed as

CONNECT_UPDATE_PROFILE, the connection loses its persistent status. Passing *dwFlags* as zero causes no such side effect. Under most circumstances, you want to pass *bForce* as FALSE. It tells NT whether it should break the connection even if the user has files currently open over it. If *bForce* is FALSE and files are open, then WNetCancelConnection2() fails. If it is TRUE, the connection is broken, and the files are left to fend for themselves.

Finding Out Your User Name

WNetGetUser() is a complementary function to WNetAddConnection2()

```
DWORD WNetGetUser(
       LPTSTR      lpszLocalDevice,
       LPTSTR      lpszUserName,
       LPDWORD     lpdwNameSize);
```

If *lpszLocalDevice* is not NULL, WNetGetUser() tells you the user name you used to connect to the resource that lpszLocalDevice names. Otherwise, it informs you who you are logged in as, and is probably the same as calling GetUserName().

Connection Dialog Boxes

The WNet API gives you canned dialog boxes you can present to your end users to let them connect and disconnect drives and printers. They are the same dialog boxes the File Manager displays when you select Connect Network Drive... and Disconnect Network Drive from the Disk menu, and are shown in Figure 17-1 and Figure 17-2.

These dialogs can be quite useful; not only do they give your users a standardized interface for connecting to network disks, they also do all the work of browsing the network and making the connection. The only thing you have to do is call WNetConnectionDialog() or WNetDisconnectDialog(). Both functions take the handle of the owner window and a constant defining the resource as a disk (RESOURCETYPE_DISK) or a printer (RESOURCETYPE_PRINT). WNetConnectionDialog() only supports connections to remote directories. WNetDisconnectDialog() will also disconnect you from a printer.

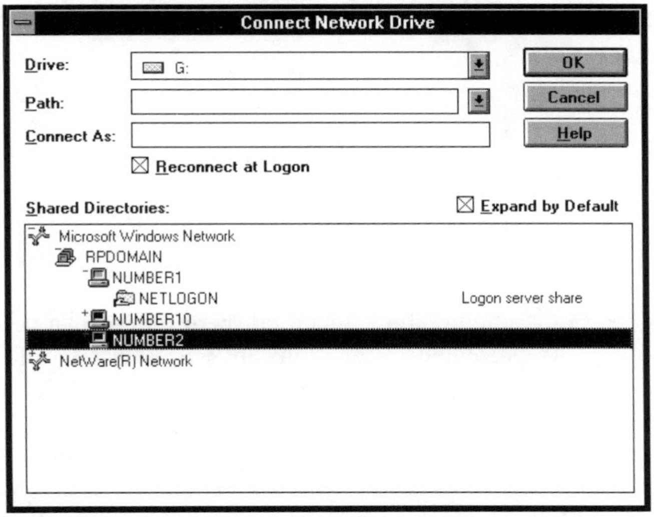

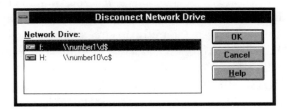

Figure 17-1.   The WNetConnectionDialog() Screen

Figure 17-2.   The WNetDisconnectDialog() Screen

Network Resource Enumeration

Win32 provides three functions to enumerate network resources: WNetOpenEnum(), WNetEnumResource(), and WNetCloseEnum(). These functions allow you to determine what network resources, such as shared directories and print queues, are available. You can take the information returned and pass it unaltered to WNetAddConnection() or WNetAddConnection2() to connect to the resource.

WNetOpenEnum(). WNetOpenEnum() begins a resource enumeration. It has five arguments:

```
DWORD WNetOpenEnum(
        DWORD           dwScope,
        DWORD           dwType,
        DWORD           dwUsage,
        LPNETRESOURCE   lpNetResource,
        LPHANDLE        lphEnum);
```

The scope of the enumeration, specified by *dwScope*, can be all resources on the network (represented by the constant RESOURCE_GLOBALNET), currently connected resources (RESOURCE_CONNECTED), or persistent connections (RESOURCE_REMEMBERED). (Persistent connections are connections that NT automatically restores for you when you log on.)

dwType indicates whether you want to enumerate disk resources (RESOURCETYPE_DISK), print resources (RESOURCETYPE_PRINT), or all resources (RESOURCETYPE_ANY).

If *dwScope* is not RESOURCE_GLOBALNET, then *dwUsage* is ignored. Otherwise, passing *dwUsage* as zero indicates that you want to enumerate all resources. The value RESOURCEUSAGE_CONNECTABLE says that you want all connectable resources (shared resources on your own or other machines). RESOURCEUSAGE_CONTAINER requests enumeration of container resources, like domains, workgroups, and servers.

If *dwScope* is RESOURCE_CONNECTED, *lpNetResource* must be NULL. Otherwise, it may point to a NETRESOURCE structure, shown again here for ease of reference:

```
typedef struct _NETRESOURCE
{
    DWORD  dwScope;
    DWORD  dwType;
    DWORD  dwDisplayType;
    DWORD  dwUsage;
    LPTSTR lpLocalName;
    LPTSTR lpRemoteName;
    LPTSTR lpComment;
    LPTSTR lpProvider;
} NETRESOURCE;
```

dwScope and *dwType* are the same as the arguments to WNetOpenEnum(). *dwDisplayType* gives you further information about the nature of the resource. Its most important values are:

- RESOURCEDISPLAYTYPE_DOMAIN: The resource is a domain.
- RESOURCEDISPLAYTYPE_SERVER: The resource is a server machine.
- RESOURCEDISPLAYTYPE_SHARE: The resource is a share being offered for public access over the network.

If *dwScope* is RESOURCE_GLOBALNET, *dwUsage* tells you whether the resource is a container (RESOURCEUSAGE_CONTAINER), like a domain or a server, in which case you can enumerate its contained resources, or is a connectable resource (RESOURCEUSAGE_CONNECTABLE), like a shared directory or print queue. If it is connectable, you can pass a pointer to the NETRESOURCE to WNetAddConnection2() without modification.

If *dwScope* is RESOURCE_CONNECTED or RESOURCE_ REMEMBERED, then *lpLocalName* reports the name of the redirected local device (F:, LPT1, etc.). Finally, *lpProvider* is a string identifying the network provider responsible for this resource. Because the WNet API is network-independent, you may see resources on non-NT machines, like NetWare servers.

The last argument, *lphEnum,* returns an enumeration handle that you then use as input to WNetEnumResource() and WNetCloseEnum().

The first time you call WNetOpenEnum(), set *lpNetResource* to NULL. Then, when you call WNetEnumResource(), it returns an array of NETRESOURCE structures. For any container resources that WNetEnumResource() reports, you can call WNetOpenEnum() with a non-NULL *lpNetResource* to do a recursive search for resources.

WNetEnumResource(). WNetEnumResource() uses the handle returned by WNetOpenEnum(). Note from the prototype that WNetEnumResource() behaves like a LAN Manager enumerator, rather than a Windows enumerator like EnumWindows() or EnumFontFamilies(). That is, it populates an output buffer with an array of object descriptions; it does not call an enumeration function.

```
DWORD WNetEnumResource(
        HANDLE    hEnum,
        LPDWORD   lpdwEntries,
        LPVOID    lpBuffer,
        LPDWORD   lpdwBufferSize);
```

hEnum is the enumeration handle returned by WNetOpenEnum(). On input, **lpdwEntries* specifies the number of entries you want to get back; a value of 0xFFFFFFFF means you want all possible values. On output, it will report the number of entries actually returned. *lpBuffer* will be filled with an array of NETRESOURCE structures. *lpdwBufferSize* points to a DWORD describing the size of *lpBuffer*. If the buffer is too small to hold even a single entry, WNetEnumResource() will return ERROR_MORE_DATA , and **lpdwBufferSize* will tell you how much memory you need.

WNetEnumResource() returns NO_ERROR as long as it has more information to report. When it has enumerated all requested resources, it returns ERROR_NO_MORE_ITEMS.

You can do nested enumerations on the NETRESOURCE structures returned by WNetEnumResource(). If the *dwScope* argument to WNetOpenEnum() is RESOURCE_GLOBALNET, the *dwScope* field of the NETRESOURCE structure is the same, and the *dwUsage* field has the RESOURCEUSAGE_CONTAINER flag set, you can call WNet-OpenEnum() again, this time pointing *lpNetResource* to the array element you are looking at. You'll see an example of this later in this chapter.

WNetCloseEnum(). WNetCloseEnum() closes an enumeration. Its only argument is the handle returned by WNetOpenEnum().

```
DWORD WNetCloseEnum(HANDLE hEnum);
```

An Example: EnumNetworkResources(). The WNETRSC sample application contains a function that enumerates network resources and performs recursive enumeration on container resources EnumNetworkResources(). Here is the listing of that function, taken from \NTNET\CODE\WNETRSC\WNETRSC.CPP.

```
void EnumNetworkResources(LPNETRESOURCE lpNet, int nLevel,
                          DWORD dwScope,
                          DWORD dwResourceType, DWORD dwUsageType)
{
    static char *szResourceTypes[] = {"",
                                      "Domain or Workgroup",
                                      "Server",
                                      "Share"};
    DWORD  dwRetcode;
    HANDLE hEnum;
    char   szBuffer[1000];
    DWORD  dwEntries = 0xFFFFFFFF;
    DWORD  dwBytes = 163840;
    DWORD  i;
```

```
LPNETRESOURCE lpBuffer;

lpBuffer = (LPNETRESOURCE) VirtualAlloc(NULL, 163840,
                            MEM_COMMIT,
                            PAGE_READWRITE);

if (lpBuffer == NULL)
   {
   printf("\nMemory allocation error\n");
   ExitProcess(1);
   }

dwRetcode = WNetOpenEnum(dwScope,
                         dwResourceType,
                         dwUsageType,
                         lpNet,  // NULL the first time
                         &hEnum);

if (dwRetcode == NO_ERROR)
   {
   while (WNetEnumResource(hEnum, &dwEntries, lpBuffer, &dwBytes)
         == NO_ERROR)
      {
      for (i = 0; i < dwEntries; ++i)
         {
         ZeroMemory(szBuffer, sizeof (szBuffer));
         if (nLevel > 0)
            FillMemory(szBuffer, nLevel * 5, ' ');
         sprintf(&szBuffer[strlen(szBuffer)],
                 "Local name:  %s  remote name:  %s\t(%s)",
                 (lpBuffer[i].lpLocalName != NULL ?
                  lpBuffer[i].lpLocalName : ""),
                 (lpBuffer[i].lpRemoteName != NULL ?
                  lpBuffer[i].lpRemoteName : ""),
                 szResourceTypes[lpBuffer[i].dwDisplayType]);
         printf("\n%s", szBuffer);

         // Do recursive enumeration of container resource
         if (lpBuffer[i].dwUsage & RESOURCEUSAGE_CONTAINER)
            {
            EnumNetworkResources(&lpBuffer[i], ++nLevel,
               dwScope, dwResourceType, dwUsageType);
            —nLevel;
            }
         }
      dwBytes = 163840;
      dwEntries = 0xFFFFFFFF;
      }
```

```
    WNetCloseEnum(hEnum);
    }
  VirtualFree(lpBuffer, 0, MEM_RELEASE);
}
```

The main() function calls EnumNetworkResources() twice: once to enumerate all network resources, and once to scan your connections to remote resources. Here are the calls.

```
printf("\n===== Enumerating All Network Resources =====\n");
EnumNetworkResources(NULL, 0, RESOURCE_GLOBALNET,
RESOURCETYPE_ANY, 0);

printf("\n\n===== Enumerating Current Connections =====\n");
EnumNetworkResources(NULL, 0, RESOURCE_CONNECTED,
RESOURCETYPE_DISK, RESOURCEUSAGE_CONNECTABLE);
```

Here is its output on my network.

```
===== Enumerating All Network Resources =====

Local name:      remote name:  NetWare(R) Network
Local name:      remote name:  Microsoft Windows Network
    Local name:    remote name: RPDOMAIN       (Domain or Workgroup)
        Local name:    remote name: \\NUMBER1   (Server)
            Local name:    remote name: \\NUMBER1\NETLOGON (Share)
        Local name:    remote name: \\NUMBER10  (Server)
        Local name:    remote name: \\NUMBER2   (Server)

===== Enumerating Current Connections =====

Local name:  H:   remote name:   \\number10\c$
```

Extended Error Reporting

When one of the WNet functions fails, your first step is to call GetLastError(). If it returns ERROR_EXTENDED_ERROR, you can find out the extended network error by calling WNetGetLastError(). This will return a network-specific error code and a printable string that you can display to the user. The kinds of errors that may occur vary greatly from one network provider to another, so WNetGetLastError() is a good way to shield yourself from these details.

```
DWORD WNetGetLastError(
     LPDWORD      lpdwErrorCode,        .  // Captures network-specific
                                           // error code
     LPTSTR       lpszErrorString,         // Returns printable error
                                           // message
     DWORD        dwErrorStringSize,       // Size of message buffer
     LPTSTR       lpszProviderName,        // Returns name of network
                                           // provider
     DWORD        dwProviderNameSize);  // Size of provider buffer
```

That, then, is the entire built-in WNet API. It is a decent API as far as it goes, but it is not a rich API. There are many more things a developer needs to do on a network than connect to remote drives.

NetDDE

In *Windows Network Programming*, I fairly raved over NetDDE:

> NetDDE is a very important enhancement that Windows for Workgroups brings to the Windows programming environment. It makes possible a whole new range of distributed computing possibilities... (page 471)

Having read this book, you will probably smile at my youthful enthusiasm. (Indeed, I was younger then.) In the context of Windows 3.1, NetDDE was quite an innovation. But in the NT environment, where Named Pipes, Windows Sockets, NetBIOS, and RPC all offer competing claims, NetDDE begins to fade into the background. It is still powerful and easy to use. It just doesn't look like many people will ever use it, as you'll see in a minute.

NetDDE is an extension to the DDE Management Library (DDEML) interface. Client and server applications use DDEML calls to communicate with each other, and there is very little difference in how they use DDEML.

Connecting to a NetDDE Server

One slight variation is that the client must provide the name of the target station when it starts a conversation. Also, the target application is always NDDE$, the name used by the NetDDE server. Standard DDEML uses topics and items to further identify the individual pieces of data involved in an exchange. For example, in a conversation with Excel, the name of a spreadsheet might constitute a topic, and cells A1, A2, A3, and A4 might be individual items. A DDE server application that wishes to offer its services over a network creates a share name that represents the service (or application), topic, and item names that it would use for local DDE. The client application then uses this share name as the topic in its call to DdeConnect(). If the application you are trying to access is not running on the server machine, NetDDE can start it for you. For example, to create group boxes in Program Manager, you connect to it using the application and topic name "PROGMAN". Suppose Program Manager creates the NetDDE share "PROGMAN$". (It does not, by the way). A client application on \\NUMBER10 would connect to Program Manager on \\NUMBER1 as follows.

```
#include <ddeml.h>

extern HINSTANCE hInst;      // Assume a global exists
DWORD   dwDDE;
HSZ     hszProgman, hszTopic;
HCONV   hProgmanConv;

if (DdeInitialize(&dwDDE, MyDDECallback, APPCLASS_CLIENTONLY,
                  CBF_SKIP_REGISTRATIONS | CBF_SKIP_UNREGISTRATIONS)
    == DMLERR_NO_ERROR)
  {
  // Use the application name \\NUMBER1\NDDE$
  hszProgman = DdeCreateStringHandle(dwDDE, "\\\\NUMBER1\\NDDE$",
                  CP_WINANSI);

  // Use topic name PROGMAN
  hszTopic = DdeCreateStringHandle(dwDDE, "PROGMAN$", CP_WINANSI);

  // Try to connect
  hProgmanConv = DdeConnect(dwDDE, hszProgman, hszTopic, NULL);

  if (hProgmanConv != NULL)
     // Proceed with DdeClientTransaction() calls for
     // XTYP_EXECUTE transactions
  }
```

Once the client is connected to the server, the DDE conversation proceeds just as if it were a local interaction; there are no further differences.

Incidentally, it has been my experience that NetDDE does not like it if you pass Unicode strings to DdeCreateStringHandle(). Specifically, the DdeConnect() fails, apparently because the target machine name gets garbled.

Making a DDE Server NetDDE-Aware

As I stated above, a DDE server that wants to make itself available to clients across a network must create NetDDE shares that symbolize its service and topic pairs. In other words, a server application must be NetDDE-aware in order for NetDDE clients to connect to it. This, as it turns out, is the greatest weakness in NetDDE; only a few DDE servers know anything about NetDDE. Unless more major applications add NetDDE awareness, it seems likely that NetDDE will be eclipsed by the other APIs discussed in this book. The very existence of those other APIs makes it unlikely that many serious server applications will choose to support NetDDE.

The NetDDE DLL, NDDEAPI.DLL, provides functions for adding, deleting, and enumerating DDE shares: NDdeShareAdd(), NDdeShareDel(), and NDdeShareEnum(). NDdeShareGetInfo() returns more detailed information about a share reported by NDdeShareEnum(). The prototypes, data types, and constants are defined in \MSTOOLS\H\NDDEAPI.H.

WNETRSC includes a section that enumerates the currently existing DDE shares, then adds the share WNPM$. The Windows Network Manager uses WNPM$ to field remote XTYP_EXECUTE requests for the Program Manager. Since Program Manager is not NetDDE-aware, NetDDE is used to establish a connection to the Windows Network Manager, who is NetDDE-aware. The Windows Network Manager then connects to the Program Manager on the local machine and sends along the command strings that he received from the partner application.

Here is the code that creates the WNPM$ share. I first delete the share if it already exists by calling NDdeShareDel(), then call NDdeShareAdd() to recreate it. Among other things, NDdeShareAdd() needs a pointer to an NDDESHAREINFO structure.

```
typedef struct _NDDESHAREINFO
{
    LONG                    lRevision;
    LPTSTR                  lpszShareName;
    LONG                    lShareType;
    LPTSTR                  lpszAppTopicList;
    LONG                    fSharedFlag;
    LONG                    fService;
    LONG                    fStartAppFlag;
    LONG                    nCmdShow;
    LONG                    qModifyId[2];
    LONG                    cNumItems;
    LPTSTR                  lpszItemList;
} NDDESHAREINFO;
```

After this, I call NDdeSetTrustedShare(). This is required because I set the *fService* flag in the NDDESHAREINFO to FALSE. After this, just out of curiosity, I call NDdeGetShareSecurity() to see what kind of security descriptor NT generated in response to NDdeShareAdd(), which I passed a NULL security descriptor to. Notice the use of NDdeGetErrorString() to convert a function return value into a printable string.

```
NDdeShareDel(NULL, "WNPM$", 0);

ZeroMemory(lpShareInfo, sizeof (NDDESHAREINFO));
lpShareInfo->lRevision = 1;
lpShareInfo->lpszShareName = "WNPM$";
lpShareInfo->lpszAppTopicList =
    "\0\0WNET|WNETPM\0";                       // Note the two leading
                                               // \0s. This is not
                                               // clearly documented,
                                               // but it
                                               // is required.
                                               // The first one is for
                                               // the DDE app and topic,
                                               // the second is for
                                               // the OLE app and topic.
                                               // We're using a static
                                               // app and topic (???),
                                               // which comes in the
                                               //  third position.

                                               // The Service and topic
                                               // are separated by
                                               // a vertical bar (|)
lpShareInfo->lShareType = SHARE_TYPE_STATIC;   // I don't know what this
                                               // means, but this is
                                               // how the other DDE
                                               // shares are typed
lpShareInfo->fSharedFlag = TRUE;               // Allow remote users
                                               // to connect
lpShareInfo->fService = FALSE;                 // Must make this a
                                               // trusted share before
                                               // it can be used
lpShareInfo->fStartAppFlag = TRUE;             // Allow automatic
                                               // startup of application
lpShareInfo->nCmdShow = SW_SHOWNORMAL;         // Show screen in
                                               // normalized state
lpShareInfo->cNumItems = 0;                    // Share all items
lpShareInfo->lpszItemList = "";                //   under this topic
```

```
uDDEError = NDdeShareAdd(
    NULL,                                       // Execute locally
    2,                                          // Info level, must be 2
    NULL,                                       // No security descriptor
                                                // Inherits security
                                                //   from somebody
    (LPBYTE) lpShareInfo,                       // Pointer to NDDESHAREINFO
    sizeof (NDDESHAREINFO));

if (uDDEError != NDDE_NO_ERROR)
   {
   NDdeGetErrorString(uDDEError, szDDEError,
     sizeof (szDDEError));
   printf("\nCannot add DDE share WNPM$: %s", szDDEError);
   }

// We have to call NDdeSetTrustedShare() since we
// set the fService flag in the NDDESHAREINFO to FALSE
uDDEError = NDdeSetTrustedShare(
            NULL,                               // Execute locally
            "WNPM$",                            // Share name
            NDDE_TRUST_SHARE_START |            // Let NetDDE
                                                // start the app
            NDDE_TRUST_SHARE_INIT);             // and initialize it
if (uDDEError != NDDE_NO_ERROR)
   {
   NDdeGetErrorString(uDDEError, szDDEError, sizeof (szDDEError));
   printf("\nCannot make WNPM$ a trusted share: %s", szDDEError);
   }

if ((uDDEError =
   NDdeGetShareSecurity(
     NULL,                                      // Machine name
     "WNPM$",                                   // Share name
     DACL_SECURITY_INFORMATION,
     (PSECURITY_DESCRIPTOR) bySDBuffer,
     dwSDSize, &dwSDSize))
    == NDDE_NO_ERROR)
   DumpDACL("WNPM$", (PSECURITY_DESCRIPTOR) bySDBuffer);
else
   {
   NDdeGetErrorString(uDDEError, szDDEError, sizeof (szDDEError));
   printf("\nCan't read share's security descriptor: %s",
     szDDEError);
   }
```

Here's the output from DumpDACL().

```
DACL explicitly assigned
Access allowed ace
Access rights 0000023D granted to Everyone on WNPM$
Access allowed ace
Access rights 000F03FF granted to Administrators on WNPM$
```

This is an inherited DACL, though I don't know where it's inherited from. The default DACL in my access token gives GENERIC_ALL rights to SYSTEM and Administrators. SYSTEM does not appear in this DACL, and Everyone does. The rights masks are represented by constants in \MSTOOLS\H\NDDESEC.H. For Everyone, the flags are NDDE_SHARE_ GENERIC_READ | NDDE_SHARE_INITIATE_LINK. For Administrators, they are NDDE_SHARE_GENERIC_ALL.

Obtaining NetDDE Share Information

To obtain information about NetDDE shares, call NDdeShareEnum() to retrieve their names, then NDdeShareGetInfo() for each one.

```
UINT NDdeShareEnum(LPTSTR    lpServer,
                   UINT      uLevel,
                   LPBYTE    lpNameBuffer,
                   DWORD     dwNameBufferSize,
                   LPDWORD   lpdwEntriesRead,
                   LPDWORD   lpdwTotalAvailable);
```

Set *lpszServer* to NULL to enumerate NetDDE shares on the local machine. *uLevel* must be zero. NDdeShareEnum() works like a LAN Manager enumerator; it returns an array of null-terminated share names in *lpNameBuffer*, with two nulls at the end. On input, *dwNameBufferSize* says how large the buffer at *lpNameBuffer* is. On output, **lpdwEntriesRead* reports the number of shares enumerated; **lpdwTotalAvailable* returns the number of bytes of information available. If the original buffer was too small, NDdeShareEnum() returns NDDE_BUF_TOO_SMALL, and you can allocate the memory required.

You can get the original NDDESHAREINFO structure for each share in the array by calling NDdeShareGetInfo().

```
UINT NDdeShareGetInfo(LPTSTR   lpszServer,
                      LPTSTR   lpszShareName,
                      UINT     uLevel,
                      LPBYTE   lpShareInfo,
                      DWORD    dwShareInfoSize,
                      LPDWORD  lpdwTotalAvailable,
                      LPDWORD  lpdwItems);
```

As usual, *lpszServer* must be NULL to get share information on your own machine. *uLevel* must be two, just as it was in the initial call to NDdeShareAdd(). *lpdwItems* must be NULL at this time. *lpszShareName* is the name of the share you are requesting information on. *lpShareInfo* points to an NDDESHAREINFO structure, and *dwShareInfoSize* is the size of the buffer at *lpShareInfo*. Any items that are included in the share will also be returned in the buffer pointed to by *lpShareInfo*; if the buffer is only *sizeof* (NDDESHAREINFO) bytes large, NDdeShareGetInfo() may well return NDDE_BUF_TOO_SMALL. **lpdwTotalAvailable* returns the total number of bytes needed to capture all of the output information.

WNETRSC enumerates existing NetDDE shares and analyzes their application/topic pairs. Here's the code, followed by the program's output.

```
printf("\n===== DDE Shares on %s =====\n", lpStation);
ZeroMemory(szDDEShares, sizeof (szDDEShares));
NDdeShareEnum(
    NULL,                                  // Enumerate locally
    0,                                     // Level must be zero
    (LPBYTE) szDDEShares,                  // Output buffer
    sizeof (szDDEShares),
    &dwEntries,
    &dwBytes);

// Output is an array of contiguous null-terminated strings,
// terminated by two null bytes
for (i = 0; szDDEShares[i] != '\0'; i += (lstrlen(&szDDEShares[i]) + 1))
    {
    printf("\nShare name: %s", &szDDEShares[i]);
    dwBytes = sizeof (szShareInfoBuffer);
    wShares = 0;
    if (NDdeShareGetInfo(
            NULL,                          // Local machine
            &szDDEShares[i],               // Pointer to current
                                           // share name
            2,                             // Level must be two
            (LPBYTE) szShareInfoBuffer,    // Output NDDESHAREINFO
```

```
        sizeof (szShareInfoBuffer),
        &dwBytes,
        &wShares)
    == 0)
    {
    // App and topic are delimited by a |
    // For example, WNET|WNETPM
    // For SHARE_TYPE_STATIC, first two bytes
    // are '\0'
    while (*lpShareInfo->lpszAppTopicList == '\0')
        ++lpShareInfo->lpszAppTopicList;
    lpszAppName = strtok(lpShareInfo->lpszAppTopicList, "|");
    lpszTopicName = strtok(NULL, "");
    printf("\n\tApp name: %s, Topic name: %s", lpszAppName,
        lpszTopicName);
    }
}


===== DDE Shares on \\NUMBER1 =====

Share name: Chat$
    App name: WinChat, Topic name: Chat
Share name: CLPBK$
    App name: ClipSrv, Topic name: System
Share name: Hearts$
    App name: MSHearts, Topic name: Hearts
Share name: WNPM$
    App name: WNET, Topic name: WNETPM
```

Only WinChat, the Clipbook Server, and MSHearts are NetDDE-aware (not counting WNet). This means you cannot use NetDDE to talk to any other major Windows applications. You can, of course, use NetDDE to build your own distributed systems, and it does have some appealing features. It is built on top of DDEML, which is by and large a very usable, cleanly architected API. It offers securable endpoints. It will execute a remote server application if it is not running when a NetDDE request comes in. This is a very nice feature that no other API offers, but you can get the same effect by writing an NT service. However, it seems likely that if some major applications don't become NetDDE-aware soon, NetDDE will wither on the vine.

Other NetDDE Functions

Table 17-1 lists the other NetDDE functions.

Table 17-1.   Other NetDDE Functions

Function	Purpose
NDdeGetErrorString	Retrieves text for a NetDDE error
NDdeGetShareSecurity	Gets the security descriptor for a NetDDE share
NDdeGetTrustedShare	Gets trust information on a share
NDdeIsValidAppTopicList	Verifies the syntax of a string containing applications and topics delimited by 'I'
NDdeIsValidShareName	Checks that a share name is in correct format (does not mean that the share exists)
NDdeSetShareSecurity	Sets the security descriptor belonging to a share
NDdeSetTrustedShare	Gives a share trusted status, and defines the startup operations that a client will be allowed to do
NDdeShareSetInfo	Changes the information pertaining to a share
NDdeTrustedShareEnum	Enumerates shares that are trusted in the security context of the calling process

The Messaging API (MAPI)

The Messaging API allows applications to easily add electronic mail capabilities. It provides a set of functions for using the Microsoft mail system. Most of the functions put up a canned dialog box, which in turn handles all the details of constructing, interpreting, and sending E-mail messages. Because the level of service is so high, applications can become mail-enabled with little trouble. Indeed, as the Windows Network Manager will show you, the single function MAPISendDocuments() will give an application complete outgoing E-mail functionality.

Table 17-2 lists the MAPI function calls. The MAPI header file (MAPI.H) that defines their prototypes is provided with the Win32 SDK, but it accompanies a sample application in the \MSTOOLS\SAMPLES\MAPI directory.

Table 17-2.   MAPI Functions

Function	Operation
MAPIAddress	Presents a dialog box to get list of recipients from user
MAPIDeleteMail	Deletes a message retrieved by MAPIFindNext()
MAPIDetails	Presents dialog box giving detailed information on a recipient
MAPIFindNext	Scans mailbox for incoming messages
MAPIFreeBuffer	Frees memory allocated by MAPIAddress(), MAPIResolveName(), and MAPIReadMail()
MAPILogoff	Logs user off the mail system
MAPILogon	Logs user onto the mail system
MAPIReadMail	Reads a message retrieved by MAPIFindNext()
MAPIResolveName	Retrieves information on a user known to the MS-Mail system; may also present a dialog box asking the user to resolve an ambiguous name
MAPISaveMail	Updates a mail message
MAPISendDocuments	Presents dialog box to send files to remote user
MAPISendMail	Presents dialog box to send mail to remote user

Under Windows NT, the functions reside in MAPI32.DLL. No matching import library is provided, however, so you have to load the DLL by calling LoadLibrary().

Word for Windows includes a Send... item on its File menu. Selecting that option right this moment puts up the dialog box shown in Figure 17-3. This is none other than the dialog box belonging to MAPISendDocuments(). This is the easiest way to mail-enable an application. The recommended procedure is to do it just as Word for Windows has—add a Send... option to your File menu.

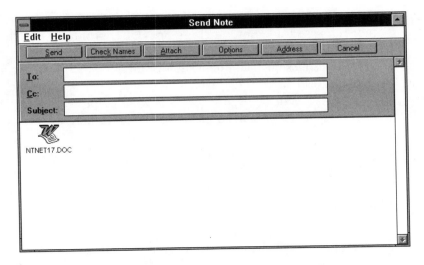

Figure 17-3. Word for Windows Send File Dialog Box

MAPISendDocuments()

When users selects Send..., you might want to ask if they want to send the active document, selected documents, or all open documents. MAPISendDocuments() handles everything else for you. By the way, the LPSTRs in the prototype tell you that MAPI does not support Unicode.

```
ULONG MAPISendDocuments(
    ULONG ulUIParam,
    LPSTR lpszDelimChar,
    LPSTR lpszFilePaths,
    LPSTR lpszFileNames,
    ULONG ulReserved);        // Pass as zero
```

ulUIParam is the handle of the window that will own the MAPI dialog boxes, cast to a ULONG. To pass multiple file names, you build concatenated strings in *lpszFilePaths* and *lpszFilenames*. The character in *lpszDelimChar* is the delimiter. For example, if you use a semicolon as a delimiter when passing D:\WINNT\SYSTEM32\WRITE.EXE and D:\WINNT\SYSTEM32\WRITE.HLP, then *lpszDelimChar* will be ";", *lpszFilePaths* will be "D:\WINNT\SYSTEM32\WRITE.EXE;D:\WINNT\SYSTEM32\WRITE.HLP", and *lpszFileNames* will be "WRITE.EXE;WRITE.HLP". Notice that *lpszFileNames* and *lpszFilePaths* both include the file names. *lpszFileNames* lists the file names without their paths. If passed as empty strings or NULL pointers, no files will be transmitted; however, the user can still compose an E-mail message or select files for transmission. The implication of this is: MAPISendDocuments() is the only MAPI call you ever need to use, unless you want to read incoming E-mail. MAPISendDocuments() does its work by presenting canned dialogs to your users and letting them make the selections they want. It corresponds to a series of calls to the other MAPI functions. For this reason, once you have entered the mail system by calling MAPISendDocuments(), you do not need to make any other MAPI calls.

Mail-Enabling an Application

The Windows Network Manager (\NTNET\CODE\%Cpu%\WNET.EXE) has two hooks into MAPI, both of them by way of MAPISendDocuments(). Its File menu includes a Send... item, and its Network menu has Send E-Mail.... The only difference in how they are implemented is that Send E-Mail calls MAPISendDocuments() with NULL pointers for the file arguments.

The Windows Network Manager adds one additional level of complexity as a service to the user. To send files, it calls GetOpenFileName() to present the standard File Open dialog box. It sets the OFN_ALLOWMULTISELECT flag to allow the selection of multiple files. If the user does so, WNET has to convert the list of names from the format in which GetOpenFileName() returns it to the format that MAPISendDocuments() likes. GetOpenFileName() places the file names into a string where the directory name is followed by the individual file names, delimited with spaces. (GetOpenFileName() presents NTFS long filenames in 8.3 format, and returns them this way.) MAPISendDocuments(), as we saw, wants two arguments: the full path names of the files delimited by a semi-colon (or whatever character you designate), and the simple file names, delimited by the same character.

Here is the WM_COMMAND handler from \NTNET\CODE\ WNETMAIN.CPP. The function is short, so I list it in its entirety. I force GetOpenFileName() to use the ANSI character set by using the ANSI-specific versions of both the structure (OPENFILENAMEA) and the function (GetOpenFileNameA()). If the user selects multiple files, the function ParseMAPIFileNames() converts the list from the format in which GetOpenFileName() returns it to that required by MAPISendDocuments().

```
void WNet_OnCommand(HWND hwnd, int id, HWND hwndCtl, UINT codeNotify)
{
    typedef ULONG (WINAPI *PFNMAPISENDDOCUMENTS)(HWND, LPSTR, LPSTR,
                    LPSTR, ULONG);
    OPENFILENAMEA ofn;
    CHAR  szFileName[MAX_PATH + 1];
    LPSTR lpFullPaths, lpFileNames;
    HINSTANCE hMAPILib = NULL;
    PFNMAPISENDDOCUMENTS MAPISendDocuments;
    LPTSTR lpszMAPILib;

    if (!ISWIN32S())
        lpszMAPILib = TEXT("MAPI32.DLL");
    else
        lpszMAPILib = TEXT("MAPI.DLL");

    switch (id)
        {
        case IDM_FILESEND:
            hMAPILib = LoadLibrary(lpszMAPILib);
            if (hMAPILib == NULL)
                break;
            MAPISendDocuments =
                (PFNMAPISENDDOCUMENTS)
                    GetProcAddress(hMAPILib, "MAPISendDocuments");
            if (MAPISendDocuments == NULL)
                break;
            lstrcpyA(szFileName, "*.*");
            ZeroMemory(&ofn, sizeof (OPENFILENAMEA));
            ofn.lStructSize = sizeof (OPENFILENAMEA);
            ofn.hwndOwner = hwnd;
            ofn.lpstrFile = szFileName;
            ofn.nMaxFile = MAX_PATH;
            ofn.lpstrTitle = "Select File";
            ofn.Flags = (OFN_ALLOWMULTISELECT | OFN_NOCHANGEDIR |
                        OFN_HIDEREADONLY | OFN_FILEMUSTEXIST);
            if (GetOpenFileNameA(&ofn))
                {
                // Call routine to parse multiple file names
                ParseMAPIFileNames(szFileName, &lpFullPaths, &lpFileNames);
                MAPISendDocuments(hwnd, ";", lpFullPaths,
                            lpFileNames, 0);
                if (lpFullPaths != NULL)
                    VirtualFree(lpFullPaths, 0, MEM_RELEASE);
                if (lpFileNames != NULL)
                    VirtualFree(lpFileNames, 0, MEM_RELEASE);
                }
```

```
         break;
      case IDM_SENDMAIL:
         // MAPISendDocuments() does this too
         hMAPILib = LoadLibrary(lpszMAPILib);
         if (hMAPILib == NULL)
            break;
         MAPISendDocuments =
            (PFNMAPISENDDOCUMENTS)
               GetProcAddress(hMAPILib, "MAPISendDocuments");
         if (MAPISendDocuments == NULL)
            break;
         MAPISendDocuments(hwnd, ";", "", "", 0);
         break;
      case IDM_DISKCONNECT:
         WNetConnectionDialog(hwnd, RESOURCETYPE_DISK);
         break;
      case IDM_DISKDISCONNECT:
         WNetDisconnectDialog(hwnd, RESOURCETYPE_DISK);
         break;
      case IDM_SYSTEM_INFO:
         if (hSystemInfoDlg == NULL)
            hSystemInfoDlg = CreateDialog(GetWindowInstance(hwnd),
                              MAKEINTRESOURCE(IDB_SYSTEM_INFO),
                              hwnd, SystemInfoDlgProc);
         else
            {
            SetFocus(hSystemInfoDlg);
            BringWindowToTop(hSystemInfoDlg);
            }
         break;
      case IDM_STATIONVIEW:
         DialogBoxParam(GetWindowInstance(hwnd),
                     MAKEINTRESOURCE(IDB_STATIONS),
                     hwnd, ViewStationsDlgProc, (LPARAM) nNameIndex);
         break;
      case IDM_ABOUT:
         DialogBox(GetWindowInstance(hwnd), MAKEINTRESOURCE(IDB_ABOUT),
                  hwnd, AboutDlgProc);
         break;
      case IDM_FILEEXIT:
         PostMessage(hwnd, WM_CLOSE, 0, 0);
         break;
      }
   if (hMAPILib != NULL)
      FreeLibrary(hMAPILib);
}
```

```
static void ParseMAPIFileNames(LPSTR lpInBuff, LPSTR *lplpFullPaths,
                               LPSTR *lplpFileNames)
{
    DWORD   i, j, k, dwLength;
    CHAR    szDirectoryName[MAX_PATH + 1];
    LPSTR   lpFileNames, lpFullPaths;
    BOOL    bMultipleFiles = TRUE;
    CHAR    *pLastBackslash;

    // This function parses a buffer of multiple file names
    // that were passed back by GetOpenFileName()

    // They come back as a space-delimited string, where the
    // first token is the directory name, and the rest of
    // the tokens are the individual file names

    // We need to build two output buffers
    // One will contain the full path names of the files;
    // the other will just have the file names

    *lplpFullPaths = *lplpFileNames = NULL;

    if (lstrlenA(lpInBuff) == 0)
        // No files selected
        return;

    lpFullPaths = (LPSTR) VirtualAlloc(NULL, 8192, MEM_COMMIT,
                                       PAGE_READWRITE);

    if (lpFullPaths == NULL)
        return;

    lpFileNames = (LPSTR) VirtualAlloc(NULL, 8192, MEM_COMMIT,
                                       PAGE_READWRITE);
    if (lpFileNames == NULL)
        {
        VirtualFree(lpFullPaths, 0, MEM_RELEASE);
        return;
        }

    // First, pull out the directory name
    for (i = 0, dwLength = lstrlenA(lpInBuff);
         lpInBuff[i] != ' '; ++i)
        {
        szDirectoryName[i] = lpInBuff[i];
        if (lpInBuff[i] == '\0')
            break;
        }
```

```
    if (lpInBuff[i] == '\0')
       bMultipleFiles = FALSE;

    if (bMultipleFiles)
       {
       szDirectoryName[i] = '\\';
       szDirectoryName[i + 1] = '\0';

       lstrcpyA(lpFullPaths, szDirectoryName);

       for (++i, j = lstrlenA(lpFullPaths), k = 0;
            i < dwLength;
            ++i, ++k)
          {
          if (lpInBuff[i] == ' ')
             {
             lpFileNames[k] = lpFullPaths[j++] = ';';
             // End of a file name
             lstrcpyA(lpFullPaths + j, szDirectoryName);
             j += lstrlenA(szDirectoryName);

             }
          else
             lpFileNames[k] = lpFullPaths[j++] = lpInBuff[i];
          }
       }
    else
       {
       // Only one file selected, we get back the full path name of
       // the file
       pLastBackslash = strrchr(szDirectoryName, '\\');

       ++pLastBackslash;
       lstrcpyA(lpFullPaths, szDirectoryName);
       lstrcpyA(lpFileNames, pLastBackslash);
       }


    // OK, that's it—no need to null-terminate, VirtualAlloc() took care
    // of it

    *lplpFullPaths = lpFullPaths;
    *lplpFileNames = lpFileNames;
}
```

Conclusion

The built-in WNet API set is small and provides little useful functionality. NetDDE offers valuable services, but at the present has not been widely adopted and is unlikely to be. MAPI is a high-level standard dialog API that allows applications to become mail-enabled with a minimum of effort. It is slated to be superseded by the Common Messaging Calls (CMC) API, which is becoming available as this book goes to press.

Suggested Readings

Davis, Ralph. *Windows Network Programming*, Chapters 13 and 14. Reading, MA: Addision-Wesley Publishing Company, 1993.

Networks Overview in the Win32 API on-line help. Published as Chapter 56 in the *Win32 Programmer's Reference, Volume 2*.

Network DDE in the Win32 API on-line help.

There is an excellent on-line help file for MAPI in \MSTOOLS\ SAMPLES\MAPI called MAPIC.HLP.

The Common Messaging Calls (CMC) API help file (CMC.HLP) is distributed with the Development Platforms CD.

Index